The Years of Theory

Fredric Jameson is distinguished professor of comparative literature at Duke University. Over the last several decades, he has developed an influential and richly nuanced understanding of the relationship between culture and political economy. He is a recipient of the Holberg International Memorial Prize and the Modern Language Association's Lifetime Achievement Award.

Also by the Author

The Poetics of Social Forms
I. *Parts of Speech* (forthcoming)
II. *Allegory and Ideology*
III. *The Antinomies of Realism*
IV. *A Singular Modernity /*
    The Modernist Papers
V. *Postmodernism, or, the Cultural*
    Logic of Late Capitalism
VI. *Archaeologies of the Future*

Studies
Sartre: The Origins of a Style
Fables of Aggression: Wyndham
    Lewis, the Modernist as Fascist
Late Marxism: Adorno, Or, The
    Persistence of the Dialectic
Brecht and Method
The Hegel Variations: On the
    Phenomenology of the Spirit
Representing Capital: A
    Reading of Volume One
Chandler: The Detections of Totality
The Benjamin Files

Theory
Marxism and Form: Twentieth-
    Century Dialectical
    Theories of Literature

The Prison-House of Language: A
    Critical Account of Structuralism
    and Russian Formalism
The Political Unconscious: Narrative
    as a Socially Symbolic Act
Valences of the Dialectic
An American Utopia: Dual Power
    and the Universal Army

Film
Signatures of the Visible
The Geopolitical Aesthetic: Cinema
    and Space in the World System

Essays
The Ideologies of Theory
The Seeds of Time
The Cultural Turn: Selected Writings
    on the Postmodern, 1983–1998
The Ancients and the Postmoderns:
    On the Historicity of Forms
Inventions of a Present: The Novel in
    Its Crisis of Globalization

Seminars
Mimesis, Expression, Construction

The Years of Theory

Postwar French Thought to the Present

Fredric Jameson

Edited by Carson Welch

VERSO

London • New York

First published by Verso 2024
© Fredric Jameson 2024
Editor's Preface © Carson Welch 2024

1 3 5 7 9 10 8 6 4 2

Verso
UK: 6 Meard Street, London W1F 0EG
US: 388 Atlantic Avenue, Brooklyn, NY 11217
versobooks.com

Verso is the imprint of New Left Books

ISBN-13: 978-1-80429-589-2
ISBN-13: 978-1-80429-591-5 (US EBK)
ISBN-13: 978-1-80429-590-8 (UK EBK)

British Library Cataloguing in Publication Data
A catalogue record for this book is available from the British Library

Library of Congress Cataloging-in-Publication Data
A catalog record for this book is available from the Library of Congress

Typeset in Minion Pro by MJ&N Gavan, Truro, Cornwall
Printed and bound by CPI Group (UK) Ltd, Croydon CR0 4YY

Contents

Editor's Preface

Fredric Jameson's seminar on postwar French thought was held remotely for graduate students and auditors at Duke University in the Spring of 2021. In the midst of the COVID-19 pandemic, the seminar was obviously quite different from those Jameson recalled from the French '60s, when Lacan's audience, for example, was so tightly packed in the lecture halls of the École normale that it was not uncommon to let one's cigarette ash fall on a neighbor's knee. In 2021, by contrast, attending a seminar required little more than opening a laptop and clicking a few links, and the evocation of a crowded room was apt to strike a pang of agoraphobia in a virtual class. The pandemic, of course, was only one of the more conspicuous differences between contemporary America and postwar France, and yet Jameson himself was not prevented from drawing a number of striking connections between the two. Perhaps the clearest of these can be found in his first lectures on Sartrean existentialism, which resonated strangely with the circumstances in which they were delivered. Through his theory of the "situation," the nexus of relations into which each of us enters, Jameson's Sartre seemed to be reminding us that we must live our new situation ("unprecedented," in the media's parlance) as if we had chosen it ourselves. Thus was the impact of Sartre's "meteorite," *Being and Nothingness*, felt across the serialized confinements of our global present, long after that immense work originally landed in German-occupied Paris.

Jameson's overarching narrative of the period carried us slowly away from those powerful examinations of lived experience in Sartre and related figures such as Beauvoir and Fanon. Over the course of the lectures, a succession of theoretical paradigms traces the departure from questions of praxis and experience—structuralism, semiotics, and all the rest of them—each receiving here an explanation in its own terms before dutifully acceding to the rapid turnover of intellectual problems that have collectively come to be known as French theory. It is true the term "French theory," an American invention, threatens to smooth over the contentious debates that attended each of these paradigms, which often spanned such distant areas as psychoanalysis, feminism, and film criticism. But, with the benefit of hindsight, the intellectual period as a whole has gained a certain coherence that would have been unthinkable for its participants, partially because the story of its emergence turns out to be the story not only of those students and intellectuals, not only of a university system, of Paris, or even of France, but also of something much larger and more difficult to grasp—namely, the expansion of capitalist relations to a scale for which "unprecedented" is not such an ill-fitting word. The final lectures will then include references to the Maastricht Treaty, the Gulf War, and any number of political and economic topics which would likely be considered aberrations by someone expecting a more traditional history of philosophy or theory. By the same token, if the seminar proposes a definition of theory as such, it does so by articulating how a certain French variant (because there are, of course, others) emerged through a historically specific interplay between thought and social process.

Even a brief glance at postwar France would suggest that it was a society in transition, changing with such speed and regularity that Lacan found it reasonable to remark, "What I always expect from history is *surprises*, and surprises which I still haven't succeeded in explaining, although I have made great efforts to understand."[1] Lacan's paradoxical pronouncement— does expecting a surprise not spoil it?—suggests that he, like so many others of his generation, still entertained a modernist reverence for "the new." In the '50s, France's rapid modernization was introducing novelty everywhere from the home (flooded with new commodities) to the streets

---

1 Jacques Lacan, "Of Structure as an Inmixing of an Otherness Prerequisite to Any Subject Whatever," in *The Structuralist Controversy: The Languages of Criticism and the Sciences of Man* (Johns Hopkins University Press, Baltimore, MD: 1967), 199. See Jameson's discussion below, pp. 187–9.

of Paris, into which the struggles over Algerian independence occasionally spilled.[2] But whatever prosperity was once promised for some by France's postwar arrangement soon disappeared, as its *trente glorieuses* gave way to the first waves of deindustrialization sweeping across the '70s; the loss of empire, redoubled by a pervasive Americanization, had long since set the agenda for many political mobilizations of French nationhood in response. Any lingering faith in "the new" likewise became an unaffordable luxury amid the decay of the modernizing project—not only in France, after that project failed to be met with liberation in May '68, but also globally, having left in its wake the ravages of climate catastrophe, a brutal legacy of racial violence, the decomposition of the working class, and resurgent fascism. It has been a long time since any of these came as a surprise.

Jameson's seminar emphasizes the extent to which the end of modernization is accompanied by a certain paralysis of action, a paralysis which encourages ever more elaborate analysis from the period's intellectuals. To be sure, their various attacks on idealism and "the philosophy of the subject" hardly compensate for the missing dimension of collective social life; nor have they brought about anything resembling the seminar's ghostly twin, "the years of praxis." But they do draw our attention to a sense of political urgency in the realm of ideas itself (as it becomes, for Althusser, another terrain of class struggle). Particularly noticeable in this regard are the proliferating concepts and theoretical languages which, from Sartre onwards, are summoned to ward off the relapse of thinking back into this or that rote "philosophy" (or into yet another discipline) and for which the Deleuzian neologisms—nomads, desiring-machines, bodies without organs—now serve as the great and properly disorienting examples. These languages can become then quite complicated indeed, and their accrual throughout the seminar makes apparent the immense effort and rivalry involved in their emergence.

At the same time, *The Years of Theory* renders this rich tradition of thought available for contexts far beyond those of its inception. In fact, Jameson's work as a whole can be taken as an extended demonstration of the uses of French theory—among many other traditions—within his own highly original Marxist project. The development of that project is partially reconstructed in the footnotes to the present seminar, from

---

2 Two closely related developments, as Kristin Ross demonstrates in *Fast Cars, Clean Bodies: Decolonization and the Reordering of French Culture* (Cambridge, MA: MIT Press, 1998).

his first book on Sartre's style, to engagements with structuralism in *The Prison-House of Language*, to his response to Deleuze and Guattari's challenge to interpretation in *The Political Unconscious*, to the critical reflections on Althusserian Marxism that extend into *Allegory and Ideology*. Across these works, the advantages of a "deplorable nonchalance" toward the various orthodoxies of the period (to broaden Jameson's more specific stance toward Greimassian semiotics) are proven to the extent that his example permits fellow travelers of all stripes "to *steal* the pieces that interest or fascinate us, and to carry off our fragmentary booty to our intellectual caves."[3]

Just as Benjamin offers a rationale for the seminar's organization (in a wonderful fragment that I leave to the reader to discover in the following pages), so too might he provide an apt model for this methodology. For both Benjamin and Jameson, the active appropriation and arrangement of concepts is not so distinct from an assent to the passage of historical time in which they appear: it is history itself which measures the distance between thought and reality, and which provides the impetus for their relation. What this means for Jameson is that thinking historically requires thinking through the movement between identity and difference, the identity and difference of historical periods themselves, whereby what appears utterly foreign and relegated to a bygone era suddenly lets off a flash of resemblance to any number of others, while everything familiar about the past morphs beyond all recognition and transforms itself into a sign of profound difference from the present. At its most powerful, the strangeness of the past projects itself into the future as nothing less than a promise of the world to come.

To attend Jameson's seminar, as the following transcript allows, is not only to relive the era of French theory with a certain vicarious enthusiasm, but also to witness a unique kind of historical thinking at work. Readers may then count themselves among the many students who have benefitted and continue to benefit from the generosity that sustains Jameson's thinking and teaching alike. It is out of a desire to retain the spirit of this pedagogy that the following transcript largely preserves Jameson's extemporaneous speech (whose colloquial style, I don't think he would mind me saying, may come as a relief even to admirers of his written works).

---

3 Fredric Jameson, "Foreword," *On Meaning: Selected Writings in Semiotic Theory*, A. J. Greimas (Minneapolis, MN: University of Minnesota Press, 1987), viii.

Transcribing and editing that speech has admittedly afforded an insight into what is lost in the process, such that it seems necessary to conclude with the obvious point that even a more or less faithful record of the lectures can only come at the price of reducing their innumerable qualities to a single, finite text.

Carson Welch

Introduction

The Seminar as a Collective Book

Hegel distinguished three kinds of history: that of participants or con-temporary witnesses; a history reconstructed around a theme, possibly but not necessarily arbitrary; and, finally, history viewed as the progres-sion of the Idea, as the realization of the Absolute. The history of French theory I propose here can be grasped from all three perspectives. If, for the Hegelian Absolute, one substitutes the evolution of capitalism, then it will gradually become clear how the emergence of French theory in the 1940s and its gradual exhaustion in the neoliberal period can be seen to be an expression of the uniquely national intellectual response to this more fundamental trajectory.

As for the construction of a history in terms of a theme, and one cer-tainly at issue throughout this whole period, the lectures foreground the relationship of the production of theory to Marxism and the varying solutions of mainly linguistic alternatives to an incomplete Marxist reading of the then current situations. This version could also be expressed as the construction of so many idealisms in the face of a philosophically unsat-isfactory materialism, or indeed, as the reverse. Finally, and this is what I want first to underscore, the book can be grasped in its autobiographical dimensions, as the account of a witness and sometime participant.

There are therefore at least three stories to be told here. The first is that of the productivity of a Marxist framework or problematic. Then the texts themselves demand periodization and reconstruction in an authorial as well as a more general thematic context. Finally there is my own (very mediated) participation in a period that runs from the Liberation of Paris in 1944 to the 1980s or '90s, or in other words to the de-Marxification of French intellectual life, the subsumption of France into the European Union, and the gradual primacy of a neoliberal or privatization-cum-austerity economic agenda.

One's seminars are, one thinks, a rather personal matter, something between oneself and one's students; and, on the other hand, a relation of performance to the texts in question. Lectures is too formal a word (although we have to use it), talks a little too informal. They are not writing either, although we have tried to reduce the spoken dimension to a respectable minimum. Meanwhile, they necessarily imply a pedagogical philosophy of some sort, but I leave that to the reader, the former or imaginary listener, to work out.

In the case of this set of lectures, I find, on reading it for the first time (since I did not write it, I had never read it before), that it is informed by an autobiographical impulse I cannot quite classify; although once identified, I find it at work in other seminars of mine in the last few years. I can only explain it by the non-chronological review of what I would call cycles of intellectual interest that have at various periods possessed me: thus, I could imagine defining myself in terms of Science Fiction, architecture, film, German culture, Marxist theory and practice, psychoanalysis, Hegelianism, modernism and maybe some more rubrics which certainly sound like seminar topics, but which have for me been dimensions of a life—on the order of France, China, Los Angeles, the Balkans, Italy—experiences or passions, in other words, rather than topics. Perhaps one could also identify these as so many different languages. In that sense, the present lectures are as much about France as about "theory," and as much about certain years, as about a steady commitment or specialization.

Meanwhile, under certain circumstances, there can be a personal involvement with the "production of texts" which far exceeds the merely vocational and also constitutes a stand taken on the debates, the research, the ideological positions, of other people, some of whom I have known personally, but with all of whom I entertained a peculiarly ideal relationship which is more substantial than the abstract or scholarly one of the researcher or the imaginary one of the fan. Nor was this relationship a purely individual one: in all its phases, it was collective and involved the participation of groups of people—students, colleagues, comrades—in its enthusiasms and its disillusionments. The theoretical positions about which I will shortly speak, that is, the written transcriptions of the spoken accounts that follow, all have the status of lessons I both learned and taught, and rehearsed in common with other people.

I first discovered my own profound acknowledgment of the spirit of Sartrean existentialism in contact with the novelist Georges Auclair, at Haverford College, and René Girard, then at Bryn Mawr. I indulge myself by remembering my intellectual excitement at unpacking that first shipment from France of the big fresh uncut volumes of *Saint Genet* and *L'Être et le néant* in the living room of my family home in Haddon Heights, New Jersey, in the early 1950s. But it was the reading of Sartre's novel *L'Age de raison* which first struck me like a thunderbolt and revealed the truth of an existentialism to which, since then, I have always tried to be faithful. I mention these personal matters because they document the ways in which an individual, and indeed a foreigner, participates phenomenologically, if I may say so, in what is in fact a collective social phenomenon. Indeed, my teachers, both at Haverford and at Yale and mostly French, confirmed the way in which a philosophy or a "theory" takes on a quasi-material and certainly historical existence by way of collective acknowledgment.

Indeed, it was during this period, as frequent stays in Paris confirmed, that the hegemony of Marxism and existentialism during the Resistance and the Liberation began to be complicated by the excitements of linguistics and semiotics and also the emergence of new forms of politics on the left and the emergence of Trotskyist and Maoist adherents alongside the party-communist ones to which I had only a limited access.

It was during this transition that I began to understand that the new semiotic activities, as well as the various "philosophies of the concept" being elaborated alongside more familiar idealisms and materialisms, were all in dialogue (a word I don't much like but prefer to the bland Rortyan term of "conversation") with Marxism. But it was also at this time that, at UC San Diego, my own intellectual participation in what by now we may call the evolution of French theory (from structuralism to semiotics, from Sartrean existentialism to the various so-called post-structuralisms) took on a more openly collective form.

One learns as much from one's students, and, in particular, from their commitments to the material, as from one's own affinities, and so my own work during this period constituted a kind of untheorized collaboration with many interlocutors—students as well as visitors, colleagues as well as comrades, teachers as well as learners, at La Jolla, and (after interludes at Yale and at Santa Cruz) at Duke, where, during the plague years, remotely, there took form these lectures to which those interlocutors, in one way or another, contributed. I cannot name them all, they know who they are, but I must make an exception for the name of my regretted friend, comrade, and collaborator Stanley Aronowitz, with whom together we founded both the Marxist Literary Group and the journal *Social Text*, and to whose memory this seminar is dedicated.

Meanwhile, from an "objective" standpoint now, I will offer a periodization which is perhaps more idiosyncratic than some intellectual histories of the period, in which the *Tel Quel* group (and various analogous movements and journals in film studies) have generally been called upon to play a central role in the French '60s and '70s. This is, rather, for me a period in which the political as well as the theoretical avant-gardes begin to break down and to constitute themselves into a variety of named ideological groups, some of them truly vast and systemic indeed: I will mention the Althusserians, the Lacanians, the Foucauldians, the Deleuzians, the Derrideans, alongside a variety of feminist movements and various subcultures. The towering edifice of Lévi-Strauss's work precedes all this, no doubt; while that of Roland Barthes faithfully accompanies these developments and adapts in wonderfully creative sinuosity to their general rhythms. Anyone who has not lived through this period will not be able to understand how one can provisionally adhere with a certain passion to all of them in turn, without abjuring the Marxism with which they were all "in dialogue" and without becoming a fanatical adherent of any one of these theoretical stances, now considered a doctrine or an -ism. But this is my personal claim, which animates these lectures and which, from another perspective, has tended to be denounced as eclecticism.

What do I mean by developing within a Marxist problematic—or perhaps I should say a Western-Marxist problematic (the latter being distinguished by an emphasis on ideology, political subjectivity, and ultimately commodification, as opposed to the centrality of questions of party organization and class struggle in the older Leninist paradigm)? I think it means an overlap of three more circles of interest and inquiry: that of existential ontology, that of Lacanian psychoanalysis, and that, finally, of semiotics and structural linguistics. When these three overlap within the more general framework of questions and problems proper to so-called Western Marxism, at that point "theory" has thrown off its more purely philosophical and systemic exterior and reaches its moment of greatest intensity. When the three zones (and their Marxian framework) begin to disengage from each other and recover a more traditional autonomy of an essentially academic nature, then that impetus is weakened or lost altogether (and much the same thing can be said for a Marxism that relapses into the technical questions of value, class definition, and the like.) Academic philosophy begins to reconstruct itself, and questions of psychology, ethics and aesthetics reassert their primacy as separate fields. This seminar does not propose some unified "field theory" in response to the current situation; but the intent is to demonstrate for those who never experienced it the intensity and originality of the problems of those older "years of theory."

Hegel would not have wanted me to theorize the end of this very rich and exciting period with the contingent deaths of its "master-thinkers." Nor is it necessary to do so. For the exhaustion of their work coincided with the withdrawal of the world-spirit (so to speak) from France at the moment of failure of the Mitterrand experiment in social democracy and the absorption of France into a Europe in which, as Régis Debray has observed, it turned from being a nation-state into a member-state, and in which the autonomy aspired to by Gaullism proved in nascent globalization to be unrealizable.

Nor does one have to posit the end of the Soviet Union as a central cause of France's loss of cultural hegemony, although among the various "overdetermined" preconditions for that outcome it must certainly take its place. I have mentioned de-Marxification as an intellectual process, which spelled the end of Sartrean fellow-traveling. The end of the concrete presence of an active and influential Communist Party is a separate matter, one cunningly engineered by Mitterrand but clearly completed by the definitive breakdown of the Soviet experiment. I have already mentioned the role played by the coming to hegemony of neoliberalism in the various tournants to be subsumed under the term postmodern. What follows culturally and intellectually is the return of academic specializations, the withdrawal of the possibility of political action (and of the sympathies with it), and a general "aesthetization" of theory and politics which Walter Benjamin already denounced in the 1930s. The return of certain neo-fascisms all over the world tends to encourage the belief in a kind of cyclical movement of politics or the Zeitgeist, which I think it would be better to avoid.

Still, something more should be said in conclusion about the preeminence of France and more particularly of Paris which is the premise of this "history." Why should there have accrued any special privilege to French theory in this postwar period, and what can possibly justify the implicit characterization of Sartre and his successors as "world-historical" figures in theory?

This is the moment to underscore and defend a level of properly geopolitical interpretation, of which the US reader is less likely to be aware than the European one. To be sure, the unique centrality of Paris—which has no equivalent in the other West European countries, let alone the United States—makes for a situation for intellectuals in which the doom of provinciality is irredeemable even for strong regionalisms. Sartre's *La nausée* is first a powerful and uniquely philosophical expression of the ennui of the provincial town; but its historical background is that of the return of the global adventurer of the 1920s. Roquentin is a caricature of André Malraux returning home from an Indochina in which he hoped to make his fortune in stolen artworks: this retreat signals the transition to a political 1930s in which fascism and Soviet Communism reoccupy the field of play and condemn the new Sartrean intellectual to historical research (M. de Rollebon and conspiracy) and thereby to that paralysis of praxis or action from which the awareness of ennui or Being springs. (In this respect, the Occupation—the Republic of Silence—is to be seen as yet another form of forced provincialization in which the choices of freedom can be analyzed in their absence.)

As a kind of metaphysics, then, a geopolitical analysis presupposes a view of the human animal as a species condemned to seek "meaningful" activity beyond social reproduction as its justification for being. I will argue that this fate holds at the level of the nation-state as well. The defeat of France by England in the Napoleonic period—the loss of world hegemony to the British Empire—is, for its citizens, consciously or not, a sentence to an essentially superstructural competition, to the exercise of action through language and the elaboration of culture (the production of intellectuals and artists as well). Ennui begins here, with the epigones, Musset's "enfants du siècle," and begins to bear those "fleurs du mal" which will culminate in the existential and phenomenological philosophies of the immediate postwar period.

It is a situation which is redoubled on the empirical level, with a renewal which will leave France stranded between the superpowers and its intellectuals productively caught between capitalism and communism, and in search of a third way which does not exist. The very geographical situation of France during the war is allegorical of its unique divisions: a reactionary yet self-governing zone and a Nazi occupation. France's intellectuals thus knew both defeat and victory. They had not, as in Italy or Spain (let alone Nazi Germany), been thoroughly purged and subjected to that hiatus of modernist production suffered also by the Soviet Union. On the other hand, they were far from having been reduced to the Americanizations of the United Kingdom or postwar West Germany. Only France, indeed, experienced both the Popular Front and the fascism of Vichy, both a Nazi occupation and a left-wing Resistance, along with a Gaullist nationalism that gave it, for a time, a certain autonomy from both the United States and the USSR. This limited free space will determine the unique possibilities of thought and cultural production open to the intellectuals read and studied in these lectures.

It only remains to admit that I and my collaborator Carson Welch have chosen to retain a (somewhat laundered) spoken text, whose advantage lies in the innumerable digressions and obiter dicta its situation permits; nothing essential has however been changed or added, save a few factual corrections.

Fredric Jameson
Killingworth, 2023

1

Les Cinquante Glorieuses

In the early years of the fifth century BCE, a famous philosopher visited
Athens. You could say that this philosopher, Parmenides, was the inventor
of ontology, and thus, in a way, the first real philosopher. Athens was a
small town, and everybody knew who he was. Being a celebrity, he met a
lot of people, one of whom was the young Socrates, who might have been
a teenager. They had a long conversation. That would have been around
450 BCE, and if you believe the reports of this, perhaps you could date
the beginning of Athenian philosophy from that encounter. Socrates will
then meet the young Plato in 407 BCE. Plato abandons playwriting and
becomes part of Socrates' circle, and after Socrates' execution for blas-
phemy in 399, he starts to write the dialogues, a lot of which are fictional,
perhaps including this meeting with Parmenides, which becomes one of
Plato's most complicated works. Did this actually happen? Who knows?
In any case, Plato will turn his circle into a kind of school, the Academy.
In about 367 BCE, a young man from the North—who is not an Athenian
and therefore never really enters Plato's intimate circle—will come to this
school to join his group. This man, Aristotle, is from the general area of the
Macedonian coast, and in 343 he is summoned by the king of Macedonia
to tutor his son, who becomes the king when Philip II is assassinated, the
figure whom we know as Alexander the Great. Aristotle then returns to
Athens and founds his own school, the Lyceum, which practices a certain
critique of Platonism. The Lyceum is founded in 335 BCE.

After that, there emerge two major streams of philosophy that shape medieval philosophy, and then Western philosophy in general. These two major branches of philosophy are, of course, Neo-Platonism and Aristotelianism, and we can abandon those to their own stories. But, if you follow these dates, if you really want to start this period in 450 BCE and end it with the foundation of the Lyceum, you have about a century of interactions and of intellectual stimulus. Lots of other things are going on, of course. There are two world wars. The Persian War has just ended at the beginning of this period, and the great civil war of the Greek city-states, the Peloponnesian War, is just beginning. It is a hot war between Sparta and Athens, essentially, and it will end with the defeat of the Athenians. So there is an initial moment in which the Athenians defeat the Persians and start a civil war with Sparta, ending with the defeat of Athens. Almost immediately, there follows the world conquest of Alexander the Great and the beginning of a still Greek but principally Hellenistic period, which is, let's say, a bilingual world of Greek and Persian, in which the intellectual center of the world will gradually shift from Athens to Alexandria. Anyway, this period seems to have a certain coherence, and it makes sense to think of it as a period in its own right.

Now, if you skip to another philosophical period, eighteenth-century Germany, you find not a period of city-states but of principalities. There is no real German capital. Berlin is to be sure the Prussian capital, but merely a larger city than some of the others. Suddenly, in 1781, from one of the outlying parts of the German-speaking world, which is later called East Prussia but has now completely disappeared, out of a city which was called Königsberg, comes the publication of *The Critique of Pure Reason*, which suddenly inaugurates a whole new philosophical school. Everything comes out of that. I won't go into a lot of detail, but we note that the publication comes immediately after the American Revolution and before the French Revolution, so this is a period of tremendous historical convulsions.

So we could date this period of German philosophy from 1781 to the death of Hegel in 1831. Hegel, Schelling, and Hölderlin are roommates in Tübingen. Fichte moves back and forth through these areas; produces an enormously influential rewriting of Kant and then the first great defense of German nationalism during the Napoleonic invasion. The group called the Romantics are all living in Jena at the time, and Hegel, an unemployed graduate student, somewhat older, comes to Jena later. Weimar being quite close to Jena, it is Goethe who refounds the University of Jena, where Hegel finishes the *Phenomenology* just as Napoleon is winning the Battle of Jena. It is said that Hegel could hear the guns in the distance as he was writing the last pages of his book on absolute spirit, and even that he saw Napoleon himself, whom he pleasantly called "the world spirit on horseback." At any rate, this is a comparable period in which you have an even tighter relationship between these various players and a monumental external world history.

What is that relationship? The history of philosophy is not a history of ideas: it is a history of problems. *The Critique of Pure Reason* is a critique, and it is a critique of types of knowledge. It raises all kinds of problems, and suddenly all those problems lead to an efflorescence of philosophical thought. After Kant come the Hegelian schools, to one of which Marx belongs, and by the time you get to 1850, suddenly all of Hegelianism is eclipsed by a very old book, written at practically the same time as Hegel's early works, which is by Schopenhauer. Schopenhauer's work, along with Lange's history of materialism, suddenly eclipse all that came before them and lead us into a new period of German thought dominated by Nietzsche.

All that is to tell you that I think there is such a thing as the periodization of philosophical problematics. *Problématique* is the word that Althusser uses for this, for a complex of problems that are intertwined and that touch on certain limits, because there comes a moment when you see that these kinds of thinking can't go beyond a certain point, where the problem itself becomes a kind of straitjacket, where the creative force of philosophical inquiry is lost and you get a period the Germans call *Epigonentum*. You know what epigones are: people who are born a little too late to partic- ipate in the great era. The younger French writers—Musset is the most famous—who came to their maturity after Napoleon had a nostalgia for this moment under Napoleon when you could become a general at twenty- five. That comes to an end, and the next generation considers itself, rightly or wrongly, epigones of this great period.

I gave you to read Alain Badiou's article called "The Adventure of French Philosophy," which tries to theorize the notion of modern French philos- ophy as a period.[1] I think it is very suggestive. It's not exactly what I would have done, nor what I am going to do in this course, but it is a starting

---

1   Alain Badiou, "The Adventure of French Philosophy," *New Left Review* 35 (September/October, 2005), 67–77. See Alain Badiou, *The Adventure of French Philoso- phy* (London: Verso, 2022).

point. The other text I put on reserve, by the way, for your amusement, is an interview with Jane Gallop, who was a student in Paris in the '60s, and which gives you an idea of this period from her perspective.[2] She was studying with Derrida at the time French feminism was just evolving, closely related to Derrida, and the interview gives you an idea of the excitement of that moment that we're going to look at in French philosophy. So that is less immediately relevant for us here, but her testimony is interesting.

Badiou writes that

> within philosophy there exists powerful cultural and national particularities. There are what we might call moments of philosophy in space and time. Philosophy is thus both a universal aim of reason and, simultaneously, one that manifests itself in completely specific moments. Let us take the example of two especially intense and well-known philosophical instances.

And then you have what I've just been describing. "First, that of classical Greek"—I would rather say Athenian—"philosophy between Parmenides and Aristotle, from the fifth to the third centuries BCE: a highly inventive foundational moment, ultimately quite short-lived"—although this is a little longer than the other ones we were talking about.

> Second, that of German idealism between Kant and Hegel, via Fichte and Schelling: another exceptional philosophical moment, from the late eighteenth to the early nineteenth centuries, intensely creative and condensed within an even shorter time span. I propose to defend a further national and historical thesis: there was—or there is, depending on where I put myself [because Badiou is still alive, of course, and still writing and philosophizing]—a French philosophical moment of the second half of the twentieth century which *toute proportion gardée* bears comparison to the examples of classical Greece and enlightenment Germany.[3]

---

2   Jane Gallop, "What Happened in the '80s? On the Rise of Literary Theory in American Academia," *Lithub* (December 2020).
3   Alain Badiou, "The Adventure of French Philosophy," 67.

I think that's so. I think this is a very remarkable period, and I propose this as the subject of our seminar this semester.

How long does this period last? I think everyone agrees—and, of course, this is also Badiou's opinion—that it starts all of a sudden, in 1943, with Sartre's *Being and Nothingness*. This is a kind of a meteorite that falls in the middle of an era which is, in France at least, a strange pause in history: the German occupation of Paris. The occupation will end the following year, in August of 1944, with the liberation of Paris, and, of course, World War II ends after that, in 1945. Sartre calls this period of the occupation of Paris the "republic of silence," and I'll read you the first lines of his account of this period. This is from a collection of essays with the title, *We Have Only This Life to Live*, which is the best English collection of Sartre's collected essays from 1939 to 1975, which are otherwise scattered in different publications. So this is where Sartre starts:

> Never were we freer than under the German occupation. We had lost all our rights, beginning with the right to speak. We were insulted to our faces every day and had to remain silent. We were deported en masse as workers, Jews, or political prisoners. Everywhere—on the walls, on the movie screens, in the newspapers—we came up against the vile, insipid picture of ourselves our oppressors wanted to present to us. Because of all this, we were free. Because the Nazi venom seeped into our very thoughts, every accurate thought was a triumph. Because an all-powerful police force tried to gag us, every word became precious as a declaration of principle. Because we were wanted men and women, every one of our acts was a solemn commitment.[4]

And the word "commitment," of course, is the famous Sartrean word *engagement*. Anyway, that is the way that Sartre and his friends thought of this strange period. Sartre's first play, *The Flies*, was allowed to be produced. The Germans were very anxious—or at least at that point the cultural attaché of the Nazi occupying regime was anxious—that Paris be seen as a very lively cultural place under German protection, so they encouraged all kinds of publications which were not explicitly anti-German, anti-Nazi, including Sartre's first play. Before that, Sartre had written *Nausea*, which

---

4   Jean-Paul Sartre, "The Republic of Silence," *We Have Only This Life to Live: The Selected Essays of Jean-Paul Sartre, 1939–1975*, eds. Ronald Aronson and Adrian van den Hoven (New York: New York Review Books, 2013), 83.

is one of the most important novels of the twentieth century. It isn't on
our list, but someday you must all, if you have any interest in philosophy,
read that. In a sense, it's the only successful philosophical novel. But to
develop that would be a longer matter. Anyway, we begin with *Being and
Nothingness* because it does set all this off. So my title, "postwar," is just
slightly imprecise.

In his essay, Badiou goes on to talk about four different operations in
this period. Four procedures which exemplify the way of doing philosophy
specific to this moment: the first one is a German one, or a French move
upon German philosophers; the second one concerns science, the French
philosophers who sought to wrest science from the exclusive domain of
the philosophy of knowledge; the third operation is a political one under-
taken by those thinkers of the period who sought an in-depth engagement
of philosophy with the question of politics; the fourth operation has to
do with the modernization of philosophy, in a sense quite distinct from
the cant of political and social journalism. Here, we find a desire for the
transformation not only of philosophical thought but of philosophical
language as such. And I think one can say that, in a sense, France is one
of the last Western European countries to modernize, really in this now
American sense, because a lot of them called all this *américanisation*.
That begins in France with de Gaulle, the second de Gaulle regime, after
he returns to power in 1958. So the Paris of this earlier period, allowing
for the destruction of the war, is not terribly different from Balzac's Paris.
What happens to Paris after that, in the following decades, will move it
much closer to a conventional world city.

At any rate, I mention that, just as I mentioned these political events in
ancient Greece and in the period of Kant and Hegel, to explain why we're
also going to have to outline, however imperfectly, a kind of history of
contemporary France. We're going to need to see what kind of effect this
extremely mobile period in French history has on philosophy, or rather the
other way around: how the philosophers tried to react to these historical
events. The France that came into being after the war was still a colonial
power. It had its colonial war, which it passed on, as you well know, to us,
after having been defeated. The French then faced something even more
cataclysmic, which ended with the return of General de Gaulle to power,
the beginning of the Fifth Republic, and the independence of Algeria. After
that, what can one say? One can say that the opposition was reabsorbed
into a kind of institutionalized space, and that France begins to be a part

of something that emerges as the European Union, losing something of its national identity. And so the France of today is not at all the France of Gaullism and the autonomous France of that period, which has its effect on the philosophers themselves, because, after all—and I am not at all talking as a nationalist—the national fact, the framework of a nation that you're in, is a collective part of your individual personality. Certainly, the primacy of Athens is all part of ancient Greek philosophy. Plato's utopias, for example, are absolutely a response to this permanent crisis, which is the Athenian state and its imperialism. In Germany the tendency is, first of all, the assumption of a German nationality with Fichte and then the attempt, as in Italy, at a unification of these provinces, which will only happen with the Franco-Prussian war of 1870. It will be hard to talk about these individual philosophers in much detail, but that is a general story I'm going to tell you about the whole movement of this period, a story which runs from the question of individual action, the kind that we just heard Sartre expressing in terms of the German occupation, to the effort to deal with larger institutional and even transnational structures, under which your own political positions, your own words, are acts that have a meaning inside of a very constrained situation.

Now I'm passing to the four divisions of our readings in terms of which I want to tell this story of modern French philosophy, or, if you would like, modern French theory. First is this immediate period of the postwar, beginning in the occupation and running up to the beginning of the Korean War and of the Cold War, I would say. I characterize that as the period of the Liberation; *libération* is the crucial French word for this historical period. It is a period of the possibility of individual action and individual identity, and it is shot through with the fundamental political movement of anticolonialism, which will come to an end in the Algerian War, since Algeria is then officially not a colony but a province of the French state. And, therefore, this is not only a war of national liberation, as they would call it in that period; this is also a civil war, and it is the most deeply festering wound of colonialism in France. As you know, the '50s are a great period of decolonization all over the world. Britain's colonies become independent. But it doesn't mean that colonialism is over. The word we use now is "neo-imperialism." France still has what are effectively colonies. There is something called *Françafrique*, which is France's unwritten partnership with all its former French-speaking colonies. You will have seen in the newspapers that whenever some group of Islamic terrorists kidnap somebody in French Africa, French parachutists arrive the next day and track them down. So, economically, militarily, there is still some kind of French power in its former colonies.

The other thing that then begins, besides anticolonialism, which I think is the fundamental impulse of this period, is the Cold War. It's very important that you understand how the Western Europeans see themselves, even in England, but in France and Italy above all, because Spain is still Francoist. They feel themselves caught between the two superpowers. It's the Korean War that suddenly proves this. The official Cold War, so to speak, begins in France in the late 1940s. The first Gaullist government is a government of national union which includes the Communist Party for the first time in modern French history. When the communists leave the government in May 1947, that is the beginning of the Cold War in France.

Caught as they were between the two great powers, France and Italy, with very strong leftist parties, entertain the possibility that each country needs to affirm a national identity, which is distinct, either from Soviet Communism or from Americanization and the Marshall Plan. The Marshall Plan includes all kinds of economic conditions. You may think that the Marshall Plan is a wonderful, gratuitous, generous act with respect to the Europeans—and, in a sense, it was—but it also very much included, for example, conditions about the import of American films. French national governments in the film area like to include foreign films in quotas so that their own national film industries are not destroyed, as in other countries, by this overwhelming export of Hollywood. The Marshall Plan included clauses which restricted the national possibility of excluding those Hollywood products. So the Marshall Plan, in that sense, can be seen as a project to wipe out national film industries. It was overall quite successful, but, in France, much less, because of both the New Wave and the resistance of Gaullism to this kind of American imperialism.

At any rate, France is caught between these two superstates. Its intellectuals have to ask themselves what side they're on. And you will see that one of the reasons why Americans don't like Sartre—and to a certain degree, Beauvoir—has to do with their positions here. In Beauvoir's novel *The Mandarins*, which people don't read so much anymore but which is a wonderful evocation of this immediate postwar period, the intellectuals are constantly asking themselves: "If it's a choice between the Americans and the Soviets, what do we do?" "Well, the Soviets of course," they say. "Socialism." They know about the gulags, but nonetheless they don't want

Americanization. So this is not exactly "fellow-traveling." This is an attempt to affirm an autonomy of French culture, if you want that kind of word, in the face of the gradual absorption of the European countries. You see this with Brexit. Some of the European states still feel the oppressiveness of the European Union, as opposed to that of the superstates, though you could say that the European Union is already an attempt to create a European superstate in between these two things, even though, of course, the Soviet Union is now gone.

Anyway, that is a first period, which is dominated by Sartre, Sartrean existentialism, and phenomenology. Suddenly, in the late '50s, we'll say, something else begins to happen, a turn toward communication and language called "structuralism." I think that is the easiest way of conveying all this. Suddenly there's a new philosophical current, not from a philosopher but from an anthropologist, Lévi-Strauss, a turn to structural linguistics and a meditation on language, on narrative analysis. All these things begin to colonize the various disciplines. So I would say structural linguistics has a profound effect on the disciplines not only in France but in other countries. So you get this structuralist period which is dominated by a whole notion of language that we will look at. And, from the point of view of anthropology, suddenly you get a very interesting phenomenon, which is that of tribal utopias, of the attempt to analyze societies without power. Lévi-Strauss's work is a fundamental contribution to that movement.

And then, in a dialectical fashion, the meditation on societies *without* power brings about a meditation *on* power. I would say that is the moment when French philosophy moves away from the emphasis on individual consciousness that you found in the first period toward a period dominated by the notion of trans-individual forces. I would say it's a little bit like pre-Socratic philosophy in that sense, or the Tao; it doesn't want to focus anymore on individual consciousness, which would be called "the subject." Focusing on the subject in this period means being confined, as Sartre was, to individual consciousness or the Cartesian subject. This older focus will then be called, with a certain contempt, *la philosophie du sujet*. The new period wants to get out of the individual subject and into great, supra-individual forces, even in psychoanalysis, the drives (*pulsions*). So, in my opinion, this period will be dominated by the two great figures of this period: Deleuze, with his notion of the philosophy of the concept, and Foucault, with his idea of power. With Derrida, it's a little bit different. We would say that Derrida is committed to undermining both the philosophy of the subject and the linguistics of structuralism. Can we say that Derrida has any positive positions with respect to these forces? I think not, but, nonetheless, his is a related project. And this is not to say that these people all worked together. Foucault and Derrida hated each other. They had a great fight. Deleuze is a little bit distant from all these folks, although he had a friendship with Foucault.

We'll see that this third period is characterized by greater forces under the impact of what I call the experience of defeat, because, indeed, I have omitted a crucial moment in contemporary French history, fundamental in any consideration of France even today: May '68, the great uprising against . . . everything, really. Everybody used to joke that even people who were self-employed went on strike. Against whom? Against themselves. Everyone was out in the street; there was an immense fraternization. You can see this, if you like, as the culmination of the utopian strain that I mentioned. This was the great moment of utopia, and it failed. It did not lead to revolution. The Communists are blamed for that. Instead, it led to Gaullist oppression, although General de Gaulle left the government at that point, and finally it led to the corporatization of France. I see this emphasis on supra-individual forces as a reflection of that corporatization, that eventual coming into being of the great transnational monopolies. And the same is true here. That is to say, when the Vietnam War was over, Nixon had prolonged it to the point that the revolutionary power of the anti-war movement was lost. What appeared when the dust settled, when the fog of war cleared away, was not a transformed world, not even the world of decolonization, of independent nations, but the world of transnational corporations, nascent globalization, and the end of a period of this or that individualism, this or that revolt. So here we have, as it were, two overlapping periods: that of structuralism, the linguistic turn, and that of revolt, the Algerian War, May '68, and so-called poststructuralism.

Then a fourth period could be this period of the epigones, if you like, but I don't like to put it that way. We will look at some of the writers from this period. It is certainly a period of globalization. It is a period of a return to the disciplines in the sense that French philosophy had broken free of the disciplines in a way that I will describe in a moment. So it is a return to institutionalization and, of course, of postmodernism, because that is really the first global American cultural movement. You can still count, for example, Foucault's aesthetics among the aesthetics of modernism. Deleuze is always a little more difficult to pin down on these things, but, in a sense, the conclusion of Deleuze's film book is not a postmodernist conclusion but a modernist one. In this period, however, little by little, the modernist aesthetic falls away and you get the beginnings of something else. The beginnings of what? I also call this the end of theory.

Now let's look at this from a different point of view. We have said that each of these philosophical periods—Greece, the Germans, and now the French—are characterized by a problematic, but a changing problematic, a production of new problems. This is, in effect, Deleuze's whole philosophy, the production of problems. But, if you put it that way, if you say philosophy's task is the production of problems, what problems could there be if philosophy has come to an end? These problematics always end up producing a certain limit beyond which they are no longer productive.

What I want to say is not that these people all knew each other, not that they exactly derive problems from each other the way Schelling, Hegel, and Fichte will derive their problems directly from *The Critique of Pure Reason,* but in a different way which turns on the matter of what is called "influence." People think influence is the reproduction of something. When people say, for example, that Simone de Beauvoir, Frantz Fanon, Merleau-Ponty, even, to a certain degree, Camus were influenced by Sartre, that is not the right way to put it, I think. I once interviewed an East German novelist who was quite interesting at the time, and we asked him the then-obvious question: "How much of an influence did Faulkner have on you?" As you know, after the war, all over the world, it is the example of Faulkner that sets everything going, from the Latin American boom to the newer Chinese novel. Faulkner is a seminal world influence at a certain moment. But what does that mean, "Faulkner's influence"? So he said, "No, I never learned anything from Faulkner—except that you could write page after page of your novel in italics."

What does that mean? It means that to be influenced by somebody is not to write like him or her; rather, someone's work suddenly opens up new possibilities that you never thought of before. It never occurred to you that you could put page on page in italics. Suddenly, you're free. You're opened up to something new, which may go in a completely different direction. What Sartre did, as someone who was not just a philosopher but also a playwright and a novelist, was to suddenly open up the possibility of writing philosophy in a wholly new way. You could suddenly get rid of all the traditions of academic philosophy. You could turn philosophy into something which was like the novel, which was really part of the novel. There was a new freedom which all these people, in one way or another—maybe except Derrida, who says he was never interested in Sartre—but all these other people—Deleuze says Sartre was "my master," *mon maître*—felt was liberating, until they reach a certain moment when that influence is no longer productive for them and they cast it away. But, even then, they keep certain freedoms that they have learned.

I think that the passage in this period from philosophy to what we call "theory" is part of that liberation. Suddenly, philosophy is freed of its systemic ambitions. Here's an anecdote. One of Sartre's closest friends in school was Raymond Aron, a conservative, pro-American political scientist. In those days, the French government had scholarships to various foreign countries. They started a whole French school in Brazil. Lévi-Strauss himself taught in that school and his early work is the result of that contact with Brazil. Roland Barthes taught on this scholarship in Egypt, because the French had a teaching fellowship in Cairo. There was one in Berlin, and when Aron had just gotten back he said, "There's this thing called phenomenology. What does it mean?" He is sitting in a cafe with Sartre and Beauvoir, and Aron says, "What it means is: you can philosophize about that glass of beer." Suddenly, the whole idea that phenomenology allowed one to think, write, and philosophize about elements of daily life transforms everything. As historically reconstructed by participants, the drink turns out to have been a *crème de menthe*, but that doesn't matter too much. That's the lesson that these people got from phenomenology, and that's what seems to me to set off this immense period of liberation from philosophy, a liberation toward theory. But, in the fourth period, this kind of thinking is folding back down, and we are seeing once again that professional philosophy has reconquered these terrains that were opened up by theory.

Before we end, let me tell you why this is going to be so frustrating and unsatisfying for all of us in this class, including me. We're trying to do everything. That means that we're going to touch on each of these people only for one or two classes. How do we do that? I had a boss once (Roy Harvey Pearce) who said that—I hate sports metaphors, but this one I've always liked—to get to know a field, you can't know everything in detail. But the first things you need to learn as a student, graduate student, or young scholar are the names and numbers of all the players. My references are not to American sports, but you know that Messi is a number 10; Ronaldo is a number 7. That's what you know about the players: you know their names and you know what they do, but you haven't seen all their games. That's what we're going to try to do in this course. Instead of numbers, what I'm going to give you are the slogans. For Sartre we would say "freedom," "bad faith," "reification," a series of slogans like that. You will learn, at least from me, what those slogans are, even if we don't have time to read *Being and Nothingness* cover to cover. And we will use these words in the language, because, in France, that's what people did. *Le pour-soi*, the "for-itself," short for *l'être-pour-soi*, means human beings, human reality, as opposed to the *en-soi*, the being of things. So, if we say the *pour-soi* in English, that is a meaningful expression.

So that is the kind of slogan we will be learning. The French get it from the Germans, of course, because, when we talk about Heidegger, we talk about *Dasein*, "being there." The whole point is that these existentialists don't want to talk about mind. They don't want to talk about personal identity. They don't want to talk about spirit. They certainly don't want to talk about soul, because they don't believe in any of those things. How are they going to talk about what's in the head? They're going to call it "consciousness." Sartre's little essay on Husserl, "Intentionality: A Fundamental Idea in Husserl's Phenomenology," is the fundamental starting point for all this stuff; it is the connection between phenomenology and existentialism, and it addresses consciousness. Consciousness does not have a personality or an identity. It's impersonal. But it's very strange. What can you say about this thing, consciousness? We each have it, but does each have it the same way? We don't know.

Anyway, *pour-soi* will be one of these slogans in terms of which we'll have to read Sartre. I have already mentioned "desire" for Deleuze, but there are plenty of other Deleuzian slogans, "territorialization," "de-" and "re-territorialization." For Foucault, "power" is one word that you get, but you can also look at "genealogy." In other words, we're going to go fast, and we're going to try to develop what was called a while ago "cultural literacy." When you talk about one of these philosophers, these are the keywords that come to mind, and we have to start with those because we're going too fast to do anything else.

There is a sentence of Walter Benjamin's that I like to quote, and it reflects both the limits of this course and the limits of our own tolerance, our frustration, and all the rest of it. It's from a collection of sayings of his. "The task is to make a stopover at every one of these many little thoughts. To spend the night in a thought. Once I have done that, I know something about it that its originator never dreamed of."[5] Now, if you were making a grand tour and you spent a night in Paris, one in Rome, then Naples, then Cairo, you spent one night in each of those places, and, afterwards, someone asks you how you liked them, what would you know about them? You have been to each of these places and seen some buildings, but, in effect, you know nothing about them. That is what it's going to be like for us with each of these thinkers. We will spend one night in Deleuze, one night in Foucault, one night in Derrida. What are we going to get out of that? Well, at least we will have a larger narrative. You may not like spending a night in some of those. You may not like some of them. Some of them you will like. And, for intellectuals, "like" means "interest." You will be interested in some of them, and others you will not be interested in. The ones you're interested in, I hope, will lead you on to further exploration, and, as for the ones you're not interested in, at least you will know who they are, why their enemies are hostile to them, what's the matter with them, and how they fit into this period of great rivalry—because the Paris of this period is tremendously rivalrous. Newer generations are coming out, wanting to write new stuff and become famous; people are divided into groups. You have Derridians, Foucauldians, Lacanians, and they are all hostile to each other in one way or another. You aren't necessarily going to be able to participate fully in that sense of rivalry, but at least you can get a sense of the way it all works.

Years ago, when I was teaching a course on the '60s, I had two visitors named Chantal Mouffe, whose work you may have read, and Ernesto Laclau, who unfortunately died recently. I asked Chantal to tell us about her experience of the '60s. At the time she was having a love affair with a guerrilla, freedom fighter, whatever you want to call them, in Colombia so she only got back to Paris in the summertime. "Oh," she says, "it's like a slideshow. Each summer I'd say, 'What are you doing?' and they would respond, 'Well, now we're studying Lacan's attack on the signified.' Then I'd go away, and when I came back the following summer I'd say, 'What's up with the signified?' 'Oh, we're through with that now. We're doing the *passe*.'" And so on. So the French '60s, the high point of all this, is a constant fight over new problems, new solutions. It is a very lively intellectual era.

January 21, 2021

---

5   Walter Benjamin, *Selected Writings: Vol. II, Pt. I, 1927–1930*, ed. Michael W. Jennings (Cambridge, MA: Harvard University Press, 1999), 122.

2
The Uses of the Verb to Be

{Sartre}

Next time, we will get involved in the philosophical problems of Sartre's idea of the look, but, for the moment, I want you simply to think of the look as a form of alienation. It is alienation by the other. The other problems we will take up are the philosophical ones, but alienation, I think, gives you a kind of limit, which perhaps makes it possible to work with the matter of the look in some practical way. The point is that, in Sartre, there are, let's say, four levels of being. First, being-in-itself, the *en-soi*. You can say three things about it, and that's it: it is; it is in itself; it is what it is. That is a fairly sterile and unsatisfying way of talking about being, and, of course, it is directed a little bit against Heidegger, for whom having some relationship to Being is of enormous importance. But it helps Sartre set up his major concern, which is not the *en-soi*, not being-in-itself, but being-*for*-itself, the *pour-soi*. Being-for-itself is of course what we call consciousness. Do we want to use the term "thinking"? Heidegger makes a great deal out of this business, *das Denken* and so forth, though by that he doesn't mean what traditional philosophy means. But he has his own word for Sartre's for-itself, and that's *Dasein*, the being-there, which is different for him than *Sein* but part of it. In Sartre, on the other hand, the *pour-soi* is going to be defined against Being. So, if Being *is*, then, for one thing, the *pour-soi*, consciousness, is *not*. If Being is what it is, then the *pour-soi* is *not* what it is, and it is what it is not. And finally, if Being is in being-in-itself, then the *pour-soi* is, obviously, being-for-itself.

So, all of a sudden, we realize that Sartre's language of being must be taken as a particular philosophical code, whereby Sartre is trying to express some things for which there really is no preexisting language. And there is a game that he is playing with the verb "to be." This game is to exclude certain kinds of ideas, like those of psychology, and to invent others. So the status of all these words is very unusual. Normally, we think that philosophy writes its thoughts down in language. But this kind of philosophy—for the moment we'll call it "existentialism"—doesn't believe that language can really express reality; it believes that language is at a distance from reality, that you need a trick to ward off error and metaphysics but above all to allow you to think something which is not even the negation of something that is. All I'm saying is that we must see this linguistic trick of using the word "being"—to be what I am not and not to be what I am—as a kind of strategy for warding off the phenomenon of reification. He invents the word in French, *chosification*, because, as you've seen from these initial oppositions, the for-itself cannot *be* something. To affirm that the for-itself, consciousness, *is* something, is to reify it. Things are obviously reified because a thing is a thing. It is what it is. But since consciousness cannot really *be* anything, then one of your major philosophical polemics is going to turn on how we can use language to talk about consciousness *at all*, to talk about it *as though* it were something when it cannot *be* anything. (Althusser will, later on, use italics in a similarly strategic way.)

We'll constantly be repeating these things. But let's start over again with where this comes from. This is supposed to be an existential ontology. Heidegger calls his a phenomenological ontology, an ontological phenomenology. And phenomenology itself remains to be defined. So phenomenology, in its modern sense, is an invention of one of these two Germans who stand behind all of this, Martin Heidegger and Edmund Husserl. Husserl wrote thousands and thousands of pages. A lot of them are now in Leuven. People go and study there for a time and work through a few of these manuscripts. Paul Ricœur is the most famous French commentator on Husserl. Eugene Fink was the latter's most notable German disciple. But if we can't really get into what phenomenology is, we can at least talk about what is phenomenological. Husserl's idea was that, to describe operations of consciousness, you have to bracket or suspend their content. Let's say it is a question of some mathematical problem in my mind. We suspend the truth of that operation, and we observe how the operation is going on. That would give us a different kind of description than if we're just thinking mathematically. It would give us a phenomenological description of the operation of thinking mathematically. Okay, well, think of Merleau-Ponty's book *Phenomenology of Perception*. Suppose I'm perceiving things now. Can I describe what that's like by removing the objects? I'm looking at some colors. All right, I suspend the colors. They're still there but I'm not interested in them; I'm interested in the process whereby I'm perceiving them.

So that would be a phenomenological description. Now that's why, as I said the other day, you have this famous moment when Sartre's friend comes back from the Germany of the period and says, "Now you can philosophize about this glass of beer." Yes, I can bracket or suspend the glass of beer, and I can try to make a phenomenology of taste, let's say. What is it to distinguish different tastes? I can dislike somebody, then bracket that person and ask myself: What is it to dislike? What kind of operation is going on in my mind? Now Husserl did not get into that kind of thing; he was much more interested in epistemology. And we'll see that the whole thrust of this development is against traditional epistemology, what Kant was interested in. How can we know that we know? What gives us the certainty of proof of a scientific statement? Kant used the word experience, but, you remember, the word "experience" in most languages—most Latin-derived languages, at least—has the same origin as the word "experiment." So, when Kant was talking about experience he was, in some sense, talking about scientific experiments. Now, when the phenomenologists start to talk about experience, yes, they mean something like that, but little by little the word "experience" opens up a whole range of things that have nothing to do with knowing, with knowledge and science, knowledge in its scientific sense. That's still there and a possibility of exploration; but what's opened up now we will call lived experience, and lived experience is everything.

So you can see the connection between Sartre's novelistic inclinations and the project of a phenomenology. And you can also see, as someone said very pertinently, when Sartre describes these things, he always seems to do it in terms of a narrative or a story. Well, that's the advantage, in a way, of having a novelist do phenomenology, because phenomenological knowledge will examine our operations, but only in a specific situation. And then the word "situation" becomes important. It's not there in Husserl very much, but it's in Heidegger and Sartre. It comes from Karl Jaspers, who was a psychiatrist and philosopher before the First World War. He stayed in Germany, lived through World War II, remained respected and honorable, never became a Nazi or anything. But, anyway, Jaspers began to use this term "situation" philosophically, and out of that Heidegger gets the term, and then Sartre makes it a principal pillar of his philosophy.

We're trying to figure out: What is phenomenology? Why ontology? And then: What is existential about all of this? First of all, you can see that Husserl's analyses are always going to be about what he calls "the living present." It's in the living present that we're performing these operations. We're feeling something and phenomenologically analyzing what a feeling is. We're thinking something and phenomenologically analyzing what that is. Time! Time itself has to be examined, and Husserl attempted to do so in his famous piece on the time sense, from which a lot of this comes. But, obviously, as Hegel says, there is an immense privilege of the present, of this living present.

So you can see a certain connection between Husserl and the *cogito*. Husserl wrote a book called *Cartesian Meditations*. This is, in a sense, to misunderstand Descartes as doing a phenomenology of the present, because the *cogito*—I think therefore I am—is the present and has to happen in the present. I think therefore I *was*? Maybe, but the present has to come first. I *thought* therefore I was? Well, that would be the memory of a *cogito*, but it would still rely on the present in some sense. So there is a way that Descartes—and Descartes is one of Sartre's heroes—in some shadowy way, is in the background of all this. I think that Heidegger is also right to say that Descartes's *cogito* is really about knowledge, and we don't want knowledge; we want experience. So our notion of phenomenology is much broader than anything that would be included in the *cogito*, but there is still in Sartre this notion of the *cogito* as a moment of truth, as a living present of some mental operation which is truer than the other ones. That will be what is called in existential language "authenticity" or "freedom." Authenticity and freedom constitute this special kind of Sartrean existential *cogito*. But we will come back to that.

That's enough of Husserl, I think, except for the word "intentionality." Intentionality doesn't have anything to do with intention. Did so-and-so really intend to do this act? It has nothing to do with that. It is a purely technical word, a foreign loan word—*intention* is not a German word, while *Intentionalität* is something invented by a previous philosopher, well-known in the nineteenth century, named Brentano—and it means exactly what Sartre says it means in an important little essay, "A Fundamental Idea in Husserl's Phenomenology," in short, that consciousness is always consciousness *of* something.[1] This has an important corollary, namely, if there isn't something there for it to be conscious of, consciousness isn't there. Consciousness has to be outside itself, as Sartre says, intending an object. Intention becomes an arrow-word, a word which replaces knowing things, feeling things, perceiving things, and so on. Intending things means everything that can be an object of consciousness. Intentionality could be a pain. It could be a feeling. It could be a perception. It could be a thought. It could be a belief. All those things can be what are called contents of consciousness, but, the minute you don't have any content of consciousness, there isn't any consciousness.

I should add that this means that Sartre refuses the idea of an unconscious. And that is a question of Freudianism that we can deal with when we come to Lacan, whom I read as a successor of Sartre. In very many ways, Lacan, who was, on occasion, Sartre's own doctor, and who was a few years older than Sartre, though they were both still young in the '30s and moved in the same circles, develops Sartreanism further with a very different sort of turn. But does Lacan believe in an unconscious? That is an interesting question too. He talks about it. He uses the word. Sartre does not use the word. I think it's best to think of the whole range of Sartrean consciousness, Sartrean intentionality, Sartrean lived experience, as a kind of preconscious. In the preconscious, you can always be aware of what you're thinking, what you're conscious of, but you don't pay any attention to it. So, we get a kind of distinction between (pre-)reflexive consciousness—and remember that is done with another linguistic trick, which is the parenthesis around the "pre-"—and reflexive consciousness, which means I'm aware of it. It's pretty obvious. Here I am, drumming my fingers, not paying attention, but, at any point, someone can say, "What are you doing?" I say, "Oh, I'm just nervously drumming my fingers." We could not possibly be reflexively conscious of everything we do. I heard Umberto Eco say once, "When I'm talking, I'm not thinking, but, when I'm listening to someone's question, I'm thinking." Okay, well that's the distinction. I do not have a reflexive consciousness of what I'm saying

---

1   Jean-Paul Sartre, "Une idée fondamentale de la phénoménologie de Husserl: l'intentionnalité," in *Situations I* (Paris: Gallimard, 1947).

to you right now. If I did, I'd start to worry, "Am I using the right word? What am I saying next?" It would suddenly get so complicated that my feet would be tangled in these problems of language, and I wouldn't be able to say anything. So we know that most of what we do is not reflexive, but it certainly isn't unconscious. We will leave the question as to whether there is an unconscious for another day, or at least until we get to Lacan.

So existence means my unique existence. Fortunately, I don't think about this a whole lot, but there does come a moment in life, apparently, we are told, when the child suddenly realizes that he or she exists. Hegel writes this moment of identity as "I = I." So, in this moment, which can be a frightening moment, the child suddenly realizes: "I exist. I have a unique existence. My authenticity is somehow my self." There is a pronominal part of this. There is a "my." What does Heidegger call it? A "my-own-ness." There is a my-own-ness that attaches to this strange thing that is my existence. And existentialism is the thought that takes that as the primal experience, and it tries to develop everything else out of that. So it can be religious; there are religious existentialisms—Pascal, for example, and maybe even Saint Augustine, to a certain degree. There are atheistic existentialisms. Heidegger was very insistent on his atheism, even though, for a lot of us, it is rather religious in tone. But this is what the fundamental experience of existentialism is. I would use as an example of this Sartre's last play, *The Condemned of Altona*, about a Nazi war criminal who's hidden away in his family's house in Altona, a suburb of Hamburg, and commits suicide at the end. I don't know whether this was before Beckett or after. You know how, in Beckett's *Krapp's Last Tape*, you have the recording machine, and he is talking back to it as it's telling about previous stages of his life? Well, in *The Condemned of Altona*, the stage is empty and there is nothing but the tape player. The hero is a kind of crazed character who has been talking to the future. "How am I going to be judged by the inhabitants of the thirty-first century?" And the final word from the tape recorder on the empty stage is: "Inhabitants of the thirty-first century, know this about me. *J'ai* été. I have been. I did exist. I was existing. I existed." And that is also a positive thing. It would be wrong to say that existentialism is obsessed with death and so on. It is obsessed with the fact that, right now, I exist, and that this is a unique thing. About Descartes's *cogito*, Sartre likes to quote a teacher of his who said everything starts with the *cogito*, provided you can get out of it. And, for this existential moment, it's the same. Yes, okay, here is this experience. But then how do I get out of it, into the world? How do I get to other people? That is precisely what Sartre's philosophy is trying to do here.

I would say it is an affirmative and energizing philosophy, existentialism. Whereas other existentialisms are not. Pascal's, for example, is about the misery of human beings, the misery of a life in time, my unique identity which has nothing to support it. In Sartre it is an affirmation.

In any case, where does Heidegger fit into all this? We have intentionality coming out of Husserl, and it will later be unmasked as an existentialism, though Husserl isn't interested in anything like that. Heidegger, who was Husserl's student and teaching assistant and successor at Freiburg—and we can leave the rest of it out of this for the time being—wants to turn this Husserlian phenomenology in an ontological direction and to ask the question of being. Heidegger says there are two questions. The existential question is: how is it that I = I? How is it that there is this I? What is the selfness that I have, that I uniquely feel right this minute? That is the question about existence. The second question, about Being, that Heidegger wants to raise is this: how is it that there is something rather than nothing at all? Why is there Being? What is Being? How can there be such a thing as Being? Does Being *mean* anything? Well, this has a long philosophical history, as you can imagine, and one of Heidegger's ambitions will be to reconstruct the history of philosophy around this questioning which he thinks has been lost. And so he uses this term: the "destruction" of the history of philosophy. His disciple, if I may put it that way, and I think it is fair in a certain way, Derrida, will modify this word a little bit: not *Destruktion* but "deconstruction." But it's the same. The destruction of the history of philosophy as metaphysics. Metaphysical philosophy believes that it has the answer to this question of Being, whereas the only way that this question can be posed is *as a question* to which it is false to give any answers. "Authentic" means recovering the living question, keeping the questioning alive.

So Heidegger wants to re-invent the question of Being, but not to answer it. And, little by little, Heidegger will move into a new kind of mystical framework in which we approach Being as such, and that's no longer of interest; but you see that with both existence and Being, language is not going to do much for us. Language is put in question here. Take a look some day at the etymology of the word "to be," the word "being" in the various languages. What are the primal words? Well, presumably, I don't know, "the hand"? That must be a primal word. "The stone." "Hunger."

I don't know. But "being"? Where would a word like that come from? Is it actually—the medievals debated this at great length—a quality of something? This is glass; it is transparent, and it is. But are the qualities of transparency and glass of the same order as being? Well, you can see all kinds of philosophical questions arise. Sartre did not show a great deal of interest in the history of philosophy, I would say, or in destroying or deconstructing the history of philosophy. I would say that it is more a question of the philosophical stand to take in the present. But Heidegger also is going to raise a question about that weird kind of being which is our existence, *Dasein*—not the for-itself, because I think Heidegger does not even talk about consciousness. He doesn't talk about mind, soul, or even consciousness, whereas Sartre will be content to keep the language of consciousness, provided he can juggle it to keep it from referring to a thing. "Human reality" is sometimes the translation of *Dasein*, which just means there is one weird kind of being that is not like the rest of it.

Now there are two more things I want to say about Heidegger that will be useful for us. One is the notion of "world." This is the period of Gestalt psychology, of eco-biology, if I may say that, the idea that there are creatures and they have their ecosystems and so on. It is a 1920s notion of holism, that a thing can't be understood all by itself but must be understood in its own native surroundings, and that thoughts have to be understood in that context too. Well, Heidegger's word for that is "world." And there is a lot of wordplay on this in Heidegger: *Welt weltet*. The world worlds. The world brings a world into being around itself. I think, with some modifications, Heidegger's world is Sartre's situation. But the situation is a much more concrete, let's say, novelistic sense of world. So Heidegger will talk about world in general, while Sartre will talk about the Paris of the 1920s, in which he is a student at the École normale, walking in certain streets, and so on. That is his situation, but it is also his world. This is very important: situation is an essential part of Sartrean existentialism, because if consciousness is consciousness *of* something, what it is conscious of is first and foremost its situation. These two things absolutely go together. It is not conscious of just one object. I'm looking at this computer. I'm looking at this color again. No. All of that is taking place in a larger situation, in which I'm going to a museum because I have to write a paper about Cézanne or I'm looking at Cézanne because Merleau-Ponty wrote a famous essay on Cézanne and I want to figure out what he meant. And that presupposes that I'm a student; I'm reading Merleau-Ponty; this is

New York in whatever year; and I'm doing this among English-speakers. So the situation is a very concrete one that can be explored all the way down, so to speak, but the consciousness *of* something has to take place within that situation.

The other thing you have to remember as you move toward the idea of freedom is that I can't choose my situation, and yet, in another way, I have to choose it, because I have to react to it. That is to say, I am not. I'm not an *en-soi*. My body is an *en-soi* but I'm not an *en-soi*. My situation, however, *is* an *en-soi*, in a sense. I'm born in a certain year, in a certain country, into a certain language, with certain parents, and all of that is something I have no control over. These are, if you like, the contingencies, or, another good Sartrean word that I don't think you're going to meet in these readings but that you may run into, "facticity." Those are the facts that I can't get around. I can't change the fact that I was born in that year. I can't change the fact that I was born in this country. But, in freedom, I also choose those facts. That is to say, I choose my way of living them. So I may bitterly regret that I was born in America and wish I had been born in France or back in the Romantic period or whatever. That's a way of living my American facticity in a negative mode. Or I could affirm it and say, "Boy am I proud to be an American in this century. We're the greatest country in the world."

I'm again kind of caricaturing here. But you see how you are thrown into a situation. Heidegger's word is *Geworfenheit*, "thrownness," and this is the characteristic of existence. Everyone who has lived on the earth has been thrown into existence, and that ultimately means that there was no reason for them to exist. Nobody picked them out and put them in that situation. This is just a basic contingent fact about all of us, that we are thrown into the world, and we're thrown into this situation which involves my body, the dates of my life, my sex, my gender, my language, and so on. All those are conditions that I'm thrown into. But I'm not free not to choose, because I have to live those things as though I had chosen them. And what if you don't like them? Well, then you live in a kind of horrible denial; you wish you were somebody else, someplace else. That's another kind of choice. One of the objections to Sartrean freedom is that this is just the old Stoic idea of being free in chains. How can you be free in chains? This is a silly idea. Sartre doesn't say the opposite; you're not choosing to be in chains, and about to be executed the next day, or something like that, but you have to live it as though you chose it, because you're stuck with it. You have to invent your relationship to this thing. You have to live it. And to live something is a choice. It's a choice of an attitude toward it, of a relationship to it. So I, in chains, can live in perpetual revolt, anger, resignation, despair, or hope.

I think it was the great Italian writer Primo Levi who wrote about certain of the prisoners in the German concentration camps who had simply lost all will. This is really what Agamben means by naked life. They were called *Muselmänner*, Muslims (although they weren't). I don't know why, a kind of Orientalism of fatality. But they sat there, hardly alive anymore. Even this most extreme example is another way of choosing your situation in chains. In any case, you choose it. That is the terrible thing about Sartrean freedom. This is not an energizing part of Sartre's philosophy. To be aware that you are free is to be aware of innumerable things you have chosen and that you have to continue choosing.

So we are in a world which is a situation, for which Sartre invents this expression: "in-situation." I am in-situation. That means that, suddenly, I'm aware that I have to take a position on this. All of us now, with this pandemic, are in-situation; we're stuck in a world and our contacts with people are through this . . . thing. We have to invent relationships to it. It could be exciting, the way television was exciting originally. I mean opening up these contacts with a whole world of other people. Or horribly confining. But we can't *not* have a relationship to it, and inventing that relationship is what freedom is. You invent it whether you want to or not. That's what being alive is.

The other thing that Heidegger did, which I think is very useful for us, is a distinction between the ontic and the ontological. *On* is, of course, the Greek word for "being." The ontic means things which are. That is the normal, Sartrean, novelistic, realistic thing or object. So I have a new kind of lamp up here—I hope you appreciate it—and I have some papers, my glasses, over here another light. All of that is ontic. Those are the existents of the world. But they also all *are*, and that is a level of being which is no longer ontic. The ontic is that each one of those existents is a specific thing. Ontology, the ontological, means the level on which all of them *are*.

Parmenides, whom I mentioned the other day, is famous for affirming that only being is. But that is a very strange philosophy, because it means *not being* cannot *be*. Nothingness cannot be. There is only what is. The ontological level is that level of the question of being, of what Heidegger calls the ontological question. This is very important. We take people's ontic existence—at least Sartre will, in one of his biographical analyses —and we ask: Why is it that my relationship to these ontic things is the way it is? Why do I like certain kinds of things, certain tastes, certain temperatures? Well, he says, because they are all ontological. They are all relationships to being.

So, in both Heidegger and Sartre, there is a way in which you can move from the ontic—the realm of everyday reality—down to the ontological, which is your choice of being. And the choice of being is a much deeper, and if you like, metaphysical choice, and everyone has a specific originary choice of being. What would that be? Why do we do that? At the end of *Being and Nothingness*, he gives us what he says is a kind of metaphysics. He says, of course, we can't do metaphysics because we don't believe in that. But, if there were a metaphysics to my system of being, the *en-soi* and *pour-soi*, what would that be? That would be something that tells us about the *why* of existence. And this is what he says: "Each human reality is at the same time a direct project to metamorphose its own For-itself into an In-itself-For-itself, and a project of appropriation of the world as a totality of being-in-itself."[2]

What is this "In-itself-For-itself"? Every human reality is a passion. This is the passion in the religious sense, what you suffer. Christ's passion is what he takes on himself as suffering. And in emotion, the passion of love. Well, it means it takes possession of you. It is not something that you can pick up or drop. It is something you can't get out of. "Every human reality is a passion in that it projects losing itself so as to found"—to ground—"being and by the same stroke to constitute the In-itself which escapes contingency by being its own foundation, the *Ens causa sui*, which religions call God."[3]

I want you to see how at this point the ontic passes over into ontology, how desires of a *pour-soi* are also desires for being. A *pour-soi* is a nothingness, but it would like to *be*. Now, there is one way it can be, because it is already its body, as well as a consciousness. It can be killed, and then, of course, it becomes an *en-soi*, but that isn't quite what the *pour-soi* really wants. Deep down the *pour-soi* wants to *be* in the sense of the solidity of being, while still being conscious of itself. God would be that, the cause of itself. God would be being itself as a conscious thing, but that would

---

2   Jean-Paul Sartre, *Being and Nothingness*, trans. Hazel E. Barnes (New York: Philosophical Library, 1956), 615.

3   Ibid., 615.

be the *en-soi* being a *pour-soi*, and it's obvious that this is contradictory, that it can't exist.

I'm going to give you an example. I'm thirsty, so I develop a project, another Sartrean word, his word for desire, I suppose, and it is to drink something to overcome my thirst. Thirst is a lack. I wish to overcome this lack, so I drink some water. When it's all over, I'm not thirsty any more, and my desire vanishes, and there's no meaning in that project anymore. But there's a very ephemeral moment when I'm still thirsty but my thirst is being quenched. That would be a very ephemeral moment of an *en-soi-pour-soi*. It's the moment when I'm still conscious of myself as a lack, but I can feel this lack being fulfilled, that is to say, vanishing into being. So that ephemeral moment when I'm both of those things, that could be a kind of symbol of what an in-itself-for-itself is. And that is what human beings deep down want to be, their ontological craving: both to *be* and to be *conscious of being*? But it's impossible.

Let me finish reading this magnificent passage. This is sort of the conclusion of *Being and Nothingness*. There are a couple extra chapters added on, but this is the great moment: "Every human reality is a passion in that it projects losing itself"—I lose myself as a for-itself—"so as to found being, to become the very reason of being, and by the same stroke to constitute the in-itself which escapes contingency by being its own foundation." The in-itself is contingent. I have no reason for being, but I would like to have a reason for being. What will give me a reason for being? Only being itself can ground that: "the *ens causa sui* which religions call God. Thus the passion of man"—and excuse these pronouns and terminology, because, in the French of those days, *l'homme* was the word for man, and was in English too; what can we do about this? Anyway: "the passion of man is the reverse of that of Christ." Remember that Christ loses himself as God to become a human being. "For man loses himself as man in order that God may be born." Because I sacrifice my contingent consciousness to be a part of being itself. In order that God, this *ens causa sui*, may be born. "But the idea of God is contradictory and we lose ourselves in vain." And this is one of the most famous Sartrean sentences: "Man is a useless passion." That is, this passion is impossible, and it goes nowhere. This is, in effect, Sartre's version of Heidegger's question. Heidegger wants to revive the question of being, but not to answer it, because it can't be answered. There is no answer to the question of being. The same with Sartre. Sartre wishes to define our incomplete being in terms of the ideal projected by that being, which would both be consciousness and actually be fully. But this is impossible, and therefore it is a useless passion.

The other way of saying this is in terms of the justification of existence. The point of being thrown, of being in-situation, is that it is completely contingent. Where did my unique consciousness come from? Why would it be born at that moment? Why would it be speaking English? And so on and so forth. There is no answer to that, and, therefore, we may say, unless you believe that a god has made you for a certain purpose, that our existence is unjustified. We have no reason for being. So Sartre says that being born is like this. You're waiting for the train. The train comes along. You get on the train, and it's filled with other people. You find a seat and sit down. The conductor comes through, and he asks you for your ticket. That is your reason for being. You look around and everybody else has a reason for being. Of course. Other people, their existence is justified. But you don't have a ticket. You have no reason for being. This is the useless passion. I'm trying to justify my existence, and there is no justification for existence, or at least for *my* existence.

This also explains what the strange role of other people in this is, the strange kind of optical illusion where I think other people *are*. Of course they are. I see them. The question of solipsism, you see, is, for Sartre, interestingly stupid. Solipsism as a philosophical problem was: How do I prove the existence of other people? And people debate this and figure out how I could possibly know they're not androids, let's say. Sartre says the point is that this problem is backwards. I never have a problem about the existence of other people. Other people exist; it's myself that I have the problem about. How is it that *I* exist?

So other people in their being come first, and that is the look. That is a different alienation. It's the fact that I am always visible. Just the fact that I'm visible, that I have an outside, means that other people exist. Now, if you want to jump ahead to Lacan, then you can say that, for Lacan, language is an alienation. Language is other people, after all. I didn't make it up, and I couldn't make it up, individually, and nobody else could either, although, of course, I couldn't necessarily know that, because they're all talking away. And I, as a child, an infant—*infans*, not speaking—I'm thrown into a world where there are all these other beings around me who are talking away.

And one of the fundamental alienations that I have as a child is my name. The name is the parents, the other people looking at me and making me into a thing. So the parents say, "Well, little Johnny is like this. Oh no, he doesn't like that kind of food. He wakes up at night all the time. Look how cute he is." And so on and so forth. These are all what other people are turning me into. In Lacan, that will be reflected in the formula of the sign. In the formula of the sign—I'm jumping ahead now to structuralism, but we can do that—you have big "S" over little "s." You have the signifier, the word, and the meaning, little "s." In Lacan, you have, let's say, the name, and underneath the little "s" is what Lacan calls the subject of desire. That's this boiling thing that's going on inside the infant. But the name is what is going to turn the infant into a thing, give it a being, the being of little Johnny, or whoever. So that is like the look, in Lacan, that alienation by the name.

Now you can see, with this business of the ontic and the ontological, the look—yes, it's ontic. Here is a weird thing in the world, the fact that human beings have eyes, and they look at people. That is not a meaningful thing. Isn't that sort of an accident? We have hands. Yes, Darwin can explain this, why we have a thumb and how that influences our history. Famously, in antiquity, they used to say that human beings are the ones who can see the sky, because they look up while animals look down. Well, because human beings, before they were humans, came down out of trees into a savannah where they had to look up, because there weren't any trees anymore. So eyes are a kind of *ontic* thing, but the *ontological* meaning of the look is a relationship to being. So ontic and ontological are functioning there as well.[4]

But we are always look-at-able. We are always visible. We are always victims of the look of other people. We are always vulnerable to the look of other people. That is why the look is an alienation. And our own look comes second; I can't see it anywhere. What comes first is the existence of other people. People are looking at me, therefore I have some kind of existence. Then, maybe, I look back at them, and then I can do something to them. But you don't need to philosophize whether other people exist because that's a certainty you have from being born.

A couple other things. I want to talk about these words, because we have to do that. Now, one word that I'm particularly insistent on a particular translation of, one that nobody pays any attention to, is the French word *angoisse*. You can imagine that freedom, which we haven't really completely

---

4 Ibid., Part 3, Chapter 1, Section IV.

dealt with, is not a pleasant experience—consciousness of freedom—and, indeed, it's identified by its relationship to anxiety. Anxiety is: you can't be free, and you can't really be authentic, unless you feel anxiety. The French word is *angoisse*, so the translator is tempted to use the word "anguish," which is the false friend, the immediate cognate of *angoisse*. Anguish, that makes it too metaphysical. In French, *angoisse* is an everyday word. At least *angoissé(e)*. It means, I don't have any cigarettes—can I go out? I'm waiting for a phone call. Then you're *angoissé(e)*. That doesn't mean you're in anguish, like one of the saints. It just means you have anxiety, and anxiety is an everyday experience.

But then how to define anxiety? Okay, here is Sartre's example, one of those that I like the best. You're climbing a mountain. You're on a very narrow ledge. There is a great drop next to you, so you feel fear. You're afraid that a stone will slip and you will fall in. Then you feel anxiety. What's the difference between fear and anxiety? There's a fundamental difference. Fear is fearing that you will fall in. Anxiety is the fear that you're going to throw yourself in because you don't want to be afraid, because that's a horrible, negative feeling. You want to get it over with. Well, there are two ways of getting it over with. They could be Freud's death wish and his eros, if you like. One is to go through this process and get beyond this ledge. The other is to jump off, and then you're not afraid anymore because the problem is solved. You have fallen. If you think in terms of your own life, you can distinguish these things. Fear has an object. Anxiety is fear of my own freedom, so it doesn't have an object. Anxiety is the fear of my not being and the fact that I have to choose everything. So whenever an estimable translator like Hazel Barnes uses the word "anguish," you must rectify it by turning it into "anxiety."

We talked a little about the (pre-)reflexive, which is sort of pre-conscious, if you want to use a less precise terminology. So you have three states of consciousness: (pre-)reflexive (I'm doing things); reflexive (somebody says, "What are you doing," and I say, "I'm doing this"); and then you have pure reflection. That's when you're busy thinking something about yourself, which is, let's say, incorrect. In a pure reflection, all of a sudden, you realize why you're really doing this, what's really going on, Hegel's *Sache selbst*.

We haven't really begun the question of bad faith. Maybe Sartre does have a word for the unconscious after all, and it is "bad faith." Bad faith is how I avoid knowing things about myself that I don't want to know, and that falls into the question of ethics. We'll get back to that, but that would also be authenticity. Most of the time, Sartre says—and Heidegger agrees—we are inauthentic. We are in inauthenticity, from which, every so often, we can conquer a little bit of authenticity. It's not as though we can become authentic and then we are heroes for good. It doesn't work like that. Conquering a moment of authenticity very much involves anxiety, and it takes place in what Sartre calls extreme situations. But, remember, he is a playwright who is interested in situations in which it is demonstrated how we come to terms with our choices.

Another pair of ordinary words that come back again and again in these texts is "transcendent" versus "transcendental." Transcendent is a very plain philosophical word, and, in Sartre, it simply means what is an object for consciousness. It is what transcends consciousness. Consciousness is a nothingness which is *of* something, and the thing it is *of* is what transcends it. Why does one need a word for that? Well, as you read this, you might see why. But it's a technical philosophical expression. Now transcendental, on the other hand, is a super ideological expression. It means idealism. This will get more confusing when we talk about Kant, but it's important to understand how Sartre is using those two terms, which are so similar. It would be important also in this context to talk about humanism and so forth, but we can do that another time. Those are just a few of the terms I wanted you to know about.

And that will be enough for today. We'll go back to the business of bad faith next time. Then we'll take on the look, and then we'll try to take on what follows from the look, namely groups and the relationship to collectivity.

January 26, 2021

3

Reification or Otherness

{Sartre}

Today, I want to try to situate all of this in terms of the history of philosophy, and then I want to situate it in terms of this segment of philosophy
which is French theory. We could think of that segment as seventy years,
if we want to bring it up to date, but it is essentially a fifty-year period,
beginning with *Being and Nothingness.* Now, on the larger issue of philosophical development, one of the ways people have talked about this
history is in terms of the idea of substance. This presupposes that the basic
theme in terms of which one could see philosophy is the subject-object
split, as we have seen it running through Sartre, and we will obviously
come back to it. In the view of many modern philosophers, the ancients
and also traditional Western philosophers are stuck on Aristotle's idea of
substance. Aristotle was a botanist, a biologist. He wanted to find concrete things, species, to name. So this notion of the substance is central
in Aristotle, and in Plato too, because the ideas are ideas of things; they
are like things. And this runs all the way through Western philosophy,
until the modern period that you could say starts with Nietzsche. Various
modern philosophers have expressed this in different ways, but Alfred
North Whitehead is the one who has been revived recently and who has
expressed this very strongly, namely, that modern philosophy wants to
get rid of the centrality of the idea of substance and to replace it with the

idea of process. So what is important is not so much things in themselves; it's how they relate to each other, which is always a process.

So we can talk about a movement from substance to process—or, in absolutely contemporary terms, to networks. In a way, this will be a movement away from things—in Sartre, that could be a movement away from the soul, personal identity, the mind—toward that "something else" which in Sartre is "nothingness." Consciousness is a nothingness, but a very strange and active kind of nothingness. Sartre is already moving away from the idea of substance insofar as substance is the *en-soi*; but, even here, there is nothing to say about substance. Being is. It is in itself. It is what it is. So, already in Sartre, we are beginning to have that movement away from substance, the idea of thingness, toward something else. That something else is going to change as we go through these stages of French philosophy, in which we can see the movement away from the static centrality of things and being toward something else. What is paradoxical is that absolutely contemporary philosophy has come back to things, and we have stuff like object-oriented ontology and networks, as I say, which are not interested at all in the subject anymore, in subjectivity, but in things. Yet perhaps it's a different version of this same movement.

We can sum all that up in a famous medieval sentence, which is often given as the definition of existentialism: "Existence precedes essence." If you understand essence as some kind of substance, as the name of a thing, then you can see how pure existence comes first, and then the thingness of whatever you're talking about begins to appear. As we know, existence is the word for human beings, human reality, in existential philosophy. Being is the word for things. We're talking about reification, and, ultimately, the sensuous. So the *en-soi* is a useful slogan, but it also defines a kind of ethic, because it means that, in a way, we are trying to *be* like things, but what comes first is this nothingness which is anxiety and a freedom of choice, but of a very peculiar kind.

Coming now to these three types of being, the in-itself, the for-itself (consciousness), and ultimately, as we shall see, the for-others. What is that? Some third kind of being, my alienation by other people? Well, we'll see. Now the point about any of these philosophical concepts is that the best way to look at them and the history of philosophy is to find out what they're arguing against, or to find out what problems they're trying to solve, or what questions they're trying to answer. An idea isn't a thing either. It isn't there all by itself. It's in a situation in which it is invented to reply to something, and what it's going to reply to is a problem or a question or another position. So, when we think about Sartre's notion of being—being is; it is what it is; it is in itself—we can ask: Why is he talking about it like that? Because he wants to discredit the use of "being" when it comes to people, and so he has to define being in such a way that it cannot apply to people. And we can only see that when we move to the second mode of being, which is existence, the for-itself.

And yet, as I read to you the other day, in terms of Sartre's metaphysics, so to speak, consciousness wants to be. Our fundamental ontological passion or drive is to be, but to remain conscious, to be an in-itself-for-itself. Why do we want this solidity of being? You can find this in all kinds of places. You can call it a flight from freedom. We don't want to be free; we want to *be* something. You can find it in social life, where people's ambition is to *be,* to be considered and to have a reputation and be something in society. We'll see that you can find it in human relations and so on. Well, in literature, this takes a lot of forms, this longing to be, this dissatisfaction with the insubstantiality of our existence. I'm thinking of a line of Walt Whitman, for example: "I think I could turn and live awhile with the animals . . . they are so placid and self-contained."[1] People brought up the question of animal existence the other day, so I thought that would be a nice one for you, because animals seem, obviously, to have an existence. They have some kind of consciousness—they look at us of course—and yet they have a solidity, apparently. Throughout literature, there is that drive back to animals, back to the earth. The city dwellers, the intellectuals, get nostalgic about the earth, the peasants—Tolstoy, for example, with the solidity of the peasant, the peasant's relationship to the earth. Well, that could be because the peasant is fantasized as having a relationship to this primordial being which is the earth itself, a fantasy we find in Heidegger as well.

So it takes a lot of different forms, this passion for being, this passion to be. But Sartre will isolate a special word for this, for what results from this process, and I gave it to you the other day: thingification, *chosification.* If you want a proper philosophical word: reification, but that's used in other contexts, too, and so maybe that's not so good. Thingification is something we have the habit of. We have the habit of seeing in terms

---

1   Walt Whitman, *Leaves of Grass: The First (1855) Edition* (New York: Penguin, 1986), 55.

of thingness, or as I said, in terms of substances. We have the habit of being attracted to being. Some people seem to be more than others, and so on and so forth. So there is a process of thingification going on here, because clearly, in another sense, there is no privileged consciousness. No one *is* in that sense. I like to refer people to a great Polish writer who wrote his masterpiece around the same time as Sartre's *Nausea,* in the mid-1930s. His name is Witold Gombrowicz, and the book has an equally incomprehensible title, *Ferdydurke.* There's a new translation that's very good. In his novel, what people suffer from is not nausea but what he calls in Polish *niedojrzałość,* "immaturity." The hero is a grown man who suddenly shrinks down into the state of a child, because, in this primal metaphysical state, we are all like children looking at the being of adults. Everybody around us is an adult, but we are children. There is a nice page in André Malraux's autobiography when he meets a priest who was active in the Resistance and who confessed—it's in the Cévennes, I think, where there was a lot of resistance activity during the German occupation—and he confesses those people, so he has a lot of experience with what the resistants feel. He says to Malraux, *"there's no such thing as a grown-up person."*[2] Well, that is this existential sense of not being that Gombrowicz tries to convey in his own way and Sartre in his. So that will have an effect on our notion of ethics that emerges from this, existential ethics, the ethics of freedom—insofar as there is one—because there's a real problem here with ethics.

Okay, so now we move on to something about which we can actually say something (some thing). We really can't say anything more about being from an ontological point of view. It just is, and that is incomprehensible. There is Heidegger's metaphysical question: Why is there something rather than nothing at all? Nobody can answer that. That doesn't mean, "How did our universe, our cosmos, come into being?" This is a question at a deeper level, which is the ontological level. Remember this distinction: ontic means the things of the world and the people of the world; ontological is the translation of all that into the language of being. The eyes are ontic, but the look, in the sense of the alienation of my being, is ontological. This is the movement of ontology as philosophy. This is what ontological phenomenology tries to do to the experiences of the world.

---

2   André Malraux, *Anti-Memoirs,* trans. Terence Kilmartin (New York: Holt, Rinehart, and Winston, 1968), 1.

You begin by describing those, and then you try to figure out how it is that they represent a certain type of being.

So this is what the *en-soi* is busy doing: the for-itself is trying to be, but it can't be anything, and that's where the language of being is useful, because we have the three characteristics of the *en-soi*, the in-itself. Then the *pour-soi* will just be the negation of all those. Being is, but the for-itself, the *pour-soi*, is not. It has no being in that sense. It doesn't mean it doesn't exist; it just means it *is not*. Being is in itself. Well, the *pour-soi* is not in itself; it's for itself. It cannot rest and be placid and self-contained in its own being. No, on the contrary, it is for itself. So that's going to mean that anything has to try to *be* what it is. I'll come back to that.

Let's take the third saying about being: being is what it is. So the *pour-soi* is what it is not, but it is not what it is. The *pour-soi* looks like it's something. It has characteristics. Each of us have characteristics, and so on, and of course we're like a centaur: we are part being—our body—and then we're something else, but that something else isn't a soul, an identity; it's nothingness. Yet, of course, it exists, and, therefore, it has characteristics. People come up to us and ask, "Why are you like this? Why do you do this?" They judge us and so on and so forth. And in a way they're right, except as a *pour-soi*, what I answer is that I am not what they had accused me of being. "You get angry too easily." Yes, I get angry, but I get angry on the mode of not-being. I am not angry the same way a table is brown or solid. I'm angry in some other way.

We were talking about aesthetics the other day—painting, staring at a painting. Gertrude Stein used to say that what she likes is oil painting, the solidified color of oil painting. Thingification, right? If it's a regular color, to be fascinated by it you have to give it a certain density. Well, in the great oil painting tradition of Western art, that increasingly comes to the fore until it explodes in Jackson Pollock, but it's there throughout. What is our experience of a painting when we stare at it? It sounds silly, but it is that we are *not* that color. We are *not* that paint. We are *not* that. That's the pleasure of this thing, that we have it before us—we intend it, to use the word "intentionality"—but we are not it, and that's what its fascination is, and probably a clue to the fascination of all art.

Okay, I want to read for you an example of how all this works. Last time I read you a famous part of *Being and Nothingness,* and now I'm going to read you another: "What are we then if we have the constant obligation to make ourselves what we are, if our mode of being is [defined as] having the obligation to be what we are?"[3] It's that we aren't something, but, obviously, we have certain characteristics that are like being, but we have to be those characteristics. They're not given in advance.

So how does he answer this question? "Let's consider this waiter in the café." They wrote—Beauvoir and Sartre—in cafés; the famous one is *Les Deux Magots,* and Sartre lived right around the corner at Saint-Germain-des-Prés. And they sat there all day long (probably upstairs), scribbling. So they're in the *Deux Magots.*

> Let us consider this waiter in the café. His movement is quick and forward, a little too precise, a little too rapid. He comes toward the patrons with a step a little too quick. He bends forward a little too eagerly; his voice, his eyes express an interest a little too solicitous for the order of the customer. Finally there he returns, trying to imitate in his walk the inflexible stiffness of some kind of automaton, while carrying his tray with the recklessness of a tight-rope-walker by putting it in a perpetually unstable, perpetually broken equilibrium which he perpetually reestablishes by a light movement of the arm and hand. All his behaviors seem to us a game. He applies himself to [linking] his movements as if they were mechanisms, the one regulating the other; his gestures and even his voice seem to be mechanisms; he gives himself the quickness and bitterless rapidity of things. He is playing, he is amusing himself. But what is he playing? We need not watch long before we can explain it: he is playing at being a waiter in a cafe.[4]

Everything we are we have to play at being, even if we don't feel it that way. That's a social function, so, of course, you have to rise to the occasion and play at being that social function. But what Sartre implies is something much deeper than that, and it has to do with other qualities. Of course, we have qualities. Every culture has its catalog, its list of human qualities, social qualities. The longest living of these lists is the four humors. These are all quasi-social qualities, but, of course, they are qualities, apparently, of your personality and so on. Does he mean that there's nothing like that? No, not at all. Of course, we have those qualities. But that's the secret: we have to be them. This is not to say we have to become them; we *are* these qualities already, but have to *be* them.

---

3   Jean-Paul Sartre, *Being and Nothingness,* 59.
4   Ibid.

And then, underneath that ontic quality that each of us has, that our characters are, is a choice of being, what he'll call an originary choice of being. And it doesn't have to be positive. That is, there's a way in which various kinds of negative things can also give us the satisfaction of being. Take for example the inferiority complex, another Sartrean example, by the way. So I constantly think I'm failing, everybody else is doing better than I am, and so on. I go to a psychoanalyst and I try to get over this. I explain that I have this problem that I keep messing things up and I'm so obviously inept and incapable and so on. And I fail. I come to a few sessions, and, little by little, I realize that this is not working. So I drop the analysis. Well, what was the point of the analysis? The analysis was ostensibly to get over this, to cure myself. But the real purpose of the analysis is to *fail* and to show that I can never get over it. So Sartre talks about the voluptuousness of failure. That is, there's a way in which, of course, in the United States, we know that success is supposed to be a voluptuous pleasure. Yes, but failure is too. All of those are modes of being. We can live our relationship to being, which can never be satisfied fully in an ontological sense. We can somehow live those in all kinds of ways. So trying to be, wishing to be, doesn't have to be this positive kind of thing. It can be negative. You can find a profound ontological mode of satisfaction in suffering or unhappiness. You can occasionally find it even in happiness. With any of these qualities—and qualities of character, for example—we're approaching the problem of the other, because qualities of character are generally conveyed to us by other people. We don't necessarily feel them from the inside. But we're talking about deeper feelings from the inside of our existence, so to speak.

One of the things I haven't brought up—and I just mention it in passing so you see how this works on another level—is an expression he gets from Heidegger, the three temporal ecstasies. *Ekstasis* means being beside oneself. And, of course, that's sort of what the *pour-soi* always is. So there is a kind of ghostly shadow of being always involved in my existence, and yet I'm never fully that in the same way a thing is its qualities. The temporal ecstasies are the past, present, and future. The past is something I *am* on the mode of not being it any longer. The future is something on the mode of not yet being it; it's also outside of myself. And the present? Well, that's the whole point. The present is also a kind of not being. I am not fully being in the present. Later on, we'll see that this becomes a central theme of Derrida's philosophy, even though Derrida claims to know nothing of Sartre and probably doesn't want to, but there's also Ernst Bloch ("the blindness of the present"), and even Kierkegaard ("the present is not a temporal idea").

This has to be grounded, I think, in two further ways. First of all, remember that our body is an *en-soi*, but not for me: for other people, and for the neuro-psychologist who's taking a picture of my brain. But, for me, my body is not a thing, because I choose it in a certain way. My body is a kind of situation. So, if you said, "Well, what is all this Sartrean business about freedom? There's genetic determinism, and our genes sort of program us to be irascible, passive, benign, or sly." I don't know if genes do that. But the genetic makeup of my body and the fact that I have a certain kind of complexion—maybe I have some inherited illnesses—that's my situation. Just as a social situation is my situation, a cosmological arrangement is my situation. I'm alive in this moment when the sun is dying, or when climate change is destroying the planet, so many years from the big bang. So also with the body. I have a tendency to fat. Okay, that's my situation. But I have to live that in some way. I have to choose that. So I keep dieting; I keep struggling against it. Or I let myself go completely. Or I become jolly like Falstaff. We are not free not to do something with this situation. Freedom is our choice of how we deal with it, but we have to deal with it, because it is us. But it's *not* us in the way a thing is a thing. We are *not* our body. We *are* our body on the mode of *not* being it. We want people to understand that we are different, that we have a personality, that we're not exactly what our body seems. And we are *not* it on the mode of *being* it, because we still *have to* react to it. It's ours.

So that's how we are at a distance from our situation. But a situation has to be chosen too. Think in terms of old-fashioned warfare, let's say. A general like Napoleon emerges into a landscape. The enemy is approaching. And this landscape is organized in a certain way; there's a hill and a river and so forth. The great general Napoleon assesses that situation. That is to say, he constructs it in his mind as a situation; and he sees that here is a place in which I have to withdraw; there is a place from which I can ambush them. And the other general does the same. But that's the sense in which the situation is a set of contingencies of raw facts—facticity, he calls this—but we always have to do something with it, and what we do with it is we construct it in a certain way, and then we react to that construction. Better still, constructing it is the same as reacting to it.

Kant said that genius was the presence of nature in a human organism. Let's say I have a tremendous mathematical gift. Where did that come from? My parents don't know a thing about mathematics. But there's something in there that I'm very comfortable with; I can remember numbers that are twenty or thirty digits long; I can solve problems in my head and so on. Where does it come from? Maybe that is in the brain somewhere, but it's not exactly me. It's something I have to react to and choose in some way.

What about my personal identity? The Husserl essay seemed to say that consciousness is nothing. Yes, I think consciousness is an impersonal thing. I think if you look at yourself carefully you will see that nothing of what other people think is a personality or an identity is in your consciousness. Most often, it comes from other people, but, of course, in some deeper sense—and this will be important in psychoanalysis later on as well—it is also something which is constructed by you. Sartre's first book, very short and readable, is called *The Transcendence of the Ego*. I once asked Badiou whether people were still reading Sartre. He says, "Well, I think there's this little book called *The Transcendence of the Ego* they're still reading." You can see why. Remember the meaning of transcendence. It means not that the ego is transcendent in some religious or Kantian sense of the soul. No, transcendence means simply an object of consciousness. So the title of that book says it all. It says, yes, we have an identity, just as we have a body, but it is an object for consciousness. It is constructed. When you think of yourself, you have a feeling of some kind of selfness. It's hard to convey. Writers have tried to convey this. Presumably everyone has a different kind, but is that true? How would we ever know, except by reading writers whom we translate into our own terms?

Anyway, there is a personal identity, but it is constructed as an object for consciousness. This is very compatible with Lacan's notion of the mirror stage, which we'll look at later on. It is clinically a fact, apparently, that there's a moment when the infant, the *infans*, the non-speaking baby, the helpless child, looks at itself in the mirror and sees something in the mirror, which is somehow itself. Before that, it's just a jumble of various impulses. It's hungry in some parts of its body, warm because something warm is holding it (that will be *das Ding* in Lacan); it also itches and it's wet. But, in the mirror, all that is unified, and that unification, suddenly, is a self. It is also an other. But that is a question we'll get to when we get to Lacan.

But this is comparable to what Sartre is talking about in terms of identity. We have an identity, but it isn't really us. We are that identity on the mode of not being it. There is a way in which, occasionally, we can pull back from that identity and we can judge it; we can see that, as the religions might say, it is full of sinfulness, that we've lied to ourselves about it. That would be what Sartre calls authentic reflexivity. We feel it in anxiety. It's the moment, very brief, very transitory, when we can see ourselves, because our selves are a kind of lie. It's this spurious identity that we have made up and about which we make all kinds of judgements. We can be ashamed of it. We can be proud of it. We can forge all kinds of relationships to it, but we have to take a relationship to it. So our qualities are at a certain distance from us. Even our deepest identity is at a certain distance from it. We ourselves are this pure consciousness which is nothing. The *pour-soi* is that; it's this pure consciousness which has to be all these other things.

Being those things is what Sartre calls freedom. It's not a very pleasant idea. People have compared Sartrean existentialism to Jansenism, which is a kind of French Catholic puritanism or Protestantism, and it is a very difficult and demanding kind of system. So being free in chains is not the way of describing this, unless you want to say that everything in that sense is a chain. Yes, we're free, but we're thrown into those chains. That is why psychology is of no use to us. Psychology is a kind of lie. The psychological novel. What are my characters thinking now? That's all made up. That's all projected. Those things are at a distance from this pure consciousness. Sartre's later novels try to show this, but, obviously, it's very hard to show because language doesn't work in this kind of situation. Pure consciousness doesn't have a language. Language will always be a construction of some kind.

How to describe this Sartrean unconscious, if you want to call it that, which is called "bad faith"? We say this in English, too: we have an argument with somebody and they're arguing in "bad faith." They're not accepting the rules of the game; they're cheating, and I get exasperated and I say, "You're not taking this seriously." So bad faith is lying to yourself, and, of course, we lie to ourselves in everything we do. That's the sense in which the religions say that human life is completely empty and we are nothing—in Buddhism, for example—or, with the religions of the book, that we are sinful, fallen, that this is fallen consciousness and so on. Those are all approximations in different languages of this initial insight that we're always at this distance, that we can never really *be* what we are because we have to *try* to be it, which means we're not it. And that's the role of anxiety in all this, this pure consciousness. We always feel it in anxiety, because it says, "Look, you're really nothing and you're lying to yourself and your whole life is a lie," and so on and so forth. Now this is why one of the answers to this—because there is a positive Sartrean answer—is that I have to assume myself and my acts. So I affirm what I have done in the past. I affirm my qualities as mine—and as not mine—if I want to. But how do we go about doing that? That's where the question of other people comes in.

So what is this concept really? I said that all these concepts are really posed against some other concept. This concept of the for-itself is against introspection, psychology, the psychological, in the sense of the psychological novel and so on, any form of thingification; in terms of ethics, it is most succinctly argued against remorse and regret. Regret is: I wish I had done that. Remorse is: I wish I hadn't done that. But, in the Sartrean scheme of things, if you did it, you wanted to do it. And maybe you wanted remorse along with it, because, like the inferiority complex, remorse is an ontological mode, and it can give also you a sense of being. That's what Sartre's play *The Flies* is about, in a sense. If you didn't do it, then really, deep down, you didn't want to do it, and that is regret, another form of bad faith. So that's the sense in which one is responsible for everything one is and has done, except, of course, one *isn't* anything like that. In Sartre's famous little book on the poet Baudelaire, he writes that, even though everyone says Baudelaire had a wretched life, that he didn't have the life he deserved, he actually had exactly the life he deserved. Everyone has exactly the life they deserve. And that's what Sartrean ontological analysis is all about. That's why this notion of freedom is very deceptive, because it looks as though this would be a wonderful thing, that we are all free and so on, but, on the contrary, it is quite a terrifying and nightmarish idea.

Let's go on then to other people. About them, the for-others, the *pour-autrui*, we can use another famous Sartrean sentence from the end of his play *No Exit*. It is the final sentence and sort of the leitmotif of the whole thing. It is a play situated in hell, which is a room in which you're locked up for all eternity with a couple of unknowns, and the whole thing acts out this dialectic of your otherness. The famous last sentence is: "Hell is—other people!"[5] So in what sense is hell other people? What is this idea directed against? Well, for one thing, it's directed against the notion

---

5   Jean-Paul Sartre, *No Exit and Three Other Plays*, trans. Stuart Gilbert and Lionel Abel (New York: Vintage International, 1989), 45.

of intersubjectivity. Yes, of course, there is a difference between my being all alone and my being in some situation with somebody else. Here I am talking to you: this is intersubjectivity obviously. But what good is this concept? How is there this intersubjectivity? What Sartre seems to be telling us is that all human relations—individual relations with other people—are forms of antagonism. Well, that's not a very nice thought. Why couldn't we say they're forms of love? Why can't we build an ethics and a relationship to other people on the basis at least of cooperation or some positive kind of thing? Well, this is ontology, and we're going to have to argue this out in some way, and the way we'll do so is through alienation. We'll see that, for somebody like Althusser, later in this development, alienation is a bad concept, a humanistic concept, and there would be reasons for being against it. But Sartre, although he says he is a humanist, is also, in this philosophical sense, an anti-humanist. Anyway, that's a question I don't want to raise right now.

What I do want to raise is this business of antagonism. "Hell is other people." This is the basis of it. It's again the subject-object position. You will remember in what you have read that the eyes are this strange, ambivalent duality. If we look at someone else, they can't see our eyes as a physical object. If we are looked at, we can't see the gaze. This also will be developed in Lacan, the idea that there's an object which is called the gaze, which is different from the eyes, but which exists on its own. Something of that is already here in Sartre: either we look at someone else and we are a subject and we turn them into an object, alienate them into objectness, into a kind of being—but this is a kind of being that's different from the *en-soi*; it's different from the *pour-soi*—or they look at us, and they are the subject and we are the object, and the other person looking at us sees our eyes as objects in the world. How does this work? How is it that we can't be both at the same time? Well, this is the logical premise of this argument, that we can't be both subject and object at the same time.

Someone, I think very intelligently, found this sentence in which Sartre said we can't perceive and imagine at the same time. Sartre wrote two books on the imaginary, by the way, and that's a very important observation in Sartre, this incompatibility of imagining, which involves a kind of negation, and perception, which is also a kind of negation but of a different type. Anyway, that's not relevant to what we're doing now, but this business of subject and object is. What does it mean that, if I'm a subject, the other must be an object? If the other is a subject, I'm an object. We're talking about dual reactions now. How can this work out? Doesn't this recall something like, in Nietzsche, the strong and the weak? When we come to Deleuze, we'll see that there is a subterranean influence of Nietzsche that runs through all these people, but Deleuze reinterprets Nietzsche in the following way. He says that being strong means being active; being weak means being reactive. So here we get action and a kind of passivity. It isn't a complete passivity, but it is a reactive passivity. I'm always carrying around something that I'm reacting to, whereas the Nietzschean active person is acting out of the center of their personality. I'm using different philosophical languages here. Well, we have to think of things like that to understand this.

You've seen how Sartre defines the look as what steals away my being, or that whereby I turn the other person into an object. So it is a struggle for positions, subject or object. In another chapter, which is one of the most dramatic chapters of the whole work, Sartre will go through seven different versions of what he calls the fundamental relations with other people. These are still dual relations. These are the seven structural types of subject-object relations into which we can translate the look. Remember the look is ontic—that's a way of evoking it—but, ontologically, it means alienation. It's a kind of being that I can't do anything about. What the other person thinks about me, that's lost to me. I'm helpless in front of that. They can think anything they want; I may never know. I can try to win back their thoughts of me in one way or the other. But the two reactions I feel—and both of them are completely insubstantial and worthless—are, he says, shame and pride. I'm being looked at. Okay, either I'm ashamed or I reaffirm myself as pride, but neither of those really allows me to recuperate this alienated being. I'm responding to it as a situation that I can't do anything about, but I can still *try* to do something about it, and these relationships are the ways in which I try to relate to the other.

I think this stuff about other people is the most original thing that Sartre ever did. Heidegger has a very ideological, conservative idea of the notion of other people, what he calls *Mitsein*, and those tend to be the kind of contempt that conservatives felt for the masses, for the crowd, in the 1920s. It's not an articulated relationship. The one predecessor in all this—and we'll come back to it but maybe not in this segment or in these weeks—is the great moment in Hegel, the struggle between the master and the slave. The look is Sartre's version of the master and the slave. When I look at the other, I am the master and the other is the slave or serf or whatever you want to call it. And vice versa, because it's reversible. We'll come back to this in Fanon, because this is one of the things that's developed in Fanon's anticolonialism, and in Sartre's as well.

What are these seven different relationships to other people?[6] Love, language, masochism. Those are the relationships in which I am object for the subject, the other. Then there's a turn and a strange relationship appears: indifference. Then there are the positions in which I am the subject and the other person is the object, and that's desire—he means sexual desire; he is one of the few philosophers, in those days at least, who theorizes about sexuality—hate, and sadism. It seems a sorry kind of list of relationships, right? But these are ontological relationships. None of them work. That is, none of them can solve this problem of my alienation by the other. But these are the ways I try to do so.

Now with love, it's very funny, and Lacan will do a turn on this when he talks scandalously about how—a very famous Lacanian sentence—there is no sexual relationship (a very strange remark, but we'll come back to that later on), Sartre is saying that we talk about requited love, when two people really love each other, but, for Sartre, that's a misnomer, because, for him, love is wanting to be loved. So, if both people in a relationship want to be loved, isn't there a kind of ontological problem here? Each one wants something different from the other. It's not that I love the other and then the other loves me. What this means is the justification of existence, because everybody knows, in all the literature of love, Proust or Wagner or whatever, love is a chance at the justification of my existence. And with love, the rest of society, the rest of the problems of other people, all disappear, because the lovers are alone in the world. They are in their own special world where no one else matters. Of course, if the third breaks in on them, then, maybe, something happens to that love. But the problem is that, ontologically, each one wants something different from the other. Sartre is not saying ontically that love doesn't exist. Obviously, it exists. What he is saying is that it is ontologically a failure, because to say that I want the other to love me means that I want to be justified in my being. I want to have a reason for existence. And the other's love for me means that I'm saved. I'm saved, in the sense that I have a reason for being. And, for the other, it's the same, but the other wants the same salvation from

---

6   Jean-Paul Sartre, *Being and Nothingness*, Part 3, Chapter 3, Sections I and II. For Sartre on *Mitsein*, see the final section of the chapter.

me, and these ontological drives are incompatible, like the parallel lines that miss each other in infinite space. They don't do the same thing. So the analysis of love is very interesting.

Now what about language? Language, he says, is an attempt to fascinate the other. Here I think you can think of eloquence. You can think of politics. You can think of poetry. Language is this attempt in which I turn myself into the object of fascination for other people. Whereas, normally, one would say in language I'm trying to do something to the other, persuade the other, argue with the other, and so on, Sartre is thinking of it the other way around. No, in language I seem to be acting on the other, but, in reality, I'm speaking in order to make myself an object for the other.

Okay, let's think of the great orators. If you think of the descriptions of Hitler, all of them say that the masses were fascinated by Hitler. It is very strange for such a large country to be fascinated by this person who is not even really prepossessing physically. What they all say is that it was his look. In the great meetings, Hitler's look is on everybody, and it seems to be saving them, in a sense; it seems to be giving them all a justification for being. But the gift of Hitler was a gift for speech. He found, just by accident, that he was a great speaker and that he could fascinate crowds of people by his oratory. And that means that he is making himself an object for an other. They are fascinated by his being. He is an object; he is his language, an eloquence that he is inventing. Language is a very funny thing in that respect. Sartre has more complicated ideas of language, but this is a very interesting one. At any rate, speaking, eloquence, language, is also a mode in which I am with people and where I make myself an object for people, and that can lead us to more thoughts about language itself, if you like.

Okay, masochism. That's the most obvious example. The masochist wants to be an object for the loved one. The great Sacher-Masoch was a novelist in Galicia, which was then a Polish province of Austro-Hungary. He was a very successful novelist, and then he wrote a few very strange little books on the side—*Venus in Furs,* for example—about being dominated by these fascinating women figures. The point is that he wanted to be an object for these women, for this form of domination. These are very interesting novels, *Venus in Furs* in particular, and Deleuze has written a great book on masochism—the novel is published with it—in which that novel is analyzed. He was a very talented writer. But, as Sartre points out, these women are not interested in this stuff. They love him for other reasons, but they don't want him as an object that they whip and things like that. They do it because they love him. So the masochist doesn't get anything out of this either, ontologically, and yet that is the primal form of being an object for others. That is the primal passion. That is the clearest version of this passion for being an object in this subject-object relationship.

Now there is a turn, and we confront indifference. Indifference is the attempt to blot out the problem, not to see the other at all. Indifference to the other means I escape the whole ontological dilemma of my alienation. I somehow do not recognize the existence of other people. I'm alone in my world. And, as he says, this is also a passion. There are people who are like this. It's a mystery. They could be very cold and so forth, but maybe that's not really necessary. But the main thing is that, for them, apparently the other is not there in this sense. But it means of course that they don't solve the ontological problem either, any more than a corpse does. So indifference is a very special, unique kind of relationship, which is a non-relationship. And then we get to desire, hate, and sadism. It's very easy to work backwards and to see that sadism is an attempt to be the subject over other people. Torture is an ontological passion for some people, who are the most abominable of all. There are people who have this passion, and the state uses them, of course, or they become criminals to satisfy this passion, or whatever. And the crucial thing here is the other's surrender. What you want is for the other to recognize your primacy. People knew Faulkner in the '30s in France; they had great translations. Sartre picks the lynching in *Light in August* as the example of how, whatever you do to the other, you can't do anything about this gaze of the other. If you kill the other, the problem is not solved ontologically, because the other will always *have been*. You will always have been alienated by the other. If you torture the other, there's still a place in the consciousness of the other that alienates you. You can't get around it. Faulkner really does express this. It's quite remarkable.

Okay, we're working our way back. Hatred is different from sadism. It means you pick out a certain other, and you wish to obliterate this other so that it does not exist, has never existed. Well, it's obvious that this obsessional ontological passion is impossible, because the other will always have been. But you see how that could pass over into something like sadism, but it is also a useless passion. Then sexuality itself. This is a very interesting reading of desire. What Sartre says is: in the sexual act, the main thing is to make the other an object, the other's body, by making yourself an object. So it's a very curious attempt for both sides to escape this subject-object tension by both becoming objects in some sense. That's also a very interesting phenomenological description, but it's a failure, because, for one thing, desire disappears, and, for another, you can't prolong this relationship. So there is an ontological distinction in Sartre between love and sexuality, between the ontological analysis of love and the ontological analysis of sexuality.

Okay, so all those things are failures. Ah, but we've forgotten something! There is also the plural. What about the plural? Is it possible that there could be ontological satisfaction there? Well, remember the plural comes in subject-object forms too. There is a *we*, and there is an *us*. His analysis of the *we*, the collective subject, is that it is simply an illusion. We can have the sense of being in a collectivity. His example is using instruments, like opening a can. The can gives you instructions. You are therefore just like everybody else when you open a can. There is no personal way of opening a can, so you are a part of a whole invisible collectivity when you're doing those things.

In the same way, if you want to translate it into class terms, the ruling class consciousness comes after proletarian consciousness. That is, the consciousness of the repressed, of the oppressed, comes first. Then the ruling class realizes that it is in-situation and threatened, and, at that point, the ruling class gets a class consciousness. The we-subject does not have ontological priority. But the we-object does. How is that possible, and where does it come from? Well, clearly, it comes from the look. It is because a group is looked at from the outside that it becomes a unified kind of collective being. But that could be an object of shame. The greatest American playwright of the twentieth century—I think nobody puts him on anymore; maybe they see this great movie, *Long Day's Journey into Night*—was Eugene O'Neill. There is an early play of his called *The Hairy Ape*, in which some stevedores are working away, sweating, ugly, smelly, filthy and everything, and suddenly a beautiful, very elegant society woman in furs, comes in and looks at them. Suddenly they feel themselves as a group. They feel mutual shame at being looked at from the outside. They are a thing together, a collective.

Or we can look at a more historical example. The French Revolution begins with the taking of the Bastille. It begins when a rumor starts that the king has summoned his troops to surround, invade, and control the working-class quarter, the Faubourg Saint-Antoine. The Bastille is this great prison and a kind of armory. So, as this spreads, this rumor, through the neighborhood, the neighborhood is united by this attack from the outside, which is supposedly threatening them all, but which in fact doesn't exist; and they unite on the basis of that look from the outside. That is the moment when they are capable of acting and seizing the Bastille.

Those two final forms of collective consciousness are then the basis of this later, much more difficult, incomplete book which is called the *Critique of Dialectical Reason*, and of which I assigned a few fragments.[7] You will see that there, the first-person *we*, this insubstantial illusory idea of collectivity, of a collective subject, is called seriality. And the we-object is called the "group-in-fusion"; I think the translation says "fused group." His example is people waiting for a bus. That's intersubjectivity, if you like, a pseudo-idea. They don't really have any relationship to each other; they're all separate, and yet they're together. But the fused group, on the other hand—think of terrorism, conspiracy, the family, or any kind of small, active group that's together against the outside world—is somehow united in a different way. For the serial collectivity, for the people waiting in line for the bus, you could say that the center is always elsewhere. None of them are the center. The center is other people, but it's not there. There isn't any center. For the fused group, everybody is the center. And that's the ontological difference between these two things.

Now one thing I want you to be aware of, because, next week, all of these readings will deal with identity, identity politics, and a special kind of alienation: all these forms of identity politics are alienated forms of otherness. They are all the result of the look. Just to give you a quick preview: in Sartre's work on the Jewish question, the first thing you have to ask is what is a Jew? It's very clear, he says. A Jew is somebody other people consider to be a Jew. Ah! So this is the alienation of the look. It means that I am defined. From inside, how do I feel? I don't feel anything. Inside, nobody can feel themselves to be Jewish, or black, or woman. We are just pure consciousness, impersonal consciousness.

So where does this situation, this stereotype or definition come to us? It comes from other people, and therefore all these examples are examples of that being which is my alienation by other people. And, finally, if you extend this politically, you see that this will include colonization, and we

---

7 Jean-Paul Sartre, *Critique of Dialectical Reason: Vol. I*, trans. Alan Sheridan-Smith (London: Verso, 1991), Book 1, Part IV, Chapter I and Book 2, Part I, Chapter IV.

are at the moment in the '40s and early '50s, right before the great moment of decolonization, which begins, I think, with the independence of Ghana in 1957. The Algerian War is already going on. This is the great moment of the wars of national liberation all around the globe. And, of course, being colonized is yet another form of this alienation by the other. And, here, it is very clear who is doing the alienating. The colonizer is alienating not just the property, the work and so on, but the very being of the colonized. Something like the work of Fanon will provide a psychoanalysis of that phenomenon, as well as a political pamphlet about it.

Okay, I think we have to stop here. We'll go on to this stuff tomorrow, but I hope you got a sense of how all this massive work derives at the very outset from this ontological question.

January 28, 2021

4

After Sartre

{Sartre, Merleau-Ponty, Beauvoir, Fanon}

I want to repeat what I said before, that the point of understanding a philosophical concept is not first and foremost simply to agree or disagree with it. We are looking at these things historically, but also in terms of their relevance for us and their general truth. I don't think you can separate those things. But the first way to understand a concept, it seems to me, is to understand what it is written *against*. When we get to Merleau-Ponty, for example, it is clear that he is writing against Sartre's idea of negation and consciousness, but that he is still within Sartre's problematic. That is, he accepts the problematic that Sartre sets up about otherness, but he wishes, if you like, to challenge or criticize absolute negativity, but also, in another sense, to extend it and to develop it. That, it seems to me, comes first, that understanding of how a concept fits into this system and how a historical problematic provides the context you have to understand it in. Later comes your own evaluation; but I think that's less important from an initial point of view.

Now the point is that we are dealing with history here, so you have to remember that, although many of these concepts will be recognizable, the historical situation may be completely different. When we come to deal with racism, for example, I think you will have to understand not only that American racism isn't the same as French racism, and they are not the same as the racism of Martinique or the Caribbean—the French colonies, for example—but also that the situation of racism is not the same in 1960 as it is today. All those things have to be factored in. And one of the ways that I like to present the dialectic is to say that it is understanding that one has a foot in both these periods, that you use the same word, "racism," for phenomena which are, however, to a certain degree distinct, and that one keeps both those things, their identity and their difference, in one's mind at the same time. This is a kind of history, this material. That is to say, we are trying to find out what the continuities but also what the breaks are between these positions, let's say, or even between the debates themselves.

A relatively recent essay by a distinguished feminist philosopher says, okay, *The Second Sex* is fundamental for us; but, she says, we don't read it all. We skip the existential stuff. We don't need that philosophizing anymore. Who asks themselves, she says, about justifying their existence?[1] Well, is it a good thing that we don't ask ourselves that anymore? Is that a loss? Should we be worrying about justifying our existence, or in other words, about ontological questions? She seems to think not, that this is ancient history, old stuff that belongs to the 1940s and '50s of France and other places, and that we can forget about it, because the philosophical problematics have changed. Yes, they have changed, but, on the other hand, that was presented as a metaphysical dilemma, justifying your existence. Can it have disappeared? If it did disappear, if people don't talk about it anymore, doesn't that tell us something about today? Isn't that an interesting matter? I would say the same about your own reactions to these texts and mine. It takes two forms. If there is something you feel is boring or not interesting anymore, that is material for an interesting historical question. It doesn't simply mean you drop it and forget about it. Yes, you could do that—none of us have time enough to do everything—but, on the other hand, if it is no longer important to us, that tells us something about us and something about it. That raises historical questions.

As for the difficulty of these texts, that is another matter, and I think everyone has these problems, because the difficulties very often lie in the language of the text, and I urge you to think of the philosophical text as a language experiment, as the invention of a set of terms which is comparable to the way poets invent their obsessive terms, and not to assume that

---

1   See Michèle Le Dœuff, *Hipparchia's Choice: An Essay Concerning Women, Philosophy, Etc.* (New York: Columbia University Press, 2007).

this thing is *a priori* incomprehensible for you, or on the other hand, that there is somebody for whom it is absolutely clear and unproblematic. There probably is not anybody like that. It is probably just as difficult for everybody else, but they don't use the difficulties in the same way. If you want an example of that, I gave you that long footnote on racism from Sartre's *Critique*.[2] That's about as incomprehensible as it gets. Sartre's *Critique* is not the kind of luminous and novelistically accessible kind of stuff that you find in *Being and Nothingness*. It is very labored, this late work of Sartre. He was under a lot of pressures, medically, physically, writing around the clock on drugs and stressed by the Algerian War. The apartment he was writing in was bombed by the right-wing OAS, the army group. He had to move. Meanwhile this huge manuscript—I guess written by hand, because a lot of them did that—didn't have page numbers. There comes a day when it is sitting on the window and the wind blows it all over the place. His friends take about a week to put it all together. So there are all kinds of reasons why this long footnote is not as readable as other parts of Sartre, but, on the other hand, one can play with that, and one tries to guess at what's going on in it.

I am trying to convey to you seriality versus the fused group, the group-in-fusion. For that, I would use the notion of center and margin. It's not an accident—this is 1961, '62—that suddenly we are talking about collectives. And this is also a reflection on the media. Sartre, in fact, does have a chapter in the *Critique* on the media, and it is clear that the question of the media—if there is to be a philosophy of the media, which is not certain, but much time has elapsed since that (McLuhanism and so on), and the media is now for us a whole separate discipline—fits into this problematic. What kind of intersubjectivity does the media present? Well, Sartre invents his notion of seriality precisely to convey that. How is it

---

2   Jean-Paul Sartre, *Critique of Dialectical Reason: Vol. I*, 300–3, fn. 88. Here is the footnote's conclusion: "In short, by the very act of repeating [*racist ideas*], one shows that it is impossible for everyone to unite simultaneously against the natives, that it is merely shifting recurrence, and that in any case such a unification could occur as an active grouping only so as to massacre the colonised people, which is the perpetual, absurd temptation of the colonialists, and which, if it were possible, would amount to the immediate destruction of colonisation. In this way, *the racist idea*, both as an unthinkable idea and as a categorical imperative, can serve us as a typical example of *the serial idea* as an act of alterity which *realises in urgency* (and for lack of anything better) the practico-inert unity of the gathering, and, in contradiction with the original exigency, manifests this unity as a fundamental negation, that is to say, as impotence grounded on separation."

that all these people at the bus stop standing side by side don't have a real relationship to each other? You remember that in the original discussion of relations with others, the we-subject is something like the people at the bus stop. All these people in their separate apartments are busy opening cans and doing collective things. They identify with each other. They watch the same TV programs for example. They are a public, but they have no concrete relationship to each other. How can that be?

What I use to explain this idea—and I believe Sartre writes a little bit about this, but it hadn't really been developed in that period—is public opinion polls. What is public opinion, this object of public opinion polls? I would like to use an example which will be, for you, ancient history. In Eisenhower's elections, his opponent was a former governor of Illinois named Adlai Stevenson, who was a very literate and very witty man. Nobody ever doubted that Einsenhower would win these elections, but the question was always raised: Stevenson's speeches are so elegant—who's going to understand them? Will the "common man" understand them? That was a common term of the period, so please don't blame me for using it in that form. So the pollsters went out and asked people who were precisely, by an economic definition, a common man. And the preponderance of common men said, "Well, *I* like the speeches, but the *common man* will never understand them."

So the common projection is that I'm just a separate individual with my own personal preferences, and the great bulk of people are outside of that. In a sense, that is to say, the self of seriality is always someone else. The center of subjectivity is always someone else, and that someone else also thinks it's someone else. It is always elsewhere. There *is* this public opinion. I feel it—it's obviously not just made up, not fictional—but what is it? It is this idea of the existence of others, myself being projected onto these others, so that in a sense I am absent to myself.

But then groups get to be formed. And this does not bear on the judgment you pass on the nature of these groups, because these militias and so forth from a few weeks ago in Washington are fused groups as well. All these groups have something structural in common. That's what Sartre is trying to describe in his section on groups. For the fused group, it's not that the center is elsewhere, constantly in infinite regress. It's that everyone is the center. And what that means is that, in a sense, these groups have no leader. Now you will say, "No, that's obviously not true; there are always ringleaders." Well, the point about this group, Sartre says, is that the leader is a temporary spokesperson, and, if the group doesn't agree—there is a sort of general will in a small group like this—then he or she is not the spokesperson anymore. So I am a center, but everyone else is a center, and there is a rotation of these centers. Sartre goes on to show that, in a certain moment in the development of the group, the rotation slows down and it stops, and a real center emerges, who is, let's say, the dictator or the leader. At that point in the collective, a whole new process of reification sets in.

But what is interesting for us historically is that here we have what Sartre feels to be the extension of the philosophy that he has developed about other people in *Being and Nothingness,* and yet what we know to be a kind of subtle shift in the political meaning of this problem. That is to say, the individual problems of commitment that these people faced under the German occupation, where they have to decide whether they individually are going to participate in the Resistance and run the risk of torture and death. That gradually is going to shift in the postwar to the problem of groups —parties first of all, but, increasingly, the problem of non-party groups and the problem of group power and of the institutions—so that, by the time we get to the end of this period, in globalization, it will no longer even be a question of the action of groups. It won't be the question of the possible action of individuals, but it won't be the problem of the action of groups either, because groups will have ceased to have power. It will be the problem of these massive institutions, which is, I would say, a problem of number and population, but that is a problem that, hopefully, we will have a chance to look at in the historical transformation of these phenomena.

The other thing I wanted to warn you about is this matter of freedom. We haven't spent enough time on it. It has to do with the structure of the *pour-soi.* As you know, the *pour-soi* can never be a thing; it can never have the qualities of a thing. But it can't *not* have them either. And that will undergo, clearly, a sudden change when the other appears. But, even for myself, thinking about myself, there is this question of what I am. Freedom is part of that, and, if you have understood Sartrean freedom, then you realize, as the Bible says—this is a very difficult thought—being free in the Sartrean sense is as painful as being a sinner in certain theologies. This is not a position of power and possibility; it is a position of responsibility and judgment.

So we have to distinguish between the ontic and the ontological again. We are talking about freedom as an ontological thing. What is my relationship to my being or to my existence? Can I *be*? If I can't be, how am I related to my not-being? What does it mean to not be something? Those are all ontological questions, and they eventually result in this business of the justification for my existence which Michèle Le Dœuff thought was not an interesting problem. The ontic version of freedom—am I free to cross the road? Am I free to rob the bank? Am I free to drive my car on the left hand side of the road?—is a very different matter, and, clearly, in politics there is going to be a slippage there. Sartre tried to make an ethics out of his ontological notion of freedom. And you can see that existentialism does not dictate a notion of the future, and therefore cannot offer you any kind of advice about the content of your future actions. Finally, Sartre gave up his project of writing an ethics. I think we here touch the limits of the Sartrean problematic, so to speak. For existentialism, there is a kind of limitation which is the present, which is my own individuality, and that is my own present of time. My future, as they like to say, is open. That is why there are aesthetic rules that they devise for writing novels, where you do not impose some knowledge of the future, of the character, on a given situation, on a given dramatization of a scene. But, if the future is open, then the existentialists have no means of criticizing your choice of one future rather than the other. The example he uses in this misleadingly titled lecture of his, "Existentialism Is a Humanism," is about a young man whose mother is dying, and he has a choice between staying with her or joining the Resistance. Sartre says this is an example of an existential choice. We can't give you any advice on that, he says, except that whichever future you choose—whether you choose to stay with your mother or to leave her and go out into the Maquis and resist the Germans—will have to be chosen with the understanding that you have completely committed yourself to it. That is to say, it must not involve regret or remorse. Whatever you do, authenticity lies in your assumption of the freedom of choice in that instant, in your anxiety of that instant. That is not a very helpful ethical doctrine, in the sense that it really doesn't give you the kinds of guidance that the religions do, or that many kinds of bourgeois ethics do. And this will go on, I think, into politics, because, as I just said, it's clear that, for Sartre, the group-in-fusion is authentic, and seriality is inauthentic. Most of the time, we are in both. Maybe we occasionally have the experience of a group. It is clear that there is an ethical preference of the group, of the collective. But what collective? There is nothing in this doctrine which is able to distinguish between, let's say, a left-wing group and a right-wing group, between the characteristic choice of that historical period, communism and fascism (since fascism is still around in the postwar era). You have to fall back on Kant, at that point, and on Kant's categorical imperative, which posits, as you know, that you treat the other as an end rather than a means. For the Sartreans, it would be: you must do nothing which does not acknowledge the freedom of the other. Yes, at that point, you have an ethics that distinguishes between different forms of politics, different forms of groups, but only by going back to Kant. That is not going forward in philosophizing.

We are going to get into all of that, but we have two directions to go today. Merleau-Ponty presents a rather different kind of problem than these other writers, and I think I would like to say a word about Merleau-Ponty first, and then we'll get to Fanon and Beauvoir, because Merleau-Ponty's problematic is somewhat different. Merleau-Ponty was a classmate of Sartre and Beauvoir. All three were students at the École Normale. All ranked very high. Beauvoir was the second highest in the exams after Sartre himself. That's where they got to know each other. That's also where Merleau-Ponty got to know them. After the war, they will form a kind of group in the production of this journal, *Les Temps Modernes*, and that will be, essentially, Sartre's internal politics. But, as for what we call real politics—that is, parties and so on, and, in particular, the relationship to the Soviet Union, the Communist Party and so forth—none of them officially join the Party, but Merleau was much more radical, while Sartre—and Sartre himself says this—was apolitical up until the Korean War. Merleau-Ponty was stridently on the Left until the Korean War. At that point, their paths are reversed. Sartre becomes a kind of fierce anti-anti-communist. Merleau drops out of politics altogether, and his main contribution then lies elsewhere, in aesthetics.

He died quite young, the same year as Fanon, 1961. The work he left was very ambiguous, so a lot of different schools felt that, had he lived, he would have been the philosopher of their school. So the structuralists, Lévi-Strauss for example, said that Merleau-Ponty would have been their philosopher. But then Lacan, not exactly a structuralist, also thought, had Merleau-Ponty lived, he would have been the philosopher of Lacanianism, because Lacan is not exactly a philosopher either. And it is certain that we approach the problematics of language in Merleau, but the principal thing is still the relationship to the Sartrean problematic and the radicalism imposed on his notion of freedom or consciousness by the choice of ontological language. To be or not to be. Being and nothingness.

He will describe—we were talking about this the other day—this fascination one can have with a painting as the relationship of my not-being
to this being, this fullness of being which is the painting, which is the
material paint in the painting. The essay I have given you, the most famous
essay Merleau-Ponty ever wrote, is an essay on Cézanne and painting,
"Cézanne's Doubt." We can't spend a lot of time on this, but I recommend
it very highly. Cézanne's experiments turned on what the nature of seeing
and visuality was. And Cézanne tried to break out of this business of
consciousness and the subject-object opposition by experimenting with
how the object is constructed by our perception. Merleau-Ponty's great
book, of course, is called *The Phenomenology of Perception*, and his great
philosophical problem is precisely how the phenomenological subject
stands in relation to the object. For Sartre, it was black and white, open
and shut. Merleau-Ponty wants to make this more complicated. Any of
you who have seen a Cézanne in real life and have stood in front of it for
a long time to try to understand it know that there's a play of distances
in which, if you approach the painting, it breaks up into small pieces of
color, and if you draw away from it, suddenly the object becomes visible.
Merleau shows that Cézanne, whose letters are very interesting, but who
was mostly very inarticulate about these things, is describing, in a way,
how the eye and subjectivity constructs the object. "For the world is a mass
without gaps, an organism of colors, across which the receding perspective,
the contours, the angles, and the curves are set up as lines of force; the
spatial frame is constituted by vibrating." That's Merleau-Ponty, but here
is Cézanne speaking: "The drawing and the color are no longer distinct.
Gradually as you paint, you draw; the more colors harmonize, the more
drawing becomes precise . . . When the color is at its richest, the form is at
its fullest." The traditional struggle in painting is between line and color,
and that's what Cézanne is trying to overcome here:

> Cézanne does not try to use color to *suggest* the tactile sensations which
> are given form and depth. These distinctions between form and sight
> are unknown in primordial perception. It is only as a result of a science
> of the human body that we find we learn to distinguish between our
> senses, between touching and seeing. The lived object is not rediscov-
> ered or constructed on the basis of the data of the senses; rather, it
> presents itself to us from the start as the center from which data radiate.
> We *see* the depth, the smoothness, the softness, the hardness of objects;

Cézanne even claimed that we see their odor. If the painter wants to express the world, the arrangements of his colors must bear within this arrangement this individual Whole, or else his painting will only be an allusion to things, and will not give them, in the imperious unity, the presence, the unsurpassable fullness which is for us the definition of the real.[3]

Cézanne says, "The landscape thinks itself in me, and I am its consciousness."[4] Well, that is the kind of relationship between subject and object which Merleau-Ponty wants to use to replace the absolute Sartrean notion of being and nothingness, the nothingness of consciousness which is apprehending the fullness of the *en-soi*. That is what he is going to theorize philosophically, then, in this other fragment that I gave you. It is an unfinished work—he died in the middle of it—but it is perhaps one of the richest and fullest expressions of what he was trying to think, namely entanglement, or the chiasmus.[5] Chiasmus is a trope, and this trope is one aspect of Merleau-Ponty's anticipation of structuralism. Here he is taking what we normally think of as a linguistic figure—a trope is a deviation from literal language, and we're going to see that a number of people, Paul de Man, Lyotard, Hayden White—take the tropes as a sort of unconscious of language itself. We are not thinking; the tropes are thinking in us. And the final result of that is that the tropes are—a deviation from literal language? Ah, but maybe there is no literal language. Maybe we are thought by language. All of that is going to come out of structuralism, but you're going to see that Merleau-Ponty is already getting to that point.

The chiasmus is the X form. It is how pieces of the subject get transformed in the object and pieces of the object get transformed in the subject, and they come together not as an opposition but as this chiasmatic relationship to each other. Marx used to love the chiasmus, especially in his early writings. It is very simple as a form, but also very dramatic. "The weapon of criticism cannot replace [. . .] criticism by weapons."[6] You

3   Maurice Merleau-Ponty, "Cézanne's Doubt," in *The Merleau-Ponty Reader*, eds. Ted Toadvine and Leonard Lawlor (Evanston, IL: Northwestern University Press, 2007), 75.

4   Ibid., 77.

5   Maurice Merleau-Ponty, *The Visible and the Invisible*, trans. Alphonso Lingis (Evanston, IL: Northwestern University Press, 1968), 130–55.

6   Karl Marx, "Contribution to the Critique of Hegel's Philosophy of Law: Introduction," *Collected Works of Karl Marx and Friedrich Engels, Volume 3: 1843–1844* (New York: International Publishers, 1975), 182.

can see how these two things get intertwined. We don't go outside the initial data. We have two data. We have the word "weapon" and we have the word "criticism," but something will happen when we change their relationship to each other, and the place where that happens—this is from Merleau-Ponty—is the place where the subject and the object get entangled. I am in a chiasmus with the object.

In Cézanne's paintings, this pure gaze of the painter is going to resolve itself, is going to be taken up and somehow put back together by the data of the object world. And that data is not just sight. It's all those other senses. The senses will be constructed out of this. So Cézanne's painting is philosophizing. We'll find this in Deleuze as well. Visuality is a concept, and it produces yet another concept. Painting is a kind of thinking in its own terms; that's Deleuze, but it's also Merleau-Ponty, in a way. Cézanne's painting is a thinking, and not just the thinking of Cézanne, but also of the landscape. Mont Sainte-Victoire, which is the great mountain in Provence that he painted from all angles; it is thinking for him and in him. So this is how—we can't go any further with this right now—Merleau-Ponty will revise the Sartrean notion of the self and other.

Let's move on to these other people now, because they come more directly out of a different feature of Sartre, which is the relationship to the other. You must understand Sartre's other two works, *Anti-Semite and Jew* and the book on Genet as a part of this sequence, which includes Beauvoir and Fanon.[7] We can see what's happening here. Merleau-Ponty is talking about the construction of subject and object, this chiasmatic construction. Once we get to these other people, we are faced with what I guess is called constructivism—not in the old Russian sense, but in the sense of an old book in sociology called *The Social Construction of Reality*. Reality is a social construction. But, for Merleau-Ponty, perception is a construction. The object is a construction. And, once we start thinking in terms of construction, all kinds of things change. These works of the so-called existentialists will be the place in which those changes begin to happen, although the emergence of constructivism as a philosophy or a philosophical position doesn't really take on its programmatic form until postmodernism. But it has its origins here, as does modern identity politics, and that's what we want to try to figure out. The great sentence

---

7   Jean-Paul Sartre, *Saint Genet, Actor and Martyr*, trans. Bernard Frechtman (Minneapolis, MN: University of Minnesota Press, 2012).

is not pronounced by Sartre but by Simone de Beauvoir: "*On ne naît pas femme: on le devient.*"[8] You aren't born a woman: you become a woman. You are constructed and you construct yourself as a woman. This is the great sentence from the very center of *The Second Sex,* 1949. From that, all kinds of things emerge. You have a notion of freedom there. You have all kinds of problems about how we become these things, and how we become our being for the other, in some sense. But how does that take place? And what does it mean individually and politically? Out of that will come the discussions of anti-Semitism, of feminism, of sexism, of blackness, and, finally, the Genet book on homosexuality, although Genet poses a much more complicated set of issues.

Let me now introduce a text from a great American writer, now over one hundred years old, but, in Sartre's day, less than fifty. Sartre would not have known this text, I don't think. It articulates in advance Sartre's notion of the relationship to the other, of the alienation of the other, of my being. This is from 1897:

> After the Egyptian and Indian, the Greek and Roman, the Teuton and Mongolian, the Negro is a sort of seventh son, born with a veil, and gifted with second-sight in this American world,—a world which yields him no true self-consciousness, but only lets him see himself through the revelation of the other world. It is a peculiar sensation, this double-consciousness, this sense of always looking at one's self through the eyes of others, of measuring one's soul by the tape of a world that looks on in amused contempt and pity. One ever feels his two-ness,—an American, a Negro; two souls, two thoughts, two unreconciled strivings; two warring ideals in one dark body, whose dogged strength alone keeps it from being torn asunder.[9]

That is W. E. B. Du Bois in *The Souls of Black Folk,* and it is one of the great moments in which his notion of double-consciousness emerges. It is not only a great text in the African American tradition; it is a great text in the American tradition and in the philosophical tradition. Du Bois was one of our great writers. He was a novelist. He was a politician. He was a sociologist. He was a philosopher, a student of William James like Gertrude Stein

---

8   Simone de Beauvoir, *Le Deuxième Sexe II* (Paris: Gallimard, 1949), 1.

9   W. E. B. Du Bois, *The Souls of Black Folk* (Oxford: Oxford World Classics, 2009), 8.

and others. He was an internationalist and a great American intellectual and figure in our general heritage. What is meant by double-consciousness? It means that in the *pour-soi*, I'm a pure consciousness. There is nothing in there, since it isn't anything that marks me as being Black. It is only when other people see me that this happens.

Fanon tells a little story in one of his books. A white woman and her little boy come past him and the little boy whispers to his mother, but loud enough for Fanon to hear, "Mama, is that a Negro?" And then he says, "I'm afraid."[10] Yes, that's the view of the outside. That is the other consciousness. So I am that, but not inside, because I can't be anything inside. I can't be a Jew or Black or a woman either. I am just a consciousness, a *pour-soi*. It is for others that I'm that. But that kind of freedom is not an ontic freedom. On the other hand, there are conditions in which some people pass, or choose to pass, and those are very interesting stories in their own right.

In modern identity politics—and this certainly develops in the '60s, as the various anticolonialist movements emerge, the various anti-racist movements emerge, the state of Israel, and so forth—there comes to be a sense that, as Sartre says in the introduction to Fanon's *Wretched of the Earth*: "Not so long ago, the Earth numbered 2 billion inhabitants, i.e., 500 million men and 1.5 billion 'natives.'" *Indigènes*. "The first possessed the Word, the others borrowed it."[11] Suddenly, something changes when the subjects, the colonized, the *indigènes*, whatever you want to call them, the objects of the gaze, begin to speak, and speak in their own language.

Fanon was a Black man, born in the West Indies, in Martinique. Beauvoir was obviously a woman. Sartre was a white man, and presumably he shouldn't be able to talk about those things, because he doesn't know from the inside what it is to be Black, what it is to be a woman, what it is to be Jewish. You can certainly look—and you have to look—at the personal situations of these people. Sartre, you have to remember, was short, very ugly, and had a walleye—that is, eyes that go in different directions. Later in his life, he loses sight in his good eye and goes blind, and that will be the end of his writing. So we can say Sartre certainly felt looked at, and he felt alienated by the look of other people. That gives him, in a strange way,

10   See Frantz Fanon, *Black Skin, White Masks*, trans. Charles Lam Markmann (London: Pluto Press, 1986), Chapter 5.

11   Jean-Paul Sartre, "Preface," in Frantz Fanon, *The Wretched of the Earth*, trans. Richard Philcox (Grove Press, NY: 2004), xliii.

his chance at understanding certain phenomena, which lots of us don't necessarily have to feel, or at least not all the time. There are only certain situations when we feel this embarrassment of being looked at. Should I be proud, or should I be ashamed? And so on.

So there are privileged situations for any kind of knowledge and any kind of thinking, and we could say that that was Sartre's, and maybe there were others. He tells his story in his autobiography, *Les Mots*, which ought to be translated as *Words* and not *The Words*. It's the one book of Sartre that people who hate Sartre like. It's quite a remarkable little book. He also has some other autobiographical essays that are worth reading, the one on Merleau-Ponty, for example. So there are things in one's situation that allow one to do certain things. They're not always negative things. In Fanon's case, it is the discovery that he is a Black man in a white society, in France. If he were a Black man in a Black society, it wouldn't quite be the same. And the Négritude poets, by the way, for whom Sartre wrote an introduction, are African poets, for the most part, except for Aimé Césaire, a fundamental reference for Fanon and one of the great poets of the modern age, who was from Martinique. You have to understand this multiple alienation. These are people who are alienated both by the colonizer, by France, but also alienated by Africa, because they are not African either. So there is a very complex situation at work in Fanon's personal relationship to this work.

But I want to take Beauvoir as an example. Does Beauvoir owe her insight into these things from sexism and oppression? Well, I think not. I think she was very privileged. Hers was a petty noble family. The "de" is the sign of nobility in French, so when we use the name of the noble in English, we leave off the "de," but if it's a bourgeois name, for whatever reason—General de Gaulle, for example—we can retain the "de." Anyway, she has the "de" of nobility. For some reason—and here too we have her autobiography, which is very interesting to look at, and which is called in English *Memoirs of a Dutiful Daughter*—what allows her to see all this was that she was never discriminated against, and she never suffered all this kind of stuff we've been talking about. So she did not have to react either with rage or with inferiority. She simply took her autonomy for granted, and, as I say, she was the second in a whole class of young philosophers from all over France. She was always in a privileged position as an individual, and, therefore, she was in a position to judge from the outside what other women had to face on the inside.

This is why *The Second Sex* is of a different kind than some of these other analyses, because she never experienced that kind of alienation, and it was a matter of amazement to her that other women had to feel those things, or that they did feel them. This book began simply as a set of notes about various women's life choices, and then she realized that she was in a unique position to write this description of women's situations, because, in some sense, she didn't feel any of them. That does not mean that, in the French situation, she wasn't constantly subject to the French version of sexism. Obviously, the French have a different relationship to gender and sexuality than we do; it's not a puritanical country, the way we are still. But, nonetheless, I think you would say that the male relationship to female intellectuals, for example—a kind of "bitchiness," as she said herself—is a kind of constant. And that is something she certainly got to know after she became famous and influential with this work.

But the other thing you have to remember is that she received hundreds and hundreds of letters from women in response to this book, many of whom told her, "Look, we never understood that this wasn't us, that all this stuff we have to live through is something imposed on us from the outside; we just assumed that we *were* that, that we *were* subordinate, that we *were* inferior to men, that our function in life *was* to bear children and wash dishes and so on and so forth." This is the kind of awakening to the distinction between the *pour-soi* and its situation that, for the most part, people didn't feel, and as far as that goes, men don't normally feel it either in relation to their situation. So the power of this book was quite extraordinary in the way that it introduced all of this. What that means, of course, is that feminism today has a very complicated relationship to Beauvoir, because she did not call herself a feminist. Nothing like that really existed at the time. What happened in France—and we'll be looking at French feminism later on—is the formation of groups and collectivities, in particular the *Mouvement de libération des femmes* and some other groups. It is only much later that Beauvoir felt she had to associate her personal authority with these movements.

I would say, indeed, the central theme of Beauvoir's work can be found in probably her best novel *She Came to Stay*, the first one, *L'Invitée*, which has a Hegelian and Sartrean motto: "each consciousness desires the death of the other." But also, if you are interested in this period historically, *The Mandarins*, I think, is a wonderful novel that holds up very well. It describes the situation of intellectuals under the occupation and in the immediate postwar period. It is supposed to be a roman à clef about Sartre and Camus. Well, there is a young figure like Camus; the Sartre figure is much older than Sartre himself, but you could take it that way. I think it is best not to think in those terms, but, rather, to think in terms of this situation that they face politically and otherwise.

But, essentially, it is *The Second Sex* which made a real impact. And you have to understand, too, that this book is, in a sense, addressed to women. And this describes the kind of works that emerge around these questions of otherness. Is it a condemnation of male sexism? Obviously, implicitly it is. There are many objective historical parts, and she shows very interesting stuff about the legalities of women's situations in the various countries. France, in particular, has different kinds of legal freedoms for women that they didn't have in other traditions, which explains the rather unique position of great women in French intellectual life, if you go back to the salons of the Revolution, or even Madame de Sévigné in the seventeenth century. Women are somewhat more in the foreground than in certain other traditions. So there's a lot of historical and personal material in this, but it's obvious what one would have to denounce if one were denouncing external constraints or situations. This is, instead, addressed to women and their authenticity. And much of her literature will be about women's inauthentic consent to their situations or their attempt to fulfill themselves inauthentically by family, by relationship to the man, by relationship to children.

Clearly, just as this liberated a certain number of women who read it, it also posed a very serious, painful problem for many, and there is a hatred that has pursued Simone de Beauvoir from women, just as there is a hatred of Sartre. There is a very strong reaction against this stuff. With Fanon, I would say, this is all a little subtler, and one finds it in the way in which the contemporary revival of Fanon has preferred not to look at the political part of Fanon. Let's look more at the psychiatric analyses of Fanon. Let's not bother about all this violence and liberation stuff. So there, too: picking out only certain parts of Fanon and so forth. Many of Fanon's works are similarly, as Sartre says of the poems in *Black Orpheus,* addressed to Black people and to the colonized. This involves a satirical portrait of the role of the colonizer, but, in effect, Fanon is doing two things, or rather, one complex thing. He is applying the categories of psychiatry, which are normally taken to be timeless, to a historical situation. You know there's a huge dictionary of psychological states which psychiatrists use, the DSM. It can be revised; those are momentous revisions, sometimes, when the diagnosis of certain kinds of mental illness is transformed by the absolute authority of this book. What Fanon is trying to say is that some of what you think of as mental illness is political; that is to say, much of what he observes is in fact the alienation which the colonized undergoes. These are not diseases of the mind or of psychiatry. They are diseases of colonization.

And this is where Fanon crosses paths with Antonio Gramsci, the great Italian Marxist theorist. Gramsci, who was one of the great organizers of the Communist Party, as you know, and who was imprisoned by Mussolini and, in the *Prison Notebooks*, invented the notion of subalternity, which is the inauthentic agreement to being subordinate to the masters. It is the Hegelian condition of the slave or the *Knecht*, the bondsman. It is my acceptance that I am a sub-person, inferior, only good to serve the masters, and so on. And it is most obvious—and Gramsci was the great theorist of the South, which inevitably means Sicily and the peasantry—in the mentality of the peasants. They don't speak; they have habits of obedience, except that every so often, in the history of the peasantry, there are great bloody explosions, which in French you call a *jacquerie*, in which the peasant is no longer this subaltern creature but rises up in a massacre.

So Fanon's is really an analysis of subalternity, but it is a political analysis. Fanon was a leading figure in the Algerian Revolution. Later on, when the freed Algeria becomes Islamicized and a military state a year or two after the victory of the Revolution, Fanon is sort of written out of the picture. But Fanon was a leading figure in the Algerian Revolution and in its theorization. His insistence on cultural transformation is particularly important.[12] It would put him in line with some of the theories of the Chinese Cultural Revolution, that revolution is a transformation of subjectivity, not simply a military victory—and that there's a whole way of building what in those days had to be called "national liberation," a liberation from subalternity, a transformation of the self into authenticity, into collective authenticity. So this is still very much in the Sartrean notion that what one does with this alienation from the outside has to be an assumption of the alienation, rather than a flight from it, a denial of it, or a submission to it. It has to come out of the assumption that you become what you are. You were never a thing, but you have to seize on it as an active weapon in your own

12   See Frantz Fanon, "On National Culture," in *The Wretched of the Earth*, 145–70.

liberation, in the same way you get, in American politics, with the Black Panthers in the '60s, an affirmation of the alienation that is imposed on you. So a lot of Fanon is written in that spirit against notions of African identity and of cultural regression to older traditions and so on. He died of leukemia at a very young age, only thirty-six.

But then we have to come to his notion of redemptive violence, which we're looking at historically, and precisely in the context of these wars of national liberation. It is a theory which is aimed against non-violence. Non-violence as a political strategy is something that is a form of resistance under certain circumstances. In Gandhi's India, or in the American South, non-violence could be a very powerful weapon, but the Algerian situation presented different political problems. Fanon gets an idea from a play of Césaire—and, as I say, Aimé Césaire is constantly present in the thought of Fanon—namely the idea that, only in the master and the slave—since this is a certain Hegelianism—and only in the struggle between these two sentient beings, is something like freedom achieved, since it's not something that can be bestowed upon the other.

People asked again about animal consciousness and so on. What I found interesting is what I believe that the biologists have found, namely that, in nature, symmetry is always a signal for danger. If a sentient being, an animal of some sort, sees something symmetrical, like the eyes, though it may not recognize them as eyes, it means that it is in the presence of another lifeform. It is in the presence of vulnerability. I think you have to see Hegel's myth of the master and the slave like that. You have two sentient beings. They struggle, and they struggle for recognition. Okay, that is also a very charged and problematic term, because recognition means recognition as a human being, as part of the human species. The slave becomes a slave by his surrender, his living surrender; he is not killed, or otherwise there wouldn't be any master-slave struggle. He "recognizes" that he is a slave, a subaltern, and the master has thereby achieved recognition. But, as Hegel says, this is an ironic victory, because the master's recognition can only be given to him by the slave. If the slave is not a human, how can the slave have the right to recognize the master? How can the master get any satisfaction out of that? The slave knows what the human is, even if he himself cannot yet be recognized as such.

What Fanon means by redemptive violence is that this relationship, once established, can only be broken by fear. It is the master's fear of the slave and the slave uprising that causes the master suddenly to recognize the former slave as a human being, as a freedom, as the Sartreans would say. Behind Césaire's work, and behind a lot of this stuff, is the one great successful slave revolt of Haiti. You have a great book by a West Indian writer, C. L. R. James, who lived for a long time in this country, *The Black Jacobins*, which is the classic study of this victory by Toussaint L'Ouverture and the slaves, but Césaire's play on the subject is also very important and is the prototype of Fanon's notion of redemptive violence. Redemptive violence is the possibility of a war of genuine national liberation from slavery. It is the one great victory of the slaves over the slaveholders in history, the one supreme success of this redemptive violence—until the '60s—against the master, against the colonizer. So these theories are rehearsals of the Sartrean positions.

That is probably all I will say today, and we will try to make a transition to structuralism next time, but we can still talk a little more about these things if you like.

February 2, 2021

5

After the Liberation

{Sartre, Merleau-Ponty, Beauvoir, Fanon}

I would like to move from existentialism to what we are used to calling "structuralism." But let me just say something about this business of periodization. We are going from 1943 to the early '60s, beginning roughly with the liberation of Paris in August 1944, a period of tremendous optimism and utopianism and political energy, in which it seems France, along with the whole world, can be recreated. It is true in America too, but in a different way. Here, we were moving toward greater consumption goods; finally, all the stuff that you couldn't buy during the war is going to be available. Alongside this you have expansion, Eisenhower's Highway Act, the construction of the suburbs, the construction of networks of roads, and women going back to the home, because the utopia of World War II in the United States was a utopia of full employment, with women in the industries. I would say World War II is almost a lost utopia of American history in that respect. But, in France, it is a different kind of utopia, a political utopia, the idea that society itself can change. That will come to an end with the beginning of the Cold War in 1947, and in particular for Sartre, with the Korean War in the '50s.

But what about intellectual life? We have this stuff that we have inherited from the history of ideas: worldviews, *Weltanschauungen*. Heidegger has a very pertinent essay denouncing *Weltanschauungen*, so-called world-pictures. These are, generally, if you look closely, patterned on the history of science. The crucial figures might be Descartes, certainly Galileo, various mathematicians. Science is the one area in which there seems to be progress, linear history, a way in which something new is discovered, the old stuff is thrown out, and history progresses. This is why I recommended to you—for cultural literacy and for your general education—everybody should eventually read this; it is still a very useful book—Thomas Kuhn's *The Structure of Scientific Revolutions*, in which he invents the idea that each period of thought is modeled on a paradigm. It allows science to progress to a certain point, and then there are structural limits and things beyond it that it can't understand and can't fit into its version of things. So there has to be what he calls a paradigm shift, and sometimes those can be dated with great accuracy. Einstein's paradigm shift had to do with, if I understand it rightly, the circuit of the planet Mercury, which never quite fit into the Newtonian paradigm. Einstein invented a way of thinking about that—we now call it "relativity," I guess—in which suddenly that makes perfect sense and it is lawful, whereas, before, it was one of the things that fell outside the Newtonian paradigm. Foucault, in his history *Les mots et les choses*, *The Order of Things*—my favorite book of Foucault—calls these paradigms *epistemes*, the Greek word for "knowledge"; and each one will be a notion of knowledge organized around a certain kind of patterning system. Althusser, on the other hand, will call these things—and he won't talk about them so much in terms of historical periods—*problématiques*, problematics. That is to say, there are problems within this problematic which are lawful, and there are others which are stupid and worthless and have no relevance until suddenly this problematic breaks down and we have to move into a new one.

Something like that is going to happen here, and I'm going to try to show you exactly how that happens and why. But, first, I want to read you Deleuze. The authority of Deleuze is better than mine. "How Do We Recognize Structuralism?" A nice title. It is not a good introduction to structuralism. But it is an introduction to something, and it is also an introduction to Deleuze himself, and we will use some of it. At any rate, at the very end, he says, books against structuralism, or those against the new novel, which was a form of the novel that was being written in the '50s and '60s, are "strictly without importance; they can't prevent structuralism from exerting a productivity which is that of our era." Note this notion of productivity. "No book *against* anything ever has any importance; all that counts are books *for* something, and that know how to produce it."[1] Well, that's not quite true. I think, for Deleuze, one would rather say that what counts—and I agree with this too—is not the solution to the problem, but producing a new problem, and if you don't produce a new problem, then somehow your work is worthless. But the fact that something is an old problem or that it's not in your problematic anymore isn't an excuse to throw the past away.

This new kind of thought which came into being in the history of science called "science studies"—I don't know when it began, maybe the '70s or the '80s, and there are some important names associated with it—had two principles. First it was necessary to explain why a discovery comes to count as true, but then it was necessary to explain why what is now false once counted as true. In the normal scientific view, and the view, for example, of Anglo-American philosophy, at least some of it, the past is just worthless. If it's all mistakes, just throw it out, start again, begin afresh. An opposite view—that could be a Hegelian one—is that you have to work through error to get to truth. You have a truth, let's say, that you've discovered in science. The scientists think, okay, biology, I'm just going to teach this truth. I'll forget about the old errors. We don't need to study alchemy to find out what chemistry is. Well, Hegel would say you can't do that, because you only get to truth through these errors. You have to work your way through them, find out what's wrong with them, find out the limits of that paradigm, and then you can see why it had to be changed, and why we have to go into a new one. We will try to do that a little bit today.

But, first, I want to go through some things. I talked to you about the four humors. I conjectured that Sartre's notion of the truth of a human being, and his interest in biography, which we will come back to, has as much to do with character as with buried traumas. Freud said, yes, I can cure your trauma, but I can't do anything about your character. You were cantankerous before and easy to find fault. Even after you are cured, you're going to stay that way. Psychoanalysis has nothing to do with that. I think that Sartre, on the other hand, in his ontology of this original choice which we make of ourselves, reverses that. At any rate, the first form of psychology, going way back in India, posits these four humors, which are

---

1   Gilles Deleuze, "How Do We Recognize Structuralism?" in *Desert Islands and Other Texts, 1953–1974*, trans. Michael Taormina (Los Angeles: Semiotext(e), 2004), 191.

various secretions of the body which predominate and therefore give you a certain character. For the ancients, there were four types of character, the four types of bodies: blood, phlegm, yellow bile, and black bile. It is almost a structural system *avant la lettre*. It's very interesting to note that. We will get back to this question of Sartre and character in a moment, because we never get done with these things.

For Sartrean notions of freedom—you might try to understand it by the idea that, for Sartre, as for Proust, there is no such thing as willpower. You cannot change by willpower, because willpower is itself determined within an all-encompassing, originary choice. I gave you my example of the inferiority complex. I'm going to change myself. I'm going to go to the psychoanalyst and I'm going to change. But, really, I go to him to fail, to prove that I'm inferior. Willpower means: I'm going to set this up so I stop smoking, and then I'm going to fail at that, and I'm simply going to be reconfirmed in the fact that there's nothing I can do about it, that I'm just a smoker. If you're a reader of Proust, you know that, for Proust, willpower is a hindrance to writing and perception and experience. I want to see what's going on in this church. I want to really explore this church. I call on my willpower to make me observe. Well, I don't observe anything, because I'm too focused on my own willpower. So willpower is not freedom. On the contrary, willpower is a kind of ruse of freedom, which makes me think I'm doing something when I'm not.

A lot of your responses to my last lecture are about violence, and this is a very important matter. But you should know that, in the '60s, there came into being a distinction between force and violence. You know perhaps Weber's definition of the state: the state is this entity that has the monopoly of violence. So, for the state, violence is called force, and what the Left wanted to argue in the '60s was that you are wrong to say that we are violent and you represent order. In France, the police are called *les forces de l'ordre*. You are not the forces of order, says the Left. Yes, you have force, but it is a different matter. Force is this institutional violence, and violence is directed against that kind of force.

Then there is the question of non-violence as a strategy, and I would like to say that, from this ontological point of view, obviously any strategy is a matter of a situation. In some situations, non-violence is a very powerful course. In other situations, not at all. Fanon is writing in a special situation, and so he is attacking the strategies of non-violence, those of Gandhi and so forth. The question of violence is an ontological thing, and non-violence in that sense, as a political process, is also violence. It is resistance, but it has another ontic form. It means you are not fighting the state with guns; you are fighting them with all these immense demonstrations of population that they can't do anything about. So, again, ontic and ontological is a very important distinction for us to make in this area.

I said that Beauvoir's slogan—you are not born a woman; you become one—is a really fundamental slogan for everything in the existential period, if you want to call it that. But there is another one, which I think is equally important, which we get from Fanon, but it is expressed in Sartre and other people: you have to take freedom for yourself. If it is given to you, it is not really yours. Freedom has to be your own act. You have to seize it, but, if it's given to you and you receive it passively, it is not going to be freedom, and, therefore, there must be a process in political action which has to do with the relationship between action and the self, how our action changes the self, how it is a transformation of the self. You have that on the last page of *Wretched of the Earth*, which talks about something like a cultural revolution, a subjective revolution, a change from subalternity, what Sartre will call a conversion. And that's a very important distinction.

I should also add something to our discussion about Merleau-Ponty. It fits in with this in a certain way. The one thing I forgot to say in defining the chiasmus and entanglement is that it's dependent on a very interesting fact about our bodies. People talk about his use of the word "flesh." Flesh doesn't really have a religious overtone—Sartre used the word, too—but it's meant as a mediation between subject and object. He wants to get rid of the absolute disjunction in Sartre between subject and object and introduce this mediatory moment which is both subject and object. Flesh is sort of that, but how is it that? I would say this is based on the notion of active and passive and on a very peculiar fact about our bodies. You can understand this in terms of your hands: you can do something with your body, and you can feel something with your body. For the hand as being touched is different from the hand as an instrument of action. The word here that I always want is "incommensurability." There is an incommensurability between the active and the passive. I think that notion of incommensurability is very important for a lot of this stuff, and we'll see its forms in structuralism, too, but, here in Merleau-Ponty, it's fundamental. There is a distinction between action, the active use of not just our hands but our bodies, as subject, and their passive reception as modes of perception. The chiasmus, however, is this place in which these two things cross, and at which there is a moment of transformation from passive to active. That's something that goes back to Merleau-Ponty's *Phenomenology of Perception*, that this is somehow a fact of perception. And all of this, as I said, you can find in this wonderful essay on Cézanne in terms of aesthetics.

Just as a footnote, particularly if you're interested in France, all of the great philosophers in France, from the '30s on, wrote on the visual arts, beginning with Sartre. Lévi-Strauss wrote a lot about painting, but we will see what he does with facial painting in the Bororo Indians. Deleuze has a whole book on Francis Bacon. Foucault wrote famous pages on Velázquez's *Las Meninas*, which we'll read. So one could really do a whole history of French thought through their relationship to the visual arts and to vision. Martin Jay has an important book called *Downcast Eyes*, which he says is a study of the denigration of vision in French philosophy. Well, I don't know about denigration. I think this tradition gives visuality a great importance. At any rate, that is a huge book, but a very useful handbook to modern French thought, and a very interesting way of approaching this whole topic of the senses and of visuality as such.

I include the name of Camus here. You have his wonderful essay on Tipaza, a beautiful little Roman garden outside of Algiers; it is just stunning in the sun and the heat.[2] There is nothing like it in the world. It *is* the Mediterranean, really, and Camus is a Mediterranean writer. For Camus, this is the plenitude of the present, of the instant. It is that plenitude of the present that interests Beauvoir as well, and she calls it *le bonheur*, happiness, but *bonheur* is stronger in French than it its equivalents in English or German. So there is a kind of choice of the present as a fullness, which is a positive side to existentialism, which, of course, is precisely this affirmation of life in the present and the problematization of the past and the future. One should maybe remember that the present is also a problem, because the stronger the present becomes, the weaker and more fantasmatic become memory, history, and indeed the project, futurity.

Kierkegaard says a very remarkable thing about this. He says the present is not a temporal phenomenon. The present has nothing to do with time. That's very odd and very strange and I think could lead to all kinds of interesting meditations, and, of course, it does in Kierkegaard, but Kierkegaard is a little too complex for our topic today. But this indicates the difference

---

2   Albert Camus, "Return to Tipaza," *The Myth of Sisyphus and Other Essays*, trans. Justin O'Brien (New York: Knopf, 1955), 193–204.

between a view of existentialism as suffering, misery, and responsibility, and this other view in which the present is this fullness, the possibility of happiness. I would say that Beauvoir's work turns really essentially on that, and on the way in which—since her emphasis is on women's experience, *mauvaise foi*, "bad faith"—that bad faith cuts them off from this experience. This also means that Beauvoir's central work consists of these immense autobiographical writings; she must have had notebooks where she noted down this stuff as it happened from day to day. You get a whole 1,000-page history of what she and Sartre did on such-and-such a trip, such-and-such a day, who they met, what films they saw, what they thought, what they discussed. Now, if you hate Beauvoir, then it's clear that her life is just a kind of tourism. Here she is, privileged, searching out new places, new people, new sources of interest, instead of being in this struggle for women's liberation, as this will very shortly be called, which is collective. And it is certainly true that, from a political point of view, you have to make a difference between the critique of your own inauthenticity and the critique of other people's. So, if you want to talk about subject and object, you can say her book is addressed to women and their choice of subalternity, their choice of obedience, their choice of various miseries and so forth. It is a call for them to liberate themselves and to acquire—I would say this is the central political or even existential word for Beauvoir, though I don't know how much she uses it—autonomy. This becomes an important word later on, in the '60s. You conquer a personal autonomy. That means you are the subject of your decisions, as she was. She tends to feel that marriage, children, the traditional roles of women are flights from this autonomy, and she tends to concentrate on these situations not from the outside, where you would wish to struggle politically for change in marriage laws, change in laws on abortion, change in all kinds of things relating to legal status; those would be properly political struggles. She is rather struggling against the psychological submission to those things, which is, in a sense—and there was a famous book by Erich Fromm on this during the war—the fear of freedom, the escape from freedom.[3] And this is an important feature in Sartre as well. There is a reason why people aren't authentic, why people flee their freedom. It is because it is much safer and much more comfortable. It doesn't involve anxiety. It is a flight from anxiety. If freedom is anxiety, then it is obvious that you would want

---

3   Erich Fromm, *Escape from Freedom* (New York: H. Holt, 1994).

to get away from it. Nobody wants to feel anxiety. So, in a sense, if she has a politics, it is that. But you can see why people actively involved in these struggles could look back at this and say she is speaking from a position of privilege in her own life and in her own psychology, and this is not what we need right now; we need people to attack the laws, the domination of patriarchy, and so forth. And she is aware of those things. She later joins collectives—she has to, really; she is the great authority—but on the other hand, the collective, maybe because of the strangeness of women's subalternity, isn't something you can organize the way you can organize other kinds of movements, the movements of the colonized and so forth. Although, of course, the women's movement addresses that.

In the whole area of identity politics, there is always this fundamental—I would call it a contradiction—this incommensurable choice. Either you choose equality—that is to say assimilation—or you choose secession. There have been women's collectives and lesbian feminisms for whom secession has been a political solution. Equality, assimilation, on the other hand, means that your cause disappears all of a sudden. Here, we get to Fanon. Remember that Sartre says in *Black Orpheus*, "I'm talking to white people, trying to show them that the Négritude movement, African poets who wrote in French like Aimé Césaire, are not speaking to them." But French is an alienation for them. It's like the Irish writers. Joyce says, "I speak the language of the conquerors." But he doesn't turn back to produce a Gaelic literature, an Irish literature. Some people have tried to do that. But the language they speak is an alienated language. In this sense, maybe all language is an alienation.

In any case, Fanon reads a passage from *Black Orpheus* by Sartre, and he says the following. This is a passage in which Sartre's Hegelianism comes out, because Sartre is asking himself: What is universal about Black struggle? I'm not Black. How can I help this? Is it particularist? Is it a secession? This would be one of the objective possibilities in these choices. I think current debates on Afropessimism are related to all that. Sartre writes: "But that does not prevent the idea of race from mingling with that of class: The first is concrete and particular, the second is universal . . ." Race is a negative moment, because "the position of negritude as an antithetical value is the moment of negativity." It is from the position of blackness that you can criticize this master position, which is empty, of whiteness. Whiteness isn't anything except its power, and it is the center. From the outside, you can criticize that, attack it, negate it. But then, he says, "this negative moment is insufficient by itself, and the Negroes who employ it know this very well; they know that it is intended to prepare the synthesis or realization of the human in a society without races. Thus, negritude is the root of its own destruction, it is a transition and not a conclusion, a means not an ultimate end."[4] So we have a Hegelian position. Négritude is the negation, and there's another moment after that in which this whole business of race versus race will disappear, and we will be in a new moment.

So Fanon responds:

> When I read that page, I felt that I had been robbed of my last chance. I said to my friends, 'the generation of the younger black poets has just suffered a blow that can never be forgiven.' Help had been sought from a friend of the colored peoples, and that friend had found no better response than to point out the relativity of what they were doing. For once that born Hegelian had forgotten that consciousness has to lose itself in the night of the absolute, the only condition to obtain the consciousness of self. In opposition to rationalism he summoned up the negative side, but he forgot that this negativity draws its worth from an almost substantive absoluteness.[5]

So Sartre's mistake was to block the very source of the experience of being Black. In a way, Fanon's critique of Sartre is more existentialist than Sartre. This is the critique of the existentialist versus the Hegelian. It is Kierkegaard's critique of Hegel. Kierkegaard as a young student, visiting Hegel's last lectures in Berlin, finds that he, Kierkegaard, torn by this religious existentialism, merely fits into a place within Hegel's system. He fits in a place called "the Unhappy Consciousness," which is Hegel's analysis of this religious idea of anxiety. And then, of course, in Hegel, that is subsumed, *aufgehoben*, canceled and lifted up in another moment which leaves it behind. So Kierkegaard suddenly feels that he has been robbed of his entire existence, because he has been told, "Just wait a while. You will get out of that moment and into another. You will get out of your particularity, your existential uniqueness, and enter a new universal moment."

Sartre has an essay on Kierkegaard, which you might find very interesting. He is quoting a scholar of Kierkegaard, who has applied to the late

---

4   Jean-Paul Sartre, *Orphée Noir*, preface to *Anthologlie de la nouvelle Poésie nègre et malgache* (Paris: Presses Universitaires de France, 1948), *xl* ff., quoted in Frantz Fanon, *Black Skin, White Masks*, 133.

5   Frantz Fanon, *Black Skin, White Masks*, 133–4.

Kierkegaard the prediction of the late Hegel. A dialectical pair is formed in which each form denounces the other. Hegel foresaw Kierkegaard in the past, as a superseded moment; that is, the Unhappy Consciousness is a moment of the historical dialectic, but it's superseded by another, universal moment. Kierkegaard gave the lie to the internal organization of Hegel's system by showing that superseded moments are conserved not only in the *Aufhebung* that maintains them as it transforms them, but in themselves, without any transformation whatsoever, and by proving that even if they arise anew, they are created merely through their appearance as an anti-dialectic. That is to say, precisely this existentialism that I defined for you in the last scene of *The Condemned of Altona*, the fact that you don't overcome this, but that what you affirm is that you exist and have existed. The unique thing is my existence. It's not my subsumption under this Hegelian moment or that. My class consciousness, insofar as it is mine, is not to be negated by classlessness. So this is a basic moment where existentialism and Marxism or Hegelianism, for example, come into conflict. If your absolute is in the present, then you can't look ahead to a position in which your present is canceled, or else that's just manipulation, to promise that, in the future, your children will enjoy a happier state. At any rate, this is how Fanon sees this kind of conflict.

Returning to Camus, I just want to mention in passing—because he is often associated with existentialism—his notion of the absurd, which is not exactly what Sartrean existentialism is talking about, because the absurd is, I think for Camus, far more dominated by the presence of death, the imminence of death. He was consumptive. He was a sickly child. He was always under the spell of his possible death, and, of course, his death in the car accident only ratifies that in our memory. So the absurd is the fact that we have to die, and that everything we do is really without a point. You should all read *The Stranger* which celebrates this moment of the present and of *bonheur* and how it does not fit into society. So it is an attack on the established order in some way. But there's a wonderful sentence in another book of his called *The Myth of Sisyphus*. Sisyphus is the one who has to keep rolling the stone to the top of the hill over and over again for eternity, and that's Camus' vision of the impossibility of the human project. But the last sentence is quite wonderful: "One must imagine Sisyphus happy."[6] *Il faut imaginer Sisyphe heureux*. We have to

---

6   Albert Camus, *The Myth of Sisyphus*, 123.

think of what the happiness, *bonheur*, of Sisyphus is. We're condemned to rolling this boulder up a hill, but there is a present in all that, in each of those moments, and that's what we have to think of as happiness.

Let me go back just for a minute to Sartre. Sartre is a biographer. Even his first novel, *Nausea*, is about biography. We talk about him as a novelist. He wrote poems, too. But it's interesting to think of him as a biographer. His final work is this huge, multi-volume, unfinished study of Flaubert. I gave you a bit of the book on Genet, which I'll say something about in a minute. He wrote his own autobiography. He tried to do short biographies of Baudelaire and Mallarmé. And, of course, Simone de Beauvoir wrote her own lengthy, life-long memoir. We have to go through childhood. Beauvoir says that all our problems would be solved if people were born grown up, if there were no childhood. It's in childhood that we gropingly create ourselves, and out of what materials? I haven't mentioned Sartre's short pamphlet on Marxism and Freudianism. It's called *Search for a Method*, and I recommend it very highly. Sartre says that, yes, of course we're in a class society, but we learn that through the home. The child learns the facts of class and class conflict through the parents, through the family, through what the home opens onto. Obviously, for example, bourgeois kids learn much less about the social world than working-class kids. So Sartre's question remains: What is this originary choice? How do we get to it? It isn't something we create out of nothing. It's a totality, a system. If we have chosen ourselves, if we've chosen ourselves as melancholy, for example, how could we change that, since willpower doesn't exist? That's a conversion, but this conversion is meaningless because change and choice only mean something within our system, and they have no basis to move from system to system. There is no reason for me to change within my originary choice of myself.

In the book on Genet, he tries to show how and why—it's a book of dialectical changes—Genet becomes a thief. He is an orphan. He is farmed out, literally, to a farm family. Obviously, they don't really consider him as legitimate. They make him do all kinds of stuff. He has to have some place to himself. He knows he doesn't belong there, so he plays around with things. He looks around in drawers, and he plays with what he finds there. All of a sudden, at some point, one of the foster parents comes in, sees him playing around with some jewelry or something, and says, "You're a thief!" This is the look from the outside. This is what reifies him and petrifies him. Now he can react to this in all kinds of ways. If he were older and stronger, Sartre says, he would just shrug it off and insult them. He might try to pretend that he wasn't doing anything. He doesn't know from the inside what being a thief is, because, of course, from the inside we aren't anything, and what would it be for an impersonal consciousness to be a thief? There's a moment I always liked in one of Sartre's novels when one of his characters has discovered freedom; it is at the outbreak of the war; he has been drafted, and he looks around his apartment he is going to pass on to a student. He sees his closet full of sheets, and he says, "What does it mean for a freedom to possess sheets? What is possession? How can a free consciousness possess sheets? What does it mean to have things?" In Genet's case, it's the other way around. "What are they accusing me of? What does it mean that they have something I'm taking?" So this first choice, this first moment of his personal dialectic will be: "I will become what you say I am. I will become a thief. I will try to become equivalent to what you see as me from the outside, based on the way you objectify me." And then, of course, he does become a thief, and he is imprisoned. The whole trajectory is meant to show how you move from that to writing, because Genet becomes a great writer and a great playwright. That's a very elaborate process. It's a long book, I think Sartre's greatest in many ways. You can say this is Sartre's own objectification of Genet. Isn't this a horrible oppression of the intellectual, to do this to someone else? I don't know whether Genet was influenced by it. Probably. How could he not be, in some sense? Sartre gets this from him; they are close friends and Genet tells him his story. But the point is that this first trauma—because it is a trauma—is verbal. "You're a thief!" It is about words. So, in a sense, Genet's whole story is going to be transforming what is done with words. It will be a Hegelian process whereby you somehow interiorize the word and then control it. First, it is something from the outside, and, of course, you could simply deny it and say you are not a thief. On the contrary, if you want to say, "I am a thief," then you enter into this strange experiment with words where you try to be something, feel their distance from you, and little by little you begin to use them differently. So that's one way in which Sartre solves this problem of conversion, but, in another sense, he never really solves it.

Now I want to tell you why I'm bringing this up. This originary choice that Sartre says we're imprisoned in—it is not the imprisonment of the situation that you have fallen into, but of your choice of reactions to all that—this originary choice is a kind of system, but it is a static system.

We can't get out of it. What would it mean to get out of that system, into another one? Ah! Here's something like our epistemes and our worldviews. Your Western science, let's say, is caught in a set of choices, in a certain system, but this system has its limits. So how does it pass from that system to a new one, in which these problems can be solved? Sartre's system has its limits. As later people will say, it is a philosophy of the subject. This is the limit of phenomenology. Even for collectives, Sartre never manages to get out of the notion that true reality is lived experience. The small groups: I have a lived experience of collectivity. Seriality: no, I don't have a lived experience of collectivity. But there are larger groups, which are maybe not serial. He is confined within this commitment to lived experience, to the individual, to existential experience. And so, while this is profound, it is also a fundamental limit on his problematic, on his thought.

What is going to change that? Well, first of all, maybe we could name this problem. Maybe we could turn the problem into a solution by describing it. That is what will happen in structuralism. This problem will suddenly get a new kind of name, and it will be called the synchronic and the diachronic. Synchronic and diachronic are, in a sort of vulgar sense, taken to mean the present and historical succession, respectively. That is a little bit reductive. Everybody uses it that way, and there is no way of getting away from it, but that is not exactly what it means in the beginning. Synchronic was a word that had existed for a long time. Diachronic is a much newer word; I believe its first use is in Lyell, who was the great geologist who discovered, at least as they knew it in the 1830s and 1840s, the age of the Earth. You all know when the Earth was created. A pastor in the late eighteenth century in England—you know these English pastors with their hobbies—calculated how old the Earth was, because we know that God created it, and we know that he created it in 4,444 BCE. So that is when the Earth begins. But, unfortunately, in the eighteenth century, they began to find these things called fossils, which are evidently older than that. So you had to figure out where those came from if God hadn't even created the earth at that point. Well, the solution is ingenious: God knew that we would be bothered by this, so he inserted into his creation elements that looked older. He invented fossils to place a kind of deep historical perspective into this world that he had just created in 4,444 BCE. If you have seen *Blade Runner*, you know how the replicants, the androids, have to have false memories invented to place inside their heads so that they think they had a previous life, even though they didn't. Well, God did something like that with fossils.

At any rate, Lyell first showed that you cannot confine the age of the earth to these biblical proportions if you really want to study geology. So diachronic has to do with that kind of inquiry about the deep past, continuity, and so forth, whereas synchronic means the present. But synchronic means system, while diachronic means some kind of evolution. Where does that come from? We have to go back to a Swiss linguist, who lived at the turn of the twentieth century, a very influential linguist in Geneva, a very famous Swiss name as well, Saussure, whose *Course in General Linguistics* resurfaces in the early '60s in the structuralist period and becomes, if not a Bible, at least the work to which everyone pays homage. Saussurian linguistics are then structuralist linguistics, long after Saussure's death, long after other linguistic schools have evolved. But Saussure's discoveries are very interesting. The two key quotations from Saussure are these. First is an early letter where he says, "I'm coming to think that nothing we're doing in linguistics right now has any meaning and is of any value." How can he say this? What's he talking about? The official school at the time, in the late nineteenth century, was called the neogrammarians; that's not important, except to say that Saussure's first work is a classic of neogrammarian linguistics. I think it was about Indo-European. But, in the same way that people attack Picasso or Jackson Pollock, not knowing that both Picasso and Pollock were great draftsmen and marvelous executors of a realistic style, so that, if they do something else, it's only because they wanted to, critics of Saussure had to reckon with his mastery of the earlier system. What Saussure was talking about was this movement of nineteenth-century grammar, which was one of the great discoveries of modernity, really. It is the discovery of the laws of sound change, of language change. You have heard of Grimm's law. A more fundamental figure behind the Grimms was Franz Bopp. These discoveries all have to do with the lawfulness of sound changes in language. So, for example—I'm picking stuff from the modern period—in German they say *besser* for the English word "better." Well, it so happens that there is a lawful change, in low German and in Dutch, between the *s* and the *t*, and one could chart this transformation. In Spanish, the *sp* has to be accompanied by an *e*, by a first syllable, so where we say 'Spanish,' the Spaniards say *Español*. So these are changes which you must look at over much longer periods. Grimm's law is about some of these fundamental changes. And, finally, we move back in time and artificially construct the primal language from which all these European languages, no matter how distant they seem, originally emerge, and that's called Indo-European. Nobody has ever seen it or heard it; nobody knows anything about it. But the linguists think they have discovered it, and it came from somewhere in Persia. Most European languages came out of it, except Finnish and Basque, which are incomprehensible phenomena in the middle of this sea of various interrelated Indo-European languages.

So the nineteenth century was a period in linguistics of the great discovery of all these historic changes, and Saussure himself contributed, as I say, a classical monograph to these studies. And these are diachronic changes from earlier languages to later ones. They are lawful; they happen, and we can demonstrate them. But Saussure, looking out at a whole century-long monument to all this, is saying that these diachronic laws have absolutely nothing to do with speech, with what we're saying, with this language that we use in the present. We do not have to know the past of these words of our language in the present. This is quite different from what Heidegger does with etymology, and sometimes false etymology; you know that much of Heidegger's notion of Being is derived from his supposed reconstructions of old German, because for him, the true relationship to Being is only found in two European languages: Greek and German. The other ones, the Latinate languages, are bastard languages. Well, you can see where that ties in with politics.

But Saussure says there is a task for linguistics which has nothing to do with these sound change laws, with the diachronic. This would be the task of describing language as a synchronic system, as a system which exists in the present. And it doesn't have anything to do with this business of subject, verb, and object, with syntax and so forth. It is a different kind of system, and its prototypes are made up of sounds—not sound changes, but the relationship of sounds to one another in the present. You know that in each language, there are sounds which have a marked difference, and other kinds of sounds that are unmarked and therefore unimportant. I use again a Spanish example. It may or may not be true, but it's handy. The liberator of Latin America is a man named Bolívar. In Spanish it doesn't matter much if you confuse *b* and *v*. It could have been *-bar*, not *-var*, whereas in English the *b* and the *v* have to be kept separate; otherwise you're confusing two different things. These are phonetic systems that were developed and really explored by a great Czech linguist, and that's why if you go to Czechoslovakia and start talking about French structuralism, they will get furious and tell you that there's a Czech structuralism that's far more basic and important than French structuralism. So structuralism is not itself a finalized thing. It could be Swiss structuralism, if you like. Anyway, the point about this system is that it is a system of differences. Language is patterned on your understanding of the difference between the various sounds that I am using. So here is the second great principle of Saussure; the second great sentence is this, and you find it somewhere in his *Course on General Linguistics*: "In language there are only differences *without positive terms*."[7] So, all of a sudden, you're turning away from the notion that the pronunciation of a *b* is interesting in itself, or that substance is interesting in itself, as Aristotle thought, and you are turning toward difference, a relationship which is that of—and this will be I think the dominant concept of structural linguistics—the binary opposition. The binary opposition, the difference between these two sounds, which have no interest in themselves, this difference without positive terms, is what makes it possible for us to identify words.

The other structural term that you could summon up in that context is what is called the double articulation of language. Language is based on this system of phonetics, and out of the phonetics are formed phonemes, which become meaningful words. So we have two levels. We have a level of differences in sound, and then out of that we have a level of differences in words. This is the double articulation, so to speak, of language itself. That is what the synchronic is. It is looking at things in terms of systems of differences, rather than looking at their history, whereas for Hegel, you can't understand anything without understanding how each thing is the subsumption of all kinds of historical strands. For Saussurean linguistics, the present is important, not in Beauvoir's or Camus's sense, not because the present is an existential present, but, rather, because it is a system. Even the sounds we're not making right now are part of this system, and this system is not an evolutionary system, a system of change, but a system of negative relationships. So, in a funny kind of way, the whole structuralist movement is born out of this.

I will next time be talking a little about the history of this, but maybe I should mention some of it now. Lévi-Strauss is, of course, the dominant figure of all this, and you will find that he is one of the great stylists of French. You will find that especially in his autobiography, which even in

---

7   Ferdinand de Saussure, *Course in General Linguistics*, trans. Wade Baskins (New York: Philosophical Library, 1959), 120.

English is called *Tristes Tropiques*. It is a wonderful book which I highly recommend to you, although we don't have time to look at it all right now. He is recognized as a great writer; he was admitted to the Académie Française. He died a few years ago at the age of 101.

But where did this leap come from? How did it come about? It's like a disease germ. Where did he catch this thing? He was an anthropologist working in Brazil. In the 1930s, he had a fellowship to São Paulo in the French outpost that I mentioned before. Later on, at the outbreak of the war, he manages to escape—from the Port of Marseille, I guess; I think Marseille rather than Portugal, where a lot of people managed to make their way—on one of the last boats to the Caribbean. Finally, he gets to New York, and there he meets a Russian linguist who had worked in Prague and therefore knew Czech linguistics, Roman Jakobson, a very important name. He didn't write any books, but there are a lot of wonderful essays, and I'll recommend a few. It is from Lévi-Strauss's meeting with Jakobson that suddenly a spark is kindled, and this notion of structural linguistics can be applied to anything—not only to kinship systems (anthropologists in those days were obsessed with kinship systems) but also to myths, to narratives, and to all kinds of other social things, literary things. So the relationship to Jakobson in all this is also fundamental.

Next time, we will then see what it was that Lévi-Strauss brought to this, including an attack on Sartre, on the diachronic and on history, and on the Sartrean dialectic, thereby unfolding a whole new world of methods. Lévi-Strauss had a very interesting life. He is obviously an enormously brilliant figure who, like a lot of such people, is absolutely untrustworthy. So you must read him with admiration and then the appropriate grain of salt, because Lévi-Strauss, as you will see as you read these essays, will not stop with a single insight. He will go on and turn it into a whole system, as is perfectly appropriate for a structural linguist. Anyway, we come back to that on Tuesday.

February 4, 2021

6

Glory to the Binary Opposition!

{Saussure, Lévi-Strauss}

I want to begin by reviewing. I gave you a few remarks on Saussure. His *Course on General Linguistics* is really just a collection of his notes and some lectures he made in Switzerland in the years before World War I. He died in 1913. He did not publish them. After his death, a version was published. That is the version that gets reprinted in the '60s and causes such tremendous shock and excitement. Since then, people have put together assemblages of all these lectures, or combined them, in more philological editions, so to speak. I'm just going to draw on a few more aspects, and, in particular, on the terminology, because it seems to me that one of the things about the structuralist period is, insofar as they are busy discovering new distinctions, new aspects of things, they are also obliged to name them. And you have to account for a certain scientistic orientation of some aspects of structuralism. Lévi-Strauss does not claim, for example, to found anthropology, and, indeed, I'm not sure you can talk about a school of Lévi-Straussians, although some of the linguists do found schools. There is such a thing as structural linguistics, but then there emerges from that something called semiotics, the science of the sign, so to speak, and so forth. And all those people will end up inventing their own terminology, and it can get very confusing. For example, we're going to talk a fair amount about myths, but Roland Barthes, in his early years, that is to say, in the late 1940s, does a remarkable series of news-paper articles on what he calls "mythologies," but which have nothing to do with Lévi-Strauss, who had not yet published in that period, I think. They are analyses of signs in the public sphere, and we'll look at them; they're quite wonderful to read, quite delicious. You will find them in a separate book, obviously enough called *Mythologies*. They are early Barthes, although he does this throughout his whole life, and it gives us a sense of how he operates and how terrifically his mind and perceptions work. But we don't want to confuse those mythologies—and I wouldn't use that word for them anymore—with the actual myths (the *mythologiques*) that Lévi-Strauss is talking about.

So there are distinctions of that kind. But then there are other technical ones. I'm anxious that you not be intimidated by these things. One doesn't have to learn them all, but, on the other hand, what you need to retain is the distinction that they name, and not necessarily the terms themselves. But, on the other hand, these terms keep coming back over and over again—all the writings of the period will use them—and so we have to learn them, as one learns a foreign language; you learn Deleuzian, Derridian. But then there is more scientific stuff. That is to say, when you come to semiotics, these people are trying to found a discipline. Now, does it catch on? In France, there are departments of semiotics. In Canada, in Quebec, there are departments of semiotics. As far as I know, in this country, there is only one, at Vanderbilt. Everyone uses many of these semiotic texts, but the ambition of founding a discipline has not necessarily caught on here. So part of this business of the terminology will be precisely this outfitting of a whole new discipline, because a discipline requires a terminology. It has to differentiate itself from related things. And we can say that these things come out of linguistics, and then that they produce other forms of research, let's say; these people love the word "research," but we don't necessarily have to follow them in this.

And for the linguistics of this period, the one writer that I recommend to you—I think you're probably not going to go and read through the *Course on General Linguistics*, and I don't think it's even necessary, because there are more advanced versions of this than Saussure's—the one writer I always recommend, who is always interesting, and who shows you that these infinitesimal philological details can be exciting, is a linguist named Émile Benveniste. There are two volumes of what he calls *Problems in General Linguistics*. That sounds about as exciting as the *Course on General*

Linguistics. But these little essays are very exciting, and I will, in fact, refer to one of them later on. He went on to do an immense dictionary of Indo-European words, which, of course, comes out of all this but is not necessarily relevant for us. But these little essays on linguistic points are very interesting indeed, and he was one of the great minds of linguistics, even if his masterwork, so to speak, is not exactly in our domain, but, rather, in that of the history of Indo-European.

So the linguistics of this period will produce three kinds of things. First of all, it produces a discipline called semiotics. One of the names we will associate with that is A. J. Greimas, a Lithuanian scholar, who found himself in Paris and whose life was very interesting, and who also worked in Turkey during the war; there was a very interesting moment in which French and other scholars met in Turkey and cross-influenced each other in the construction of this discipline called semiotics. Anyway, some of his work is translated. It is not fun to read, but it is fascinating, and, since some parts of it are very suggestive, we'll touch on it later on. Then, alongside semiotics, another branch of inquiry that comes out of this— and their boundaries are fluid—is what is now called "narratology." And you can see already that Lévi-Strauss is contributing something immense to the study of narrative, in this case myths, but that gets widened into narrative in general. Finally, I would say, a third thing that is produced by linguistics—I wouldn't call it a discipline, exactly, but an ideology, and linguistics is not its only source—is the ideology of communication. You will find that in the postwar period, in the '50s and '60s, little by little, that ideology, coupled with computers, with cybernetics, with all kinds of other things, becomes a general notion that information somehow comes first, before production, before other things, that somehow communication is the fundamental human activity. One of the outcomes of that shift is Habermas's philosophy of communicative practice. But there are lots of other theories of information and communication, and I think we have an interest in identifying them as ideologies as well.

And then there is another branch, which is related to these ideologies —and I think these people have a relationship to it, but not all of them adopt it—and that comes more specifically out of anthropology. It comes from the nephew of one of the founders of anthropology. You know that sociology and anthropology really are founded at more or less the same time in the late nineteenth century; and I would say there are twin fathers of sociology: in Germany, Max Weber, and in France, Émile Durkheim.

Their sociologies come into being to address this interesting, frightening new phenomenon, which is the great industrial city and its proletariat, its underclasses. What to do about that? Sociologists have in general been called upon to offer ideas about what to do with the city and these modern effects. As for anthropology, it has another source, which is the work of people in zones not of the city or of the modern, but rather of so-called primitive societies. That is not a good word; I will just say "tribal societies," "pre-capitalist" or "pre-feudal societies," "societies without writing," or "without power," if you prefer. And the principal source of that material comes from the missionaries, because when one of the founders of anthropology—a very important figure for Marx, Lewis Henry Morgan, an American—invents, so to speak, the idea of kinship and the importance of kinship in these societies, he writes around to get information, and who does he write to? Well, in all these different colonized places he writes to the missionaries, and the missionaries are the ones who tell him who can marry whom, what to call your mother's brother, and so on. Anthropology is a sort of circuitous effect of colonization. Morgan is a very great figure. If you like, you can see the mid-nineteenth century as organizing itself around three explosions at ten-year intervals. There is Darwin in 1859; Marx's *Capital* is from 1867; and Morgan's *Ancient Society* is from 1877. Out of Morgan much flows, and, indeed, Lévi-Strauss acknowledges him as the founder of anthropology, for reasons we will see later on.

But Durkheim's nephew was not a sociologist; he became an anthropologist. Alongside those materials, and the myths that people like Frazer are collecting in the isolation of their home, without going out into the field at all, there are a few daring but also scientifically oriented minds who go into the field and live there with these tribal peoples, and of course the greatest name among them is Malinowski, at the beginning of the twentieth century. We won't be touching on Malinowski. In fact, I don't see a whole lot of references in Lévi-Strauss to Malinowski—but Malinowski studied one other form of this other ideology I'm about to mention, which is the circulation in the Trobriand Islands of cowrie shells. You could call it a form of money. With this research, and with the research of Durkheim's nephew, Marcel Mauss—another very important name, even though he wrote almost nothing, the most well-known writing being a book called *Le Don, The Gift*—here we have, at once, an ideology which I will call the ideology of exchange. This is not the exchange of commodities that we find in capitalism; it's pre-capitalist. It's a form of both exchange and communication, the basis of which is supposed to be found, according to these people, in these so-called primitive societies. So there emerges an ideology of the gift or of exchange which offers to replace capitalist life with something else, which could at the outer limit become a kind of utopian space, and we'll look at that later on. But there is definitely an ideology of the gift and of exchange which is a little bit different from this ideology of communication, but which is related to it. And exchange—that's speaking, right? We are exchanging words. Of course, these anthropologists had to learn the so-called primitive languages, many of them much more complicated than our own, others not at all primitive in any sense, and this was already so in the early nineteenth century, with the so-called discovery of Sanskrit. It's an odd thing, like the discovery of the new world, as though there weren't people there already, and as though Sanskrit scholarship isn't far older than anything one finds in Europe. Nonetheless, in the late eighteenth century, working for these British companies who finally conquer India, scholars discover both Sanskrit and a proto-language which would play a big role in the development of the historical linguistics that I spoke to you about last time.

Anyway, those are various things that come out of linguistics. But, as I was saying the last time, they come out of Saussure's break with that historical linguistics, and, after having made what is apparently a great classical contribution to it, proceeding on a different path, which will be called synchronic. I think it is pretty inevitable that we tend to think of synchronic as the present and diachronic as a continuous past of some sort. That's not exactly what it means, but everybody thinks about it in that way when they're not watching themselves. I propose to look at the synchronic rather as a cross section. That's not a temporal idea. In a cross section you somehow see all the elements of a system frozen before you, and you're able to put them together and see how they interconnect and how their binary oppositions are arranged. That is a much more satisfactory way of thinking of synchrony, because clearly synchrony is not just the present of time but rather a systematic phenomenon of some kind.

As for the diachronic, however, there are lots of versions. It certainly means a certain kind of continuity. Does it mean causal history? Yes, bits of the past begin to generate other, newer phenomena, and that all fits together causally in some way. But maybe it would be better from our perspective to think of causality as a narrative form, that is to say, causality produces a kind of story over time, and stories and narratives must always have this element of continuity. In any case, even though I don't think there's any absolute agreement as to what the diachronic might be, it certainly produces a new problem. That is, if you're describing things synchronically as a system, then what do you do with the past and with history? It is very clear that this is exactly what happens with Saussure. He has the diachrony of this neogrammarian school of linguistics, of the whole great movement of nineteenth-century linguistics looking at the history of languages, and he realizes that they have nothing to do with our speech, with what we mean when we're talking, because if we started to think of the history of every word that we used, we would be in great trouble and we would be tripping over our feet. In fact, it is impossible because of the changes, the sedimentation involved in these etymologies. But then you can see how immediately the questions will arise. That is, what is the relationship of synchrony to diachrony?

If you project this onto other areas, in literature, for example, you could say that maybe a certain period has a synchronic aesthetic; that is to say, in a period—it could be the '20s or the '60s—there's a certain notion of what art is, no matter how variously it's practiced. There is at least a dominant notion of art. There are survivals of all this stuff; there's stuff that won't yet come to fruition, a certain kind of subversion. Okay, but how is that connecting up to the past of art? And this is one of the ways diachrony has been thought of, and people have been anxious to criticize it: is there a telos in this? In modernism, for example, there is a telos of the modern. Once you start out from—where do we want to begin?—let's say Manet, then the next painters who really want to change the paradigm have to make it new, to use Pound's expression. They have to do something new. So modernism will have a telos of innovation and constant change. And, when it comes to the end of what seemingly one can do with the novel or poetry or whatever, when it looks like all these innovations have exhausted themselves, then there's a kind of crisis of the modern, which one tends to call the postmodern. So that diachrony of the modern would seem to bring a certain teleological ideology with it, that is, a false ideology, if you like, because all these painters are working in the present, and yet they wish to somehow outbid their rivals and their predecessors and make something new. Harold Bloom's *The Anxiety of Influence* is another version of that idea. We could go further, and we will a little bit, because we're going to see that Lévi-Strauss, although a revolutionary in his own way, draws a line in terms of aesthetic taste, and one cannot consider him an absolute revolutionary in aesthetics. You can find that in this remarkable introduction to *The Raw and The Cooked*, the overture about music, which we'll talk about at some point, hopefully today.

So we have then a first set of terms, which comes out of Saussure's break with diachrony and his discovery of synchrony. This discovery turns on the sign, and I will warn you then about another confusion. The French use the word "symbolic" a lot, especially in this period, but they do not necessarily mean by that "symbolism." We would tend, I think, to make a distinction between symbols and signs, and you can see that in film studies, where you have the iconic, the mimetic, the religious totem, the meaningful image, and so on. But *symbolique*, the symbolic, does not have to do with symbolism in the old Freudian sense, as he is interpreted in an orthodox way. It simply has to do with signs and language. So, when we come to Lacan and the symbolic, he's not talking about symbols; he's talking about language.

Now one would naturally think of starting with this business of the sign and linguistic structure. The older idea of the sign was dual: a word and its meaning. Here, we have a paradigm shift. Instead of thinking of this in two ways, we think of it in three ways. Here is a pencil; there is also an idea of the pencil, and the word "pencil." That is a thing in the world, an object. There is a sound. Then, to that signifier, there corresponds a signified, which is an idea of the pencil. And then, as a kind of third thing, there's the referent. That's this pencil. So, whereas the older thinking about language saw a duality between a word and a meaning, now one sees three aspects of this relationship: signifier, signified, and referent. If you're interested in the logic of the signifier then the referent will disappear into a kind of Kantian thing-in-itself. It is there, of course, but language doesn't seem to have an immediate purchase on it, only a purchase on its meanings. But then, with Lacan, we see that the meanings fade away, and we have only a logic of the signifier. That will be an interesting development, but we don't want to get there yet.

Indeed, I already regret having given you that Deleuze essay, in which Deleuze, as is his habit, annexes the whole of structuralism to himself and turns it all into something Deleuzean. But what Deleuze has used to organize that essay of his is Lacanianism, and not Saussurean linguistics. It could also be misleading, because Deleuze will divide his opening chapters, the ones I wanted you to read, into the Imaginary, the Symbolic, and the Real. Those are the three dimensions which are fundamental to

Lacan; at least you can think of them that way if you like. The Imaginary is a dualism. The Symbolic sort of comes out of a canceled trinity, but then, with the Real, he goes back to the one, in some sense. The Real will pick up this reference that seemed to be dropped when we concentrated on the Symbolic. But don't worry about that right now. We will get that in much more detail with Lacan.

So we begin with a sign, but we begin with the arbitrariness of the sign, and much depends on that. Older languages, older philosophies of language and older mysticisms, thought that a word had its own inner meaning, maybe by onomatopoeia or something else. For example, if you're positing a mystical character to written language, then there is something in the number of letters or something in the form of the thing, that contains the meaning of the word. What Saussure insisted on is that language is absolutely arbitrary. There is no relationship between, let's say, *le lait* and *Milch*, in the words other languages have for this same substance, which we call 'milk.' But, in another way, we mustn't overestimate that, because, at another level of the language, it is not arbitrary anymore. That other level is the phonetic level and the level of system. So we must distinguish between phonetics and phonemics, between the pure sounds of a language and the syllables that it gets formed into, which become words. And you must also realize that linguistics is a domain that's limited, as Benveniste says, at two ends. First of all, it's limited by the science of sounds. He says, yes, of course, in the laboratory, they can go deeper into this, but that doesn't contribute anything to the active use of language by individuals, whereas the distinction between sounds does. And these are binary distinctions, which separate the various kinds of sounds the mouth can make into meaningful oppositions, marked oppositions, so to speak, and we use this terminology of marked and unmarked to convey some of the nuances of this true system, which is that of phonetics. This is, in a sense, the deeper level of linguistic meaning. But that means that, as far as we speakers are concerned, the sound of a word in our particular language and the dialects of that language, the sounds of those things are arbitrary sounds. They don't tell us anything about the meaning; they are conventional. But the fact that they're arbitrary does incite us to look for the deeper system, and that's the point of this idea of the arbitrariness of the sign. Benveniste points out that linguistics, as a discipline, is limited at both ends. It is limited on the one end by phonetics and the phonetic systems, the sound patterns and oppositions, that it explores, but, on the other end, it's limited by the sentence itself. The sentence is the absolute limit of what linguistics can do. It can try to get out of the sentence, beyond the sentence. Obviously, any kind of writing is a set of sentences, but, as he says, unfortunately, you get over the boundary of one sentence, and what do you find? Just more sentences. So, in a way, that is the upper limit of linguistics, but not necessarily of semiotics or of what is going to come out of all this in other areas. I told you last time what the system produces for us and the form it takes in Saussure: differences without positive terms. It doesn't mean the other terms are negative; it means that they are just placeholders for this fundamental thing, which is the binary opposition.

A great many of you have reacted against binary oppositions in your papers, and therefore I want to say something in defense of the binary opposition. It is not a dualism. A dualism is a difference and a relation between positive terms, but, in language, for example, these sounds mean nothing in themselves, and that's why linguistic differentiation, the linguistic notion of the binary opposition, will be one of a negation, a differentiation, in which it is the differentiation itself that is meaningful, not the two individual terms. Now, I consider that this is really part of the dialectic, although, in Hegel, it gets much more complicated, and I don't think that Hegel's notions of language are very interesting, nor are Sartre's for that matter. These are people who have a kind of linguistic optimism that you can say everything, that there is no zone of experience that you cannot express. That's kind of funny, because we said, if you remember, that for the existentialists, in a sense, you can talk about essences, but you can't really say anything about existence. It is an ineffable experience; it is something for which there are no words, and so about it you can only say that you can't say anything. It seems to me this is a starting point on which this linguistic optimism can build. That is, there is a negative energy where you really can talk about what you can't say by explaining why you can't say it. All right, that is another matter . . .

We are coming to another form of the binary opposition. Here, I think the point is that we are able through it to look down at the building blocks of meaning. So it's not that language is incapable of saying everything, but that we have to look at its atomic and subatomic levels to see how it says anything at all. I believe that when we move up the ladder toward semantics (rather than pure semiotics) we find that this has a useful effect on ideas; that is to say, it suggests that everything you think of as an idea in its own right is defined by its negation in some sense. Determination is negation, as per a famous Spinozan saying. That means: to say what a thing is, you have to say what it's not. Well, the binary opposition suggests more than that. It suggests that, in our thinking, all these ideas and values and meanings that we imagine to stand alone are, in fact, parts of systems and involve negations; and one way of exploring ideas is precisely through these hidden oppositions that they are caught up with, a whole ideological spider's web of these things that can be explored. People don't just have *an* idea; they are caught in a whole series of these complex binary oppositions, and sometimes they are able to readjust them and break out of them. In my book on structuralism, I think I mention a German philologist (Jost Trier) who showed that, at a certain moment of the Middle Ages, *List* was part of a binary opposition with *Kunst*. But then, in the next century, suddenly a third element (the Middle High German *Wizzen*) appears, so the whole paradigm shifts a little bit, and now a new paradigm takes the place of the old.[1]

So examining binary oppositions can do that as well; and I also think that there is a reason why I have always been struck by a historical passage from existentialism to structuralism, which involved the movement of people who had considered themselves Sartreans into semiotics, and, indeed, I can sort of count myself one of those, insofar as I was at the time, and still am, a kind of fellow traveler of semiotics and a more-than-former Sartrean. But why would that be the natural place for Sartrean existentialists to go? As for Marxism, you understand that, in France, all self-respecting intellectuals after World War II, up until about 1980, maybe a little later, were Marxists, however they understood that. Marxism is the baseline ideology of all these people, unless, indeed, they are something else entirely, and, in the later '50s, some of the older fascists began to come out of the woodwork and you began to see that there was another ideology in play somewhere. That is not surprising. But this movement from a philosophical position like existentialism to that of structuralism is an interesting one, and I think that Sartre's phenomenologies of the present, the ways in which the body is involved in sensations and in thoughts and so forth, were crying out for semiotic analysis. It wasn't just that people suddenly realized: What happened to language in all this? Where is language in Sartrean existentialism? Why does Sartre really have no theory

---

1   Fredric Jameson, *The Prison-House of Language: A Critical Account of Structuralism and Russian Formalism* (Princeton, NJ: Princeton University Press, 1972), 19.

of language, except to think of it as a kind of *en-soi*, as a kind of object that is to be worked over, or as a kind of transparent relationship to the other? Well, with Saussurean linguistics, suddenly it becomes possible to map out a phenomenology of these things in much more tangible and concrete linguistic terms and systemic terms, and I think that would be one of the reasons for these intellectual evolutions. And it relies on the notion of system, which is projected by binary oppositions, and they can take all kinds of forms, and we will probably see a few of them. In other words, in terms of what I said the other day, arguing against something means that you're still caught up in its problematic. It involves binary oppositions, and an idea that opposes another one and tries to correct it is still deformed by its struggle to oppose that other idea. So there are all kinds of contacts which I think are fruitful if they get us out of this notion that there are individual ideas, that people think a certain thing. That's opinion, and opinion is a system in its own right, *doxa*, which we can also call "ideology." Certainly, when we get to the public sphere, we will find that there is a level of opinion, in Barthes's mythologies for example, that can be explored semiotically, but it is best to think of positions in this deeper sense.

Now we have some other kinds of things to consider. Where is this all taking place? It is hard to translate these ideas, because we have different words for them. French has two words: *langue* and *langage*, both of which mean "language." If we wanted to get a second term out of this in English, we would have to say "tongue"—your native tongue and the language that you use—but that doesn't exactly work. In structuralist French, let's say, there is a fundamental opposition between *langue* and *parole*. *Parole* means spoken speech, and *langue* means the system of the language; and you can immediately see how Lévi-Strauss projects this opposition onto his myths. If you were a linguist, somebody would not come to you and say, "You're studying syntax? Well, how can you do that unless you've registered all the different sentences in the form that this language can project?" Obviously, no one can do that. Language is creative—you can always project a new kind of utterance, a new kind of sentence—but the language itself as a system is separate from that productivity. If you like, yes, it is a constructed object. Nobody can see it. They would have said in the olden days that each foreign language has its own particular genius, but we can at least say each has its own style, its own mode. Very recently, the philosophers have discovered this, again in France. They have published what is called a dictionary of untranslatables.[2] And this reflects the fact that, whereas the translators of philosophy blithely find equivalents and get on with it, philosophical terms occupy different positions in different languages. Take a word like *Vorstellung*. *The World as Will and Idea*, *Die Welt als Wille und Vorstellung*. In German, *Vorstellung* is something you put in front of yourself. Is that "idea" or "representation"? Plato was not thinking of visuality or anything when he invented his doctrine of the ideas. So even translating something like Kant or Schopenhauer into French or English is going to deform it, because there is no exact fit between any of these terms, and, at best, we have to explore the meaning of these terms by way of binary oppositions, by finding out in those languages what system they come out of, what they fit into. Some of that is etymological. As I said earlier, Heidegger loved to find things in etymology, to explore phenomena in terms of etymologies.

The idea of the untranslatables gives you a sense of how each *langue*, each language as a system, has its own parameters, its own logic. But now there is the *parole*, the sentence that you speak in this language. There can be an infinite number of those. They are unpredictable, and therefore linguistics cannot occupy itself with individual pronouncements. It must study the system of language. Since then, we have gotten the production of speech acts, as well as Chomsky and the production of felicitous sentences. There is a lot of work on how the individual sentence is produced, but, in the Saussurean period, the great discovery was the idea that *langue*, language as system, had its own unique kind of objectivity that could be studied in its own right.

And now we come to something of the greatest importance for everything that we've been looking at here. Think of Lévi-Strauss with myths. You have some kind of system, and then each of these tribes produces its own myths, and each generation of the tribe rewrites them a bit. So, in a sense, each individual myth is like a *parole*, like a "discourse"—one word they have used to translate *parole*, but that is not right, so we will just go on saying *parole* or enunciation—whereas the system of myths is very different from its individual instantiation, so that exploring the individual myth will not be quite the same as the mythic system as a

---

2   Barbara Cassin, *Vocabulaire européen des philosophies: dictionnaire des intraduisibles* (Paris: Seuil le Robert, 2004), translated into English as *Dictionary of Untranslatables: A Philosophical Lexicon*, eds. Barbara Cassin, Steven Rendall, and Emily S. Apter (Princeton, NJ: Princeton University Press, 2014).

whole. Lévi-Strauss will make this absolutely scandalous and ridiculous proposition that any and every later version of a myth is to be added into the corpus. So we have the Oedipus myth here. Sophocles made his own version of a much more ancient legend, but Freud rewrote it as well. So we will add Freud in, and Freud's version of the Oedipus complex will also be part of the Oedipus myth. In fact, anything that comes along that deals with this material is a proper variant of it, but it is a variant of something of which there exists no original. There is no original Oedipus myth. It's not in Sophocles. Does that mean there is no first written version? No, it means more absolutely that there is no original to begin with. And that notion of copies without originals is very stimulating in some way. It certainly poses problems. What are we studying if there is no original? Can we just study the variations? One could begin to talk about modern music in that case with its perpetual variations. But I think the idea is that it is the system of that particular myth that we're studying, the form of it and not its content, nor any of its individual versions.

But now we come to something which is going to be even more important for us. It is the notion of the double articulation or the double inscription. You remember I talked about phonetics and phonemics. Phonetics is the lower level of language, for Benveniste, the ultimate physical level of language, which is made of these sounds and their oppositional relation to each other, because each sound allows us to differentiate the word, the utterance that we're making, from other ones. But then this phonetic level will produce another level which is that of phonemics, the way in which syllables are formed. With syllables, we're already on the way to a recognizable notion of the word, and then there will, presumably, be a syntactic level on top of that. Syntax is neglected until we come to Chomsky, which we will not do in this course. But you have levels of organization of these things. You have lower levels that are then organized into higher levels, and, presumably, the highest level will be that of the sentence. Well, if we are talking about stories and narratives, does it mean they are like sentences? This will be what people like Barthes and Metz and the narratologists think. Hold that idea, as they say in the silent movie theater, and we'll come back to it.

But for us what counts is that, while even here there are these levels, then, alongside them, there is another set of relationships, which is that of the horizontal and the vertical. That will be the form taken by the double inscription. It is another opposition, like diachronic and synchronic: that of the syntagmatic and the paradigmatic. If you're like me and you use a lot of oppositions like this, there comes a moment when sometimes you can't tell which is which anymore. We are going to get to a famous opposition, which is that of metaphor and metonymy in Jakobson, something also very important in Lacan. But it has been pointed out that, in one of Lacan's major essays, when he is talking about a metaphor, it turns out not to be a metaphor at all, but a metonym. Lacan has just gotten them confused! The whole point of the identification of a binary opposition is that, in another, dialectical sense, they are the same. They are related to each other, so you are forgiven in advance if you make those mistakes, which I often make.

The syntagmatic and the paradigmatic. We have found the word paradigm before, so we can maybe build on that. A paradigm is something which gets replaced by another paradigm. So, when you're using a noun, though paradigms don't always have to be nouns, you can replace it with other objects. You can say, "I chased the dog," and then in the paradigmatic, the vertical, you can replace "dog" by "cat," by "child," by other objects. And for "chase" you can say "find," "heard," "saw." So all those substitutions will be the paradigmatic level of the sentence, the vertical axis of an utterance or a sentence. But the other level, the horizontal level, will, therefore, clearly be the succession of types of words in your sentence, or in other words, syntax. So that is horizontal, and that can be replaced by other kinds of sentences, but it's not a question of replacement there so much as it's one of contiguity, the way in which this word gets related to that word in a horizontal sequence.

Let me stop then and go back to Roman Jakobson, the great Russian linguist and philologist who ended up in the United States, having made a stop in Prague, where he encountered the whole system of phonetics. Trubetzkoy was the name of the phonologist who discovered this system; Jacobson took it with him to New York, and in New York he met Lévi-Strauss, or vice versa, and so something gets going in that confrontation. The spark between those two sets off structuralism, in a sense. One of Jakobson's great points is to point out, on this business of tropes, that we talk all the time about metaphor. Metaphor is the hallmark of genius; that's either Aristotle or Proust or both. Everybody thinks that the very essence of the poetic gift is this ability to invent striking, marvelous metaphors. But, he says, we've forgotten another trope, another use of figurative language which is equally preeminent but which we never notice, because it is the trope of prose, and not of poetry: metonymy. Metonymy talks about what's *next to* things. Metaphor talks about what things are *like*. So metaphor is similarity, and metonymy is contiguity. This is already, I think, present in eighteenth-century associationism, when they were trying to figure out how the mind works, but not in these linguistic terms. Now how can we think of this new opposition? Jakobson says metaphor is the essence of poetry—it doesn't have to be of all poetry, clearly—whereas metonymy characterizes prose, the great novels, for example. Now think of something like this. Both these examples are invented examples, but I attach them to Balzac. Balzac liked comparing his characters to animals, so he would say, "This man was a lion," or "a weasel," or whatever. You can compare the character with whatever he or she is like. But, suppose you said instead, which Balzac will also like to do, "This character was very slovenly. He wore an old, worn-out overcoat. His shoes were worn and unpolished. He tended to frequent a down-and-out part of Paris. His own house was ramshackle and needed a coat of paint." That description is metonymic, because we're not saying what the character is like; we're saying what's next to the character. So the character is characterized by his clothes, his immediate living space, his area of frequentation. Even bodily descriptions are metonymic, because the body of someone is not the essence of the character, but we tend to figure character in terms of the body and bodily descriptions. So the true field of the novel does not lie with any kind of comparisons or with metaphor in general. It lies with metonymy.

How did Jakobson prove this? He looked at the clinical phenomenon of aphasia, a condition that affects one's speech. I'm not going to follow it into all the details, but what he found was that there were two types of aphasia, which correspond to two types of language or two tropes, and those tropes are metaphor and metonymy. The one kind of aphasia is a paradigmatic disorder, while the other is a syntagmatic impairment. So, in this analysis of clinical pathologies of actual speaking, you have located some of the very functions or mechanisms of language itself.

Well, in this business of the syntagmatic and the paradigmatic, you can see at once that you have these two things at work. The paradigmatic is the realm of metaphor and substitution, whereas the syntagmatic is that of metonymy or contiguity, order, continuity. And you can go on and multiply your relations to these things. Of course, you will want to go back to Freud, where you find out that this is a fundamental form of dream analysis, and that the logic of dreams is that of *Verschiebung* and

Verdichtung, condensation and displacement. Condensation would be the metaphoric. Displacement is the metonymic. And dreams create their own private languages by way of these two processes, as do jokes, wit, and the like. So you can see that this will become a fundamental way of thinking about and analyzing language, or, at least, it gives us the dual organization of the processes of language.

Now, as soon as you say that, you are going to think of Lévi-Strauss's analysis of myth. What does it consist of? It consists of taking the various episodes which make up the Oedipus story and finding paradigms in them. Remember, he compares it to a set of playing cards, and then he says we should divide these myths up according to their similarities and their differences. And we'll see that his analysis of myth turns on the relationship of the paradigmatic and the syntagmatic. One line is to the other line as C is to D, in this analysis. And you can see, then, why he can fit as many versions of this in there as he wants to, because you simply add the additional pieces into each of these lines, and they become like the playing cards, the red cards, the black cards. That is why it's so funny when, in the overture to *The Raw and the Cooked*, he writes about some Martians who arrive on Earth. At first, they find these things that seem to be marks—probably something to read—and they go from left to right; maybe they go from right to left. Do you know what *boustrophedon* is? *Boustrophedon* is the pattern of furrows that an ox makes in a field. You let the ox pull the plow down to the end of your field, and then it turns around and pulls the plow back in the next furrow the other way. Well, there's a form of writing in which you read from left to right, and when you get to the end of the line, the next line goes from right to left, and so on. Given our modern habits, it would be very onerous to follow these oxen of words back and forth across the page. Anyway, that is the first thing the Martians find. And then, suddenly, they find something else, and given Lévi-Strauss's own interests, you're not surprised to find that the new manuscript that they look at is a musical score, an orchestral score. Here, indeed, we have the syntagmatic—the development of the theme—and then under it the orchestration of that theme and all the notes. How to read that? That would be Lévi-Strauss's image or method of analysis, and he pretends it's inspired by music—I'm not sure that's true—but, clearly, he thinks in those terms, and, at any rate, it is absolutely covered by this axis of the paradigmatic and the syntagmatic. Of course, he shares the Wagnerianism of his youth. In the late nineteenth century, Wagner was in France a kind of religion of the aesthetes. It's been said that, back in the late nineteenth, early twentieth century, more books had been written about Wagner than anyone except Jesus Christ. There is an enormous new volume called *Wagnerism* by the music writer Alex Ross of *The New Yorker*, which I highly recommend, if you are interested in this kind of thing, because it traces how the study of Wagner, though not just Wagner, developed up until our own time in all these fields. Lévi-Strauss is, of course, a great Wagnerian, and, in a way, I think that a decisive moment in Wagner must be this moment in *Parsifal* when, lacking modern technology, Wagner has to make his characters walk without walking. They have to walk to the Grail castle without really moving, and the one who's leading Parsifal says, "*Zum Raum wird hier die Zeit.*" "Here time becomes space." When we get to this decisive business of geology in Lévi-Strauss, you must remember this: here time becomes space, and, for the geologist, that is so too.

Maybe we should go on to that. Do you know what the watersheds are? The watershed is where all the water from various streams gradually works its way down and drains into a central ocean or sea or whatever. Many of you, I suppose, and myself, spiritually, are in the state of North Carolina, so you should know that one of the great drainage divides is the continental divide, up in the Smokies. It corresponds to the Blue Ridge Parkway. Everything on one side of that divide drains into the Atlantic Ocean, and everything on the other side ultimately into the Mississippi and the Gulf of Mexico. So you have an absolute division. And on one side you have plants that don't exist on the other side of this line, and you have animals, maybe also insects, that don't exist there. This invisible line is itself a kind of structural boundary, defined by things underneath it, by geological formations, by changes in soil, in the movement of tectonic plates. This is what Lévi-Strauss is doing in his analysis, for example, of the Bororo face paintings. You have a certain kind of surface formation, in which several axes are moving in a certain way. Okay, what causes that? Nothing in the face of the tattooed person. No, he says. Underneath that, in some kind of tectonic unconscious, what's going on is an incompatibility between two types of social organization, a dualism and a tertiary formation. We'll look at what that is next time. It is a very fundamental, interesting problem for Lévi-Strauss, and it is the class problem, really. It is a question of classes and power.

What do we want to say about that? Do we want to say that the art which is symptomatic of that deeper contradiction expresses that contradiction?

Maybe it conceals that contradiction. Maybe, says Lévi-Strauss, it gives the artists of this tribe the feeling that the contradiction has been resolved. They can't resolve it in reality, so they resolve it in form. And this is a kind of formalism, but it's a formalism in which you have base and superstructure, in which you have an aesthetic system, which somehow reflects a contradiction, although "reflects" is a very impoverished word for it. But that's the point: It reflects a contradiction. It doesn't reflect a static system. This opposition of two and three in the tribal village, for example, is a deep contradiction, which is sort of resolved formally in the art, or is appeased by it, or gives the utopian sense that it could be resolved.

So we have a whole aesthetic there in which art comes out of contradictions, but not just the banal contradictions of the surface of these things, but deep tectonic plates that are moving underneath the surface. These are the categories. You know that the word "category" in Greek means "stumbling block." It means a problem of some kind. So the categories underlying these things are themselves contradictions. For Hegel, I guess you could say that a contradiction can never be resolved; you can only transcend it. That is to say, in practice, you expand it. Hegel has nothing to do with thesis-antithesis-synthesis. There are no syntheses in Hegel. There are only expansions of basic contradictions, and we see that in history. Today, our contradictions are now expanded to the very global level, to the world market itself, so everything that was unsolvable earlier is solvable by enlargement. So the impossibilities of the Greek city-state are solved by the new contradictions of the Roman Empire and of Christianity, and there, the contradictions of empire are then solved by this breakup and this newly emergent system of the fiefs and then the nation-states, and now we have a wholly new set of contradictions, of perpetuations of those things in the global system and its possibilities.

At any rate, that is the way in which all this linguistic speculation that I have been talking about works. And that is the sense of the double articulation: we have an articulation which is purely formal in the facial tattoos, but then there's another level on which it's articulated, which is the twos and the threes of binary social organization and tertiary social organization. The tendency would be to talk about this in terms of an unconscious. That's okay, provided you know that they don't fit; they are articulated into each other. It is a *double* inscription. They can't solve each other. They can't even express each other. They are, in some sense, distinct from each other and yet related. Now the relations, what do we want to call those? Mediations? In Lacan, it's called *point de capiton*, "quilting points." I don't know anything about quilting, so I prefer the other translation, which is tacking nails. You tack your cloth on a piece of furniture. So mediation would be these quilting points or tacking nails. That is what's happening at the end of this essay on the structural study of myths, when he comes to the Zuni myth of creation. That is the problem he is raising. Can mediations serve to conceptualize creation? Origins? Beginnings?

Well, I think we have to stop there.

February 9, 2021

7

Saussure in Brazil

{Levi-Strauss}

We're dealing with some difficult stuff here, and I recognize that. But remember that our task is not so much to go into all this in detail as to identify it and outline it. The names and numbers of all the players. I gave you the example of a trip where you stop in Rome for one day, Naples for another day, and obviously you don't see anything, but at least you know, because your guidebook tells you, that if you want to find the Caravaggios, there are four churches in Rome you need to visit. So, if you get interested in Caravaggio, you will know where to look when you return. Of course, you have to know where the Caravaggios are, where the churches are, and so on. That is a little bit our situation here, especially with structuralism, which is constantly trying to realize its unconscious wish to become a science. One part of it will call itself semiotics. Another part will call itself narratology. And, of course, Lévi-Strauss has already made a science, which is anthropology. To be sure, there's a way in which he makes it up himself, so Lévi-Straussian anthropology is not the same as other kinds. A science is going to constantly invent terminologies, and I recognize that they can be confusing, particularly when they begin to rhyme with each other, that is to say, when the paradigmatic axis kicks in and we find the substitutes for all these things, substitute names, substitute languages. There can be so many of them, and maybe I confused you last time by throwing them all together.

What I'm trying to do here is to make a map of what's there, and I am also going to tell you a story about it all. I have already told you what that story is: the gradual diminution of the study of action and free choice, and a movement toward the study of the great forces and finally the institutions which dwarf individual action. I think that is characteristic of the history of this whole period, from the postwar to what I consider the turning point in 1980, up to our time, but, of course, once we get up to our time, I don't necessarily endorse any particular version of this. It seems to me that's the story we are telling.

These are not all examples of my attempt to make a historical narrative of this period. But it does suggest why narrative is important, because it's very hard to see how you can have any kind of history without a historical narrative. History is a historical narrative. It's not the facts. Or rather, yes, it's the facts, but the facts arranged in a narrative. Arthur Danto, who became an art critic and a painter later on, started a series of philosophical monographs, in one of which he claimed that all history could always be turned back into a narrative. You are always in history telling the story of something. Then Hayden White came along and tried to categorize the different kinds of stories we could tell about history, at least in the nineteenth century. Those were four—comedy, tragedy, romance, and irony—and he endowed them with other frills in a book called *Metahistory*, which you should all read, the categories of which he got at least partly from Northrop Frye, whose *Anatomy of Criticism* you should also read. Well, you can say, is that philosophy? Yes, I think there are philosophical categories involved in this. I think this move via Lévi-Strauss into the problems of narrative is a philosophical question. Philosophy has been appropriated, tugged, side-tracked into logic and into science. It is as though philosophy can only deal with causes. Well, causes are narratives too, and, when we get to Althusser, we will explore that part of it in more detail. But the question of narrative comes up in many ways, and it even comes up in popular speech. If you know how to use your computer, which I often don't, you can find a certain place in which you can trace the historical statistics of the use of a certain term. It goes back into the twentieth century, but it kind of works also on texts before that, so you can get a general idea of when a term is invented and how often it is used. For example, we have a very interesting one emerge in precisely the moment when the whole language of transnational corporations gets subsumed under a far more widely used term, which is "globalization."

I think there is a kind of historico-political lexicology to be done here, because when a term overtakes another one, there are reasons; there is a need, although it may be a false need. There is an ideological need, at least, which may be real or false. It is always imagined, but let's leave that aside. So the term "globalization" begins to replace all this transnational stuff, and so its number of references far exceeds the others'. Well, I would bet anything, and I don't even have to bet, that there's a moment when the word "narrative" takes over in popular speech. Before that, people argue about facts, about causes. There's a certain moment when all of a sudden the newspapers start telling us, "This is the narrative of this. This is so-and-so's narrative of that."

So this matter of narrative is a good deal more significant than a simple change in intellectual fashion. But this is simply to show you that there may be philosophies of narrative. I doubt if they're very interesting—but there are certainly also theories of narrative, and the predominance of the problem of narrative is historically significant, especially for us here, because it emerges in France from semiotics and structuralism, and then migrates into the other disciplines. How fast this happens depends on the rigidity of the other disciplines. These are uneven rates of speed, and I don't even pretend to guess how that works. Clearly, since Lévi-Strauss was an anthropologist, anthropology will be hit by this very quickly, and there emerges something called narrative or cultural ethnography. Ethnography is the same as writing, how you write up your experience of a society. The big book there is George Marcus and James Clifford's *Writing Culture*, and it dates from 1986. All kinds of things in anthropology are changed when this final tacking nail, this final articulation of the importance of narrative is brought to bear on anthropology. The other sciences take longer.

We talked about linguistics last time. I gave you various, scattered features of structural linguistics. I don't at all pretend to offer you a complete picture of linguistics, except as this sort of hidden source or spark that is going to make its mark in a lot of these different disciplines, either via structuralism or on its own, in some cases. We talked about Jakobson's metaphor and metonymy; we're going to put that aside, because it will come back in Lacan, when we get to Lacan. Then we talked about double articulation. This is a doctrine of levels. This means that in language itself we have at least two levels. One is the level of words; the other is the level of sounds; and, on top of all that, some third level, could be meanings, but that's not what the linguists work on. They work first of all on this level of phonetics, of the sound systems in each language which are absolutely unique, then phonemics, how those sounds get formed into intelligible syllables. Each language has these levels, and they're sometimes rather different from each other. There are some formations of sound that we English speakers can't even understand, let alone articulate, and vice versa. And, finally, there would be this level of semantics or syntax. So double inscription says there are at least two levels of these things that we have to look at.

Now I want to suggest to you that Lévi-Strauss is working with a double level. Those of you who are interested in Marxist criticism know that there is always a double level. You have the levels of superstructure and base. The given text is a part of superstructures, and Marxist criticism, generally— we're talking about very broad generalizations—will try to articulate that with a lower level of class or production realities, and indeed Marxism itself has two codes for these things. One is the code of social class and class struggle; the other is the code of capitalist production. Those are also kinds of levels. Actually, they are alternatives, I think, but their relationship also demands articulation.

Lévi-Strauss thinks, from time to time, that he is a Marxist. He says so. Every year, he rereads *The Eighteenth Brumaire*, the most dialectically dazzling of Marx's texts, which all of you must read some time. He believes in superstructures and bases. He says his work is a contribution to a theory of superstructures. He has a somewhat different pair of things that he constantly alludes to, which is nature and culture. That's also a double inscription; you take something at the first level and turn it into something on the order of the second level. He himself says that this is not a rigorous distinction. Do we believe in nature? What do we mean by nature? Wouldn't nature always be a part of the superstructure, that is, culture? Our idea of nature is a cultural idea. It has to be. When the Pygmies think of this immense thing which is the forest, this is nature for them, but it is certainly a cultural and religious idea that they have. This idea is not quite so important. What is important for Lévi-Strauss, as we will see in a minute, is kinship.

I would say there are three periods in the work of Lévi-Strauss, and, of course, there is this wonderful book *Tristes Tropiques*—indeed a sad book. It is about the deterioration of time. This is true throughout Lévi-Strauss, and it's visible in his aesthetics as well that things are deteriorating. It makes sense for an anthropologist. Sociologists deal with modern cities, modern societies. The anthropologists deal largely not only with these tribal societies, but with societies that are disappearing, along with their languages. I think he says when he was first writing some of his books, there were 2,000 different languages on Earth, but, today, there are perhaps only a few hundred left. Various ethnic groups, some of them, if they have enough social power, try to recuperate their language; they try to set up schools which teach both the dominant language and the native one. Of course, the state at times represses these languages and forces people to speak the dominant languages, but, today, they are tolerated, and we have this sense that, yes, the self-determination of these groups has thus, at least outwardly, been recognized.

I read about one language that has only one speaker, an old lady, and this anthropological linguist visits her and tries desperately to make a dictionary and a grammar of this language before it disappears with her. Of course, this reminds one of the fates of Ishi, which Lévi-Strauss refers to here. Ishi was a Native American who was found wandering about by himself near Berkeley somewhere in the early twentieth century, and he is brought to Kroeber, who was a very distinguished anthropologist and maybe the chair of the anthropology department at Berkeley (and, in case you're interested in science fiction or literature in general, the father of Ursula Le Guin, whose work turns precisely around these questions, utopias of Native American life, other kinds of utopias). Anyway, they find that this poor soul Ishi is the last of his tribe. There is nobody else alive. Nobody else speaks his language. Nobody to marry. All by himself. Kroeber takes him back to the department, arranges for him to live, finds him things to do. He doesn't live very long. That is a very sad story, told in a book, *Ishi in Two Worlds*, written by Kroeber's wife, Theodora.

This sadness is truly everywhere in this book of Lévi-Strauss, which, however, tries to do a great many things. It talks about his own formation. It talks about his first great anthropological expedition to Brazil, the Brazil of the '30s, São Paulo. São Paulo is the biggest city in the new world, and one that North Americans know little about. Lévi-Strauss was also a photographer, and there are two wonderful books of his photographs that have come out recently that show you São Paulo in the '30s. It is wonderfully nostalgic. There are also lots of portraits of the tribal peoples that he met in the month or two that he was able to dedicate to field work.

Now, if you're an anthropologist, presumably, you do field work. Before that was the case, there were anthropologists who just relied on missionaries' reports, but they didn't have much material to work on. So it has always been held against Lévi-Strauss that he evolves these incredible monuments of anthropological study on the basis of one or two months in the field. But obviously that is part of Lévi-Strauss's intelligence and his arrogance, you could say. He thinks about everything; he has theories about everything. For example, two types of fans in a certain area of Brazil from two different kinds of palm trees. How are they constructed? What are they for? They lead you back into other questions. Does each of these fans correspond to a certain social level? Lévi-Strauss is always thinking. The Fire Island comparison interested many of you. He was traveling in the United States and somebody took him out there, where the gender peculiarities of Fire Island became a kind of symbolic system. So you have a mind that is constantly making up theories, and sometimes these theories are outrageous, and he says so himself. He says, "Look, they want me to teach the same course over and over again. I can't do that. I can't be interested in what I did last year." But, if he is lucky, each interest will lead to further problems in that area, and therefore will allow him to con-struct ever more complex theoretical edifices. There are a lot of off-hand generalizations of great brilliance, especially the aesthetic ones, which are scattered throughout this, and maybe we will mention a few of them.

So *Tristes Tropiques* is this wonderful autobiographical summa of all the things that he has been interested in, and it is written in an extraor-dinary style which is rather old-fashioned, beautifully belle-lettristic. It is the most elegant French of the old style. That will also give us a clue as to why Lévi-Strauss is a kind of anti-modernist. How could he, with his devotion to the past and to his observation of the destruction of the past, really be an artistic modernist? Or even an analyst of the modern world? This constant deterioration is hanging over him. In Brazil, for example, he notes how many towns in the interior of Brazil—the great problem for the Brazilians: How to populate the interior of Brazil?—get populated on the basis of one mode of transport: river traffic. Then suddenly it is replaced by highways. Then, at that point, those towns dry up, become ghost towns, and new ones spring up someplace else. So the interior of Brazil is this constant deposit of ghost towns and the emergence of new towns all over the place. This was a process in Brazilian Brazil, not that of the Mato Grosso or the Amazonas or the areas in which earlier peoples lived.

So back to the three stages of Lévi-Strauss's career. The first stage is a much more orthodox anthropology, and it deals with kinship. Kinship for him is the very foundation of anthropology. There are multiple kinship systems in all the tribes of the world, from Indonesia to Siberia, from Australia to Brazil. How can one reduce all that to a single set of laws? Well, he thinks he has done that. A lot of mathematics is involved. If you want a thoroughgoing account of this—and I say it because it involves another one of our people—you read Simone de Beauvoir's long article on kinship. When it came out in the late '40s, she was commissioned by her journal, *Les Temps Modernes,* to write a review of some recent work. Simone de Beauvoir was a serious person; she sat down and worked on this for months. She then prepared a long essay, which you can consult, and which includes her account. Sartre also has a critique of this in passing in his *Critique of Dialectical Reason*, so this is a work with which people had to reckon. Reassure yourselves: we're not going to go into it in detail. But it is based on some categories that come up again and again: exogamy and endogamy. You know what monogamy and polygamy mean, and therefore you know what exogamy and endogamy mean. Exogamy means you can't marry a member of your tribe. If you want to go further than that, you can't marry your sister or brother. Endogamy means you can only marry members of your own tribe, clan, whatever the system of relationships is. So kinship will turn on the opposition of exogamy and endogamy. It will also turn on something else—and I think people don't exactly believe in it anymore, but it was one of the great utopias of the late nineteenth century, for Marxists as well as for the Left more generally—namely matriarchy. Did a matriarchal society ever exist? Well, you can see what that would do to kinship systems, because, in a matriarchy, it doesn't matter who your father is, because it's your mother who counts. Students of power, students who don't believe there were utopias and that all societies are power societies, will point out that of course there is a man present in matriarchal societies: the mother's brother. The maternal uncle, and he reasserts the power of patriarchy. So there have always been men running the show according to that position, and matriarchy as this dream of equality never existed. But it still has this aura of utopia, that a society run by women is less likely to be oppressive than the usual society run by men. And, as Engels shows, the rules of patriarchy basically come into force when you have money because the money has to pass to someone and he has to know who the legitimate child is, whereas, in matriarchy, it doesn't matter. Anyway, you can see how kinship will revolve around these ideas of matriarchy and patriarchy, exogamy and endogamy.

Elementary Structures of Kinship is an incredibly complicated work using all kinds of mathematics, and it boils down to the incest taboo, which, for Lévi-Strauss, is at the center of all kinship systems.[1] Anybody interested in adopting a philosophy of history is going to have to decide at what point hominids become human. For some of these people, especially the anthropologically oriented ones, it is the incest taboo, and, for Freud, as a matter of fact, this is also the case. The forbidding of intercourse with the mother is the very foundation of culture, as opposed to nature. Even Morgan, whom I told you about the other day, this American predecessor of anthropology, talks about three stages: savagery, barbarism, and civilization. These terms are not, except in the case of savagery, pejorative. Civilization includes writing and all the mechanics associated with that. Barbarism is the great highpoint, just as it is for Engels in its climax in the Iroquois nation. Morgan was actually a blood brother of the Iroquois. Military democracy, as he says, is the noblest of all social forms. Morgan was also a founder of the Republican Party (Lincoln's, that is) and an admirer of the Paris Commune. It's a very interesting combination. The end of his book praises the Paris Commune and says that it will lead us back to the kind of society embodied by the Iroquois confederation.

So what is the difference between barbarism and savagery? The split comes with the incest taboo. He speaks about savagery as this "stupendous promiscuity." Well, that means before the incest taboo, before the rules of kinship. The rules of kinship are established on the basis of this primal, foundational thing in society which is that law. One can think about that as one wants. But, for Lévi-Strauss, returning to the Marxist notion of base and superstructure, what would be the base? What's the mode of production here? It is not capitalism, not feudalism, not slavery. It is not an antique mode of production as in Greece, as in the city-states. It is not so-called oriental despotism. It is kinship. The original society's base is kinship. It is kinship that will divide up the production positions. So women do one kind of thing, men do something else. The young do one kind of thing, the elders something else. In the Zuni myth of creation, humans are first formed when the primal deity pulls them out of the mud. He gives them various tasks. This first group, he says, "You can be the hunters." To this next group he says, "You can be the farmers." When he comes to the final

---

1   Claude Lévi-Strauss, *The Elementary Structures of Kinship*, trans. James Richard von Sturmer and James Harle Bell (Boston: Beacon Press, 1969).

group there's nothing left for them to do. He says, "Okay, you can be the politicians. Since there's nothing productive for you to do, you might as well run the state." Here we have a first distribution of labor. As in many tribal societies, it is the elders who run the state, so to speak, who are the dictators by virtue of their age.

So that will be the part of Lévi-Strauss—this study of kinship and primitive societies—that involves a fascination with the utopian and will evolve into the question of power. We have kinship. We have these restricted Rousseauean groups. Are these utopias or not? That is, where does power come from? For the utopians, these are pre-power societies—we'll see this next week, I think—but for the others, no, power is already there in the elders and the generational organization or in the division between men and women and so forth. We'll come back to that. That is one thing which is going to lead us on into a new kind of theoretical interest in the midst of this tremendous, boiling, political society which is France in the 1960s.

So the second period of Lévi-Strauss's work is one which is signaled by a book which is called in French *La Pensée sauvage*, and which has been poorly translated as *The Savage Mind*. Well, that's not at all what Lévi-Strauss meant. First of all, *sauvage* in French doesn't only mean "savage." It means "wild," "state of nature," or "spontaneous." There's an expression for a kind of strike, *grève sauvage*. Is that a savage strike? No, it's a spontaneous strike, "a wildcat strike," we call it, so we do use natural imagery for it. So *sauvage* means "state of nature," and as for *pensée*, which, of course, does mean "thought" or "mind," it is also a cognate of the word for "flower," "pansy," and that's the image on the cover of this book of Lévi-Strauss. So Lévi-Strauss is saying that tribal science, tribal thinking, is a thought growing in the wild: a thinking in terms of objects rather than abstract classifications. It is a thinking in terms of plants, for example, which uses plants to think about plants. It is a thought without abstractions, but abstractions are supposed to make up science from a Western point of view. People ask when philosophy starts. It's obvious. It starts with Plato, because Plato invents a science of abstraction, the ideas. And so, from then on, philosophy will be not only the love of wisdom but the primacy of abstraction. What about these societies that don't have any abstraction? I think of set theory. I don't know if that's right or not. You have something like what the philosophers call nominalism. We know that these various tribal societies have incredible knowledge of plants. We know that there's such a thing as local knowledge, and even now, for example, it hasn't been completely explored, all this kind of stuff. Now suddenly the big pharmaceutical companies are very interested in this knowledge. India, which right now is pursuing a very regrettable path within neoliberalism, dictatorship, and a lot of other nasty things, is flirting with the idea of allowing foreigners and pharmaceutical companies to patent these various kinds of local medicines, herbs, and potions. That would take all of that kind of *pensée sauvage* into the domain of private property, into the ownership of these companies. Who knows, there may be some plant that cures cancer. Well, somebody like Merck necessarily has to own that, right? You can't put that out in the public domain and just go to your shaman's store and ask for this plant so you can cure your cancer! This has to go through big pharma, to be a part of the market and to cost a lot of money.

So there is a tribal lore or science—science means knowledge after all—which involves an incredible knowledge of plants. He tells a very funny story of a young anthropologist just doing her field work. An English-woman goes to a tribe in Brazil, and she wants to learn the language. They say that's fine, so she gets a teacher, and he begins to teach her the language by showing her the various plants. They all have different names. She is finally in despair. She says, "Listen, I don't even know what those plants are called in England! Do I have to learn the language by first learning the English words for these plants?" The point is that this is a knowledge of plants without the abstraction "plant." Poison ivy, oak leaves, blueberry bushes, and so on. What are you going to call them all? These people know something very precise about each of these things but don't have specific words for them. We call them "plants" because we don't know anything about them. They all have leaves. That's about all we know. So you call the ensemble of those things by the name of one of them. You call them all poison ivy, but of course they're not all poison ivy. In other words, this is a concrete science, which does not have generalized or abstract names for its objects, but it is profoundly a science, and one of the objects of this book of Lévi-Strauss is to show that these so-called primitive peoples have as complex a knowledge of the world as their counterparts do, but they don't express it in the same way. He will finally, later on in the third period, say that what's happening here is the end of Western abstraction. Now, he says, the complexity of myth, of *pensée sauvage*, of primitive science, is met by a new kind of thinking, a thinking beyond Western philosophy, which is the mind of the structuralist. My mind, as a structuralist, will finally meet the knowledge and the lore of these peoples. And it is superior to Western knowledge. It is a concrete knowledge. It is a knowledge of relationships, the way structuralism is. So this is a political position that goes well beyond anything the anthropologists normally think, because it is, for him, an invention of a new kind of thinking, which recaptures the complexities of these older kinds of thought.

We will come back to *pensée sauvage,* because that is the place in which he attacks Sartre, but I will just say, for now, that it's about classification systems. He wants to show how the knowledge of the individual object is profoundly complexified, if you like, by this whole elaborate classification scheme in which it is embedded. That's like the kinship system. Now we have a new set of systems, which are the classification schemes. Take names. We think, for example, that the name is the most unique—I'm using the Lacanian word for how you connect these two levels—the most unique way in which we relate to the singular. I am a singular person; I have a singular name. Yes, but a lot of people have my two or three names. In fact, he says, names are not at all singular or unique, but they are part of immense classification systems. Many of you have occasion to be around newborns, and you know that the parents are looking around for names. You may also know that names in the United States, as elsewhere, have fashions, and there is a moment when everybody is named Justin, and then another moment when everybody is named Kevin. So there are waves of fashions that are statistically documented. You think you're picking a unique name for your unique baby, but you're just participating in a fashionable classification scheme. Well, he demonstrates this by the most remarkable *tour de force* that you can imagine. Dogs, cats, racehorses, and birds each have a system of names. I'm not going to go into it in great detail, but it suffices to say that you don't call your cat Fido. You don't call your prize racehorse Fido. You don't call your dog Constitution, or whatever these great racehorses are called. And you don't call your dog Fluffy, or whatever you call cats. Each one of these animals has its own separate system of nomenclature. So, underneath this seemingly individual choice of a name for your pet is a whole classification system and system of nomenclature that the anthropologists can explore. And that is what *pensée sauvage* is.

Then he comes to Sartre and his counterattack to Sartre's objections to all this. Sartre's objections are very simple; we know what they are. He is talking about positions in the kinship system. He is talking about structures and relations. Sartre is saying, for example, there are human beings who perform marriages. You are quite right that those practices can get sedimented into laws and rules, but, first of all, they are actions. They are practices. And the great anti-Lévi-Strauss book, the great critique—I guess you could say the end of his hegemony over a certain kind of French culture—is by Pierre Bourdieu. His most famous book is *Distinction*, and we'll touch on that later, but his first big book is entitled *Outline of a Theory of Practice*, in which he wants to pursue the Sartrean legacy and to show that these positions which are frozen over into structures in Lévi-Strauss are all the reification of practices in the present. So structuralism is bounded on each side by some critiques. The first is a kind of existential critique, and the second is a critique in terms of more general practice, in which practice precedes laws. The laws are sedimented versions of social practices, and we should examine the practices. Well, of course, he is talking about modern societies.

Anyway, Lévi-Strauss responds in the last chapter of *Pensée sauvage*. He says all these French theorists talk about history, because, in a sense, France is the homeland of the first moment of modern history, the place of the French Revolution; this first moment of political modernity is experienced by France, before anybody else, and therefore France had to invent a whole new terminology and way of thinking about it, which is actually borrowed from Roman historiography. And the French Revolution is really still alive, and constantly it is the paradigm in which all French politics is always articulated. There is a double articulation for you. Well, Lévi-Strauss says, you're talking about history. And then he makes a chart, which is just a square full of dots. You have dot, dot, dot, dot. Then another parallel line, dot, dot, dot. The point of this chart is to show that what they call history is in fact a jumble of various models, because the year—such and such happened in 1916—comes out of one system, but the category of revolutionary months comes out of another system, and then the category of the day constitutes another. If you like, you can say that Joyce in *Ulysses* invents the single day, the idea that there is this intelligible unity which is the day. But there are also revolutionary days. All of what you call history is a jumble of these different models. Or, going back to our first description of the double inscription: things on the surface, different kinds of plants, and then, down underneath, geologically, the slippage of different kinds of tectonic plates. So what looks like a variety and a combination of all kinds of things on the surface is articulated as this underlying phonetic system, which is that of the changes of the tectonic plates, or in this case, of the way in which the mountains rear up and then the rivers flow out in different ways. This is what the double inscription is, this underlying slippage of the categories, the deep, underlying categories, into each other, which produces a surface effect of a wholly different kind. What you call history, he says, is nothing other than that, and it has no philosophical priority. And then he will go on to say that in your politics, your history, you take sides. You take sides with the losers, the proletariat, the underdogs. Well, in earlier histories, how can you do that? The Tupinambá have vendettas with other tribes that have lasted over a hundred years. Whose side are you going to take in these vendettas? You have to write their history. They have a history, though hard to get at, because they don't have writing. But are you going to take sides? In other kinds of history, in narrative history, you take sides, and that's one of the whole points of writing such histories. Anyway, those are the powerful but maybe superficial objections of Lévi-Strauss to Sartre, his later work in particular, and in a way to phenomenology itself, to the primacy of individual consciousness.

Okay, well now the third stage. It's these famous *mythologiques*, "myth-ologics," perhaps. It is these four immense volumes, the first and most famous being *The Raw and the Cooked*. It is precisely the working out of this idea of the myth as a set of playing cards. It begins with the Bororo myth in the Mato Grosso of Brazil, and finally, in the fourth volume, it arrives at the Northwest coast Indians, the home of the Thunderbird, of potlatch, of the totem pole, the most glorious artifact of all, in a way. It is important for us in America. After how many pages? It is as long as Proust. This first volume is already over four hundred pages, so over a thousand pages of myth, and I don't know how many different myths. Here, we have each one with a slight difference from each other, turning into a variety of forms that seem to be completely at odds with each other and have nothing to do with each other. Was this a worthwhile enterprise? Well, first one has to say that what is amazing is that he managed to complete it. Since he lived to be a hundred, he goes on to write a few more analyses of myths, and then a book on art, so he didn't stop with this, but at least he managed to finish these things, so we have these monuments even if we don't know what to do with them. I don't know that I would recommend you reading through all of this. I did give you the overture, and it's all arranged in musical terms, so these are musical variations, and, of course, variation is a fundamental musical category.

So there are various modes of organization of these stories. This is, at any rate, something one has to know about. One has to know that this exists. And these mythic narratives are often quite interesting, and as I say, especially these Northwest coast myths are of a special interest to us. Some of our poets have explored these things. There are modern poets, Dennis Tedlock and others, who have tried to translate them in different terms. They are taken down by individual anthropologists around 1900 or so from informants who were themselves great storytellers. We tend to think in terms of simplified stories like the Greek myths. Probably, in Greece as well, these things were as complex and differentiated as all these myths of the new world, but we just don't see that anymore. These are long, segmentary oral narratives. How to read those? And what is their organization? What holds them together? What secures their transformations from one into another?

So those are the kinds of questions that this final work raises, and to understand it we go must back to "The Structural Study of Myth." Vladimir Propp's discovery, whom I'll talk about next time, and who is at the origin of some of this stuff, is that there are universal structures of narrative.[2] Before him, there had already been lots of collections of fairy tales, especially in the Romantic period. A lot of people went out, like the Grimm brothers, into the villages and listened to their stories and wrote them down, or at least wrote down one version, and, with luck, you would have other people getting another version, so you have several that you can compare and see where they differ structurally, but it always depends a lot also on the artistry of the storyteller. This is oral storytelling. In China, even in the 1980s, on the radio you had traditional storytellers, who were registered by the radio, telling these tales. These are like the griots, the traditional storytellers. These are, in their own way, experts in producing a certain kind of popular culture. And by now all that is gone, or much of it is gone. With the Greeks, we only have the literate versions.

But, at any rate, Lévi-Strauss puts them all in these various columns, and if you have your text you can look at these four playing-card-like columns that he has divided up.[3] He has taken the Oedipus story, which we know. What we don't know, maybe, is that Laius' father, Labdacus, means "lame."

2   Vladimir Propp, *Morphology of the Folktale*, trans. Laurence Scott (Austin, TX: University of Texas Press, 1968).

3   Claude Lévi-Strauss, "The Structural Study of Myth," in *Structural Anthropology*, trans. Claire Jacobson and Brooke Grundfest Schoepf (New York: Basic Books, 1963), 214.

And you know that Oedipus means "swollen foot," because Oedipus as a baby was exposed in hope that he would die; the feet were bound together and so he limps. Laius, he thinks, means "left-sided," and, of course, the left-hand in early cultures means bad luck—the word "sinister" comes from this idea. That the father would be left-handed is itself significant. This is the way he has lined up some of those names. This is a Theban myth; Oedipus is the dictator, *tyrannos*, of Thebes. The *tyrannos* is somebody who is not from the noble, dynastic family, an outsider who's brought in to rule. Oedipus is precisely that: he has wandered in; he has killed the monster, and therefore, in the absence of their king, who was mysteriously killed, he becomes ruler. But Thebes is a funny place, because it doesn't have a good reputation in later Greece. It has a culture but not an interesting one for the rest of Greece. Well, maybe it got that from Oedipus, maybe from its founder, Cadmus. Cadmus founded the city. How did he found it? He landed in this area with his men and confronted a dragon. This dragon killed all of his men, and he killed the dragon. And then the god tells him to take all the teeth of the dragon and plant them. From that planting arises a race of human beings, and they people the city of Thebes. So we have several monsters being killed—Cadmus's monster, Oedipus's monster, the Sphinx. There is also in this family semi-incestuous stuff. Oedipus, obviously, but also Cadmus and his sister, Antigone's relationships to her brother, all of whom are unusually close; Judith Butler has written on that.[4] So we have one strand of this story that has to do with killing monsters, one strand of these combined legends which is about deformation of some sort, because left-handedness is considered deformation, and one strand that has to do with incestuous relations; and, finally, we have the various murders and butcheries and so forth. So, he says, let's line those up. Let's find a way of expressing their differences. First, blood relations: incest would be, he says, an overrating of blood relations. On the other hand, civil war, killing your neighbors and the people of your city, is an underrating of blood relations. Now killing the *dragon*, the *sphinx*, would have something to do with the earth—human beings versus some kind of chthonic creatures of the earth. So here is a human hero killing a creature of the earth. And, when we get to the lame people—lame, left-handed, swell-foot—we have to deal with something somehow unnatural, that is,

---

4   Judith Butler, *Antigone's Claim: Kinship between Life and Death*, Wellek Library Lectures (New York: Columbia University Press, 2000).

that has to do with the deformation of the body. It is thought, Lévi-Strauss says, that one of Cadmus's warriors failed to pull himself completely out of the earth as he is being born from the teeth, and so the body is a little bit deformed. So we'll say that that is the autochthonous origin of mankind. "The dragon is a chthonian being who has to be killed in order for mankind to be born from the earth."[5] So this has something to do with the emergence of people from the earth, and we already saw that in the Cadmus legend. And the final one is the denial of the autochthonous origin of man, that is, the way the human body is still caught in the earth.

Of course, he knows his interpretation in advance, so that's how he has arranged these things; in a way you have to know your answer first, so then you can put your system together. If you look at these columns, we have here two relationships that are being compared to each other. One relationship has to do with blood relations between humans. The other has to do with human beings' relationship to the earth. Remember I said this double articulation doesn't mean you're finding the same things on both levels. It means that you are comparing two sets of relationships. This is analogy. You're saying that one relation or contradiction is analogous to the other relation or contradiction.

So, Lévi-Strauss says—and this then is his "interpretation," so to speak—that the overrating of blood relations is to the underrating of blood relations as the affirmation of autochthony is to its denial. What does that mean? First of all, it means that these two kinds of relations or contradictions are analogous to each other. We can now see what Oedipus means. The myth works on the belief that mankind is autochthonous, that it comes out of the earth. Humans are like plants; plants provide a model for humans. The myth therefore addresses the inability

> to find a satisfactory transition between this theory and the knowledge that human beings are actually born from the union of man and woman. Although the problem obviously cannot be solved, the Oedipus myth provides a kind of logical tool which relates the original problem—born from one or born from two?—to the derivative problem—born from different or born from the same? By a correlation of this type, the over-reacting of blood relations is to the underrating of blood relations as the attempt to escape autochthony is to the impossibility to succeed in it.[6]

---

5   Claude Lévi-Strauss, "The Structural Study of Myth," 215.
6   Ibid., 216.

Now we can immediately compare this to the Caduveo face painting. Since Lévi-Strauss says this is all amateur stuff—I'm not a classicist, so I'm just playing around with these things to illustrate something for you—I take it on myself to do the same and to suggest that, since we talked about matriarchy and patriarchy, this is what this could be about. In matriarchy, you have a single parent, really. In patriarchy, you very much have two parents, one of whom is taken as superior to the other. Oneness and twoness. This is about numerology, really, and in all this anthropology you will see that the question of numbers is crucial. The myth would then be wondering whether it is matriarchy which is the dominant model or patriarchy, whether the one comes first or the two. The myth doesn't solve that, but, by a kind of sleight of hand, it puts them together in such a way that you can think both things at the same time, that you can hold this contradiction together in your mind, and that means, in a sense, that you have solved it. Then, if you think of this Caduveo face painting, you remember that the Maya, who are the older form of Caduveo, are a society which has three castes. It is a class society, so to speak. So it is a ternary society; it is in three groups. Its villages are built around these three castes. But there's another form of village organization which is dualistic, and which is organized around what are called "moieties," from the French *moitiés*, "halves." What Lévi-Strauss says is that this is a question about hierarchy. The hierarchical model involves nobility; it involves social domination. The dualistic organization is a sort of equality or a striving to or thinking of equality, because the two moieties are equal to each other. So, in the mind of the Caduveo there's a kind of conflict between the notion of caste, hierarchy, domination, class, and the notion of democracy. In the way that the face paintings are organized around two axes, the two and the three are put together and are visibly articulating each other. It is as though the face paintings say, yes, it's not a problem; they can coexist: look at it. You can see how in this organization of the axes these two things coexist. So it solves a social contradiction. We have the underlying tectonic plates, the underlying contradiction, the social contradiction, but, on the level of form and of art and structure, we have a play with that which pretends to harmonize and solve it. So this is what Lévi-Strauss is trying to show with these images and relations.

Another question will come up—and we'll deal with it next time—in the later part about the Zuni creation myth, and that's the question of how the two levels relate. Generally, that's called mediation, and in that second part of "The Structural Study of Myth," Lévi-Strauss will look into the matter of mediation and mediators. Can there not be between these two levels something that relates them? So already a dialectical term here is being used in structuralism.

Today I think we have been talking about the double inscription and paradigmatic organization. Next time with Barthes we will look briefly at syntagmatic analysis before we go on to this whole interesting question of utopias.

February 11, 2021

8

Victory of the Paradigmatic

{Levi-Strauss, Barthes}

You can assume "Can you hear me?" means "Good morning." You can translate from one code into another, and speaking of that, we might as well begin with codes. I have been insisting on this business of double inscription. I like the double inscription, rather than the double articulation, because it brings in this omnipresent structuralist theme of writing that we haven't gotten to yet but that will be inescapable soon. I want to show you, without sowing confusion, that we will find this double inscription everywhere, and, in fact, if you leave out writing and the rest of it, it is not unlike the opposition of the conscious and the unconscious. We tend to think that this is the strongest form of that duality, which is really present in all forms of hermeneutics, with hermeneutics meaning interpretation. You get this in Rabelais, even in Plato. The idea is this. You have a box. It has Socrates' face carved on it, absolutely hideous, but, within it, rests this marvelous balm. Hermeneutics is that process whereby you open up the outside, and inside you find this kind of meaning. You can say esoteric and exoteric. In all the mysticisms, and indeed in cult formation and so on, you always have the exoteric—that is the language you speak to outsiders—but inside the group is the esoteric. Plato's teaching was arranged in that way, so that the insiders, the students, received a different coded message from what he presented to the outside world.

I simply want to say that, in a sense, this double inscription is common to all forms of interpretation, all forms of reading. Freud would interpret symptoms. A critic might interpret a different kind of text. Lévi-Strauss, you will remember, even interpreted botany. This is the sense in which his great discovery was that this variety of plants—growing, as I might suggest, on the continental divide, on the divide between two watersheds—constituted the outside, the phenomenological layer of things. That is what we see, what is accessible in the language, in the code, of botany. So we look at different plants and we see what kinds of plants are growing here and what kinds there, but that code, the botanical code, is articulated in another, unrelated code, which is that of geology, while underneath the surface, down in the earth, another phenomenon is at play, which is the movement of these plates that cause a mountain to rise up and to create this kind of divide. Lévi-Strauss found that distinction very exciting, and it defines his intelligence, his genius, the kinds of things that he noticed; he was always noticing, especially things that had this dual character, that could lend themselves to this kind of analysis.

So there are various ways in which one can read this, but this is the paradigmatic association of things. There is one paradigm to both sets of things, but, remember, they don't connect up to each other on a one-to-one basis any more than the language of botany would be immediately translatable into the language of geology. But English, you might say, is immediately translatable into French. Well, maybe not quite so easily, and indeed, a linguist would say, all kinds of different things are happening in English syntax than in French syntax, or in the history of the words. So the correlation between these two levels—I call them levels—would be very boring if it was a one-to-one correspondence, because then you would only need one code. You wouldn't need to trace the way in which the one is articulated into the other. And remember that the basic model here is still that of language itself. We have a perceptible layer, which is that of speech. We take that apart into sentences, and then we syntagmatically separate out nouns from verbs and we construct continuities of sentences. Surface and depth—that is one way of saying this. One doesn't have to accept that. But, at any rate, to this surface correlation with its syntax and its words corresponds a different system altogether, which is the system of its sounds, the phonetic system. That phonetic system, in terms of the other system, is meaningless. It has its own history, maybe. But, for example, where does the difference between *b* and *p* come from?

That is pure contingency. Just as, from the point of view of the botanist, these geological things belong to another order of explanation. And then the relationship between those two will involve maybe what we would call mediations, and we will come back to that.

Let me give you another example of this, because I have always found it interesting. It is the research of one semiotic sociologist, Aaron Cicourel, who was interested in the passage from one language or code to another. So, he said, you go to the doctor, and for the doctor you use one language. You say, "Oh, I've got this dull pain." The doctor says, "Where? How often do you feel it?" Meanwhile this doctor is translating your language of pain, dullness, or aching into a wholly different language which is that of medical diagnosis. What is called diagnosis is precisely that translation from one code to another. Here's another one: police interrogation. "What did you do at this point? And at what point did you do this and that?" Meanwhile, the policeman is translating all of this into the code of felonies, motives, alibis, different kinds of offenses to the law. So you have interrogation itself as a process of translation. I want you to see that this is running throughout this whole period, and it could be what's called interpretation. For example, I would even like to say that Heidegger's initial distinction, ontic and ontological, belongs here. How could you go beyond Being? What is there to say beyond Being? But I think it is another example of double inscription. You have the phenomenological level. That is the level of daily life, the ontic level where we see recognizable, namable things, and we have our normal language to describe all that, and then we translate that into the ontological. For Heidegger, some of the things we're describing in ontic terms are distractions from Being, while other ones, such as anxiety, betray an approach to Being. So out of this double system, this translation from ontic into ontological, we can make moral judgements of some kind; whatever he would say about morality or ethics as a mode of thinking, these are nonetheless judgements of something as inauthentic or authentic, judgements, in his case, of Being. Well, Sartre doesn't do this any differently, except that Sartre is able to supply a whole wealth of mediations that Heidegger is maybe not interested in, because Sartre is a novelist; he is interested in everyday life, and he wants to see how everything, from drinking this glass of water all the way to your emotional reactions to things, to the kinds of films you like, to the style of your writing, to the way you live your body and so forth, are all going to be ultimately ontic, yet, in some sense, are also modes of relationship

to Being, forms, says Sartre, in which we live our *pour-soi* at the same
time that we aspire to a kind of being-in-itself.[1] We try to be, in the sense
of the *en-soi,* at the same time that we hang on to our *pour-soi,* because
we don't want to become *en-soi* and lose our human consciousness. We
want to turn our *pour-soi* into the density of the *en-soi* while remaining
conscious. This is the human passion. This is, in a sense, the metaphysics
of Sartrean existentialism, I suppose, and it is notable that, when a famous
feminist philosopher like Michèle Le Dœuff says to forget about all that
"being" stuff, she is really saying that those ontological questions don't
interest us anymore; we are interested in the ontic facts of these situations.
Maybe that is a more general cultural development, and that is one of
the questions around which I wanted to frame this broader narrative I'm
trying to tell about the movement from the postwar to modern times, and
we can come back to that as we like.

Now Deleuze talks about double articulation too. He doesn't call it
that as such. "A structure only starts to move [. . .] if we restore its other
half. [The] symbolic elements that were previously defined, taken in their
differential relations, are organized necessarily in series." Okay, he doesn't
mean the Sartrean definition of series; he means what I'm calling levels.

> But so organized, they relate to another series, constituted by other sym-
> bolic elements [. . .]: this reference to a second series is easily explained
> by recalling that singularities derive from the terms and relations of the
> first, but are not limited simply to reproducing or reflecting them. They
> thus organize themselves in another series capable of an autonomous
> development.[2]

That is to say, each of these series is a separate language, a separate code. It
is autonomous. A medical language or geological language is autonomous.
These are languages that have their own consistency, that have no necessary
relationship to each other. Interpretation here tries to relate them. This is
a confrontation between these two systems of differences. Each of these
levels is a system of difference. Differences without positive terms, this
Saussurean motif. But there are different differences, so we are comparing
two kinds of differences. That is exactly what happens in Lévi-Strauss's
playful, hypothetical analysis of the Oedipus myth.

---

1   See Fredric Jameson, *Sartre: The Origins of a Style* (New York: Columbia University
Press, 1984 [1961]).
2   Gilles Deleuze, "How Do We Recognize Structuralism?," 182.

Anyway, what I wanted to suggest is that we have this example of Heidegger. Where else do we find this? When we get to Julia Kristeva, we will see that she has a system—and again you have to be careful of this language; we say Kristeva's language, and not somebody else's—but she uses the terms symbolic and semiotic, and what she means is a level of meaning and a level of the body. So the level of meanings has an organization, and the level of the body has its own organization. In her first book about poetic language, she wants to show that modern poetry represents a kind of eruption of the semiotic into the symbolic.[3] The body has its own meaning—the upthrust of bodily existence into the abstract world of language. We have all these things going on. The mind-body correlation, or uncorrelation, if you like—the oldest philosophical problem in human history probably—and from them would come various forms of both aesthetics and philosophy.

Remember that the organization into opposites is not necessarily going to be an equality. Maybe I should open up another digression here by going back to the business of botany and geology. And of course, just to add to this mind-body opposition, this is again clearly what is meant in Marxism by base and superstructure. The base is felt to be somehow primal, bodily, the organization of production and so on. The superstructures are all these thoughts and cultural things that are generated by the base. So there, too, whether it is the Freudian unconscious, the Marxist notion of ideology, or then all these structuralist problematics, they are still organized around this same problem, which not only can't be solved—you don't want to solve it—but for which structuralism proposes another way of dealing through the path of notion of double inscription. What I wanted to add to the discussion of Lévi-Strauss—because I'm going to do a little more of that before we get to Barthes—is a different notion of the geological, which you recall from the first example. You remember that the Caduveo have a different kind of art than ours; it's the facial painting—originally a painting of the whole body—these tattoos which reflect, he says, a question about their social structure. I just wanted to observe one point here, because he has a very brief discussion of social structure, which turns on an anthropological question. It's also numerological and kind of crazy. Do dual organizations exist? Is there such a thing as a dual organization? The question turns around the shape of the village. We have a kind of

---

3 Julia Kristeva, *Revolution in Poetic Language*, trans. Margaret Waller (New York: Columbia University Press, 1984).

materialism here. The ultimate materialism in Lévi-Strauss is, as you remember, the kinship system, and that ends up being reflected in the way that the village is laid out, as we discussed last time. He has pictures of the village: the huts are in a circle; there's a center, but there are groups of huts opposed to each other. He believes that these can be organized into either dualistic or ternary structures, which will, obviously, have to do with gender, but it also has to do with totem, in the sense of the different clans, each clan having a totem, and finally with social class, because, in this kind of society, some totems are superior to others, and therefore even in the most classless societies that we know, there is something that corresponds to class, even if it isn't exactly class in our sense. So, when he discusses the Mayan aristocracy in the beginning of that chapter, he says the Maya are an aristocracy. They have three classes. Now, at some point, there is a cut across this organization of threes, which is reflected in the geographical structure of the village. At some point, a dualistic system comes into play, which represents an attempt to institute a democratic system, where the two entities are equal to each other, whereas the ternary system is a hierarchical system, in which one has to be superior to the others. So, for whatever historical reasons, in these tribes without writing which are small but which go back who knows how many thousands of years—we don't have the history of the emergence of these distinctions, but clearly they're somehow incompatible. They would be compatible with class structures. When we think about class structures in Marxism, we talk about ruling class and proletariat or underclasses. Yes, but in the United States, everybody calls themselves middle class! What is that? Are there three classes then? Do we have a ternary system, and, if so, how to think that in terms of an opposition? Let's say politically you're on the left, and you're in the Occupy movement, and you want to separate the ruling class from everybody else, so you say: 97 percent versus 3 percent, for instance. Then you have a dualistic opposition. But, if you have a ternary system, in which a lot of people say they don't belong to either of those groups, then we have a different kind of system. So, in our political unconscious, there would be a struggle between two ways of thinking about things, between a dualism of class struggle and a ternary "liberalism" of lower, middle, and upper classes, which is certainly hierarchical, but which also masks this other dualism.

Lévi-Strauss is saying that something like that is going on in these facial designs, the geometry of these two systems trying to find a kind of articulation of itself in these designs, and it is trying to work out a way in which that social contradiction is not any longer a real contradiction. Aesthetically, it has been resolved in these beautiful patterns in which one axis turns on another in an interesting way. I won't go into the symbolic value of these visual things, but it would be very interesting to do so, and, obviously, his specialty is precisely that. How to read out of dynamic patterns in the visual an analogy with the social, which, however, does something to the social? You will always have this antithesis when you're performing the social analysis of a form. Does it simply reflect the under-lying social reality? Does it replicate class society? Or does it try to solve its problems? Is it a utopian projection? Is it an imaginary attempt to resolve the contradiction? I don't know whether one can decide those things. That is to say, rather, one has to decide that when you're writing an analysis, but the decision is always political. What do you want this analysis to do? Do you want this analysis to show that this art simply replicates your moment in history, your culture, your capitalist culture, or do you want to say: no, this is a genuinely utopian attempt to resolve the antagonisms at work in this society? So that's another matter.

Several of you wrote on Barthes, and in particular on how, in a sense, Barthes is saying that everything in a story is meaningful. The point is that, from the point of view of one system, the ontic system, the system of familiar actions and objects, there is meaning. You know that in such-and-such a story, if a pistol appears in the first pages, somebody is going to use it later on, either as a clue or as a weapon. Yes, but there are a lot of things in these stories that are just in there. So, later on, Barthes is going to have to invent a new idea, and this will also eventually be of great interest to us. He begins to talk about something he calls "the effect of the real." He looks at some pages of Flaubert and finds a whole list of objects that have no function for the story. Flaubert isn't going to use these objects for anything. What do they mean? Well, he says, the point is to put these seemingly contingent things in a story—a barometer, a clock, any kind of little statue you like—as signs of the real. They are all meaningless in terms of the story, so you can pick any knickknack you like, but to have several of them like that simply "means" that this is a real house. There are a lot of real things in it, but they are there for the effect of the real. And that is how Barthes gets around this matter of contingency, that a narrative will not have anything contingent.

Let's look at two things. Somebody, in one of your responses, happened upon the word "effect" and made much of it, and I think that was quite right, because what we're going to see is a whole language of effects in this structuralist and poststructuralist work. Why? Well, partly because there isn't any truth, so all you are getting is effects. You are getting effects of the real, but there isn't any real. So that is simply to orient you, looking for that word "effect," because when it appears, it is going to be a telltale ideological proposition. Why use "effect," rather than just "reality" or symbol? In suspending questions of truth or referentiality, the word "effect" will be one of the minor symptoms of structuralism and poststructuralism.

The other thing is that, of course, in life there is contingency. In a very interesting moment in Sartre's later work—he didn't write anymore because of his blindness, but he did a lot of autobiographical interviews—he tells about how his mother would take him to the movies. We're talking about 1910 or 1911. Movies are already getting quite sophisticated. The first real formal innovation in film is by an American, Griffith, who also made some ideologically more than doubtful movies, but he first puts these things together. In early cinema, in the famous shot of the train coming into the screen, people in the audience see this train coming forward and they're all scared because they think the train was real and would run them over. Well, then, putting these shots together produces a structure, a syntagmatic structure. They call it montage, cutting, if you like, or simply—a funny kind of jump in language into English—editing, because in editing you cut up a film and you arrange the pieces, moving from one shot to another. So editing is a syntagmatic process whereby, little by little, larger and larger entities appear, and the final entity will be the fiction film. One of Barthes's disciples, Christian Metz, whom we will come back to in a minute, calls this *la grande syntagmatique*, the big syntagmatics of the overall film narrative, which is sort of a collection of the various little syntagmatics put together.[4] Anyway, at an early age, Sartre is often taken by his mother to the movie theater—I suppose theaters are starting to emerge then—and the little Jean-Paul is, of course, stunned by filmic things. Then they come out into the streets and, suddenly, he realizes that reality is nothing like a film. In film, as in Barthes's stories, nothing is without meaning. Everything in the film is meaningful. When you get out into the world and into the light, all of a sudden, there are all kinds

4 See Christian Metz, "La grande syntagmatique du film narratif," *Communications* 8 (1966): 120–124; Christian Metz, *Film Language: A Semiotics of the Cinema*, trans. Michael Taylor (New York: Oxford University Press, 1974 [1968]).

of things that are not meaningful, and we call those "contingent" things that could be there or not, that don't necessarily have any reason for being.

It is a very ancient theological category, contingency, and as you know, it will become central in Sartrean existentialism and everywhere else in the twentieth century. Contingency is the question of non-meaning. However, a funny thing happens here. Some of these existentialists fall into this trap. Camus, for example. Camus is somebody who lived very strongly the fear and absurdity of death, and, finally, he makes this notion of absurdity into a philosophical thesis or idea, that life is absurd, that life is without meaning, because we die. As somebody says in one of Sartre's plays: God is the first criminal because He made us mortal. God killed us all, and therefore He is the first murderer. Anyway, absurdity is then this metaphysical principle. Well, the minute you say that life is absurd or meaningless or you take a philosophical position called nihilism, you have meaning again, because absurdity has now become an abstract philosophy. So life gets a meaning again precisely because it's absurd. And then we get Sisyphus, who is, of course, the very image of this absurd life, but now it's turned into a meaningful image. It is a metaphysic. Existentialism has to guard itself against metaphysics, because metaphysics is always an answer to the question: What is the meaning of being and what is the meaning of human being? And, anytime you answer that question, you are in meta-physics, even if you say it has no meaning. Heidegger saw this right away, and that's why Heidegger called for a wholesale destruction—Derrida makes it a deconstruction—of Western metaphysics, because Western metaphysics is the kind of thought that is constantly attempting, in very tortuous ways, to give a meaning to life, even though life doesn't have that kind of meaning. Heidegger calls for a revival of the question of Being, not an answer to that question.

So narrative itself is somehow meaningful. The story rescues life from meaninglessness and gives it a meaning, because in the story everything is meaningful. Even absurd things are meaningful. This is then the sense in which, in Sartre's *Nausea*, we find a first statement of this kind. When he hears the jazz song "Some of These Days" in the cafe everything suddenly becomes meaningful. Whereas nothing around him has meaning, the jazz song has a beginning, a middle, and an end. The minute time takes on that quality, you're back in meaning and you're saved from contingency. But that is an artificial, let's say human, construct.

So some of those things appear in Barthes's structural analysis, and you can say structural analysis is, in a sense, an analytic that wants to destroy the meanings of narratives. Narrative, it tells us, is a constant attempt to make meanings, and structural analysis, semiotic analysis of narrative, is going to tear those meanings apart and show how they're constructed. And then, if it's constructed, you're going to say it's not natural, and so life is meaningless. And then there's another step one can take, certainly another kind of existential step, through which you can simply confirm that the fact of construction itself is meaningful. That's what we do. We construct and give ourselves a metaphysic. That's no longer nihilistic. That's giving ourselves a meaning, and, of course, Sartrean existentialism is founded on that process.

Now let's go back to Lévi-Strauss's analysis of Oedipus. We just saw how these two codes of the village organization, which presuppose class by way of the aesthetic formation of the facial paintings, are related. So how do they articulate each other? How does our interpretation of Oedipus work? These two languages are put in place—people come from the one or people come from two: "the inability for a culture which holds the belief that mankind is autochthonous [. . .] to find a satisfactory transition between this theory and the knowledge that human beings are actually born from the union of man and woman."[5] Okay, so do we come out of the earth? Are we one? Or are we born of man and woman? That is, do we come out of two? We're going to run into this kind of numerology over and over again. A lot of later poststructuralism is against the one. The one is unity. The one is metaphysics. The one is totality, and it is pernicious and wrong, and we must fight for . . . what? Well, in Deleuze, the opposite of the one is not the two; it is the multiple, and that throws this whole thing in a different direction, but numerology is still in there somewhere. It can become as mystical as you like, or you can try to demystify it and use it in a more normal way. You could also read this in terms of classical Freudianism. Matriarchy versus patriarchy. In matriarchy, there is simply one principle: the feminine. I am part of that as a child. The men are part of that. We are part of the one. Now, with patriarchy, suddenly you get two, because the father intervenes. The father is now identified. There is only one father. The male principle enters this unitary system of matriarchy and breaks it up, so now we have two. So, in a sense, Lévi-Strauss's interpretation could be used in that way, and you could think of all kinds of other ways of talking

---

5   Claude Lévi-Strauss, "The Structural Study of Myth," 216.

about it, but it seems to me that you always get this kind of numerological play, and that's going to account for the fact—think of the village again; think of these facial paintings—that beneath the language of science and knowledge and so on, there is another process, and it is that of topology. It is a language of the geometry of solids, and some of you will know more about this, but in modern mathematics there's a very complex theory of the topological, of the relationship of shapes to each other, and indeed, the forms that shapes can take, which can be irrational, as in "irrational numbers." How can a number be irrational? Well, that's going to lead into all kinds of problems. How can a process be put into numerical terms? That's the whole drama already of equations in the time of Newton and Leibnitz. With topology, for example, one of the things that inevitably comes into play—and this is going to anticipate a few of the topics that are going to come up next week with Lacan—is the Möbius strip. Imagine a band of paper. If you take that band of paper, and you cut it and turn one of the ends to reattach it to the other, then you have a strange object in which the movement of the thing is infinite on both surfaces, so that you can't tell which is the outside and which the inside. It is more than a labyrinth. This is a topological object, if you like to think of it that way, for meditation. You want to think this, but you really can't. This is a kind of spatial continuity which is not in nature, so to speak. Those kinds of topological objects get into art later on, and they get into mathematics, but there is a science of them. So topology becomes an underlying feature of all this structuralist stuff.

Let me put it this way very rapidly, because it is one of the things that interests me. I want to go on from Oedipus to the end of this essay, where he talks about the Zuni creation myth. I read through that for a while, until suddenly I find something very strange: the function of A is to the function of B as the function of B is to the function of A - 1.[6] This is going to be called by the Lacanians—we're not going to be able to get away from these things anymore—a matheme. What's a matheme? It isn't exactly an equation. It's something else. We'll see that, in all of Lacan, these mathemes are constantly struggling to come to the surface, and Lacan is constantly struggling to invent various forms of mathemes, because he thinks there's a way of attaching absolute truth to a mathematical formula which can't be attached to words. Of course, the first thing a psychoanalyst

6   Ibid., 228.

knows about words is that they're deceptive and that they're used just that way. As Umberto Eco once said, language exists to lie, not to tell the truth. Language is what allows you to lie. A perfect language is therefore inconceivable, because nothing in it would be a lie. In a way, mathematics becomes the place where there aren't any lies, and this is why, when you get up to recent poststructural philosophy, especially in Alain Badiou—you read his essay about modern French philosophy where he sees himself perhaps as the last surviving embodiment of this—he now calls himself— although he's also a Marxist and a Sartrean and a Lacanian and all these other things—a Platonist, because, all of a sudden, he believes there is something which is eternal, which is beyond anything any individual human can experience: numbers, mathematics. His mathematics is that of set theory. I don't pretend to understand anything about it, but you will find his books riddled with all kinds of mathematical equations, or rather mathemes, and he gets that from Lacan.

Okay, so what is this? I put it to you that there is something I will call schematization—a term we get from Kant—in which language tries to turn itself into something which is non-linguistic, a form of truth which is non-linguistic, and therefore cannot be refuted, and cannot know the negative. It is like the unconscious in that sense. The unconscious has no negative, and it will be topological, mathematical, or, in the case of Lacan, both of them, because we'll see Lacan playing around with all these figures, from the Möbius strip to mathemes and back to Borromean knots. But I think it is a very interesting process that the second level then turns out to be something somehow irreducible to the first, and yet it somehow is connected to the first level. It is the unconscious truth of the first level. Here is truth coming back, but in a way in which that word has no longer any meaning. This should not sound so crazy in a society in which the algorithm is triumphant. What is an algorithm? Here is a thing which you can connect to a language of desire, consumption, and lack, the commodity, but it takes a mathematical form. And the fact that such an imposing and polyphonic contemporary philosopher as Alain Badiou will affirm the eternity of number suggests that this has some interesting historical relevance that we need to explore. At any rate, keep your eye on these schematizations. Deleuze, for example, is going to write a whole book on schematizations in the work of Michel Foucault, whereas Deleuze himself is trickier than that. He won't reduce himself to schematizations. He will use them and then translate them back into language. Deleuze is almost as protean as Kierkegaard in his philosophical masks, but, nonetheless, he is aware of this phenomenon, and will deserve more attention from us.

With that, we have to say goodbye to Lévi-Strauss. I hope you have understood the fascination of his work. Over and over again, we're going to meet what they called at the time "master thinkers" with prodigious bodies of work that we can't fully explore in this class, but that is sort of what characterizes this sequence of modern French . . . is it philosophy? Well, the richness of French thinking in this period is that, no, the philosophical impulse deconstructs itself. It doesn't want to be a metaphysics or a philosophy anymore, and so all this tremendous intellectual energy pours out into other areas. It expresses itself in anthropology, in literary studies, in statecraft, in psychoanalytic forms, and it becomes what we call not philosophy but theory, and we'll come back to what that might mean another day, because it is something I try to explain, for example, to the trustees of this university on certain occasions, and nobody ever understands what I'm talking about. So I will leave that for the moment.

What I do want to say is that, with Barthes, we have a shift from the paradigmatic to the syntagmatic. In Barthes, of course, there are paradigms. The diachronic is inseparable from the synchronic, after all, but, for purposes of exposition, they can be kept separate from each other. For a while, you can work in the diachronic or the synchronic, but, finally, the syntagmatic and paradigmatic have to come back together, and, of course, in a certain sense, they do in Barthes. But his conception of narrative analysis is a syntagmatic one. As he says, to know what's going on in these stories, you first have to break them up into their smallest units. Well, that is kind of obvious in a way. What else is Lévi-Strauss doing when he sets up these columns of the individual events and elements of a myth? He is separating out little bits of these things. Narremes, do you want to call them? This business of -emes is omnipresent here. So you are establishing syntagmatic unities. You are chopping this up into distinctions which are like those you use in syntax: nouns, verbs, adjectives, subordinate clauses, and so on and so forth. So, in a sense, Barthes's final image of this superformation which is a story, a narrative, would be a single sentence, a single immense sentence. In literature, we have that, and it is Mallarmé's great poem from the 1890s, *Un coup de dés jamais n'abolira le hasard* (*A Roll of the Dice Will Never Abolish Chance*). Chance is contingency, so, all of a sudden, everything is here: the single sentence, the abolition of contingency by the sentence, and so forth. It's an immense sentence with all kinds of subordinate and dependent clauses, and it's generally published in a big book which is maybe twenty pages long, but it is then what you could call the Book of the World. Now, remember, the single sentence is the unity to which linguistics itself is condemned, and the narratologists want to tell us we have a frame, a narrative, under which all these single sentences can be arranged. So maybe we can talk about "text grammar." A grammar is normally confined to a single sentence. Suppose we have something that included a lot of sentences. Maybe that would be a larger unity. In that case, what kind of unity would that be? Why does a story have to be closed? Well, we know why, in one sense: beyond the single sentence there is contingency and meaninglessness, so, if you want to preserve meaning, you have to keep the closure of the sentence. In a sense, Metz's or Barthes's idea that the film or the story is one big sentence is an attempt to do that.

Now I have to confess that I don't find this persuasive and that I think it is a dead end. It was once very important. I mentioned Metz, Barthes's disciple, and Metz can be said, in one way—I don't want to be absolute about this—to be the founder of film semiotics, and, like Barthes, he will be interested in the syntagmatics of film, dividing it into its various categories, and one can see how in film, much more than in literature, that would be important to do, because montage itself is going to depend on several shots that are put together. How many of you study film? It seems to me that film studies is one of the basic developments of semiotics. One branch of it comes out of Barthes, and out of the work of his student Christian Metz, and it will involve this business of frames and of how you put the frames together, how you construct a little cinematic event out of the clash of various frames, if only the famous shot-reverse-shot. In any film in which you have two people talking to each other, the camera is going to look at one and then it's going to look at the other. If you don't have that back and forth, it can be very strange, because you are going to be overhearing one of the characters. So there is a little syntagmatic unity in the shot-reverse-shot, which is the face-to-face conversation. There are those who say this form is ideological. People's relationship to each other isn't like the shot-reverse-shot. This is made up. This is going to give a meaning to human relations that they don't have. And, with that, film criticism becomes ideological criticism. But leave that aside for now. Barthes's syntagmatic method has been more successful in producing film semiotics (although that also has had its day and is superseded), much more than in literary analysis, although the famous narratology also comes out of this. I don't think narratology has been so successful because they don't have a separate object like film studies. Metz never analyzed a film concretely. He just invented all the abstractions that go with it, and, later on, he will connect those to Lacanian psychoanalysis in, to my mind, a very interesting way, which proves not necessarily anything about film but something about Lacanian analysis, namely that it is a supersystem, and we will see that maybe next week.

One of the things I need to do in this course is to tell you what is at work in these people's ideas. Barthes himself we will revisit a little bit later on in another context, and Barthes's own work is extremely varied. There are periods and so on. What we're discussing today corresponds to his scientistic period. Barthes wants semiotics to be his science, and he will do a certain number of things to create this science. One of them is contained in this book I mentioned last time, S/Z.[7] This is an immense syntagmatic analysis of a short story by Balzac called "Sarrasine." Okay, is this s an s or a z? In French these things are indistinguishable. Behind that—I don't know that he talks about it—is Balzac's own name, which has this odd z in it, and which comes from a family which was originally called Balssa. And by the same token, I believe that Barthes's own family name was once Barthez. So does that z have some unconscious meaning? What is that, with its sharp edges? Well, in a way, if you read this in a deep, sort of symptomatic way, you will find that it has something to do with castration, but that's not of interest to us. Anyway, this two- or three-hundred-page volume is all organized around a single story, which is cut up into pieces. He sort of set an example here, and I'll name the other people who have imitated him, taking a single story and writing a whole book of analysis. Greimas, whom we haven't talked about very much, this Lithuanian semiotician, wrote a book about a short story of Maupassant, "The Two Friends," which is an equally fascinating story. It takes place during the Franco-Prussian war, and his book is called *Maupassant: The Semiotics of the Text*. Then Umberto Eco, not to be left out of this, took a story of Alphonse Allais—I may tell you anecdotally that I found this story for him and gave it to him; it's a very strange story—and he wrote a book called *The Role of the Reader* on this short story. Alphonse Allais

---

7   Roland Barthes, *S/Z*, trans. Richard Miller (New York: Farrar, Straus, Giroux, 1974).

was a sort of French Mark Twain, a kind of narrative humorist without the countrified side. And, finally, in our own day, if you read science fiction, Samuel Delany, who went through his semiotic stage at one point, wrote a huge book called *The American Shore* about a story of Thomas Disch called *Angouleme*. I don't think it's a very good story, and, just between us, I think all of these nitpicking syntagmatic studies, the frame-by-frame analyses of these short stories, can have some very tiresome moments, but we should try to find what's interesting in them.

So Barthes identifies five different codes at work in this narrative, and I only have time to give you an idea of the multiplicity of things he is doing here. They are as follows. The code of action, the empirical code. That means somebody does this and they do that. Then the hermeneutic code, very strangely named. That means something is happening, but you don't quite know what it is. There's a secret involved. You have to decipher it, because that's what hermeneutics does. Then there's the cultural code, which has to do with the local evaluations of things, local wisdom, local understanding in this period—1830 or so—of the text. Then there's the analysis of semes. Okay, I told you about the -emes, matheme, lexeme. Seme is the smallest unit of meaning, and this mysterious code will have to do with connotations and meanings, and we can't go any further into it than that. And, finally, there is the symbolic code, which takes multiple forms but which is somehow organized around the body. Anyway, he takes this text apart and sees these various codes appearing. You know the word text comes from a word meaning "to weave," so a text is various strands that are woven together. His image of "Sarrasine," which is a very interesting, strange story, but still a realistic one, is that it's a polyphonic text. It seems to be linear, but in fact all these different things are going on. Someday, maybe, some of you will look at this book. I don't know that it is read so much anymore. But, for me, the problem is that I'm more persuaded by Lévi-Strauss and the paradigmatic method. It seems to me if you want the story to mean something, it has to be on the paradigmatic level. It has to be on the level of story, rather than on the level of individual semes. But I think it's also extremely interesting that these semioticians, these narratologists, cannot really deal with anything beyond individual stories. Nobody has ever done a semiotics of the novel, for example. My God, if you think about what might come of locking a semiotician in a room with a two-hundred-page novel, you would have five- or six-hundred pages of analysis. It's just not possible, and, indeed, there is a reason why semiotics finds its limits in the short story, just as linguistics finds its limits in the sentence. The sentence is a unity. The short story is a unity. Something happens, and the semioticians, the narratologists want to find out what happens. What makes a story a story? What is it that happens? But can you do that with a novel? Maybe you could with little parts of it, like a film, but I'm not sure that kind of analysis even works on fiction film. But Lévi-Strauss, as we've seen, is able to show how an entity like a mythological tale, or a painting or facial painting, has a meaning, and I don't think the syntagmatic people can do that.

However, all these people are preceded by a Soviet anthropologist, and I just want to refer to a text of his in conclusion. It is from the 1920s. It is also like Saussure in that, from out of the past, from out of another country, comes this strange object, translated in the 1950s by Roman Jakobson's wife, Svatava Pirkova-Jakobson, a Czech, by the way. This is Vladimir Propp's *Morphology of the Folk Tale*. What he found was that everybody had been collecting these folk tales. It starts in the Romantic period. The Grimms go out and do field work and collect all these stories. But what do you do with it all? There are too many tales to do anything with them, so you make typologies, classification schemes, a sort of *pensée sauvage*. You take all the fairy tales that deal with bears, and you put them in one group. Then you take all the fairy tales that have to do with water, and you put that in another group. So you classify them by their surface elements. Propp said this is crazy, because it isn't their surface identification that's important; it's the function they have in the text. So you could have a bear as a villain, as a horrible obstacle in your project, in your way. You could have a white bear whose capture would be that of a desirable object. You could have a friendly magical bear which is a helper in the text. The bear could mean all kinds of things, and you could substitute all kinds of other things for it.

So Propp made a list of the functions of the elements of these fairy tales and analyzed them in terms of these functions. Then the functions give us a kind of closure, the closure of the quest. He finds thirty-one functions, and they start with the hero setting forth and end with his triumph. As it's a fairy tale, a folk tale, the peasant folk tale is sort of a wish fulfillment. It is a happy, glorious thing. The hero overcomes all these obstacles. He finally wins the princess or the treasure or what have you. So these are very positive kinds of things, but he must face the villains. There are various actants or function figures that aid him in this process. And it will be from that sorting out of the actants that syntagmatic analysis originally comes, but that still has a kind of closure. That still presupposes a beginning and an ending. You know that Godard the filmmaker said his films always have a beginning, a middle, and an ending, but not always in that order. In Propp, they are always in that order, so that's one of the criticisms of these stories. These are peasant stories. What is their relevance to the present day? That is an interesting historical question, too. But what we can say is what has been said by all these people: they start with order, and then order is somehow disrupted, and they proceed through a number of events and reestablish order. Now, for the generation that went to school on these structural analyses, that was a very conservative, if not reactionary notion of what the tale does. Who wants to reestablish order? We want the narrative to do something else, something new. We don't want it to reestablish order. So there is a deeper ideological objection to this. And incidentally, the most brilliant study of Propp is by Lévi-Strauss himself. It's translated in the second volume of his collection, *Structural Anthropology*, and it is a very probing analysis of the limits of Propp.

But here is another question: isn't the novel an attempt to undo this order of the story and replace it with something else, something larger, which may try somehow to re-establish order or may not? Isn't there a reason for the historical decline of the short story? In the short story of the nineteenth century, there were great masters, from O. Henry to Maupassant himself. Then there comes the anti-story, where you leave off the ending, as in Chekhov. Then, little by little, people don't exactly write stories anymore, or the stories become part of certain kinds of sub-genres, like science fiction or mystery stories; mystery stories are perhaps the most crystallized modern version of this kind of plot scheme, and yet mystery stories themselves have two levels. Anyway, I do want to come back next time to Lévi-Strauss on music and painting. That will be a final footnote to all this, because it's some very great stuff. And then we go on to another feature of anthropology. It's the whole business of these tribes. What is this ternary, dualistic stuff? Lévi-Strauss reintroduces the whole question of utopia here at a certain point. Well, that's what Baudrillard and Clastres are all about, so we'll come back to that on Thursday, and then we forge ahead to Lacan. Yes, Lacan is very difficult. He's fooling around with us, so you should not worry that you don't always understand what he says (or even often). This is deliberately enigmatic, and you will find, maybe, that the seminars are a little more accessible, but it will be our business to get some meaning out of all of it, because in a way, for me, Lacan is the central figure of theory in the '60s. Everything either feeds into Lacanian psychoanalysis or emerges from it, and everybody has to take a stand on it. In a sense, he is, as I have said somewhere, the Hegel of our time, insofar as we have one. So it is worth putting up with his mannerisms, which are what some of these stylistic things are. We'll come to that next week.

February 16, 2021

9

Utopia: But Where Does Power Come From?

{Baudrillard, Clastres}

Can you hear me? Which is translated as "Good morning," as you know. I'm very pleased that we've kept up with the syllabus. I rarely manage to do that. So, at the risk of leaving out almost everything, we are on schedule. But I do want to prepare you for next week. I should have made the next two weeks a separate section of our course, which is divided into these four periods. This is a kind of fifth period—third in the sequence—and it is the moment in which theory confronts the two great monuments of modern twentieth-century thought, which have been excluded up until the Second World War from the university, and I am talking, of course, about Marxism and Freudianism. Marxism is thought to be subversive and disreputable, and Freudianism is, of course, nothing more than dirty little secrets. So, in France, these had not been a part of the university curriculum or official philosophy for the most part. It is after the war that, in the period we are looking at, we will get a number of new ways of introducing these things into the current of contemporary thought. The other thing is that their very exclusion from the university meant that each one of these kinds of thinking—Marx and Freud—were ghettoized into a kind of orthodoxy. So, if you talk about a Freudian reading of something—well, we know what that is: it is the Oedipus complex. If you talk about a Marxist reading—well, that has to be about class. After the war, this is going to be much more complex and interesting. I am talking about Lacan next week and Althusser the week after. I don't say that these are the only two representatives of this process, but in a way their relationship to structuralism and to language is going to be for each of them a Trojan horse. You can get Marxism or psychoanalysis into the mainstream of discourse by way of their relationships to language, structure, and semiotics. We will start to see that next week.

Anyway, this is a sort of separate section—Lacan and Althusser—and I wanted, as Lacan is notoriously difficult, to prepare you a little bit for the kinds of things you're going to meet. I would do that simply by pointing out the crucial thing in Lacan, which is that he presupposes three dimensions. These dimensions are interrelated, but, in his seminars and in his work, there is a sort of progression from one to the other in the following way. The first dimension is the Imaginary. This is not just imagination or imaginary ghosts or something like that. It is a capital "I," and it is a specific relationship to the self. It forms in infancy, and among our texts I would say that the little essay on the mirror stage is the moment of the Imaginary.[1] The Imaginary comes first, if you want to think of it that way. Then the Symbolic. This is the area of linguistics and language, because, in French, *symbolique* doesn't mean symbols; it means language and it means the sign. You can talk about the sign, the signifier, or the Symbolic. When Baudrillard talks about symbolic exchange, that will end up being the exchange of language, and, as I said, he gets this from Mauss and from anthropology. But this is a basic premise of modern linguistics, this identification of language and exchange. So there is the Symbolic level, which is a distinct one in Lacan.

Finally, there is the Real. What can the Real be? That gets different answers every time you ask the question. It is, in a way, Lacan's version of the *Ding-an-sich*, the thing in itself, except that this *Ding-an-sich* is capable every so often of exploding into your life, into your experience, of coming out of this unknown area and suddenly having a palpable effect in real life, and of course psychoanalysis is one of the moments in which

---

1   Jacques Lacan, "The Mirror Stage as Formative of the *I* Function as Revealed in Psychoanalytic Experience," in Écrits, trans. Bruce Fink (New York: W. W. Norton & Co., 2006), 75–81.

that happens, as are any number of other crises. Anyway, keep those three things in mind, if you've never encountered this before, the Imaginary, the Symbolic, and the Real. The Real, when it is capitalized, is likely to be used in a Lacanian way. I have pointed out, of the things I have given you to read, that the mirror-stage is a beginning expression of what is going to be the Imaginary. I would say the piece on the insistence of the letter, which is all about metaphor and metonymy, is not a bad illustration of the Symbolic.[2] And, finally, when we get to Seminar XI, we begin to get to something associated with the Real, namely the drives. Slavoj Žižek has been very good in arranging this periodization. This is a moment of a break in which Lacan's seminars will move into the problem of the Real, as opposed to the language of the unconscious or the Imaginary. There is a historical reason for including the fourth piece, "Of Structure . . ."[3] You can grapple with it. I think the lecture is the most approachable, because you hear Lacan's voice. It is very attractive, very interesting. It is also incomprehensible, but it is much more fun than the written texts. Okay, more on that next week.

Then a few more things about Lévi-Strauss. I don't want to bore you. First of all, on schematization. You understand that schematization can also be these diagrams. Lacan said—and this would be the model of this idea—there is no metalanguage. What is a metalanguage? It is a language about language. But his point is that you can't get out of language that way. You can't get out of language by way of language. There is no linguistic way of talking about linguistics. So we have to talk about it in a non-linguistic way, and that could be mathematics, the matheme, or it could be these various kinds of diagrams that we will maybe have occasion to see, but which are also being represented by another branch of semiotics, the branch codified by A. J. Greimas and his Greimas square. I haven't put anything of Greimas on the list because that really is unreadable, but you have my little introduction to a collection of Greimas's stuff.[4] Fool around with that. The Greimas square is a wonderful toy to play with. Beyond that lies Hjelmslev, the Danish linguist, with his four-part series, I would say,

2   Jacques Lacan, "The Insistence of the Letter in the Unconscious," *Yale French Studies*, no. 36/37 (1966), 112–47.

3   Jacques Lacan, "Of Structure as an Inmixing of an Otherness Prerequisite to Any Subject Whatever," 186–95.

4   Fredric Jameson, "Foreword," *On Meaning: Selected Writings in Semiotic Theory*, A. J. Greimas (Minneapolis, MN: University of Minnesota, 1987), vi–xxii.

rather than two. I would love to show you those things if we have time. I don't know when we'll ever have time. At any rate, all these written, visual, diagrammatic things—at least for the writers of this period—try to do the impossible, to become metalanguages.

Coming back quickly to Lévi-Strauss. Someone said that Lévi-Strauss was a racist. If these terms are to be useful, even politically, I do think we have to be somewhat judicious in how we use them. A man who believes that primitive peoples—alas, his word—are smarter than we are, and who believes that *pensée sauvage* and the thinking of myth is more elaborate and more interesting and more complicated than the Western thoughts that we think, and who believes that the utmost progress in Western thought will be the moment when we arrive at being able to understand tribal thought—I don't know how you can call this man a racist, really. He believes that history did not have to take place, that it is an accident— history, meaning the passage from cold societies, tribal societies, to hot societies, in which the dynamics end up in capitalism. I suppose Lévi-Strauss would say that, once you get going with hot societies, the arrival at capitalism in one way or another is fatal, but primitive societies didn't have to do that. There didn't have to be history. There didn't have to be modernity, and in fact we would be better off in primitive society. You can think what you want about that, but it's part of the utopian thinking of this period.

You remember—well, you don't remember—but you know that in the '60s there were communes, and, of course, even before the '60s, people go back to the land and try to create some simpler form of society. All of those are attempts in a non-utopian society to reinvent something utopian. We will see this in Baudrillard. I think that Lévi-Strauss was certainly a leader in this. People also ask about Franz Boas. Yes, of course, Boas was the great German-American anthropologist who precedes Lévi-Strauss. He made a huge encyclopedic study, especially of the Northwest coast peoples. Theirs are the stories on which Lévi-Strauss draws. And, if nothing else, even if you don't read Lévi-Strauss, I wish that we had time for me to show you some of these Northwest coast tales, because this is really—I don't rule out the other First Nations or Native American tribes—but we have a tremendous richness of these things in the Northwest coast, along with an art, the totem pole, which is prodigious, and if nothing else I hope that some of you will get interested in this work. There is a volume which I would recommend to you, *A Story as Sharp as a Knife* by Robert

Bringhurst, which is a new collection of these Haida myths.[5] This is the first great North American literature, and it's really a shame that people aren't enough aware of it. As for Lévi-Strauss, I would recommend one work of his: "The Story of Asdiwal."[6] This is the most comprehensive study of a Tsimshian story or epic, if you like, and it is very impressive (you could say that it is his *S/Z*).

Now the final thing I wanted to say with Boas. There are a lot of anecdotes about these people that one would like to tell. If you ask Lévi-Strauss if he knew Boas personally, he says, "He died in my arms." In New York, he is up in Columbia having lunch with Boas, who dies there, and Lévi-Strauss holds him as he is dying. I don't know that they were close—two different generations—but, certainly, Lévi-Strauss had immense admiration for Boas and his work and claims to follow him.

Finally, I wanted to draw your attention to this section on art in the overture to *The Raw and the Cooked*, the first volume of *Mythologiques*. We can't discuss it in detail, but there is clearly a whole aesthetic there. It's an aesthetic of the double inscription, the double articulation, and he shows how music is inscribed on sounds, how painting is inscribed on colors, how there's a double relationship between these things. Very interesting, for me, is what he says about music and the rhythms of the body. I don't know if this is so. Does our heart beat at a different rate from our breathing? I have no idea. Some of you maybe know something about anatomy. But it is on the rhythms of the body that the second level of music would somehow be able to inscribe itself. And I draw your attention to this also because you might think that he is against these early forms; on the contrary, he is not a modernist, and there are two polemics there—one against concrete music, one against abstract art—which are really quite old-fashioned but very powerful in a way. The problem, he says, is there isn't a lower level of inscription. Colors only come to us in objects. They don't have a separate existence. Concrete music, yes, it has this separate existence of the cars in the streets and so on, but that's not interesting; it is the body which is its source. The relationship to music and the body is why I compared this to Schopenhauer, because the other great writer on music, in the early nineteenth century, is Schopenhauer and his notion

---

5   *A Story as Sharp as a Knife: The Classical Haida Mythtellers and Their World*, ed. Robert Bringhurst (Vancouver, BC: Douglas and McIntyre, 2011).

6   "The Story of Asdiwal," trans. Nicholas Mann, in *The Structural Study of Myth and Totemism*, ed. Edmund Leach (London: Tavistock Publications, 1967).

of the relationship of music and the body, his idea that music is somehow the supreme art that transforms bodilyness into the most idealistic form.

And now Baudrillard. He had a very interesting career, maybe an anti-theoretical career. You will see that both Baudrillard and Pierre Clastres are anti-Marxist in some way, that is, that they are against Marxist anthropology, the attempt to somehow imprison the realities of tribal society in the Marxist framework of superstructure and base, which, as I remind you, is another double articulation. First, Baudrillard's attack on Marxism. Baudrillard was a student of Henri Lefebvre, probably the greatest modern French Marxist philosopher, who stayed in the Communist Party, unlike many others, but he wasn't very popular there either. He left in '56, as so many people did. Lefebvre invented two very important ideas. One, which he shared with the Situationists—we'll read Guy Debord later on, when we come back to Baudrillard, actually—is the notion of *la fête*, the festival, and the other notion that he invented, so to speak, is that of daily life.[7] You might be surprised. How can daily life be invented? The sociologists did not make a category for daily life, but they studied daily life, in fact, in older societies. But, really, it is Lefebvre who sets himself to study daily life as a uniquely modern category, and there are some very accessible books of his on that idea, as well as on modernism itself. He wrote a great deal about art and literature. And I would say his little book on dialectical materialism from the late '30s is quite amazing for a party writer, very Hegelian, and is one of the best introductions to the dialectic that I know.[8] In any case, a whole generation of French intellectuals learned Marxism from that book, so Lefebvre was a major figure. Baudrillard said once that he should have been the Marcuse of May '68. You know the enormous symbolic importance of Marcuse in this country, but Lefebvre never quite made it in France. I don't know why that should have happened, but there is some truth to that. Anyway, Baudrillard was his student, probably a great disappointment to him.

Baudrillard began at first in the study of the commodity form. He began to study "the system of objects," and, of course, as he is beginning

---

7   Henri Lefebvre, *Critique of Everyday Life*, trans. John Moore and Gregory Elliott (London: Verso, 2014). See too Raoul Vaneigem's *The Revolution of Everyday Life*, trans. Donald Nicholson-Smith (Oakland, CA: PM Press, 2012), originally *Traité de Savoir-vivre à l'Usage des jeunes Générations*.

8   Henri Lefebvre, *Dialectical Materialism*, trans. John Sturrock (London: Jonathan Cape, 1974).

his own work, he returns to the reign of language and semiotics, but now it's a question of the semiotics of commodities, the rule of the sign. So Baudrillard is going to end up in this trajectory: from orthodox Marxism, the base, into superstructures, commodities, and into semiotics, then a utopian period, and, at the same time, a wholesale rejection of both Marxism and semiotics, and, finally, a development into another theory of the weird nature of modern society, or let's say postmodern society, which he will call "simulation."[9] We'll come back to that at another point, because I think it ties in with another connection to Lefebvre, namely that of Guy Debord and Situationism, his notion of spectacle. That is a later Baudrillard, but you will be able to see today where that would come from. It will characterize a later period that I would simply call the postmodern period, but I don't insist on that kind of vocabulary.

So what is it that Baudrillard ends up doing here, such that he along with Clastres should be among the rebels against Marxism? The whole '60s in France is a gradual revolt against Marxism and a kind of attempt to do something else or to go over into Maoism, let's say (if you associate Marxism with the Russians), or to develop a post-Marxism of some kind. You've seen Sartre's attempts. The frustration is that, in France, the Communist Party is a separate power. It has its own culture. Communist workers read communist books; they read communist newspapers. Their contact with bourgeois thought is policed by the Party itself. Sartre complains that he can't write for the workers because he is canceled, so to speak, by the Party. They have no access to his works, and you can imagine for intellectuals that this is a very frustrating kind of situation. In the history of France, around what I consider to be a very important turning point around 1980, the Socialist Party under François Mitterrand comes to power in alliance with the Communist Party, and everybody is terribly afraid. Oh, my God! The Communist Party will not have been in power since they left at the beginning of the Cold War in 1947. So here they are in 1980, coming back into power with Mitterrand, who gives them a couple of minor ministries, and as you can imagine—well, maybe you can't imagine—it is a part of political logic that one has to take into account. The minute Mitterrand includes them in his government, they disappear. That's the end of the Communist Party. After 1980, the Party

---

9   Jean Baudrillard, *Simulacra and Simulation*, trans. Sheila Glaser (Ann Arbor, MI: University of Michigan Press, 1994).

is nothing. Of course, it is even less than nothing after the dissolution of the Soviet Union. There is still a Communist Party in France, of course, but its power is broken. Mitterrand's political act here is a very cunning tactic of cooptation, which does them in as rivals to his socialist government, which itself ends up being not very socialist. But, in this period, the Party is a presence; it can irritate all these intellectuals. They revolt against it in various ways.

You will see how Clastres's argument is really an argument against Marxism. But nowhere is this anti-Marxism more intense than in a little text of Baudrillard's, *The Mirror of Production*, a very powerful argument against Marxism, but also, in another way, against semiotics.[10] Why? And how? He thinks that Marxism is a theory of productivism. I think there are several alternatives here. Yes, it could be that Marxism sees the communist outcome, a communist state, as being the end of the exploitation of labor, as the place in which labor is no longer alienated, but you could just as easily argue—and there have been Marxisms of that kind—that communism is by these others thought to be the end of labor, the jobless future in which nobody is going to work anymore. People aren't aware that there is a sort of utopia at the end of the Soviet Union, in the Brezhnev era, the so-called era of stagnation, for which lots of Russians nowadays are nostalgic, in which the workers' saying went something like this: we pretend to work, and they pretend to pay us. Work doesn't mean anything, because you are in some other space altogether. So there are other kinds of Marxisms, and I myself think Marxism is, I would say, a philosophy of activity, of *Tätigkeit*—a Hegelian word—of production in a spiritual sense.

But Baudrillard refuses all that, because he refuses the notion of goal-driven activity. He refuses the idea, that is, of value, because, if you don't have the idea of value, there's no point to doing anything. If you do something, when you have a project, it's because, in one way or another, it produces value. Well, capitalism is, as Marx sees it, above all, the society of value, and we know what these values are. They're use-values and exchange-values. Exchange-value is a surplus work, labor, which is added onto use. And Marx says, on the first page of *Capital*, there is such a thing as use-values, but this is the last time I'm going to mention those. Use-value is what Marxism calls quality. It means different activities,

---

10   Jean Baudrillard, *The Mirror of Production*, trans. Mark Poster (St. Louis, MO: Telos Press, 1975).

and your objects serve different purposes. So, to say that a book, some clothing, a steak, a house—to say that all those are somehow the same is crazy, if you are talking about use-value. You don't want to be given a suit when you're hungry and you want a steak. You don't want to be given a steak when, instead, you want to read, and you want to study something. These objects are not comparable. But, in exchange, of course, they are absolutely the same, and you have something called money by which you're going to measure all those values. I'm going to have to pay for this with the same money with which I'm paying for my clothes, my steak, my rent. So, in Marxist theory, it is exchange-value which will transform the world of qualities, which is all distinct and different, into the single realm of quantity.

Well, Baudrillard will even refuse that. Yes, he is a Marxist, in the sense that this is still his problematic, but he refuses this theory. Why? Here is the thing: it will have to do with something that he calls "the code." Very mysterious in Baudrillard. What is the code? I don't remember the date exactly, but there is a phenomenal moment in modern science when, all of a sudden, Watson and Crick discover DNA, the genetic code. It forms everything. Every part of consciousness, life, and the body is produced by this magical code. In fact, they just found the DNA code of a mammoth that's over one million years old. The Jurassic Park stuff comes out of the idea that you can take some ancient DNA and revive all these dinosaurs and so on and so forth. Anyway, when Baudrillard uses this expression, "the code," he means the production of the same. He means, in other words, a formula which creates the double articulation, because you have some genes here, arranged in a pattern, and they will produce another set of realities, which is the organic. So it is the double inscription again, but now we must think of the double inscription like a fraction. If I had the blackboard, I could show you this. The semiotic version of the code— the semiotic code if you like—is a fraction. On top is the signifier. On the bottom is the signified. In English we write this Sr on the top of the fraction and Sd on the bottom. In French it is *signifiant* and *signifié*. The referent has long since disappeared. Forget about the referent. And, in a sense, that disappearance is also part of Baudrillard's argument. Baudrillard's argument is that this code, and above all the signifier, produces the signified. That is a Saussurean argument, that meaning comes not from the fact that one word *means* something but from the juxtaposition of these signifiers. This is against meaning as an idea. It is not that a signifier, a word, has a meaning or a signified. It is that the sequence of signifiers produces a meaning; there is a logic of the signifiers which then produces the signified. Well, in a way, Baudrillard accepts that, but, for him, this discredits any use of signifieds to understand reality.

Let me put it another way. Exchange and use. The notion that exchange-value is a new kind of signifier, which subsumes use-value, Baudrillard says, produces an illusion. It makes you think you can just get away from exchange-value and get back to use-value. You can have a utopia in which there is nothing but use-value. And this is the form that most utopias take. Throughout human history, people have been anxious to get rid of the most evil thing of all, which is already there in exchange-value, and which is, of course, money. Money is this incomprehensible, toxic thing that corrupts everything, that makes everything quantifiable, and if we could only get rid of money, if we could only get rid of exchange and the market, we would be back in a utopian society. What Baudrillard wants to say is that this double articulation, this code, produces use-value. If you don't have exchange-value, you don't have use-value either. You don't have either of them. It is the signifier that produces the signified, in a bad sense. So the Marxist code of production is always going to produce the idea of value, and it's the idea of value that's going to corrupt everything, just as the semiotic code of signifier and signified always produces meanings, which are an illusion as well. So Baudrillard's work becomes a critique of these two versions of the code, which are somehow transforming all of reality. It is the idea of exchange and use that's producing the alien-ation of exchange society. It is the idea of signifier and signified that is producing this alienation of language, which is the idea of meanings. That is, in both cases, meaning is the value of language, something that dictates my every move. I have to do things for some reason, for some purpose. Value is that purpose. Value is the end or reason for my activ-ity. This notion of the "end," Baudrillard says, is completely corrupting. In utopia, you would do nothing. You just would do what you want to. What is this utopia?

Someone mentioned another writer who was in Paris at this time, an American anthropologist. His name is Marshall Sahlins, and he used to run the University of Chicago Department of Anthropology. He and Baudrillard must have known each other in those days when Baudrillard was writing his notion of utopia, because, for Baudrillard, there is also a utopia. It's the utopia of symbolic exchange, but we get to it only by abolishing the code, only by abolishing Marxism and semiotics and going back to something else, which can be found in Marcel Mauss's book *The Gift*: symbolic exchange, not in any structuralist sense, but in the sense of talking, the exchange of *parole*, of words, rather than written language. So Marshall Sahlins writes a book called *Stone Age Economics* that touches on similar themes. I recommend it to you highly. He says, yes, all these people are talking about revolution. Baudrillard is against that too, because he thinks that just means more productivism, more value rather than less value. Sahlins says that people think of the stone age as one of primitive society. They have to have a certain circuit to survive, because they live on hunting and finding berries and so on. The minute you pass to agriculture you have labor. So this is the first stage of society, the stone age. People don't understand, says Sahlins, that this was the happiest society on Earth. Never before have people worked so little, slept so much, had so much sex, given themselves over so fully to artistic activities, than in this golden moment, and, in a sense, that is this distant utopia that we have in the whole anthropology of this period, and certainly in Baudrillard. Baudrillard and Sahlins are sort of a pair in this respect.

So how would that come about? It is the end of the idea of production, the end of value. This end is to be found in the gift. The gift is this non-money system, says Mauss, in which there are three kinds of activities that you are obligated to do: give, receive, and reciprocate.[11] But, for Marx, this is the origin of money. One tribe is in a place where they have a lot of wood. Another tribe is in a place, one would think much less propitious, in which they have a lot of salt. So exchange comes into being on that frontier, when they have to figure out how much salt they're going to exchange for the lumber they need, and the other ones are going to have to figure out how much salt they need and how much their lumber is worth. So this frontier between two unrelated things is the very moment in which the notion of value has to appear, because you have to exchange in some way. If you were hungry and I asked you how many books you would give me for my steak—there's no common denominator for that kind of exchange until you get money. So the first form of the gift is this kind of exchange without money. It is prestation, the technical term for giving, and it doesn't involve money, but it involves a return. So I give something to someone, but then they are obliged to give something back.

11　Marcel Mauss, *The Gift*, trans. W. D. Halls (London: Routledge, 2004), 50.

Not right away, maybe. Maybe in ten years, twenty years, but there is an obligation of return and an obligation of giving, he says. You have to give back. You can't refuse this demand. You know the stories where you admire somebody's watch and then they have to give it to you. Everybody says, in such-and-such country, don't ever admire anything, because the minute you admire something they're going to have to give it to you. So keep your admiration to yourself. If they see that you like it, they would give it to you, and you would have to give something back. So, in the beginning, there is total prestation. One tribe gives something to another one and the other gives something back. Then there is individual prestation, but it remains an obligation.

Finally, there is another form, which is very interesting. To refuse to give, to neglect to invite, as to refuse to take, is the equivalent to declaring war. In the realm of symbolic exchange, you must give, you must take, and you must return the gift. "Reversibility" will be one of Baudrillard's words for this. In modern societies of value, there is no reversibility. You destroy the value by consuming it, or you go into debt. In this utopian society, it is reversible, and you get back something else. Now that becomes the parody of spoken language. I speak and you can speak back. In the '60s, when the Left comes to criticize the media, it's on that basis. The television and the radio speak to us, but we can't speak back. It is non-reversible, and therefore non-utopian. A lot of schemes in some of the experiments in the '60s were invested in trying to figure out how you could arrange to use the radio or the TV in a more productive way. I remember a story that Dave Dellinger used to tell about one such set-up in New York, in the 1960s, in which anyone could speak on television for their fifteen minutes. And this was a utopian situation where people could actually reply. It all ended, he said, when some crazy man got on there and shot his dog, and with that the experiment was over. Well, for Baudrillard, in those societies, yes, it is reciprocal. It goes in both directions because it is nothing other than speaking.

So you can see how out of certain semiotic conceptions will come a utopian notion of life in general, of a form of human life, which is not—you can't even say not alienated. This is a critique of the very idea of aliena-tion, because alienation supposes that the top of the semiotic fraction is alienated, that the bottom is non-alienated, that there was a pure plenitude of non-alienation first, that naturally we were non-alienated and then we became alienated. They don't want that kind of historiography, that notion of nature as plenitude, and we'll see many other forms of resistance to anything resembling an original plenitude. But one of the things you can say about this kind of society of the gift—the one problem with this utopia—is that nobody enjoyed it very long, and everybody died in their twenties, except for a few lucky elders.

So all of that stuff is the very beating heart of the positive side of the '60s, but the negative side is of course this ferocious attack on Marxism, on structuralism, on all forms of what will become ideology. This is the birth of ideology critique, and that will be one of the other great things of the '60s. But, finally, that question about utopia will lead to other questions. This one, for example: If earlier societies were so great, why did they disappear? What made them disappear? When did they become something else? I would say that one answer—people don't like this, and it's associated with the name of Malthus—is population. Hunters and gatherers—"nomads," they will be called in Deleuze—get more populous, and, at a certain point, the tribe doesn't function. It breaks in two, like an amoeba, and half goes off to another place. There has to be a certain amount of land for them to hunt and gather on, otherwise they run up against scarcity and then all kinds of other miseries. But, with more population, little by little, there is less and less hunting land, and so they break off and start all over.

Okay, but I have neglected to give you the ultimate answer to this. Sahlins has one version of this society, presupposed in Baudrillard, although he never really wants to give us a direct picture of this vision, because he knows it's inaccessible, nostalgic, and nostalgia simply is yet another way of ratifying the present. But there is another book, which is the supreme anthropological realization of this utopia. It is a book called *The Forest People* by Colin Turnbull, and it is about the Mbuti Pygmies, a society without power. Later, as the '60s begins to unfold, as politics begins to separate itself from the Communist Party, the various other forms of *gauchisme*, leftism, begin to appear. There is a Trotskyist revival. There is anarchism. There is Maoism, above all. There are all kinds of little groups, so-called groupuscules. All of those groups are going to begin to ask themselves, what is power? And what is the state? So the real question about what happens to this utopia is: Can one imagine society without the state? That is in fact the title of one of Pierre Clastres's books. And can one imagine a society without power? Of course, in the essay of his we are reading, where does the question of war come into this?[12] Clastres reminds us: You all are talking about primitive societies. My God, take a look at indigenous Brazil! There is no place on earth where there is such constant warfare, where there are these vendettas that last a hundred and fifty years, where these groups are constantly at war with each other. There are immense amounts of blood shed by these allegedly utopian groups. Where does that come from? How does that fit into the system? He does have an answer to those questions, and we'll take a look at it in a minute.

So you can see how out of this initial problematic, if you want to use that Althusserian word, there are going to come two kinds of interests. One will be trying to find the utopianism in this, and that will prolong itself into science fiction and other things. You understand that, before this time, "utopia" was a bad word because it meant Stalinism; it meant Marxism and it meant revolution. People like Pol Pot who try to make a perfect society are going to end up killing everybody bourgeois, and so, for the bourgeois countries, utopianism is bad. Now, suddenly, we get another idea of utopianism coming through, which is that of groups without power, and on the other side we're going to get, climaxing in Foucault, an inquiry into what power actually is. So we want to know what happened to those societies. Or, better still, how did they last so long? These are the oldest societies in human history. They lasted thousands and thousands of years. When did these societies end? What happened to them? Why aren't we still at that point? So the question is where the break is, where the fall is, original sin. What was the fall into history? What was the fall into power? Where did the state come from?

Okay, well there are several answers. The first is the surplus. Rousseau gets to be revived during this period, because Rousseau's second discourse, an admirable work, one of the first great modern treatises, along with *The Social Contract*, says that everything comes from the first person who says, "This is mine," who invents property. This is the original fall out of the state of nature. Okay, well, where does property come from? Property comes from the surplus. Let's say the original tribe, the hunters and gatherers, are a family. If you're looking around for some soap, and you ask your parents or your sister for a piece of soap, she doesn't say, "Well, give me twenty-five cents." The home is meant to be the final place

---

12   Pierre Clastres, "War in Primitive Societies," in *Archaeology of Violence*, trans. Jeanine Herman (Los Angeles: Semiotext(e), 2007), 237–77.

where you don't have exchange of that kind. So, in this society, if you need something, your neighbors have it, and they will give it to you, and then you will have to give them something back. This is the society of symbolic exchange. Okay, but suppose, all of a sudden, you have too much. Let's put it this way. The perpetual present of this society is one in which nothing is stored, in which everything is used up. Now I haven't mentioned the final form of the gift in Mauss, and also the Northwest coast peoples. It is the potlatch. Do you know what the potlatch is? You get to be a wealthy member of society, and, at a certain point, you demonstrate your wealth by destroying it. You take out all your objects and your money and so on, and you burn them. It is a ritual. So the Canadian government—because most of these people are in Canada—said, "My God! This is capitalism! We can't have money burnt!" So, beginning in the 1880s, they banned the potlatch. But the potlatch is the final form of what you do with a surplus if you're in a gift society. You have to destroy it. Then, instead of your wealth, which is worthless, you get prestige, and then your neighbor, in a kind of countergift, has to burn all his stuff. It's a very interesting ultimate form of *le don*, of prestation. Otherwise, surplus means you can attach people to yourself by giving them the surplus.

Now let me tell you how Clastres, in his first book about the Guayakí people in Paraguay, a very readable book, discovers a rule for these societies.[13] How do they prevent power? How do they prevent, for example, the surplus. It's very simple, he says. The hunter cannot eat his own kill. It's on the hunter that you depend for your meat. He is going to bring back venison or whatever the animal is, but he cannot eat his own kill; he has to give it all to everybody else. If he were allowed to eat it, save it, he could build up his stock, his surplus of meat, and then he could say to others, "Follow me and I'll give you extra portions." With that a leader would be formed, and there's your origin of power. So the surplus would feed this unnecessary group which is going to be dependent on you and be the source of your power. And then, because, as Gramsci says, besides physical force you need some spiritual force, what he calls hegemony, cultural consent, we need another bunch of people who are doing nothing at all, whom we'll feed and who will become the priests, executors of another kind of power. This is what will happen to primitive society, and this will

---

13   Pierre Clastres, *Chronicle of the Guayaki Indians*, trans. Paul Auster (New York: Zone Books, 1998).

form around a chief, and the chief is the first form of power. No, he says, not quite, because they have chiefs before this, but the whole function of the chief, he says, is not power; it is talking. You have a problem? You have to lay out a number of solutions to the tribe. So the chief talks and everybody laughs at him, because he is just a talker, but that is his function. Now, once he gets a surplus, then he is a little bit different; he becomes a so-called big man. Then we get hierarchy, then we get power, and we get the first power societies.

Okay, so there would be two other, somewhat different ways of thinking about this. Where does writing come from? It comes from cataloging the surplus. In Mesopotamia, where you have a granary, they had to invent ways of keeping track of how much you had stored. They had little tablets on which they would make marks, which end up being cuneiform, and those marks are the source of the earliest writing. So writing and the surplus are connected just as writing and power are connected. There is a wonderful chapter of Lévi-Strauss's in *Tristes Tropiques* called "The Writing Lesson." One day, in one of these tribes, he's busy writing up his notes and he sees that the chief has gotten ahold of a piece of paper and he's scribbling away on it. Of course, the chief doesn't know how to write or anything, but he has understood that writing is where power comes from. The chief enhances his power by this pretend writing. It is different from language. It stays. You can write laws.[14]

Those of you who are interested in this idea of the anthropocene, which I find a little puzzling, will however be interested in knowing—although if you're interested in this you probably know about it already—that there's another way in which this utopian society is destroyed, and that's agriculture. There are too many people. You have to start planting, and planting is the source, of course, of the end of planet earth, because the minute you plant, all kinds of gasses are released which are going to lead to present day pollution, and all the rest of it. But it also is the end of leisure, because an agricultural society is hard; you have to spend a lot of hours on that. This is already in Marx, this business about machines. The machine, you would think, is labor-saving. That is what everybody says, but, in fact, workers are even more oppressed by machinery than when they didn't have machinery. Hence the Luddites. The Luddites were not stupid. They

14   Claude Lévi-Strauss, *Tristes Tropiques*, trans. John Weightman and Doreen Weightman (New York: Atheneum, 1974), 294–304.

understood that you had to destroy these machines, because, far from marking the reduction of labor, they bring about an increase in it, and along with the increase in the labor of the employed, unemployment for everyone else. So that is what *Capital* is really all about. In the realm of industrial capitalism, the so-called labor-saving device, the machine, is certainly a source of alienation.

About the first power society, agriculture, we can say the same thing. Agriculture is the beginning of the end. Agriculture will tie you to the soil. You can no longer move around the way the hunters and gatherers did, and so it gives rise to the next fall into power, which is the city. Michael Mann has a very interesting theory of early history and the emergence of power (Michael Mann the sociologist, not the film director). His idea is that the city is the beginning of the end for these societies, because what the city does is something he calls "encagement." There are lots of villages that are still functioning in the older way around this nascent city, which is Ur, a so-called hydraulic society, because it has had to marshal groups of people to make dams and tame the rivers. So you make the villages depend on you by way of commerce, and then they are "encaged"; they can't extricate themselves any longer; they become part of the city, and the city becomes this imperialistic thing which grows and grows. Well, in a system where you gradually build up so many different kinds of exchange that you can't get out of it, you end up with things like Brexit. Take a look at what's going to happen to England now that it's released itself from all those obligations; they somehow become independent, free from these links that it's had with Europe and with other places. At that point, the trouble begins.

So this is the final form of power that will be theorized throughout the '60s. Clastres, unfortunately, died very young in a car accident, and so we just have these few works of his. I think his theory is very interesting, and it still rests on the idea that every mode of production wishes to keep itself in being. The hunter and gatherer society wished to keep itself in being. Therefore, it wished to ward off the things that would transform it into something else. Hence the law about the hunter and his kill. Well, that means that you have to protect your society against outsiders, and therefore, according to Clastres, this is why—as in Carl Schmitt, where politics is the decision about friends and foes—you have to protect yourself against foreigners. These societies don't have a name. They call themselves the people. We are the humans. Those are the barbarians. They are the enemies, and obviously to keep them out means a state of perpetual war. Now I want you to go back to Sartre and to the groups and the look. Remember how a group forms itself out of serial society by the look of the other? The look is a form of danger. You're threatened, and therefore the group pulls together as a single form of being-for-others. So the very structure of an organic society is based on the other, danger from the other. Clastres doesn't cite Sartre, but it is exactly the problem of warfare in these societies. It is that they are menaced in their very being. That being is never *my* life; it is what will keep alive this group that I belong to, this form of society. How can I ward off these threats to make me over into something else? War would be one of the ways of doing that. So, he says, we have both. There is a society of the gift that circulates inside of your society, and outside there is warfare that keeps everything in. So it's an anti-utopian idea in the sense that, if the identity of your utopian society depends on excluding the others and on warfare, is there no way to imagine something without that? Well, you have defined the group as being precisely what comes into being by virtue of a threat from the other. Sartre says this too: the only way that the whole Earth could be a kind of organic society, globalized society, is if we are threatened from the outside. The Martians, *War of the Worlds*. If we're threatened by the Martians, then yes, we can have a peaceful society on earth, but only if we are threatened from the outside (see Ursula le Guin's *Lathe of Heaven*). That is the only condition under which a unified, global society comes into being.

Okay, I'm introducing you to a problematic. This will be the beginning of a different line of being in the '60s, and after we get through Lacan and Althusser we'll come to the real poststructuralists where these questions of power are posed in Foucault and others. But I think, to conclude, I want to tell you a story about Clastres. You know Paraguay has two official languages. This is quite astounding. One is Spanish, and the other is Guaraní. Well, the people there told me, that's not quite the language that the indigenous people speak. The upper classes speak it too. They speak it in school. So, if you're an Argentine or somebody else who goes to Paraguay, and they don't want you to understand what they're saying, they talk in Guaraní. It's also the place in which the famous Jesuit utopias are formed. The Jesuits decided in the eighteenth century to set up these utopias for the indigenous people. For us, they're not necessarily that; but they are places where you can study utopian thinking and utopian organization. But the people who Clastres does his field work with have a reputation for one of the most awful things that can be associated with a tribal society, and that's not necessarily incest; it's cannibalism. So he asks them about that. No, they say, we don't do that. He lives there for a year or so. Nothing of that kind. Then, one day, just by accident, toward the end of his trip, somebody has died, an old aunt. The body disappears. There's funny stuff going on. And he finds out that they are cannibals after all, and that they've eaten her body. So, he says, what's going on here? Why do you do this? Now, normally, when an anthropologist asks cannibals why they do it, they say for the power. So these guys say, "Listen, we didn't want to tell you this. The half-breed in the store told us that Westerners don't like this and that we should never tell you that we do it, so we've hidden it from you, because we like you. We don't want to offend you, but sure, once in a while, when we have occasion, we do this." So he asks why they do this. For the power? "No, no," they say, "because it's delicious! We don't get a chance to eat meat like this otherwise. This human flesh is really great stuff." If you want a film, not exactly the same as these descriptions, but a wonderful film, I recommend *Como Era Gostoso o Meu Francês* from 1971. It's a film by one of the first filmmakers of the Brazilian new wave, Nelson Pereira dos Santos, and it's called *How Tasty Was My Little Frenchman*. It is a marvelous film about precisely these warlike societies and about, as the title indicates, cannibalism as a ritual.

The other thinker, sort of an aberrant or independent thinker, whose work comes out of this business of warfare among these tribes, perpetual warfare, vengeance and so on, is René Girard. I think anybody interested in the novel should read his *Deceit, Desire and the Novel*, which is based on his theory of mimetics. After that, he converts to Christianity, because, of course, Christianity has a better mediator: Christ, who is the figure outside of the community, who will replace the enemy and therefore permit an organization. Girard's thinking—he died a year or two ago—which is very influential in the Catholic church, for example, is yet another distant, unexpected offshoot of this problematic of utopia.

Okay, we'll go on next time to Lacan and to the next segment of our thought, and we'll find the Symbolic in use as a word, but now in a rather different sense. So I hope you survive the ice storm and all the things that are happening in the weather today.

February 18, 2021

10

Enter Lacan

{Lacan}

We could begin with a little bit of biography. I hesitate to say this, but it sort of gives you an idea: Lacan, you could say, was a society doctor. He quickly became known in the '30s for all kinds of reasons. He traveled very much in the circle of the Surrealists, where of course he knew Breton, Picasso. I read somewhere—and, incidentally, your internet is useful for all kinds of things like this—that Picasso was a patient of his, although maybe it's not true. Somebody like that could go and talk to Lacan about problems and he would spend some time with them and that's that. Sartre—they were about the same age—also had a period when he was having hallucinations. He went to see a young doctor about this to consult with him, and the doctor was again Lacan. Finally, Sartre decided that he was sick of being crazy, and so he stopped having hallucinations, which could be for you an example of Sartrean freedom and choice. Anyway, Lacan was very much a fellow traveler of the Surrealist movement.

At that time, there was an orthodox Freudianism in France run by Anna Freud, Freud's daughter, who was thus the legal heir of his system, and who was always an enemy of Lacan. They hated each other. Lacan was always fiddling with the outside of the system. It's said that some of the quirks of his personality, about which you can hear anecdotes—I won't take up too much time this week with telling them, but you will find many in Roudinesco, some of which are quite delightful—these quirks existed because he was never completely analyzed.[1] His analyst, so to speak, Clérambault, was a psychiatrist, and not a psychoanalyst, but of course you could say the same thing about Freud himself. When Freud's authority was challenged, by Jung for example, he had fainting fits. This is not normal, but Freud could be as neurotic as everybody else. It is hardly a surprise. But it could also be said of him that the reason was that he was not analyzed, because there wasn't anybody to analyze him, except his friend Fliess, and, in a sense, that was an analysis, but an incomplete one. Incidentally, it's just a remark, but when you have a completely analyzed person, who would generally be a psychiatrist, it's like somebody who is a complete communist. These people are of a massive calm and certainty which boggles the mind. They are quite different from the rest of us. Their belief has a kind of solidity of being. That is not necessarily a compliment, but I just throw that out. In any case, Lacan was not of that type.

You can see him on YouTube. There are two television filmings of Lacan in action. One is the little film he did for Benoît Jacquot called *Psychanalyse*, later published as *Télévision*. That is much more mannered, because he is very self-conscious. And then there is another one in which he is giving a lecture, but it has no subtitles. At any rate, it gives you an idea of the personality and of his bearing in these lectures. What happens is that, in the early '50s, he begins a small, semi-private seminar with his students and young associates, most of them analysts in training or young doctors who are getting a psychiatric degree, and that acquires a certain following and becomes more public. That's 1952. Beginning in that year, there are about twenty-seven of these seminars. They are the teaching, the doctrine. The last ones of course are very fragmentary—he was not in good shape—but each one was a mode of exploration and tried to push his thoughts further, and they are wonderful reading. You had the chance to look at Seminar XI, a very basic seminar, because it comes at a fault line (a watershed?) that I will discuss. But, anyway, you've seen that they are very delicious, and his replies are idiosyncratic, and his digressions and so on and so forth, and if you look at the official writings, which are called *Écrits*, a huge volume, of which we now have a new translation, those are

---

1   Élisabeth Roudinesco, *Jacques Lacan and Co.: A History of Psychoanalysis in France, 1925–1985* (Chicago: University of Chicago Press, 1990).

extremely dense, and let me say Mallarméan. But they reproduce what you find in the seminars. He has reduced, in the way one would reduce a liquid, let's say, to this densest of formulas, which he conveys in a Mallarméan way, that is to say, a sort of mixture of preciosity, winks to the audience, but with a density of formulas and mathemes. So I recommend, really, first reading the seminars. I think the seminars are more readable, as you might have seen from the section on the look, which, by the way, has its Sartrean connection, as you can well see.[2] The seminars, paradoxically, are readerly—the *Écrits*, writerly.

By 1953, for various reasons, he broke with the official psychoanalytic society of France, and then the International Psychoanalytic Society. This is a decisive break, I suppose traumatic for him. He certainly talks about it very much in these seminars, but it was the occasion for him to form his own society, and that immediately begins to grow. You know that in France—or perhaps you don't—Freud went to Paris as a young man and participated in seminars. The teachers would take the students to Sainte-Anne, a psychiatric hospital, and exhibit various sick people to their students and show this or that neurosis or psychosis. For Charcot, in the youth of Freud, this was a great spectacle. Charcot was a showman. And, in fact, these patients knew that very well. They participated in this with great gusto and showed themselves off as various cases of their illnesses. I think in Huston's movie of Freud you can see this. But Lacan would also take his students to Sainte-Anne and explicate various things about the neuroses and psychoses. I'm telling you this because the audience of each changes, and thus Lacan is obliged to make rhetorical gestures in the direction of all these multiple publics. This first audience is made up of analysts in formation, and he is explaining clinical things to them. Later, as he gets more and more famous, Lacan moves to the École normale, Althusser's hangout so to speak, and begins to attract a different kind of public, that of the students, Althusser's students first of all. However fascinated all these students are with Althusser's Marxism, they hear his secret subtext and are practically all Maoists, including the man who will marry Lacan's daughter and become his intellectual heir, Jacques-Alain Miller.

---

2   Jacques Lacan, "Of the Gaze as *Objet Petit a*," in *The Seminar of Jacques Lacan, Book XI: The Four Fundamental Concepts of Psychoanalysis*, trans. Alan Sheridan, ed. Jacques-Alain Miller (New York: W. W. Norton & Co., 1998), 67–119.

So we have a Maoism going on beneath all of this. There is an interesting pattern to Maoism, which is reproduced in various ways, which has little enough to do with Marxist or Maoist doctrine. It has an abstract form. You have a master, who has lost control of his organization. He secedes from the organization and organizes a sort of populist attack on it. And so the formula of all this becomes: "Bombard the headquarters!" Mao Tse-tung, from the outside, is asking his following, who will become the Red Guards later on, to bombard the headquarters, which is, of course, the official Communist Party. So Maoism was an attack by the leader of the Communist Party, from the outside, against his own institution. Well, that's what Lacan is doing. Lacan is thrown out of the official psychoanalytic society, and then is attacking it. And, by the way, if I may permit myself a topical allusion, that's exactly what our forty-fifth president did, and if you want to consider him a follower of Mao, that would be very interesting. I doubt he ever studied these useful doctrines, but that is also an order to bombard the headquarters. You get your followers on the outside to destroy this institution of yours from which you've been expelled.

Anyway, there is more than simple Maoism in this larger and larger public of Lacan. They will be thrown out of the École normale for what the French call *tabagisme*, that is, excessive smoking. If you ever went to one of these, you were so tightly packed in like sardines that people would drop ash from their cigarettes on your knee. Well, finally, they had to be thrown out, and Lacan moved into a much larger space, which was the school of law, *la faculté du droit*; that was where all the final seminars were given to a vast public. *Le Monde* used to list these things under a rubric called *mondanités*, that is, social events, high society events. People would go to these things out of curiosity, and these were grand public events later on. And, of course, in connection with the students, these gatherings will eventuate in May '68, and so, in a sense, Lacan's political seminar could be counted among the causes—a very minor one—of May '68.

Now the great year for all the people we're going to consider is 1966–1967. This is when the full *Écrits*, the collected essays, are published. So, suddenly, Lacan moves from these smaller journals that his people have put together to a big public, which doesn't necessarily know what to do with these things. 1967 is also a year in which Derrida publishes his first three books and in which Foucault's *Madness and Civilization* comes out. That is the year in which something, which is really no longer what we want to call structuralism, what nowadays everybody wants to call poststructuralism, makes its explosive debut. Now, today, the French consider that the term poststructuralism is an American invention, illicit because of course all these people are very different from each other. Well, yes of course, but what do you want to call them? They are not structuralists anymore, but different in their various ways. We'll deal with that.

But Lacan and Althusser are a little bit different from that. I wouldn't call them poststructuralists. I wouldn't call them structuralists either, but that's because nobody wants to be called structuralists anymore, even at that time, but certainly linguistics plays a role for both of them, and they are interrelated, as you're going to see next week. The point is that what Lacan is developing is a doctrine. The seminars are this immense teaching, and the teaching evolves over time. Another thing that you should know is that, if you want to consult Freud, you don't go to German. You go to English. The great edition of Freud, of all of Freud, called the Standard Edition, is Strachey's English translation, published by Hogarth Press, the press of Virginia and Leonard Woolf. It is, or used to be, the gold standard of the Freudian texts. The Germans only later on get around to doing the complete thing, and as for the French, they don't have everything translated. So Lacan is working in a public which has a very fragmentary knowledge of Freud. One can say the same for Althusser. There is not a complete Marx in French or in other languages. A complete Marx is actually still coming in all these languages, because there are a lot of unpublished manuscripts. But both Lacan and Althusser are working with fragmentary texts from their masters, and, at the same time—and this is like the original Protestantism—they consider that these two great doctrines, which as I told you last time have no place in the university, have been distorted by their popularizers or their practitioners, as the case may be. And I wanted to say that, for Lacan, it's not just the European psychoanalysts who are the enemy, but also the Americans, a lot of them German refugees by the way, who developed ego psychology, which Lacan considers doubly toxic. First of all, it's American, and, second, the whole notion of strengthening the ego is according to him absolutely against the spirit of everything that Freud stood for. I have already told you that one needs to know what problems a given concept tries to solve. What are its intellectual adversaries and so on? This is partly to situate Lacan in this system.

On the texts, you should also know that Jacques-Allain Miller is busy collating all these seminars. He is busy cleaning them up, organizing them, and so on. This first one that he does, the seminar of 1964, only comes out in the early '70s. It takes a long time. If you have ever tried to transcribe a tape recording, you know it is very laborious. You have to get rid of all the spoken stuff.[3] So I don't blame Miller, but, later on, people will start to blame him and say that he has distorted a lot of this and pulled it in his own direction. And there springs up therefore another group of—more orthodox Lacanians, should one say?—people who claim to possess a more faithful text of the seminars, who publish them illegally alongside the much slower publication of Miller and that is now mostly translated into English. It's not complete. The French is complete, and now there is also probably an illegal American translation of those illegally copied seminars.

So we have several versions of this, and if you ever get into it you must take that into account. It has great fascination. I remember, in the early days, one of my students decided to learn French in order to read Lacan. That was already a spark. Later on, one of my students actually became a Lacanian psychoanalyst, and certainly there's an infectious enthusiasm to all this, partly based on the fact of the incompleteness of these things. This is why these immense texts like Gramsci's *Prison Notebooks*, like Pascal's *Pensées*, if you know the history of that text, are tantalizing by virtue of their very incompleteness. It is not quite like a personal journal, but journals fascinate in that way too. So the system is in the process of change all the time, but that's partly what fascinates, and I would say that it is also in the various dimensions of Lacan. There are clinical dimensions, there are philosophical dimensions, scientific dimensions, linguistic dimensions, and so on. All of these things can take you in various ways and I think that's one of the things that has made Lacan what the French call a *maître à penser*, a master whom one consults for thought and for thinking. Later on, there will be a group of young writers at the end of the '70s called *les nouveaux philosophes* who will attack the notion of mastery in all of these discourses as a form of domination and illicit power. But I think one reads the attackers less today than one does the masters.

But Lacan knew that, and that's why I'm going to begin by indicating to you what he called the four discourses, and since I don't have a blackboard, you will have to write down this very simple schema. It has four terms. On your upper left-hand side, you write "the discourse of the master." On your upper right-hand side, you write "the discourse of the hysteric."

---

3 Unlike what we've decided to do here!

On the lower left-hand side, you write "the discourse of the university." And on the lower right-hand side, under "the discourse of the hysteric," you write "the discourse of the analyst."

Now what are these discourses? The discourse of the university uses proper names. That is sort of what I'm giving you now. I say the Lacanian this and the Lacanian that. I use Lacan's name. I use other people's names. This discourse is a discourse of reference. Is it neutralized in some sense? Perhaps. But the main thing is that it is a discourse which takes its authority from other people's writing. The master is this distant thing. Lacan has another word for this, *le sujet-supposé-savoir*, the subject supposed to know. That means that for those of us on the outside the master is this distant figure who represents all of knowledge. We will never know what that is. But the authority is this absent knowledge, so to speak, that the master incarnates, in the sense in which, in popular culture, Einstein might incarnate knowledge itself. Einstein knew everything, right? And, at that point, he is a figure of otherness, what one might call the big Other. The master is that big Other, and it's the person whom you invest with this enigmatic authority, and then who becomes a reference to the discourse of the university.

Now the discourse of the hysteric. Lacan divides neurosis into two basic types: the hysteric and the obsessional. Those are not psychotics. Psychotics are people who have foreclosed the symbolic order; *forclusion* is the word he invented for this, "foreclosure." They don't possess their language, and, therefore, their language comes at them from the outside. If you want an example of this, it's your classic psychotic hearing voices. That's what psychotics are supposed to do, right? Their voices speak to them and tell them to do this and that. They're either demons or angels or whatever. Well, is this just imaginary in the ordinary sense of the word? No, they hear something, but what they hear is their own voice. They hear their own voice coming in from the outside as though it didn't belong to them, and therefore, yes, they are spoken to, but by themselves, and they don't know that because language is out there and coming back in. So the analysis of psychosis has always been very difficult for generations of doctors and psychiatrists and psychoanalysts. Normally, Freud skirts that, because his business in Vienna is to fix people up. People don't function, and they come to him. Mahler, for example, consults Freud when both of them happened by chance to be in Holland, and Mahler tells him a little about his childhood and Freud gives him a little advice and that's that. A longer-term analysis is more serious. As you may know, the classic analysis is five days a week, an hour a piece . . . for how long? Three years? Five years? Freud said you don't make decisions for this period of analysis. You are sort of outside the world. Your life is to be suspended. Well, that can't always happen. I think I mentioned that Lacan had, in this case, a schizophrenic patient whom he analyzed for eight years or so, but the man went on living. He had a family, a job. He wasn't cured, but he functioned. And, of course, at the end of their careers, both Freud and Lacan will begin to wonder about the cure. Is a cure possible? I suggest that, for Freud, the cure is what for Marx is the revolution, because these are total changes. Is it possible? Can it happen? How can it happen? We can come back to that.

Freud only dealt with psychosis through a book. He found a memoir from the nineteenth century by a distinguished jurist who had gone through a schizophrenic period and wrote up his experience. It was a certain president Schreber—"president" in French and German often means something to do with presiding over the legal system, that is, a jury or a set of lawyers—who wrote these memoirs. Freud obviously never met Schreber, who was long dead, but he had this document. So Freud's analysis of it is quite astounding, as is the thing itself. But this is what I wanted to illustrate to you about Lacan. Lacan's seminars were this immense kind of meeting place for all these people. Lacan starts to talk to them about Schreber. There is no French translation. Well, then somebody goes out and translates it! When Lacan makes a reference, suddenly, all over Paris, people want to read that reference—whether it's to Jakobson's linguistics, Schreber's memoirs, Hjelmslev, or whatever. So I would think that Lacan's seminars were really central, in the sense that they were a gathering place for all kinds of currents of thought and also a source of new references. Lots of people's seminars functioned that way in the '60s and '70s. Greimas had a seminar. It wasn't very big, but Kristeva would show up. Todorov. Other people. They would give their papers. Later on, Deleuze would have an immense seminar of thousands of people, much of which has been recorded, by the way, and if you know French you can find it on the internet. Of course, there was Althusser's seminar, which was more limited to the students of the École. But these seminars were much more than simple seminars like ours. They were public events, and you have to feel that atmosphere around these texts.

So the minute Lacan launched a slogan or a reference, it would be all over Paris. Everybody in Paris would be talking about this, whether they liked Lacan or hated him. In retrospect, as I look at these again and again, and look at some of the other stuff of the period, it seems to me the references to Sartre have disappeared. They have been iced. They have been canceled. But they are everywhere in Lacan, of course, and we're going to see that.

Back to these discourses. We have the master, the university, but what is the hysteric then? What is this difference between hysteric and obsessional neurosis? The obsessional neurosis has to do with life and death. The obsessional neurotic asks himself or herself: Am I alive or dead? Am I really alive? What does that mean? The hysteric, on the other hand, asks himself or herself—and in that case, it has traditionally been associated with women, but it's quite obvious that there are male hysterics as well: What do I desire? Do I desire at all? So, for the very emergence of psychoanalysis with Freud himself, this is a new disease, so to speak, which is coming into its own in the 1880s, this new thing called hysteria. The word is invented around that time. Psychoanalysis is a science based on these questions. What is desire? What is my desire? Do I desire? Why do I desire? And that's why, eventually, of course, Lacan will be, in a sense, the philosopher of desire, as will others, but this is where it starts. So the hysteric is asking questions, and who is he or she asking questions of? Well, the master, of course. Who else are you going to go to for your truth and so forth? And, if the master isn't around, I suppose the hysteric might consult these books by the epigones and the students and so forth, these discourses of the university.

But what is the analyst? Here is the final discourse. They tell us that there aren't any orthodox analysts anymore. In the United States, we have all kinds of therapies. Primal screams, for example. Therapy itself, which is not done by analysts and not necessarily Freudian in any way. There are fewer and fewer analysts because nobody can afford it. An analyst has to have so many patients a day to survive. A patient has to pay money five days a week for who knows how many years. This gets to be a big investment. So, little by little, we're told there are fewer and fewer American orthodox analysts. I had an Australian colleague once who was interested in finding out what the different American schools of analysis were. He found that there were three in Manhattan. One around Wall Street. One in the center of the city, and one up around Columbia. So he would go to these people, most of them ego therapists, and talk to them. They would say, "Oh, you're talking to those crazy people downtown, huh? What are they talking about? What do they do? What are their obsessions?" So you see they had a fragmented system. Janet Malcolm wrote a book years ago about American analysis from a social point of view, from the point of view of this crisis in analysis.[4] But what I'm asking you to think of is what it would be like to be an analyst. D. H. Lawrence called psychoanalysis listening to dirty little secrets and shameful childhood experiences. It is also resistance, people not wanting to tell you what they are supposed to be telling you. No, no, I don't think of anything when I think of my dream. Can you imagine what five or six hours of that would be? Yes, but, for Lacan, remember that you're listening to signifiers, not signifieds. You don't listen to the meaning of those things. *L'écoute*, the psychoanalytic listening process, means listening to the rhythms. So the analyst may be thinking something else, but he or she is listening to the rhythms, noting when the speaker is withholding something, when there's a breakthrough, when there is another kind of rhythm. The analyst rarely punctuates this, only sometimes to hurry the speaker along.

Now one of the great scandals of Lacanian practice is the short session. Lacan took to trying to use frustration as an instrument of analysis. So people go in there, pay their money for an hour, and after fifteen minutes he tells you, "Okay, that's enough. Get out. You're not functioning today. You're wasting my time." So the short session became a scandal. I believe that most Lacanian professionals have dropped this custom, which is not only very annoying but also very expensive for the analysand. But you should know that Lacan is associated with this practice, and this is one of the reasons why his reputation is variable. I have also heard people say, however, that Lacan was a great diagnostician. That is, he really had an eye for what was the matter with people, what was going on inside them. Alongside all these seminars, he had a steady practice with patients over a number of years, so he knew exactly what he was confronting, and that makes this possibility of elaborating this whole system, with all of its complex philosophical references, with its psychoanalytic references, quite amazing.

In a way, you can adapt this to politics, if you like. You have the master, some distant leader. You have the discourse of the university, the discourse of the "-isms," your orthodox followers who are busy telling people what to think, what not to think, what is wrong. You have another following who

---

4   Janet Malcolm, *Psychoanalysis: The Impossible Profession* (New York: Vintage Books, 1982).

wants answers from you; these are the hysterics. And, finally, you have *l'écoute*, the analyst. The analyst would be the someone, the Lenin, who listens for what the public really wants. What are its problems? What are the rhythms of this thing? And you can see that, for Lacan, the master is Freud. The interpreters are these university people, but he himself is the analyst. For other people, of course, he becomes the master, and then you play this out all over again. Jacques-Alain Miller is a part of the discourse of the university, but, later on, he becomes—or he tries to assume the position of—the master, or at least the spokesperson for the dead master. Maybe the masters are always dead. But I think what Lacan identified himself with was this position of the analyst.

So let's then try to get into this whole thing. I haven't told you where we are with neurosis. There are the two varieties I mentioned, but there's also perversion, which is a wholly different area. But what a neurotic is, Lacan says, is someone who believes that happiness exists. So, suddenly, you can understand a little better what the whole point of this idea is. Happiness, in other words, is an idea of the other. You know about all the suicides that take place around the holidays. That's because the subject believes that everybody else is happy in that period, all except me. Well, this requires you to believe—it's a kind of Sartrean seriality—the other is happy. That's something that happens to other people. They're happy, but I'm depressed and stewing with all kinds of dissatisfactions. Well, with the neurotic, this is even stronger. So the neurotic has, in some Sartrean way, frozen his or her choices in the form of the other's happiness and made of their unhappiness this static sense of hopelessness.

So I think the point here is that what we call happiness is, as I say, a projection onto the other, a form of plenitude that doesn't exist. And we will find that, for Lacan, first of all, desire is never satisfied, and that, in a way, this lack of satisfaction can become a kind of desire in its own right. Is this a form of pessimism? Not exactly. There is a difference in Lacan between desire and this other thing, which is going to be called *jouissance*, which I'll explain in a moment, and which is a kind of desire that knows there isn't any satisfaction to desire, and which Lacan associates with Freud's death wish. We will get to that in a minute. So, in a sense, this notion of plenitude—we will see it in all these people—is at the source of something else, which you get right away in some of these essays or fragments that I've given you, and which is fundamental, I think, to all of poststructuralism. It is the notion of what in French is called the *schiz*, the gap, the *béance*, the opening, the distance between, the crack, the cut. When we get to Althusser, we will see that he is fascinated by this historical break which is the epistemological cut or break. There is always this idea that there is never a fullness. There is not a fullness of the present. There is not a fullness of satisfaction. Everywhere, there is this structure of the break. Where does it come from? Well, in Sartre, clearly, there is no *en-soi-pour-soi*. We are constantly pursuing this notion of being. We want to be an *en-soi*, but one that has consciousness. That is a kind of fulfillment of our split identities, but it is not ontologically possible. Throughout Sartre, I think, it isn't so pronounced a term. I don't think you have a Sartrean notion of break, or something like that, but it is present. It is a distance from oneself. But, in Lacan, it is the unsatisfaction of desire, and we'll see what it is in other people. I think it is a very fundamental way in which all these people are what Badiou wants to call anti-philosophers, because philosophy, somehow, is always telling you how things *are*. Ontology wants to tell you what being *is*. But, for these people, there isn't being. There are only gaps in being. Heidegger is a funny transitional case here, because even though he affirms that *Dasein* is *not*, in this sense, he is still chasing after *Sein*, after these experiences of Being, which, for him, are really reserved for poetry or for regression to a fuller, more primitive state, a kind of Heideggerian utopia of the ur-Germanic village and forest, just like what we find later on with our utopian anthropologists. So you could enlist Heidegger either way on this.

Let me immediately then deal with this matter of *jouissance*. The verb in French is an obscene verb referring to orgasm, but the noun *jouissance* is a word you're allowed to use. What could it be in English? Žižek has invented a nice translation of it with hyphens: en-joy-ment. The joy in the center of this is to have a very strong sexual overtone for Žižek. But, en-joy-ment is this notion of a super-enjoyment. And you understand that the satisfaction of desire for all these people is not pleasure. Pleasure is a defense against anxiety. Pleasure is the contrary of *jouissance*. When you seek pleasure, it is to fill up and ward off this anxiety. So the satisfaction of desire, were it possible, would not be a pleasure. Socrates compares it to scratching an itch. I gave you the example of drinking a glass of water when you're very thirsty. At any rate, that's a very evanescent pleasure. So what is this *jouissance* as a super-pleasure? I think, in a way, it corresponds to Kant's movement from beauty to the sublime. You have beauty, which is a pleasure in harmony. Then there is this other thing, which is the sublime, which is much more frightening, in the sense of the overpowering force of the Alps, let's say, or the sea, or something which dwarfs and destroys human beings. That's sort of what *jouissance* is in Lacan. Are there moments of *jouissance*? Well, to be sure, but they are of a different order than the satisfaction of desire. They are comparable to Sartrean *en-soi-pour-soi*, I think, to a certain degree.

But we need to know what Freud's distinction was, his late idea of the death-wish. It comes out of his experience of World War I, where he finds in the shell-shocked soldiers this experience of trauma that he hadn't stumbled over before. Trauma in classical Freud is sexual trauma. It can be abuse by an adult of a child, any of those things, all kinds of stuff. But the talking cure can uncover it and get rid of it. Now, all of a sudden, there is a trauma of terror, bombs, death, killing, that you can't quite deal with in the same way. For some reason, the experience keeps coming back. A trauma is something that's not liquidated in you. You come back to it, over and over again. You can't get rid of it. The repression fascinates. The very pain of it fascinates.

So what is the death wish? Freud says organisms are organized by desire, by keeping itself alive, and faced with desire, the organism has two ways of dealing with it. This is the eros and the thanatos. The eros is the life wish, the erotic wish, the thanatos is the death wish, the death drive, Lacan will prefer to call it, *pulsion*, or "drive," rather than "instinct." The eros says, "I will take the long way around and finally achieve my desire. It's very complicated. I have to go through the world." The thanatos says, "It's intolerable. I will satisfy my desire another way: by dying." Death means I don't have any desires anymore. Death satisfies immediately. Death gets rid of desire, whereas the other route, the eros, the point of that is also to get rid of desire but by satisfying it. I think, since we've been talking here, it occurs to me the Sartrean example I gave you of anxiety is not irrelevant. It is not read the same way by Sartre, but it's the mountain climber on the cliff. How do I get past this horrible drop along this narrow ledge on the abyss? I can live through this. I can very cautiously make my way, hang on to certain things, make my way through. That's a conduct dictated by my fear of falling. Or, he says, I can throw myself in. That also gets rid of the problem, right? That's sort of what the death wish would be. Now we no longer have to suffer anxiety.

What does that mean then in terms of desire? It means that, for Lacan— and this is a fundamental difference from Freud—there isn't any life wish.

There isn't any eros. Everything is thanatos—and thanatos is a vitalism—because desire can't be satisfied. Even your satisfaction of desire is going to be a failure, because it will not satisfy this primal desire which is that of the organism. This is the point, I think, where Lacan begins to touch the metaphysical, just as Sartre did, the very function of living. Again, we can come back to that, because it has to do with the Real.

So we come back to this initial periodization in Lacan: the Imaginary, the Symbolic, and the Real. The first two are matters of development, let's say, and they are based on the fact that human beings are born as incomplete organisms and have to develop in some way, unlike some forms of life, which are fully developed when they emerge, if they even emerge. So the relationship of the Imaginary and the Symbolic, the Symbolic being language, comes from the fact that as a newborn you are *infans*. "Infant" means not speaking. So you're thrown, in a Heideggerian way, into this situation of being. In it you will discover, first of all, the Imaginary, and then you will emerge into language. These things are inseparable finally, and yet they are distinct stages about which we can say different kinds of things, and we can make different diagnoses. As for the Real, you really never can cope with that. The Real, as I said the other day, is this *Ding-an-sich* that explodes into your consciousness and that sometimes means psychosis, at other times that you can't get over it. Here is one official definition by Lacan: "the real, or what is perceived as such, is what resists symbolisation absolutely."[5] The Real is what absolutely resists linguistic formulation. So that gives you an idea of what we can't say the Real is, because that is exactly what it is: we can't say what it is. We just have to learn to do something with it.

So it turns out that Lacan's career is organized around these three things. The first seminars are about the Imaginary, or rather, they are about what the Imaginary is and how we have to develop a kind of thinking which is a little more than the Imaginary, and that would be the Symbolic. In our terms, in this class, we can say that the Imaginary is what the phenomenologists discover. Then linguistics comes along and shows that the phenomenologists are right but insufficient. They don't understand that there isn't such a thing as pure consciousness. They don't understand that there's a gap, a break, a crack in this pure consciousness. That's what the

---

5   Jacques Lacan, *The Seminar of Jacques Lacan, Book I: Freud's Papers on Technique, 1953–1954*, ed. Jacques Alain-Miller, trans. John Forrester (Cambridge: Cambridge University Press, 1988), 66.

linguists come along with. And then, at a certain moment, Lacan begins to discover the drives. There are three Freudian drives, which you know, no doubt: the oral, the anal, and the genital. That is fairly obvious stuff by now. Lacan wants to say there are other drives beyond that, because, if you extend desire and this super-desire which is the death wish, you realize that all kinds of other things can be desires. So we have the scoptic desire, the desire of looking, of visuality, for example. You know the Germans talk about eye people and ear people, *Augenmenschen* or *Ohrenmeschen*. Some people are susceptible to paintings, other people to music. Well, this is sort of Lacan's idea, because Lacan and Freud have a big problem with what Freud has to call sublimation. That is, we are not dealing with these three initial desires all the time. We do other things. How do we get libidinally invested in those other things? Well, by sublimation. But what is it? Lacan will reach the moment when he has a theory of sublimation. It's going to be called *le sinthome*, and the seminar of that name is about Joyce. Lacan, apparently, met Joyce as a young man and was always fascinated with him. But we'll leave that for now, and how that fits into the third stage will remain for us a kind of mystery.

But the work is divided along these lines—the Imaginary, then the Symbolic, then the Real and the drives. Slavoj Žižek has worked out a very interesting, elaborate, but rather convincing way of dealing with these three moments.[6] He says that in each one of them there are different emphases. Let's say you're somebody who is dominated by the Imaginary. Yes, but you can have an Imaginary set toward the Imaginary, a Symbolic set toward the Imaginary, and you can have a Real set toward the Imaginary. And the same for the Symbolic and the Real. So that gives us not three but nine different kinds, let's say, of interpretation.

Now, in the readings I have given you, the first text, "Inmixing . . .," is a talk Lacan gave at a crucial moment. I mentioned 1967. In that same year, the Americans finally realized things were going on over in France, so, at Johns Hopkins, they organized a big conference and they invited a lot of the big names. I think only Foucault and Lévi-Strauss were not there. We had Derrida. We had Barthes. Lacan agreed to come. So this was his first great trip to the United States. This text that you have is from a book which is sometimes called *The Structuralist Controversy*. The earlier versions will call it *The Languages of Criticism*. Some of it is old-fashioned. These are

---

6   Slavoj Žižek, *The Sublime Object of Ideology* (London: Verso, 1989), 145–148.

things that were current in the '60s, questions that humanists had, but a lot of it is still very pertinent, and it's a handy thing to go through, at least this one talk of Lacan, which he wrote in his Franglais. I happen to know his translator on this occasion, who was once a colleague of mine, and it would drive him crazy. He'd say, "Give me your French text so I can prepare my translation." Well, Lacan wanted to make it up as he went along. He wanted to talk it out himself, which he finally did in his broken English, and this is a kind of revision back into a little more standard English than what Lacan had. He held his audience, and he had things to say, but it is not like most of these essays. That is, he realizes that the audience knows nothing about this stuff; he has to explain everything to them, which is impossible, so he will pick up various topics. My favorite one, one of the most famous, is his account of the unconscious. I have always assumed, maybe wrongly, that he was staying in New York, and he took the train down to Baltimore for the conference, a very early train, maybe even a sleeper. So, early in the morning, he wakes up, and there, in the dawning light, is Baltimore. The upshot of this will be: *l'inconscient, c'est Baltimore à l'aube*. The unconscious is Baltimore at dawn, the scene that I'm glimpsing out of the window of my train. "When I prepared this little talk for you"—it's a lie, of course; he didn't prepare anything—"it was early in the morning. I could see Baltimore through the window and it was a very interesting moment because it was not quite daylight, and a neon sign indicated to me every minute the change of time, and naturally there was heavy traffic, and I remarked to myself that exactly all that I could see, except for some trees in the distance, was the result of thoughts, actively thinking thoughts [driving a car, opening a business, selling things, walking somewhere] where the function played by the subjects was not completely obvious. In any case the so-called *Dasein* [Heidegger's human reality] as a definition of the subject, was there in this rather intermittent or fading spectator."[7] That is to say, you're seeing the objects, the places, the buildings, the cars of all these human beings, and they're there, but you're not seeing the human subjects. The unconscious is that, Baltimore in the early morning. It is this landscape which is a landscape of human activity in which the subject is not visible.

That is not a bad notion of the unconscious, and we'll see others. Lacan's has a little extra flourish. The first definition Lacan gives of the unconscious

7   Jacques Lacan, "Of Structure as an Inmixing of an Otherness Prerequisite to Any Subject Whatsoever," 189.

is: it is structured like a language. Or the other definition: the unconscious is the language of the Other. So which is it? Let's go back to the *infans*. What is language for this *infans*? It's a murmuring all around him. He, she, whatever, doesn't know what language is. The baby has no language, but it has this *milieu*, this environment of sounds, and, occasionally, it has a warm body holding it and satisfying its wordless, unnamed desires. That warm body will be called—and this is another sort of Lacanian puzzle—*das Ding*. And we'll come back to it next time. Lacan gets it from a very early unpublished scientistic text of Freud, before the real Freud, called *Project for a Scientific Psychology*, but don't worry about that. So there is something about a primal relationship involved in this business of the Imaginary and the Symbolic. In fact, the Symbolic order is always the other. Who else would it belong to? It doesn't belong to you, but it doesn't belong to any individual other either. It is Sartrean seriality. We know the other is in it. It's like light. It's spoken all around you, and maybe even—and this is part of structuralism in general at the outer ends of its ideologies—it speaks you. Maybe you are not speaking. Maybe language is inhuman. Maybe defining what human beings are by the fact that they are speakers is not human at all. We're animals on whom this painful experience of speaking has been imposed. There are some stories to that effect. In the early nineteenth century, a child was discovered in the south of France, a feral child. Like poor Ishi, who was however grown up, there was nobody around him. He was not raised by wolves like Romulus and Remus, and he had no language. One of the great psychiatrists of the era took this boy on, and the story of this experiment was made into a movie by François Truffaut. It's called *L'Enfant sauvage*. You now know that *sauvage* means not "savage" but "wild." *The Wild Child*, it's called in English, from 1970. It tells the story of this psychiatrist's attempt to raise this boy and to teach him language. And you will see—this is the one part of the movie that's illustrative for us—learning language is this horrible pain for the child. It is a terrible racking punishment, this attempt to assimilate language. From that you can see that maybe language was not meant for us. Maybe it is not a human thing. Maybe it's something else.

In any case, the learning of language does something to us as subjects. So that's the discovery of the Symbolic. And, later I will learn that language has all kinds of places for me. I can be a subject, an object, even a verb. Lacan will illustrate that in his analysis of Edgar Allan Poe's "The Purloined Letter," which shows that the letter, which, for him, is language, has different positions, and the subject can fit into those in different ways. So I'm not just one subject. I'm multiple subjects in this structure that language has designed for me. But what about the Imaginary? Where does that come from? Language has multiple positions. Or let's say it's a three. There's me; there's an other; and then there's language, as a third position outside of both of us. But the Imaginary is two. It is always this binary thing, because it's what I see, as you now well know, in the mirror.

I'm hesitant, because one must not abuse these things, but Diderot, the editor of the *encyclopédie* in the eighteenth century wrote a very interesting text called "The Letter on the Blind." It was of great interest in that period. There was a very famous blind mathematician. Can the blind understand shapes? How can they understand shapes if they're blind from birth? Someone in fact asked that question about the mirror stage. How would a blind child possibly understand the mirror stage? You will understand that the mirror stage, like Sartre's look, is an ontic version of unity. The point of seeing the body in the mirror is that it is a unity. Before that, for the child, the child doesn't know that it's all there. It itches at certain parts. Parts of it are wet. Parts of it are hungry. It is just a mass of sensations, and now, suddenly, it sees that all those sensations are part of a central thing which is a one, and that one possibly can be my self. But we know that the idea of self is itself illusory, and we will see that the notion of the One, throughout all these thinkers from now on, is also going to be the conceptual enemy, because there is no "One." It's cracked. It's split. There is a break in it, and so on and so forth.

We will continue this next time, and we'll use this "Insistence of the Letter . . ." Briefly, for the Symbolic as he portrays it here: just limit yourself to metaphor and metonymy. That will be enough for now. And then we'll concentrate on this business of sight as an object and the look and so forth. In the meanwhile, since everything is related to everything else, we'll go through as much of Lacan as possible.

One more thing: the Freudian premise of all this is castration. You understand that, for Lacan, in Freud the male wants to avoid castration by the father. That's the Oedipus complex as well. But, in Lacan, you have to have castration. Castration means, metaphorically, that desires cannot be satisfied, and if you fail to be symbolically castrated, then you think desires can be satisfied. You think that happiness exists; you think there is such a thing as fulfillment and so forth. So take the notion of castration very symbolically, if you like, in the ordinary sense of the word, but you will come across it again and again, and you ought to know what its position is here. It is the central anchor of Lacan to orthodox Freudianism, let's say, but also its central reversal. Okay, we will go on with all this next time.

February 23, 2021

11

Genealogy of the Look

{Lacan}

I've been worrying about how we are going to fit Lacan and Althusser into this narrative we are trying to construct about the evolution of French theory, because each of them has a complicated body of work of his own. How do they fit in? As for Lacan, we can't possibly finish with him yet, because you never do that; but we can ask in what sense he influences the evolution of this theoretical-philosophical narrative. To begin with, I would say that the attacks on the ego were significantly advanced by Lacan. This will eventually result in a famous and rather idiotic poststructuralist slogan: "the death of the self." If you don't have an ego, do you have other parts of a self? No, Lacan will say: you have the drives. So these impersonal drives will supplant the personal choices of individuality and of the self. I think this can be likened to the coming of postmodernity and the emergence of the transnational institutions that operate above the nation-state. These institutions are, obviously, very far above individuals, and that determines the difference of the framework in which you and I today are living. There is a wonderful expression for this in the situation of the European nation-states: the transformation of the nation-state into the member-state. The European countries that are part of the European Union are no longer nation-states; they are member-states. I don't know what that corresponds to in this country or in Asia, for example, but it is an external sign of the larger transformations that philosophy will grapple with; we will see it reflected in Deleuze, for example.

On this point, I want to stay with Lacan for a moment to clarify his relationship to what the communists called "revisionism," which means watering down a theory so that it is liberal and agreeable to everybody. This is what Althusser will object to in so-called existentialist or humanist Marxism. Likewise, we will always have to remember that, while Freud's thought is not a sexology, it is certainly about physical symptoms. It's about sexual and psychic malfunction. So that has to be kept in the center, although, in a funny kind of way, maybe you could say that Lacan does water down that idea. Making it more metaphorical allows people to think of it in philosophical terms rather than in purely clinical terms. And the point about the clinical is, for Freudians, that this thought can never only be a theory or a philosophy. It is what in another domain is called a unity of theory and practice. That is to say, the theory is only meaningful in terms of practice, while, of course, that practice will have to be theoretical. As you might guess from the more frequent use of this expression, that is true for Marxism as well. You can't just have a Marxist idea. There has to be a practice attached to it. If there isn't, then you are already in revisionism and idealism. You're just thinking from the outside about idealistic systems. In a sense, this is true of Lacanianism as an "-ism," as the discourse of the university. Yet, despite this whole new public that he has acquired, he begins with training analysts, young doctors. So his thought begins by addressing their practice. Subsequently, he gains an immense student public, most of whom are Maoists (at a certain moment anyway), and, finally, the world public of academics, theoreticians, and all the rest. At the heart of it all there's still this problem of theory and practice. Few of us, I assume, are analysts or doctors, so we are not going to be able to read this as we should, and we ought to be aware of that.

At the very end of the last lecture, I mentioned castration. I have to say a little more about that, because it's a strange but important instance of Lacan's relationship to revision and doctrine. To begin with: Why would you want to keep the figure of castration? In Freud, the fear of castration emerges from the Oedipal situation. The father is powerful, and you might fear that he is going to do something terrible to you, as in the animal world. So, in Lacan, we will have the requirement of castration. If you aren't castrated in this figural way, you are going to be psychotic or at least neurotic. Why? Because, for Lacan, castration means giving up on satisfaction. There is no satisfaction of desire, whether figurally castrated or not. If there is something like satisfaction, it is only something that prevails for a moment, leaving us back in the same situation. There is no happiness; there is no full satisfaction or fullness.

And now we are required to talk about another thing, something always embarrassing to talk about, but we can't avoid it with Lacan. It's the term "phallus." You understand that phallus is a term of statuary. Phallus is not a penis. It isn't an organ of the body. The phallus, from an organic standpoint, is the penis in erection. That's not a thing that lasts very long, if you see what I mean. So he is not talking organically about human male bodies. No, he is talking about a moment of desire, of arousal, which comes and goes; the word he likes is "fading." Remember this notion of anamorphosis that he uses, which we see in Holbein's *Ambassadors*. The anamorphosis, for Lacan, is sort of like the phallus. It is the sign of the impossibility of satisfaction.

So don't be intimidated by this kind of language. There are ways of understanding it that are more figural, although we must constantly keep in mind that this also has a clinical aspect. This is a medical doctor evolving a contemporary adaptation of clinical work. Now, of course, people talked about the translations of these things between German, French, English, and other languages, not only between the languages of theory and praxis. Yes, there is a difference between the languages. You can say things in one language that you can't say in another. I recommend looking at the *Dictionary of Untranslatables*, edited by Barbara Cassin, because it will give you a very interesting idea of how you cannot just have a philosophical word in one language for which you have a translation. If it's an accepted translation, it's probably not right; it's probably going to be inaccurate, because there's always a slight difference between all these languages. Now this is why Lacan will have recourse not only to his diagrams, but also to the famous mathemes, these attempts at mathematical formulas. Why? We already know from structuralism: differences without positive terms. We have words for positive terms, but what about the differences between them? Every term we choose is going to betray a lack of that process-oriented relationship. And even the word "relationship" is a pretty pitiful term for this. Therefore, Lacan thinks, if you get out of language, and you understand that there's no meta-language to discuss this, then you have to invent something else, and mathemes would be one way of doing that. I would argue that these pictures and graphs are another way of doing it. Do they succeed? Well, that's another matter.

There was also a question raised, a very important one, about Lacan and history. I just want to say that, yes, you could extract from Lacan some vague kind of culture critique. In *Society Without the Father*, Alexander Mitscherlich theorized the idea of the historical weakening of the father. In Germany, after the war, either the fathers were dead, in Russian prison camps, or, if they came home—guess what?—they turned out to have been Nazis. Hence the ferocity of the German youth movement in the '60s. Three of the countries in which there were really strong youth rebellions were the three axis powers: Germany, Italy, and Japan. Why? Well, because their fathers were fascists, and the younger generation reacted strongly against that. Anyway, Marcuse used to say that the one problem with getting rid of the Oedipus complex is that you don't have that powerful authoritarian father to revolt against anymore. If you prize revolt as an expression, as a way of forming yourself, and if the father is weak or absent, then you lose that possibility of formation through revolt. So the Oedipus complex, in one sense, serves a purpose, according to him. I call these characterizations of history "culture critiques." It is the kind of thing that was often done in anthropology, or, very popular in the states a few years ago, in books like Christopher Lasch's *The Culture of Narcissism*. I don't consider that kind of theory to be anything more than impressionistic and ideological. Lacan will occasionally give voice to something that sounds a little bit like that, as will Deleuze in his theory of "control societies." I think these characterizations of the present are not terribly valuable. What I think *is* interesting in this question is his interrogation of Lucien Goldmann's question about history, to which Lacan responds that history is nothing but surprises.[1] Ah! So he is still a modernist. He means the new, change, something different. And, in Lacanian language, this response will answer a very interesting, speculative question. There can be historically new signifiers. He takes his example from Plato's Socrates. They're going

---

1   Jacques Lacan, "Of Structure as an Inmixing of an Otherness Prerequisite to Any Subject Whatsoever," 199. Goldmann's question, posed to Lacan in the discussion following his lecture: "There is no subject without symbol, language, and an object. [. . .] Is the formation of this symbolism and its modifications linked solely to the domain of the phantasm, the unconscious, and desire, or is it also linked to something called work, the transformation of the outside world, and social life? And if you admit that it is linked to these also the problem comes up: Where is the logic, where is the comprehensibility?"

to a dinner and Socrates is struck by an idea all of a sudden, so he stops. As was his custom, he stands there immobile, thinking. They leave him and go on. Night falls. And there stands Socrates at night, thinking. These societies know night in a way that we can't anymore. The upshot of this, for Lacan, is that day is a new signifier. Here, I think he is thinking of Joyce. After *Ulysses* you understand the single day as a new kind of form, which has its own unique logic, and maybe people didn't understand it that way before. So, in that sense, the Joycean day, which will become Lefebvre's everyday, becomes a new signifier. Anyway, surprises I think mean that aspect of the new: discontinuous history, a history of breaks. There is a whole theory and problem behind that which I think Lacan is getting at in his response to Goldmann.

What I'm going to try to say is that Lacan includes history in a way Freud doesn't because he includes the other. Freud is working with the sick individual. Of course, the individual has a concrete background, comes from a specific country, and so on. But, nonetheless, Freud's focus is on the individual. With Lacan, the individual is built into the system, because our individual desire is the desire of the other. So Lacan considers the social in a way that remains unelaborated in Freud. To put it even more strongly: Lacan's Freudianism, with the other built into it, is social in a way that classical Freudian psychoanalysis could never be. And I think its use to us for history and politics comes from that: any internal analysis of the psyche is going to involve this discovery of this internal dimension of the other, which Sartre had initiated after Hegel. So we'll see how this is a continuation of Sartre, in many ways, as well as a reaction against him.

Now we will go through Lacan's three stages: Imaginary, Symbolic, and Real. The Imaginary is a dualism whose illusion is based on the notion of the one. So you see how contradictory this is. This is an experience of oneness. I am that body. Of course, the child doesn't think that; it doesn't think anything. It doesn't have language yet. But it feels unity in a way it didn't before. It is on the way to discovering what Heidegger calls "my ownness." These fingers are mine; these feelings I have are mine; the skin divides me from the outside world and within which everything is somehow mine. So you are on the road there to identity, and identity is oneness, the object of attack of these poststructuralists from now on. Whenever they see the word "totality" they think "one," and that's a bad concept. Totality is bad; unification is bad; unity is bad. Why? Because, once you're locked up in the one, what do you do with the one and identity and so on? Well, for Lacanian theory, you make an ego out of it, and this is why Lacan is so violently opposed to ego therapy. Of course, he is opposed to it because it is American, although the Germans initially bring it over as psychiatry. Yes, Deleuze is an Americanophile in his way. Sartre was quite taken with America. Beauvoir says, right after the war, we loved these young Americans, our liberators, and then we got Korea and the attack on the third world; the Americans turned into just another version of oppression. But the word "Americanization" is already a word in the '20s, and it's already a bad word, because the Europeans don't want to be Americanized. So that context has to be incorporated into this kind of thinking.

But the main point about the ego is that it is a defense. It's a castle. It's all the fortifications you build up around yourself. You want to protect yourself and to defend yourself. That's your ego. So, he says, these American analysts, with their ego therapy, are encouraging people to build up all these defenses. We don't want the defenses! To be alive is to be open to all these things, including anxiety, including fear. The first one to really theorize that in the psychoanalytic tradition, a very interesting figure, was Wilhelm Reich. In his book *Character Analysis*, which Lacan endorses, he approves of Reich's description of the ego. Reich invented his own theory of sexual politics. Alone in the Freudian circle, he was a communist. He was thrown out of the Freudian circle, to be sure, and then, later on, he was thrown out of the Communist Party as well. He came over to the United States and the rest of his career is rather sad. But he made an early analysis of fascism based on sexual repression and the idea that it's only by getting rid of all these sexual taboos and so on that you develop a force of resistance and revolt among the workers. So a very interesting figure in the '20s, but that's the line in which Lacan inscribed this critique of the ego.

However, we do have an ego, and you could call it "identity" if you like. Remember that Sartre thought we all had it, but only as an object for consciousness, because, in the Sartrean language, we can't *be* anything. Every so often we feel that. Is this "my ownness," *mein Eigentum* (as in Stirner)? I think Heidegger is talking about something even more deeply existential than that, or something that can't be named, because you only have one "my ownness": your existence, *je mein Eigenes*. So we are really deep in existentialism when we say that Identity is what Deleuze would call a bad concept, because it would seem to apply to everybody else. Everybody has an identity. But that isn't the way it works. We have no access to other people's identity. So there is an existential situation here which we are not able to generalize. Identity is part of that. Identity is a kind of popular version of Freud's notion of the ego, which is a little bit different. He calls it the superego, the interiorization of the father. It is the place of commands and the law, and, of course, it is that for Lacan as well. The place of the *cogito*—I think therefore I am—should be the place for unity, because there is only that, but even unity requires another number, doesn't it? How can you think the one all by itself? Now that is why this place of unity, bad unity, will also be the place of dualism. I see myself in the mirror, and so the mirror stage is both those things. And, of course, it is Imaginary. It is the realm of images, because images are what I see in the mirror, and they can be of at least two types: visual or auditory, which Lacan will identify as two of the drives. So, in a sense, when you talk about the movement from the Imaginary to the Symbolic and then the Real, it looks like it's going forward, but, in another sense, he is going back to this bad unity of the Imaginary and trying to turn it into something more tangible, which is the visual image, the scoptic drive, the drive to look, and the acoustic image. He doesn't say much about the acoustic image, but I should recommend to you a wonderful book by a colleague of Slavoj Žižek. This is Mladen Dolar, who has often been with us at Duke, and his book is called *A Voice and Nothing More*, about the auditory and the voice as an object of desire.

So is there a good dualism? After all, linguistics was supposed to be the place of the binary opposition. Yes, but, in this dualism, there are two positive terms, that is, there's me—I'm an identity—and then there's my image, whatever that is. Presumably, that is my image of myself, or maybe my image as seen by other people, by the big Other. It's also, in a way, my name; that's the auditory part, if you like. As I've said before, the parents call me a name. They reify me into the unity of personhood by naming me. For Lacan, that's a repression of the so-called subject of desire, and its replacement by this reified term, which is my image in the eyes of others and in particular of my parents. So when we talk about identity, we're talking about all kinds of pictures of myself that are formative for me. These are Sartrean alienations. These are my being-for-others, and I can't get away from that. I always have to deal with that in a funny kind of way.

We go on now to the Symbolic. There is an uncertainty here. Is this developmental? Is it diachronic? Is it telling us something that happens to the *infans*? Of course. What is the timing of this development? Lacan really doesn't particularly want to respect this synchronic-diachronic opposition, so these things overlap in a way. But we do have several events. We have the mirror stage, and then, later on, we have the Oedipal stage. How is he going to deal with that in his linguistics? He will come to this idea: the name of the father. It isn't the father. Who knows what that is? As Joyce says, the paternal function is always a matter of fantasy or conjecture. But the name of the father is very precise. It is part of this whole linguistic network into which we are taken up when we fall into language, because, in a way, we do fall into language. We are thrown into language, Heidegger might say. Language is all around us when we're born. We don't know what it is, just all these noises. Little by little we will recognize some of them. Some of them will operate, like the mirror, by reifying us. You have the example of Genet, of another kind of reification. I'm called "thief," and then I'm stuck with that word. Is it just reputation? No, it's a word which has immobilized me. But the important thing is this fact of being assumed into language.

Now we get to the Lacanian unconscious. What is it? It's structured like a language. It is the discourse of the other. What does all that mean? In a sense, it's a losing proposition to begin with, because the unconscious always makes us think of consciousness. For Lacan, consciousness is this varying thing. The French have a nice word, invented by an early psychiatrist: *niveau* or "level." You know, some people in various stages have lower or higher "attention." That is, they are less aware, more susceptible to things. So consciousness can now be thought of as this variation of *niveaux*, but, probably, this is not the way to talk about it, inasmuch as consciousness isn't some thing. Think of dreams. In dreams, there is no self-consciousness. I pose that as something for you to explore. Sometimes you are in a dream, but you're in it as an actor in the dream. A dream is the place in which the nature of consciousness is clearest. You think you're not conscious during a dream, but in fact, yes, that is what pre-reflexive consciousness is: this dream-like state without a center. Only then do you get centered by language. I would say that none of these people really believes in self-consciousness, or that they think that's an imaginary concept, that you can't really be conscious of yourself. At any rate, the problem with unconsciousness is that it's constantly throwing you back. Unconsciousness might seem to mean pre-consciousness, only slightly conscious, but Lacan wants to say it's none of those things. It has nothing to do with consciousness. It is preferable not to think of it as a state.

According to Lacan, the language of Freud misled us and him in all kinds of ways. Lacan is reinventing Freud, making people read Freud for the first time. They have never seen these texts properly. This is like Protestantism, where you take a population that has never read the Bible before, and maybe have never read at all before, and you go back to the original Bible, an original, pure Christianity. Lacan will thus introduce us to the real Freud, but, in doing so, he is going to make some changes, because, he says, even Freud didn't quite know what he was doing since he didn't have linguistics. Yes, innovations in linguistics were going on at the same time, but Freud didn't go to Geneva. He would go to the mountains in Switzerland or—where every good German-speaker wants to go—to Italy. Freud was a great amateur of archeology. Italy, Rome, Pompeii— that's paradise. So Freud didn't know about Saussure or linguistics, but he anticipated cut much of it, so Lacan just puts them together to give us what Freud *would have said* if he had known what he was talking about, if he had had the language of linguistics. Althusser will do something vaguely like that with Marx. Anyway, that's the premise of his work.

Freud will say, for example, that the unconscious is a boiling cauldron of desires. I'm conscious, but, underneath, there is all this stuff going on in me that I can from time to time become aware of, but not all the time. I don't want to be aware of it all the time. Lacan says forget about the cauldron, about that image of the unconscious. The so-called unconscious is really a language. Let's just limit ourselves to two aspects of this language. First of all, it is a set of categories. I have all kinds of things going on in me, memory, trauma, desires in the present and so on. But I don't know how to think those things. So the unconscious will be these linguistic categories that turn all these formless, unspoken things into something with which I can operate. The two basic ones will be metaphor and metonymy, the great dualism that both Lévi-Strauss and Lacan learn from Jakobson. We can just limit it to that. "The Instance of the Letter" introduces this idea. Lacan is going to say that meanings will take care of themselves. It's the relationship of the signifiers to each other that's really going to count. These signifiers are discontinuous. They're words, but they're also more than words. Images can be signifiers. We can have new signifiers, as I've said. Meaning comes about by the sequence of these signifiers, and since we're talking about linguistics, that means the sentence. You all know what the hermeneutic circle is. The hermeneutic circle means, if I'm starting to say something, you don't know what it's going to be about or what it's going to end in—it is even worse in German because the verb doesn't come until the end—so you're holding on to each of these words as time passes, and it's not until you get to the complete sentence that you know what I meant at the beginning. How is that possible? It is a circle. In the beginning, I am understanding something that I can't possibly understand until it's all over. That is what the movement of signifiers is, but in our psychic life it's the basic experiences that I retain and remember. Each of these various moments is a signifier forming the signifying chain. But everybody has their own signifying chain, and that will be the movement of these signifiers from one to the other.

So that's what's called metonymy, and I described its operation for you earlier in the semester. It is defining a thing in terms of what's next to it, what is in proximity to it, its contiguity. Then there's metaphor, defining a thing in terms of what it's like, that is to say, in terms of substitution. And when Freud works on the dream, he finds that it has two essential processes, which is *Verschiebung* and *Verdichtung*, displacement and compression. Displacement means I move from this to that on the horizontal, metonymic line, whereas condensation means I associate all these things with one another. This means that my unconscious organizes my experiences in these categories for me, but this organization is not immediately visible or obvious to me. The unconscious—in that sense, yes, the poststructuralists are right—is speaking me, is organizing me, and language is something . . . outside of me? Remember that language is other people. It is other people who have language, but in a serial sense. No one possesses it, but everybody else possesses it, and none of those possesses it individually; but someone else does, until you make the whole tour. So how does that work? It begins with the idea that desire is metonymic. Let's say, just to be very crude about it, that your first love object is your mother. Then the next ones will all be substitutes for your mother, right? So this is a contiguity, a horizontal path of metonymy. Desire is that metonymy which moves from one of these objects of desire to another.

What is metaphor? Ah! It is the symptom. Instead of one thing, you substitute another. For some deeper problem, which you don't want to think about, you're going to substitute a pain in the arm. The great conductor Bruno Walter went to Freud because he had a frozen, paralyzed arm. For a conductor that's not very good, right? So he thought Freud would ask him all about his sex life and childhood. He just gave him a check-up and told him to take a vacation—in Italy, of course, which is where you take a vacation if you're Viennese; and, of course, the symptoms went away. But normally this matter of symptoms is what you discover as the replacement for the real thing.

Okay, so the unconscious is those two things. The minute we think we're thinking about one thing and doing one thing, we're already doing all those other things, and it's organized for us in those terms. In that sense, it is structured like a language. *Like* a language, because it isn't a language. Baltimore at dawn. A lot of buildings and empty cars and nobody in the streets. But it is also a set of signifiers. Signifiers are also not people, only signs of other people. Other people have been there and are there still. Okay, but there's something else. How else is the unconscious like a language? Well, a language includes syntax, and that means that a language is going to have a very weird thing in it which we call the first person. What is the first person? I don't know if anybody plays bridge anymore, but in bridge there are two sets of partners. One partner runs the game, and then the other partner can withdraw, and that's called in English "the dummy," and in French *le mort*, the dead man, the place of the dead. Well, in a sense, the first person is sort of like that. Jakobson called these things "shifters," because anybody can use them. Everybody else *does* use them, but they have no reference. When I say "I" I think it means me, but when you use it, it obviously means somebody else. So it is a syntactical place. In that sense the unconscious is also a set of syntactical positions, and we know what those are called. Those are the subject, the I, but they could also be the object, the verb, whatever you like. This was the allegory that Lacan was using for Poe's "Purloined Letter," because the letter moves around to different places, different people have them, it means different things, and so Poe's letter was a perfect symbol of how, for the unconscious, you could be in various positions all at once.

We have to look at what fantasy is, by the way. Fantasy is a narrative, a primal narrative. It's a narrative that the subject uses and places himself or herself in, but which is not a kind of permanent set-up. The emergence of this primal narrative in French is called *fantasme*, which doesn't mean "fantasy." We say "phantasm," as well. It means a narrative, this primal story, and we all have this. Our desires are molded around this first narrative. Evidently this fantasy is an impersonal fantasy "a child is being beaten," to take Freud's famous case study—but you can see how it is subject to all kinds of permutations. I, a child, am being beaten. I beat a child. Someone else beats a child. So, in a way, this primal fantasy has in it a number of psychic positions. And, if you want to talk about cures, then you should note that in Freud a cure is when symptoms go away, when a person can function, though, later, he wonders whether there's ever a cure in that sense. In Lacan, at least as Žižek interprets him, the cure is changing the primal fantasy. You never get rid of the primal fantasy, but you can modify it. So it would be modifying this primal syntax in which you take a position. A position is assigned to you . . . by what? By language? Althusser is going to call that "interpellation." The Brits translate this as "hailing." You hail a cab. It's someone designating that position for you. At any rate, we can modify ourselves maybe by changing those fantasy positions. It is a modification of this language into which I'm thrown. The phantasm, the primal fantasy, is also contemporaneous with the way I'm seen by the other, my image from the other. In fact, any image I have of myself comes from the other. I don't have any way of seeing myself, because the self in the mirror is not a self, really; it's just an idea. So my unconscious is the discourse of the other, of course, because the child emerges in this discourse which *is* the other and finds images of itself readymade within that discourse. Its desire is put together out of these already alienated things. In other words, we are not exactly alienated by language, since language is alienation in advance. So it is not as though we became ourselves and then we were alienated. No, we are assumed into language, which is supposed to be this powerful moment for Lacanians, moving from the Imaginary to the Symbolic, this sense of articulation by language, but it is already an alienated one. Presumably, in Lacan, the cure would then entail knowing the degree to which I am alienated by the other.

Then the drives. What is all this scoptic stuff? This bit about the look is a little set-piece in the seminar. That's why I gave it to you. It's sort of complete in itself and a brilliant performance. Roger Caillois was a remarkable essayist of the period and worked a lot of scientific material over. He wrote about, for example, *mimétisme*, the way butterflies disguise themselves against their background, the camouflage that certain kinds of insects and animals make, and his whole point is that, no, they don't imitate their surroundings.[2] How could they do that? They don't even know their surroundings. It's that they are a dimension of the butterflies, that

---

2   Roger Caillois, "Mimicry and Legendary Psychasthenia," trans. John Shepley, *October*, no. 31 (1984): 16–32.

their surroundings are sort of invented by them. I don't know how exactly one would follow this notion of *mimétisme* through, but it's important for Lacan because it shows that there's something other than the look at work here. Remember that the look is divided. This drive is split between, let's say, the eye and the look. I use my eyes to see things, but the look is something else. I want to say, obviously, that this is very Sartrean. It comes from Sartre's look. Lacan finally obliquely signals Sartre as the origin of this. What he does with Sartre, of course, is to say that this look he is talking about can be thought of as a guy peeping through a keyhole. It is not a neutral look; it has an ontic content because it involves shame, sex, desire. So Sartre was wrong. The look is not about being; it's about desire. Okay, so Lacan makes his point. To enter Lacanianism from Sartreanism, you have to abandon all this language of being, all this ontology and being-for-others, and move into a place in which your fundamental drive is derived from exactly that: desire.

So when Goldmann asks Lacan if he doesn't believe in work, the prole-tariat, and so on, I think the question is poorly posed. That is, we should have asked Lacan, "What about the project?" In Sartre and Heidegger both, the whole idea of time is bound up in that of the project. If you want to call that desire, that's fine, but the project doesn't always look like desire. So what is the place in Lacan for the project? That involves notions of sublimation and the like, which have, I believe, never really been solved by psychoanalysis. But, at any rate, that would perhaps have made for a more interesting discussion.

Here I put it to you that Lacan gets involved in a discussion of Diderot's "Letter on the Blind," which is a very dazzling mise-en-scène of problems about blindness and about number and perception and so on. He uses this Caillois stuff. But essentially what he wants to say is: Sartre limited his notion of being-for-others to one look. That is, we have the other person looking at me, reifying me, stealing my landscape, appropriating everything around me. I'm no longer a center. I am a periphery of this absent center who is the other, absent because I can't look back, or, if I do look back, suddenly that is a reaction, turning myself back into a center. I've recuperated the world, but my world is stolen from me by this look of the other. What Lacan wants to say is: let's not limit it to that other. And, of course, in Sartre, there doesn't have to be anybody there. As he says in his example from the war, you're trying to go through some area, and you notice there is a house up there, so suddenly you feel visible, vulnerable; you don't know if anybody is in that house, but if there were, you could be seen, and therefore your dimension of being-for-otherness is there. So Sartre doesn't necessarily identify it with a person, but there has to be an other for this experience to be fully felt. Now Lacan says what I'm calling the look, as an object—it will eventually be an object of desire—is the fact that I am always visible. I am always vulnerable. My world is itself visible. That visibility includes me as an object. The other has now become the big Other. You can see that this is an enlargement of the Sartrean interaction between two people into a whole structure of the world. Worldness is being thrown into being-seenness. I put it to you this way because it comes up here and Merleau-Ponty is being drawn on, and, little by little, one gets to understand what the point of the earlier discussions of painting are: in a way, this is sort of a dimension of the world itself, this being-looked-at. Therefore, we could say—and, in a sense, this corresponds to the very history of ideas and religion and even modern science—this look, to which I am fatally exposed in my very being, is what we call light. Light is the look. Do we see light? I see some light, but light itself as a phenomenon is everywhere. You might be tempted to go back to Zoroaster and light in Iranian religion, the sacredness of light and the struggle of light and darkness, all the way up to Einstein and the speed of light. Light is this very strange thing which modern science claims to have turned into an object, or to have discovered as an object, but, in fact, it is the element of my vulnerability as being in the world.

I'm mixing, as you see, languages from various philosophers here, some Heidegger or Sartre into this Lacanian process, because I think that is the basis of it all. What do we do with this vulnerability, this break, this schism, between the eye and the look, which is there in Merleau-Ponty? I told you that, in Merleau-Ponty, you have the passive and the active. That is to say, you touch with your hands, but you can also be touched in your hands, and those things are incompatible. You don't feel them at the same time. Some of you were scandalized that Sartre would say either you look with your eyes or your eyes are looked at, but you can't do both. Think then about passive and active. In Lacan, it's this schism, this *schisme*—that will become schizophrenia later on—between the eye and the look that provides one form of the break that I can never get rid of. So that's the point at which, miraculously in some sense, we get aesthetics. We get to painting, and we find out what painting really is. It is the place in which the gaze is given a place of rest, so to speak. The painting is going to absorb in itself all the light, all the look, and suddenly, the look as vulnerability and anxiety, as this alien object, will for me be somehow momentarily safe. As he says also, it is a trap for the gaze. It is a place in which the gaze can roam around and be safe. It is a way in which the anxieties of the look can somehow be domesticated and given a moment of rest—I think he actually uses that expression—and therefore the very aesthetic of painting is defined in a way. And Lacan, of course, as a follower of Surrealism, is in the very world of painting all the time, and he is a collector. He collected one of the great and mysterious and obscene paintings of all time, which is the Courbet *Origin of the World*. So this matter of what painting does for us: yes, why should people be wasting their time on painting pictures, buying them and selling them? Isn't it just representation? No, it's not representation. It is this place in which my gaze can be captured and can roam around as in its own reserve, and, in fact, he uses the term reserve in the sense in which we talk about reservations, enclosed spaces. And, here, you get this little story of the can, which I will return to in a moment.

There are several anecdotes of his that I want to mention. The one in the essay on the Symbolic involves two children and two doors. It's very touching, I think. On the doors are a pair of foreign words, and what they both signify is: "bathroom." They signify the lower bodily functions. The children are on a train, and it stops in front of these doors, and they assume that what's on the doors is the name of the place that the train is stopping. So the boy says, "Look, we're at *dames*, we're at 'ladies.'" He assumes that's the name of this place. And his sister says, "No, you idiot. Don't you see we're at 'gentlemen?'"[3] This goes very far, this touching anecdote. These children, their whole future, their destiny is there in this little story, the destiny of gender or sex and love is there in this misunderstanding. So this is the way, in a sense, that the chain of signifiers functions. They are all alike, and yet, in their likeness, they are different, and that difference is the difference of gender.

Now with the little tin can. He's out on a fishing boat. There is this burst of light from the tin can, pure light being transmitted. Then there is this stupid joke from the fisherman he is with: "*Do you see it? Well, it doesn't see you!*"[4] It stands out. It is a stain, a spot. The stain, the blind spot, is the

---

3   See Jacques Lacan, "The Insistence of the Letter in the Unconscious," 119.

4   Jacques Lacan, *The Seminar of Jacques Lacan*, Book XI, 95, italics in original.

place of the subject in all this, because, in Lacan—like in Sartre—the eye and the gaze are incompatible. And in this world of visibility, there is a blind spot, or a kind of stain like the anamorphosis of the painting, which is you, but you're not there, because you can't see yourself. Look at how he describes this. Here are these fishermen. They're in Brittany in the old days, a poor area. They're eking out a living. Here is this not wealthy but privileged kid with them, this bourgeois adolescent who goes to school and can read and write and is cultured. He sticks out like a sore thumb. When Lacan is telling this story these guys are all dead. Tuberculosis reigns in this area. This industry is gone. All of a sudden, you see that he is the blind spot socially in the middle of all this. And, in a sense, everybody knows this. So this is one of the moments—I won't say Lacan is in History—but he is certainly in the world of classes in this anecdote. You are the blind spot in other people's world. It's a blind spot for you, this piece of floating garbage in this group of working-class people who have agreed to take you out fishing. So the "I" is there, but in its absence. That's the kind of play that is characteristic of Lacan.

One more term that I haven't had occasion to talk about here, because I don't think that any of our readings really deals with it directly. It is the *objet petit a*. The object *a*. Why little *a*? Because big-letter *A* is the big Other, *l'Autre*. And small-letter *a*, what's that? That's the object of desire. It is a separate object, but it has some relationship to the other. Does it have to be the desire of the other? Yes, because, in some very general sense, it comes to me from the other. It doesn't have to be a sexual matter, or even a matter of love. It is something that has a kind of symbolic meaning for me, this *objet petit a*, and throughout Lacan's career, in any case, the specialists have shown us that he changes the meaning of it all the time. But it is important because, if we're going to have desire—lack and frustration and death drive—we need an object for this, but it has to be something that has an intimate relationship to the subject and to the other. And so it is this little piece associated with the other. Does that mean directly associated with the other? Let's say it is associated with an otherness which is, of course, that of language. The tin can, I think, is an *objet petit a*. But so are many of these things. The *tâche*, the stain, is the *objet petit a* which I can't see anymore, the blind spot, and you know how the blind spot functions. Scotoma is when part of your field of vision is blocked off, like a *tâche*. Related to this is the *ocellus* that he talks about, which is, apparently, in camouflage, the spot that reacts to light on the organism but is not yet an eye. I understand that, in evolutionary theory, one of the most complicated problems of all is where the eye comes from. Darwin didn't solve it. The eye is so complicated that you can't simply say the eye is an evolutionary product of the need to see. But the relationship between that development and these things that look like eyes on the organism is very curious as well. Lacan is just dumping all of these ocular paradoxes in here for this tremendous demonstration of his.

But what does that do to the mirror stage, this whole business? It means that, in the mirror stage, we can see everything but ourselves. It means that the idea that we're looking at ourselves is a complete illusion; we're not seeing ourselves at all because we can't. Meanwhile, there is this whole dramatization of lack, where the whole point of desire is that it is not satisfied, that we lack it. So too with this famous phallus, a symbol of lack. He writes it Φ- because nobody has it. And, of course, at least so he believes, this is not a gendered reference, because women don't have it either, so it's a universal in that sense, this lack. Meanwhile, later on, one of the most scandalous ideas of Lacan is the famous idea that there is no sexual relation, in which the two sexes are posed as having incompatible modes of what I guess you have to call "satisfaction," but that's not quite what he means. I once heard a brilliant lecture by Badiou in his broken English in which he luminously laid out this field in which one sex or gender is trying to achieve something which the other doesn't. Well, this is Sartre again, isn't it? In love, the point is that each person wants to be loved, but you can't have both of those things together simultaneously. Either I get loved and get satisfied, but the other doesn't, or the other person gets loved and satisfied but I don't. These are like passive and active. These are incompatible ontologically. It doesn't mean people don't fall in love, or that people don't have sexual relations. It means that, ontologically, the point of these two things—if they are two—is that they are ontologically incommensurable. That is later Lacan, over which much ink has also been spilled. You may want to say that this is sexist, though there is a Lacanian feminism. One of the feminist schools in Paris today is very heavily Lacanian. I think French feminism, which we'll look at later on, has really two tendencies: a lot of them are Derrideans, but certainly there is a Lacanian formation in which feminism is very strong indeed. So one can always make these accusations, but there are also other ways of thinking about this problem.

Next time we go on—I won't say to the Marxist version of this—but to the form linguistics is going to take when it comes to Marx in the work of Althusser. And, as I've told you, there's a relationship there. Jacques-Alain Miller is a Maoist student of Althusser's. Althusser invited Lacan to come and lecture at the École normale, so there are intimate relations. Some people think Althusser was analyzed by Lacan. I think he was analyzed by a student of Lacan. But there are enough relations there to raise all sorts of supplementary questions. So we leave it with that today.

February 25, 2021

12

Class Struggle in Theory

{Althusser}

Lacanianism, or Freudianism, doesn't seem to be a very political affair, and you may not have understood the meaning of this immense enlargement of Lacan's audience in the '60s, but, with Althusser, it will become more significant. We might think of the '60s, first of all, from an American perspective, where the two major domestic political events, which are conjoined, are the civil rights movement and the expansion of the university system. The first expansion of the university is very important. It is the one that happens after World War II with the G.I. Bill. Suddenly, universities take on all kinds of people who could never have afforded college before. The university of the '30s is a very class-restrictive thing, even in terms of teaching, limited numbers of professors and so on. Europe continues in that vein much longer. It never has an expansion on the scale of the United States. European colleagues of mine only recently had lecture classes of a thousand people. Of course, we have many private universities, whereas the European universities, at least on the continent, are public.

Anyway, you can see the expansion of the American university system from 1958, when the new campuses in California open and the 1960 Master Plan for Higher Education is promulgated. There is a tremendous influx of students. And the '60s will, of course, be the epoch of student revolutions, great student movements not only in America but in all these countries. Remember that, beyond this, there is another presence—I've insisted on it a little bit—that of China and the Red Guards, in which student-age people travel all over China and bring about all kinds of changes, not always non-violent ones. If we're talking in terms of mass demonstrations, maybe there have always been mass demonstrations, but I think this is a much more recent phenomenon, as with parties, inasmuch as the very systems of representative government have been relatively recent. Yet the first great mass demonstration was the May 4th Movement in China in 1919, which was the revolt of Chinese students and lots of others against the Treaty of Versailles, which reimposed the treaty ports and was favorable to Japan. So you will have to keep the Chinese '50s and '60s in the background as well.

In France, this is not immediately connected. May '68 begins as a student revolt in Nanterre and continues in that way. But you have to remember that France has known, besides its own Vietnam, the Algerian War, which is ended by treaty in 1962, but which brings General de Gaulle back to power in 1958. 1958 is then the beginning of the Fifth Republic, which is to say the beginning of the modernization of France. France before 1958 in politics and in other ways is a relatively traditional place. I like to say that, in most places, architecturally and so forth, Balzac still would have recognized rural France and many parts of Paris. After de Gaulle, after Gaullism and the Fifth Republic, that begins to change, and France then becomes a modern technocratic capitalist state with a different dynamic. The Algerian War was a period of universal repression. That is, you didn't make protests or anything in the middle of the Algerian War. Boris Vian wrote a song called "The Deserter" and was immediately prosecuted; the song was banned. The Communist Party was not really against the Algerian War and therefore the government would pursue Party members so loosely that the one rather famous and successful network of opposition to the war would hold its meetings in the cellar of a French Communist Party member, because the government never thought to surveil him. So you have all kinds of things going on. There is obviously a connection there, once again outside of France: the Vietnam War. There, the American student protests will have their reverberation in France, in Germany, in England. The first big student demonstration against the war is actually in Berlin in the early '60s, and the Vietnam War will always be there behind the scenes as this fundamental mobilizer.

So much to explain. Why is this population of students so important for the development of theory? Althusser has a relatively small group of students, Althusserian students, Marxist students, but the influence is far more general, and I would say people are frightened about this. Althusser is seemingly a frightening figure. Now that we know a good deal more about his personality, we understand that he was, on the contrary, a very conflicted person, very unsure of himself, not at all an authoritarian personality, and we may come back to that a little later. But, in this period, the Althusserians terrorize everybody, and this will be part of what we want to look at, because they bring about a new kind of what's called "ideology critique," or better still—because the German registers it better, I think—*Ideologiekritik*. This is a little more than just ideological analysis. This is a form of linguistic terrorism, as it were, and, in France, this is deeply rooted in Althusserianism for reasons that we'll want to show. Another fact of interest, and I don't know what to make of it, is that Althusser was an Algerian. In Algeria, you call the French settlers *colons*, which comes from the same word as "colonizer," obviously. He is a *colon*. So is Derrida. And, of course, Fanon was involved in the Algerian war as well, but as a *Martiniquais*; and that's a source of a different mode of thought. But, of course, Althusser was also in World War II, and all this is marked a little bit, by people of a certain generation, by the Resistance. So all of that is coming together in this period of the '60s.

I hasten to say that Althusser did not support the student movement in May '68. The students felt that the time was right for revolution in France. The Communist Party decided the time was not ripe for revolution, and instead they made an arrangement with the government which increased wages and was based on the very powerful communist unions. It was advantageous to a lot of people and the Party, but the students felt it was a betrayal. So May '68 is both a moment of jubilation and triumph and also a moment of defeat, but, after that, the intellectual experience of France will essentially be that of defeat, so we have to take that into account. Much of what we call the '60s is therefore really happening in the '70s. This is rather complicated. But that background has to be there as you understand how these seemingly very technical texts that seem to be about minor problems—even in terms of communism or Marxism—create such a commotion, all these petty distinctions of Althusser's. That is part of the interest for us.

After '68, Althusser remained in the Party. I told you it was a period of institutionalization. In the government, that means Gaullism and the strengthening of France, but France had always been a centralized state. You have to understand that. But, on the Left, it means the increasing sense that the Party is too rigid, too orthodox, and too repressive, and so new forms of oppositional Marxism will begin to appear. One was there already for quite a while: Trotskyism. After that, underneath the surface, there is, of course, Maoism, and we'll see today a little bit what that means theoretically for Althusser, because at least two of Mao Zedong's texts "On Contradiction" and "On Practice"—are fundamental to his work. After that there are varieties of other oppositional Marxisms, and, finally, there's anarchism. I would say that many of these anti-communisms lead to anti-Marxism. Foucault is in particular a complicated case, because he was of course a Party member when he was a student of Althusser. He is expelled from the Party, and he has been understood to be anti-Marxist—that isn't so clear, as we will see when we get to him—but certainly anti-communist in some way which is still on the Left. And, in France, a country in which there was a fascism in World War II, there still is still a very powerful religious presence of the church, so the words "Left" and "Right" still mean something. We will have occasion to come back to some of these things.

Now I want to show you several things. First of all, the two major concepts I want you to be aware of, which I think are the fundamental contributions of something that you might want to call "Althusserianism" to theory—I would rather consider it theory than philosophy, although Althusser is a philosopher. He is training young philosophers in the central place in which philosophers are trained in France, the École normale supérieure. Sartre went there and got the highest marks. Beauvoir went there and got the second highest marks. Lots of the people you're going to read passed through the École normale. And, while Althusser is there, there was also a young instructor working there whose name is Derrida. Althusser's student Foucault has just graduated and will shortly publish his first book, the famous *Madness and Civilization, Histoire de la folie*, which Althusser admires greatly. And then there are interrelationships. We don't even know all of those. I was surprised to learn Althusser had connections to Deleuze. Of course, they were both Spinozists, and Spinoza is somebody we're going to have to talk about in a minute. But I was doubly surprised to find out that the very essay I gave you, "How Do We Recognize Structuralism," had a profound impact on Althusser himself. They had a correspondence about it.

So you have to understand that centralization in France not only indicates the state, but also Paris. There are reasons for people not to want to live in Paris, I guess. The provinces are attractive. You could be a regionalist. There was a famous *Breton* movement. You know the question that Montesquieu raises in his Persian Letters: How can you be a Persian? *Comment peut-on être Persan? Comment peut-on être Breton?* How can you be a Breton? Because Brittany is a place in which the language has been repressed by centralization, and in which a standard French has been imposed, as all over the rest of France. And there are all other kinds of funny things I could say about this centrality of Paris, but Paris is this Petri dish in which all this stuff is going on, in which people are either talking to each other or fighting with each other, in which everybody knows what everybody else is saying, and therefore is taking a position with respect to their "discourses," another fundamental term in this period. In that respect, since I've mentioned this, I want to mention also for those of you who really want to look much further into Althusser, this fine book, I think, by Warren Montag called *Althusser and His Contemporaries.* It is a remarkable piece of historical reconstruction. Montag knows this period very well, knows all the people involved. And I will be drawing on that a little bit, although I have a somewhat different reading of Althusser than he does.

I think everything connects to the two most important concepts in Althusser. The first is one that you might not have noticed in all of this. It's what one can call the "mode of production." This is the Marxist word for society, but a mode of production is more than a society. It's a much more general term. So our mode of production is capitalist, yes, but there is an American capitalism, a Russian capitalism, an Indian capitalism, an English capitalism, and each one has its own specific histories and peculiarities. Would we want to say—the old expression was "socialism with Chinese characteristics"—that today we have "capitalism with Chinese characteristics"? I don't know. Each of these social formations has different characteristics, but, overall, the universal form of society is called a mode of production, and, in that sense, capitalism is distinct from other modes of production. In the Marxist tradition, you will find one place in which Marx develops all this, and it is in these notes published as the *Grundrisse.* There is a long section on modes of production that precede capitalism.[1] They are, first of all, tribal society, primitive society,

---

1   Karl Marx, "Forms Which Precede Capitalist Production," in *Grundrisse* (London: Penguin, 1993), 471–514.

whatever you want to call it. Then there is ancient society. That's Greece, and that mode of production is a certain form of slavery. Then you have the Asiatic mode of production. That's a moment of the great empires, and a tributary mode in which the villages and peasants pay tribute rather than taxes to the central empire, and that's of course China, Japan at a certain moment, various states in India. Then there's feudalism. What is the difference between the Asiatic mode and feudalism? In feudalism, the emperor is gone, and feudalism is dispersed among smaller units which are self-sufficient, and the peasants, who are being protected by a given noble—that also involves tribute—they support the noble with goods and so forth. And, finally, capitalism.

Is this a direct line? Well, people have said capitalism has never emerged from any other mode of production but feudalism, and the proof of that is not only Europe, where capitalism did emerge, but also Japan, which had its own unique kind of feudalism. But there is a quarrel then about linear evolution. Is this a straight line out of these things or are there multiple paths, multiple evolutions in society? That is one problem. Another one is a very serious debate on whether there exists such a thing as the Asiatic mode of production, or, as it's sometimes also called, oriental despotism, what has also been theorized as hydraulic society. These are societies in which the entire population has had to be mobilized for the great projects of irrigation and dams, and therefore that kind of society necessitated the centralization under some kind of despot or emperor. But this has been a source of dispute. After Marx's death, Engels would leave it out of his version of all this, and the more suspicious and certainly anti-communist theories of this (Wittfogel!) suggest that it's because he—like Stalin after him—knew unconsciously that that was what their socialism was, an oriental despotism, and therefore that they would do well to leave it out of their public statements and never mention it again. Well, that's an interesting theory in its own right. The third dispute that springs up about all these things is how power is organized. This is, obviously, going to come in the wake of the questions that were raised by Marxist anthropology. As we saw with Lévi-Strauss, there was an awakening of interest in so-called primitive societies, how they function, which then became, on the one hand, a utopianism, and on the other hand, a question about power and how power starts. What is the relationship of power to these various modes of production? Now you're going to see that that involves all kinds of secondary problems that you might not expect. It involves questions of the structure of society, the famous base and superstructure, which is allegedly found in classical Marxism, even though Marx only mentions it once, and in the introduction to an earlier version of the money section of *Capital*, which he published in a hurry in the late '50s under the title *A Contribution to the Critique of Political Economy* before he went back to work on *Capital*. This is the so-called critique of political economy, which absorbs some of that, but it is only mentioned once in this rather important introduction.

This interest in power will then gradually move to how power and authority is enforced, and there will be questions which, in the Marxist tradition, relate of course to questions of revolution. The first theorist who asked questions like this in a rather different and original way is Gramsci in Italy, and Althusser will have his differences—his "conversation"—with Gramsci. And, finally, there will be Mao Zedong's pronouncements on these things, followed by Althusser's notion of what a mode of production is and how it functions. So that's one strand out of which a whole lot of different positions will emerge, and in which Althusser will be trying to solve theoretical problems about this rather traditional formulation in the Marxist tradition.

Althusser's second great innovation has to do with the concept of ideology. You will see how one of Althusser's problematics is going to be concerned with the functioning of society, another with the structure of subjectivity. Now that means there will emerge from these two lines of inquiry a certain way of interrogating texts and of identifying enemies. Let's look at those before going on to ideology. There are three basic critiques of Althusserian positions. It is easier to identify the enemies than to identify his own positions, which are constantly evolving. He is questioning himself, constantly issuing new versions of his ideas, but the adversaries remain the same. Let's first look at the principal enemy, which will take us to one aspect of the revision of the notion of ideology. Before this, in the Marxian field, you have a kind of generalized notion of ideological content. You have a notion of certain kinds of fascist ideology, petty-bourgeois ideology, the ideology of the great industrialists. You have various leftist ideologies, anarchism, and of course for the Communist Party, Trotskyism. Well, with Althusser, you have to go back to something more basic: the division between idealism and materialism. Althusser will fervently insist on materialism. You understand that, in the '60s, materialism is also a slogan for unifying the forces. Even if you weren't exactly a Marxist, you could be a materialist. I will just mention materialist feminism, for example, which then is able to ally itself with various forms of Marxism or socialism on the strength of a materialist view of things, even if Marxism has not, in its notions of reproduction, solved all the problems of gender.

So materialism certainly raises some questions, but I don't think we fight over that quite so much as they did in the '60s, and, in particular, maybe we don't have a very good idea of what idealism is, except that it's some belief in transcendence, religion, or something like that. That's not exactly the case for these philosophers. I want you to think of the Pythagorean theorem. It specifies that for any right angle, the sum of the squares of the two upright sides of the triangle is equal to the square of the hypotenuse. This is one of the weird mathematical discoveries of the ancient world, and what Plato suggests is that this theorem will be true even if the world is destroyed. Plato doesn't say this exactly, but I'm saying this: even if the human race dies out, it will still remain true that the sum of the squares of the legs of a right-angle triangle are equal to the square of the hypotenuse. This is eternal. It is not based on reasoning, but it is also not objective or empirical. There are no triangles in the empirical world. This is a purely intellectual object whose truth is beyond subjectivity and objectivity. So an idealist will say no, there are eternal things. They're not historical, although Pythagoras may have happened on it at some point in his life or teaching. They are not relative or subject to change. Obviously, there are a lot of other ways in which idealism will be manifested, but to understand the force of idealism in philosophy I think you have to keep this way of thinking in mind.

For Althusser, this is something that you fight about in philosophy. When facing the question "What is philosophy?" Althusser has said: it is class struggle in theory. What we're fighting about is not so much the truth of this or that theory as about the error of the other theories. So ideological critique will mean, first of all, tracking down the remnants of idealism in all of these theories to which we have been exposed. Althusser is the next generation after Sartre, but he is trained in this very heady world of Sartrean existentialism and phenomenology. Althusser will ultimately say that Marxism is itself a science, so we're going to get another concept here. Idealism and materialism have something to do with science, with knowledge, so what Althusser will want is a materialist science. He wants to cleanse science of these idealistic remnants. There will then be two consequences of this. First of all, he will have several enemies, one of which will be historicism. I'll explain what that is. Another one will be, let's say, the phenomenological, which includes existentialism. And the third will be the hermeneutic. And how will he be waging those struggles? By way of a rigorous process of critique. If Althusserianism meant anything to anybody it was rigor, and that's what terrified everybody, because you write something, and then the Althusserians pounce on it and rigorously demonstrate that you have all kinds of nasty idealisms squirming around in your work. So this is going to be a doctrine of language, and it will necessitate a certain kind of reading, and that's why, when you get to this famous seminar, *Reading Capital*, there will be a whole first section on reading. What is that all about? Why should a Leninist take the time to bother about reading? It's like Lenin and the New Criticism were combined here. What is the point of this? What is the value of this? All we want to do is get people out in the street and make a revolution. If you look at Althusser's text, you will see that, every so often, you get a word in italics. It's as though Althusser were saying, "Here, this is really an important word. Keep your eye on this one." And, in all these cases, when you see a word in italics in Althusser, you know that a fundamental distinction is being established, and you're being alerted to a whole set of phrases and terms which replace the ones you must not use any longer because they are irredeemably idealistic.

Althusser would write to a psychoanalyst, René Diatkine, two years after the composition of "Marxism and Humanism" to criticize Diatkine for using this same vocabulary. So he writes this:

> you make use of extremely dubious psychological-philosophical con-
> cepts ('lived experience' [*le vécu* is a crucial Sartrean word] 'meaning,'
> 'intentionality,' 'human experience,' etc.). To be sure, you make use of
> them in passing, and that entails no *direct* consequences in your anal-
> ysis. But if one aligns the right you arrogate to utilize psychological or
> phenomenological concepts (phenomenology is the religious psychol-
> ogy of our time) without criticizing them with the fact that *nowhere* do
> you denounce, by explicitly naming it, the *psychologizing* temptation,
> which is at least [as] dangerous for psychoanalysis as is the *biologizing*
> tendency (if not more so), that alignment may become pertinent.[2]

---

2   Louis Althusser, "Letters to D.," in *Writings on Psychoanalysis: Freud and Lacan,*

If you give yourself the right to use these kinds of concepts, then their results could be dangerous, because, as Althusser informed him, no concept exists in solitude, but is always a member of a conceptual community. "The use of such concepts, unless they're clearly differentiated from their meaning and function, would risk burying new questions and problems under the appearance of an already existing 'theoretical community.'"[3] So what Althusser is saying is that, even in the passing language of a given piece of writing, you can find things that must be avoided. You cannot use the words for these concepts, even in passing, without summoning up a whole set of ideological consequences. To talk about *le vécu*, the lived, is suddenly to drag in behind you all this phenomenological and existential baggage. Words like that must be excluded.

Okay, so what words are left? This makes Althusserian Marxism a very rigorous exercise in writing, because if you're not going to use some word—like "experience"—then where is subjectivity here? Where are the people who are using these concepts? If you can't mention the subject, can't say "I," can't talk about personal experience, what are you going to say about ideology? How can you say something objective about ideology without somehow inventing a way of talking about the subject and subjectivity which is not already tainted and poisoned by existentialism or phenomenology? You can see that this is a very difficult thing.

But why should phenomenology be the religious psychology of our time? Because capitalism begins by breaking up communities. To create the enclosure of the farmlands in the English Renaissance, existing social relations must be broken up. Look at the beginning of Thomas More's *Utopia*. It's very astonishing and violent. Sheep are eating men, he says. When enclosing all this land, you throw out the farmers. The farmers then become landless peasants, and thereby, Marx shows, those landless peasants become the population which will be then recruited for factory labor. Now that's one form, but there are other forms in which capitalism breaks up traditional communal unities, whether they're unities of farmers, religious unities, or familial unities. Capitalism calls forth individualism. Capitalism produces isolated individuals. Then theories emerge —psychologies—which are, in fact, theories of individual psychology,

eds. Olivier Corpet and François Matheron, trans. Jeffrey Mehlman (New York: Columbia University Press, 1996), 43; translation modified.

3   Warren Montag, *Althusser and His Contemporaries: Philosophy's Perpetual War* (Durham, NC: Duke University Press, 2013), 113.

and phenomenology is sort of then the final flowering of this view of an individual subject, preceding from the *cogito*, from Descartes, who has only one subjectivity in mind, going through Kant and finally climaxing in Husserl and then, if you like, in Sartrean existentialism. So this psychological philosophizing is based on the individualization, the privatization of the biological individual; but before that, the biological individual as such didn't exist. What existed were groups and communities of various sizes, all the way from hunters and gatherers to churches and linguistic communities. Althusser's objection has a deep historical and sociological basis, but he is going to make it in the form of a philosophical critique. Part of class struggle will be showing what capitalism does to people, but, in philosophy, it will be showing how the philosophical field is distorted by the way in which capitalism imposes individual consciousness as an intelligible unity of study on all of us. And what ought to be a Marxist psychology doesn't exist yet. There should be some way of showing the fact that the biological individual is not even in consciousness a complete intelligible unit of study, but that's a more difficult task. Marx didn't do that. The Marxist tradition didn't do that. Althusser will not quite do that, but he uses it. He is able to use it as a negative critique. That's the result of the idealism imposed by capitalism.

Let's look at these other points of critique: historicism, phenomenology, and hermeneutics. We've done phenomenology in some sense. For hermeneutics, I told you about Rabelais's box, the outside and the inside, the outer appearance and the inner truth. You must open the box and take apart the appearance and find behind it the truth. Althusser feels that that's another form of idealism, in the sense that it posits some absent essence which is at work in phenomenological appearance. This is going to be very important in all kinds of ways, but it's a kind of basic philosophical question. Is the purpose of philosophical and scientific thought to get behind appearance and find some essence, which is purely constructed? We can't see it, and it's not exactly the same as a thing-in-itself, but it is a kind of universal. You find this in Sartre; I don't know if I insisted on it enough. You find it in Husserl, of course, and in other forms of idealism. It is the notion of the concrete. The concrete—and Althusser will continue to use this word—is the surface plus its meaning. Althusser wants the outside and the inside together, and, indeed, words like "meaning" and "essence" are as bad in that respect as the whole business of the subject.

So a hermeneutic operation will look for opinions behind things. It will look for an unconscious. It will look for false consciousness which hides truth. Of course, that is a Marxist or party slogan; it will search out *doxa* instead of *episteme*, opinion instead of truth. The targets here of a hermeneutic mode of thought are going to be similar to those at work in the attack on phenomenology: the subject, experience, psychology. But this is more of a methodological attack. You know that hermeneutics is a key part of German thought. So, in a sense, this is an attack on the German tradition. Nobody in France at this time knew what the Frankfurt school was up to; this is a counterattack against them *avant la lettre*. Hermeneutics is a word that one of Heidegger's students, Gadamer, brought into circulation. So is it really Heideggerian? Certainly, Heidegger has a hermeneutic, but it's not exactly this. Anyway, from Gadamer on, even dialectical thought will be hermeneutic. I think "essence" is the best word for this. It's the positing of an essence that lies behind appearance, and that has all kinds of consequences. For example, in this kind of ideological critique that we've been talking about, the older kind of ideology critique will simply say, "Oh, this is fascism," or, "This is really conservatism." That's not acceptable to Althusser, because it implies that there is an essence called "fascism," "conservatism," "petty bourgeois thought," which is expressing itself in this text. That's hermeneutical, and it suggests that there's an appearance of this text behind which there is an essence of thought. He doesn't want to do it that way. He wants to find in the very text the signs of something else.

Now the ally in all this is somebody whom we have to mention in dealing with Althusser, and, if this were a full-fledged study of Althusser, we would have to go into this in more detail. I'm not necessarily the best guide to it, but I will tell you what I think Spinoza means for Althusser. Spinoza means a lot of things to a lot of people. Spinoza has been called an atheist philosopher. That's something which could be positive for many people. Spinoza's notion of psychology is very interesting. His notion of the sad passions of negativity is extremely modern and has its counterpart in all kinds of more recent doctrines of *ressentiment*. And, finally, his notion of the relationship of human beings to their destiny has always been a remarkable resource—maybe like Stoic thought for the ancients—for modern people, and it's related to his notion of the totality. That would otherwise be a bad word in this context, but, in Spinoza, remember, the crucial role of the word *or*: God or nature. The "or" means that these are the same. There is a vast totality, of which, therefore, our existence as individuals is only a part, and, so, if we're attached to our own individuality, we think things about life which we, in fact, don't have to think if we understand ourselves as part of this immense totality. Much of Spinoza's tremendous, liberating power for so many people has come from this notion. But that's not exactly the Spinoza that's important for Althusser. The most important thing for Althusser is that, first of all, in Spinoza, there are dimensions of God, of nature, which are separate but the same. The body and the mind, for example. For Spinoza, the dimension of the mind is radically different from the dimension of the body, and, yet, those two realities are the same. And this identification of Spinoza you can read in two ways. You can read it as a radical Cartesianism, in which these two things are the same, modulated by the "or." One of the marvels of Descartes as a historical figure is that he is at one and the same time the source of modern idealism and the source of modern materialism. Spinoza also unites those things in a funny kind of way. But, for Althusser, it means there are no ideas. There is just matter, just materiality, just bodies. Ideas are materiality, and we'll see that when we come to ideology.

How can that be? Well, for the moment, all we have to do is think of the notion of immanence, which is so important to both Althusser and that other Spinozan we haven't met yet, Deleuze. That also involves the attack on a hermeneutic view of things. You have things, and then, behind them somewhere in history, are causes. We have historical events, and they were caused by something in the past. Okay, so what we have there are phenomena, and then, behind them, something which no longer exists except in an ideal state. Althusser wants to get rid of that idea of causality, a project which is, in any case, the great discovery of Hume, the paradox that sets off all of Kant. Kant says that, when he read Hume's critique of causality, he was awakened from his dogmatic slumbers. So this notion of causality is a crucial event in eighteenth-century philosophy, and now it comes back again. Althusser wants to say, following Spinoza, that the causes are immanent in the effects, which is why, as I warned you before, we're going to get this word "effect" all over the place from now on, and it generally has this kind of flavor. Are these effects without causes? Well, in a funny kind of way, yes, because what's also going on in modern theory there is this kind of retroactive movement where, since the causes are not present anymore—the past is gone and you have only the effects—when you locate a cause, it's as though the effect has produced the cause. Freud called this *Nachträglichkeit*, the way in which the present produces a past. There are different translations. I would translate it as "retroactivity."

Some people call it "afterness," which is not strong enough. What Freud discovered was that a child would have a trauma at some young age, a sexual trauma. At that age, sexuality disappears, becomes latent, as Freud says, and the child goes through a non-sexual period until it reemerges with puberty. So there is a cause here, but it doesn't do anything. It gets submerged in this period, and then the effects revive when the child is twelve or thirteen and plunge it into schizophrenia or some other disorder.

So, in that respect, the present, the symptom, reactivates the cause for Freud. It's a very funny kind of temporality. Look out for this kind of inversion of time, because it's characteristic of a lot of our people from now on, and certainly you find it in Lacan as well. But you can find it in other ways. Think of the James-Lange theory of emotion. William James says—and this is always the great counterintuitive example of this kind of thing—people might think that, when they get angry, their anger causes their face to get red, their hands to tremble, and so on. No, no, he says. It's quite the opposite. My face getting red, my hands starting to tremble, are the *causes* of my anger. This is the famous James-Lange theory of emotion. It is absolutely consistent with Spinoza and with this *Nachträglichkeit* we're talking about. But how can you believe it? When I react to something, first I start to get flushed, then I start to feel bodily things, and only then is anger produced.

At any rate, this will give you an idea of what Althusser wants to do with effects of all kinds, and it will be especially important in dealing with history and with modes of production, where it will mean something for the so-called structuralism that's going on all around it. In Lévi-Strauss, you will remember, there is a structure, and it has some effects, some manifestations. Althusser does not want to have this mysterious essence called structure behind reality. He wants reality to include structure. So, when he is talking about the mode of production, what he wants to show you, through the concept of overdetermination—a word that he borrows from Freud but that he uses in a completely different way that has nothing any longer to do with the Freudian meaning—is that a vast array of phenomena are related to each other but are not related to some deeper essence of the social formation.[4] They form a kind of effect, but they're not caused by something behind them, which is the social formation. This will be an important position, because, in the Marxist tradition, what finally causes

---

4 Louis Althusser, "Contradiction and Overdetermination," in *For Marx*, trans. Ben Brewster (New York: Vintage, 1970), 87–128.

everything is the ultimately determining instance—a very important phrase—which is to say the economic. Marxism is supposed to be the primacy of the economic. If that's the case, and if Althusser is indeed a Marxist, then the economic must somehow be somewhere behind all these things. Althusser does not want to posit that mysterious essence of the ultimately determining instance there. But how could he be a Marxist if he denied the primacy of the economic structure? It's a big problem. I try to graph it this way. Normally, in common Marxism—unless you want to say "orthodox"—all these levels are running in parallel lines. You have the superstructures. You have law, art, philosophy. You also have the kinds of production. Fordism in the factory. You have union ideology. And all of this stuff, each in its own way, reflects a moment of capitalism. But where is that moment of capitalism? You remember—maybe I've quoted it before— that that great philosopher Margaret Thatcher said there is no such thing as society. That was very Althusserian of her. There is no essence. There is no such thing as capitalism, these people will say, because such a thing can't exist. It's only an essence. So how do you understand this thing which you can't call capitalism? I try to graph it not as parallel lines, but as lines emanating from some central trunk, like a hand of cards, but maybe that's not the right way to do it either. In any case, it's a big problem for him. This is the central problem of Althusser's notion of overdetermination: how can he have a notion of modes of production from which this ultimately determining instance is absent? You found the sentence, probably one of the most famous and scandalous sentences in Althusser, in which he says that the lonely hour of the ultimately determining instance never comes. This is very tortuous writing, because he has to avoid this word and that one, but, every so often, you get these flat statements. "Ideology has no history."[5] That becomes part of a list of things that every Althusserian has to carry around in their pocket and know as absolute truth.

E. P. Thompson wrote a big, indignant book against all this stuff in which he says it is not true that the lonely hour of the final instance does not come.[6] Sometimes there are moments when it does come. The Lacanian Real would be something like that. Where is it? It's not there. It's never there. Is it an absent cause? Well, no, because the unconscious is only a bunch of categories. But the Real, every so often, does explode into

---

5   Louis Althusser, "Ideology and Ideological State Apparatuses," in *On the Reproduction of Capitalism*, trans. G. M. Goshgarian (London: Verso, 2014), 174.

6   E. P. Thompson, *The Poverty of Theory* (New York: Monthly Review Press, 1978).

Lacanian consciousness. And there are mathematical formulas—Galileo and so forth—that live together for a time with the truth. That would be the eternal for Lacan, the mathemes. Mathemes cohabit with the truth for a time.[7] That is the Real somehow bursting out. For E. P. Thompson, one of the great historians of the Left, there are moments when suddenly—and those would be revolutionary moments—the Real does burst through.

Remember what Althusser is living through. He is living in the moments of the '60s that are extremely unsettled and full of all kinds of incidents and wars, but the revolution hasn't come. Any true Marxist, I think, has to believe in a revolutionary future of some sort, one of radical change. And if you don't, as so many Marxists in our time don't any longer—either because they feel capitalism is this ultimate system for which there are no alternatives or because there seems no path out—then you end up outside of Marxism. The title of Althusser's autobiography was *L'avenir dure long-temps* (*The Future Lasts Forever*, a patently ideological mistranslation). In his final writings—they're very interesting to read about in Montag's book—Althusser finally ended up believing that the notion of the future was an idealist illusion, that there is no future. There's just the present, of which the future is a dimension. Is that no longer believing in revolution? I think it's a version of this, but maybe it's also not exactly a denial.

Althusser's last years were very unfortunate, and I guess I have to tell you what you maybe already know, the anecdotal stuff, which is maybe more than anecdotal. Althusser was a schizophrenic. He began in the Christian youth movement. He was a left Christian as a young man, as was his wife, Hélène Rytmann, but she was far more radical politically. She radicalized him and helped him throughout his life, but she was also a schizophrenic. They helped themselves through their crises. This is the way I've heard this story; there could be others, but it seems to me very plausible. When Althusser told his colleagues that things were going very well, very, very well, they knew he was going to have a crisis and would have to go into the clinic for a while. There's a kind of rhythm in these crises sometimes. Supposing these rhythms coincide, the hypothesis is that, on this particular occasion, they both had a crisis. In whatever state of demented rage and fury they were in, he strangled her. He was then

---

7 "*Il y a des formules qu'on n'imagine pas; au moins pour un temps, elles font assemblée avec le réel.*" (Jacques Lacan, "*Radiophonie*," *Scilicet*, no. 2–3 (1970), 75). See Jameson's comments in *The Political Unconscious: Narrative as a Socially Symbolic Act* (Ithaca: Cornell University Press, 1981), 34–5 and 35, fn. 18.

tried in court. In France—you may think what you like about this—the state has a different set of values than in the United States. You know the old saying about Oscar Wilde. When Oscar Wilde was imprisoned for homosexuality, the Americans said: Is this the way your poets behave? And the French said: Is this the way you behave to your poets? Well, French legality is of a different kind from ours, which is more puritanical, and, clearly, there were a lot of clinical factors to consider. Althusser was confined to a clinic, then released on a kind of house arrest where he spent the rest of his life. Even his disciples dropped away from him. The only person who was faithful to him and visited him regularly and finally handled his papers was Derrida, and I think it says much to his credit. We'll see how Derrida and Derrideanism—I won't say derives from Althusserian ideology critique—but is very closely related to it, and there are all kinds of other things to say on this matter, but we'll hold those until we get to Derrida.

Anyway, in the last years of Althusser's life, he invented his theory of aleatory materialism, the contingent encounter, which is certainly related to some of this business about overdetermination in his early essays. If you're curious, as I say, a lot has been written about these things, but on the other hand, I think there's plenty of writing to avoid. It's not only offensive but stupid when a rather well-known anti-communist French specialist writes an article called "Marxism and Murder." I think this is a rather ignorant way of handling this. But it's not unlike Heidegger and Nazism. You could decide, on the strength of Heidegger's various pronouncements, that Heidegger's work is so permeated by Nazism that it should be completely removed from the shelves and never taught again in philosophy courses. That would amount to removing a lot of stuff, I think, besides Heidegger. I think that it's rather a question of what one does with these pieces of the psyche. If you were an Althusserian, you would say that's imposing what Althusser calls "expressive causality" on a phenomenon.[8] If you have a little bit of schizophrenia here, some philosophizing here, and in some other part of the brain you have aesthetic sensibility, a relationship to politics, and so on, well, it's you, and if you are a unit, if you are a single homogeneous organic unity, then, to be sure, the schizophrenia is going to be inseparable from those other aspects of you. We can say let's not read

8   Louis Althusser et al., *Reading Capital*, trans. Ben Brewster and David Fernbach (London: Verso, 2015), especially part 4, ch. 9. See Jameson's discussion in *The Political Unconscious*, ch. 1.

this schizophrenic murderous stuff into everything, as though everything in Althusser were tainted by this horrible killing.

At any rate, what Althusser objects to with his other version of modes of production is expressive causality. He associates it with Hegel, and, despite the fact that he wrote works on Hegel when he was young, one always assumes that, if Althusser is anything, he is profoundly anti-Hegelian. Why? Because he attributes to Hegel the notion of an expressive causality, through which, in a given society, or a historical moment, everything in that moment will be somehow organically related to each other. There will be a style, a period style, which will permeate everything. So you will have the baroque state. You will have the counterreformation, the Jesuits. You will have a baroque architecture. You will have a baroque statecraft. You will have a baroque mathematics and physics. The entire style of a period will be captured in this essence which is the baroque. This is what Althusser calls expressive causality, and this is what he has a problem with, because he thinks orthodox Marxism works the same way. Orthodox Marxism will say there's an essence of capitalism, and therefore everything in this historical moment, which is capitalism, will be somehow the same, will be analogous.

Now this kind of thinking will entail what is called historicism, the notion that every moment of history is this unique, synchronic synthesis of a certain style, and that will also entail some notion of truth. Ranke said every age is immediate to God. That means that each age has its own truth. Then, of course, everything is relative, or so say the modern critics of all this, and therefore you can say Marxism is not a timeless discovery, not science, but rather just the way they thought in the nineteenth century. That's what Foucault effectively argues in *The Order of Things*. So you can have truths in those things. Althusser wants to resist that and wants to resist the notion of expressive causality. I think, myself, that expressive causality is one way of learning history, because one does explore the relationship of the various practices to one another, but this means, in practice, considering society as this unified, organic thing. It's clear that, for Althusser, that's an idealist operation for which we should find a materialist alternative. We'll get to that next time. But that's why structuralism will, despite his attacks on it, be of a certain use to him in overcoming this expressive causality that he finds everywhere.

So, three enemies: phenomenology (the philosophy of the subject), hermeneutics (the idea of finding the essence behind things), and historicism (the notion of the expressive causality of a period). We'll go on with all this next time, and we'll finally get to the most exciting part of Althusser, which is the whole theory of ideology and of the state apparatuses.

March 2, 2021

13

The Lonely Hour of the Last Instance

{Althusser}

Today, I realize that there is more to be said about this business of over-determination. As I mentioned last time, overdetermination is a term Freud uses for analyzing the dream work. But how the dream itself comes together is another matter. At a basic level, one can say that the dream puts different pieces of reality together. Have we talked about bricolage? It's a term that we now use in English owing to Lévi-Strauss. In bricolage, you collect all these bits and pieces, and then you put them together in some way. At any rate, Freud understands the dream as a bricolage of all these things, so in interpreting the dream he will invent a system of free association. This word "free" sounds wonderful! You can say anything you want! But, in Freud, you can never really say everything you want. The things you say, even if you think they're crazy, will always have some meaning, and therefore free association is not as easy as you might imagine. Take any piece of the dream. Let's say an apple appears somewhere. How does it trace its way back into meaning? In other words, how do you free associate it? When you free associate, you will find that you come to a point where it's so silly that you yourself are going to think and tell the analyst, "I don't think of anything." "What's your next thought?" the analyst might respond. "Nothing," you say. "I don't think of anything." Well, obviously, you do, and that's the point of resistance. The training in free association operates through this self-discipline in which you find out what you really think, despite the fact that you think you think nothing. So, amid all the pieces of a dream, the analyst will ask what this apple is doing over here. Any one of those pieces, if pursued rigorously enough, would lead back to the core of the dream (the core of the apple, so to speak), which is to say, the wish, the unfulfilled wish. In Freud, this unfulfilled wish is something very ordinary, something out of daily life, but which conceals the deepest, even unformulated desires of the first years of childhood, the most important desires for your formation.

So overdetermination names the way in which the dream has put together something that looks unified out of all these different elements. Now Althusser borrows that idea, even though he is not talking about dreams, obviously; he is talking about events, and he is talking about climactic events, very often revolutions. There are moments when order breaks down. Suddenly, things cease to function in a general breakdown, opposition, resistance. This could lead to revolution, or it could be put down, but, in any case, it is a crisis. What he is saying is that—and this is a lesson for the communist theoreticians and historians as much as anyone else—if we believe in causality and history, we might think that, in some period when the harvest is very poor and people are starving, they necessarily make a revolution. Actually, history often shows that that's not so. The famous revolution of rising expectations: only when things start to get a little better do you have real discontent. If things are really at their worst, nobody has any energy to do anything, so nothing is likely to happen, or you think this is the end of the world. But, when things get a little better, you begin to wonder why they couldn't get a lot better, why things couldn't change. Okay, but that's still a single cause. What Althusser wants to say is that all kinds of accidental things have to come together. The Communist Party used for a long time this formula: the situation is or isn't ripe for revolution. It is a little out of chronological order, but one of the illustrations of this would be May '68. The Communist Party had to decide: Is this a revolutionary situation? Should we make an attempt to seize power? Or is the situation unripe? "Ripe" is always the word here. They decide no, it's not ripe. In 1917, there was, as you know, a crackdown in St. Petersburg. A lot of the party-affiliated communists fled or went underground. Lenin himself fled to Finland. The idea was, for most of the Central Committee, that this was not the moment for a revolution. But when Lenin came back, he said it was necessary to make a revolution right now. "You stupid people think that the time is not ripe. The time *is* ripe, and we seize power right now." This is what we find already in the April Theses. Lenin was in a very small minority. Even Stalin was against this in October.

So that is just one illustration of this business of whether things are ripe or not, which always means reading the future as though reading tea leaves and seeing what elements were there. What Althusser is saying, in a funny way, is that you can't read the future. You never know how many tea leaves are necessary. The example I use for this is what has more recently been called a "perfect storm," but that's a very precise expression. They made a movie with George Clooney called *The Perfect Storm*, about a fishing boat out in the Atlantic. A number of things can obviously go wrong at sea. Something could be the matter with the ship. You could run out of oil in a storm. Or the storm could destroy this or that part of a ship. Or the sailors could be sick. Any number of things could go wrong. If only one of them went wrong, maybe you could get out of this. The perfect storm is when they all go wrong together, simultaneously, when there is a unique conjuncture of all these circumstances, some of them chance circumstances, some of them foreseeable. So the Althusserian notion of overdetermination is that all these so-called determinants come together in that "perfect storm," and then you have a revolution. That is why they're so rare.

Now this idea is tied in with Althusser's work on the mode of production, so I want to finish up with that. Keep in mind, in all of this, that the big test of things for Althusser—if you want to call it his ideology, I don't care—is this business of idealism versus materialism. And I want to say that this is impossible to solve, because it's the mind and the body, and nobody is ever going to solve that, but they're going to provide different kinds of solutions. In Kant, the idea is that the body is determined by causes, whereas the mind is free, but those are two different dimensions that can't overlap. So you have the spiritual dimensions—the soul and so forth—the problem of beginnings and endings. These things are sort of like things-in-themselves; that is, we know of their existence, but there's no way we can use the language of cause and effect to deal with them. The soul is there somewhere, but only as a thing-in-itself. It is outside of consciousness or scientific examination. Well, that's one form of the mind-body problem, and it may not be the way we experience it now, but my position would be that the reason it is always somehow cast in an ideological form—that is to say, that it's insoluble in some scientific way—is because consciousness is, as Sartre might say, a nothingness. We can't have a theory of consciousness because we're in it, and we can't see it from the outside. The fish can't have a theory of water because it doesn't exist outside of it.

Anyway, Althusser believes that there *is* a solution: that of Spinoza. If I understand him correctly—and it is very possible I don't, and any Spinozan expert would show that I'm interpreting this very crudely, and I would certainly accept that—the way I'm going to put it to you is that, in Spinoza, you have a notion of what I'm going to call "dimensions." Reality has dimensions. It has a great many more dimensions than we're aware of, but that is of no importance to us. The dimensions we know are matter and mind, whatever you want to call those things. And, in Spinoza, those levels, those dimensions, are the same, except that they are described in two different languages, so to speak. There are two different systems, but they are in fact one and the same. When we get to ideology, Althusser's imitation of Spinoza will take the form that ideology seems like a thought—it is therefore mental—but in the realm of the body it exists as the apparatus. Those two things are the same. But how are they the same?

That is the theory of ideology, but, first, let's deal with this mode of production stuff. Several things come together here. It is sort of a perfect storm of its own. For example, Mao Zedong's influence will be an important part of this. There are two essays that he used, "On Practice" and "On Contradiction." These Maoist writings become very important in the '60s, especially the notion that you can retranslate ideas into practices. Practices would be the materialist version of ideas. What does that mean? Well, I think you can get a little idea of it from one of our more general slogans from the '60s: "the personal is political." These two things are the same. Your actions in daily life or in private life are somehow the same as your political life—or they are the critique of your seemingly abstract political ideas. In other words, there is a correlation—to use a not very satisfactory word—between practices and ideas. So that would be one explanation for the omnipresence of the word "practice" in the '60s. In the '60s, everything gets to be a practice, which emphasizes the role of process in things, as opposed to substance. From this perspective of the mid-sixties, Baudrillard is not completely wrong to say that Marxism is a productivism. There is increasingly, all over the '60s, this notion of production as a form of action, as a form of practice or process.

So we have read about Althusser's epistemology, Generality I, II, III.[1] The production of knowledge, of what in French is called *science*. In Generality I, you take an established and accepted idea, but you take that as knowledge. You apply to it Generality II, which is more of an instrument, and, of course, we know that, in this context, the instrument is called Marxism. And, out of the materials of Generality I, you produce a scientific idea, which is Generality III. And, once you have Generality III, you can go back and see that Generality I, which you thought was scientific, is, in fact, profoundly ideological in some way. I suppose the famous analogies are alchemy and chemistry. At a certain moment, alchemy looks like a systematic set of ideas and operations. Scientific thought operates on that and produces that very different thing, chemistry. So, in the same way, Althusser is taking this mass of social ideas and preconceptions, which apply to situations, but which are not scientific, so to speak. He will use his instruments of analysis and show that they are not scientific, which is to say, in a simpler way, not materialist. So that will be how the notion of mode of production functions, but it functions everywhere. The students and writers, for example, want to say we are workers, culture workers, this famous '60s phrase. "Culture workers" means those producing something out of culture. You are producing a theory of culture out of culture. Sex workers are also workers. Everybody is producing, except maybe for the *rentiers*. Famously, in English, they are called coupon-clippers because they get their income every month by clipping the coupons, getting their interest and so forth.

It is easy to make fun of it, but I think it reflects a deeper problem, which is that of the intellectual. We live in an anti-intellectual society, and nobody likes to talk about it. Intellectuals have this peculiar status. They are always outside of their class. They are, in a sense, class traitors. It doesn't mean they are always rebels. Intellectuals can defend the system, but the people who run the system always know that they're just intellectuals. They're being paid, and you can't really trust an intellectual. And the same, of course, for the other side. The Communist Party knew very well that even the intellectuals who were supporting it were not really to be trusted. Intellectuals have a special status with respect to classes. So how does one justify this? Althusser is sort of on the margins of the Communist Party, from which he is criticizing it. He is an intellectual.

---

1   Louis Althusser, "On the Materialist Dialectic," in *For Marx*, 161–218.

How is it that the system pays him to be a professor in one of the most important French training schools? And where does the authority of all these critiques come from? I would say that, under those circumstances, this is an intellectual phenomenon that hasn't been sufficiently studied, as they might say in the '60s. But Sartre gives us a clue. He says they were petty-bourgeois intellectuals—in the jargon of the time, intellectuals were classed as petty bourgeois, which is not a very meaningful way of talking about it—but they knew that there were masses out there, and the fact of all these people who were not in the system exercised a force of gravity on them. So their thought changed. Their relationship to their own ideologies and the intellectual conventions and values that they grew up with was modified by this sense of a social reality, a mass far away and far larger than them.

Now, in a way, you can see this on an international level. In the old days, when the Soviet Union existed and it had real power in other parts of the world, there were areas for which it was energizing simply to know that socialism existed somewhere. Not here, in Africa or Latin America, but somewhere. There is this distant force of gravity of a phenomenon that you don't really know completely but that you know exists. And I would say that somebody like Althusser certainly knew—as he was in the Communist Party, he had plenty of contact with workers—that there was a mass of people out there whom the Party did not always completely represent, and he drew on that dissatisfaction. He also knew about China, to many, including Brecht, a more authentic revolution. The idea that he was a free-floating intellectual in the conventional sense is misguided. Certainly, there would be critics who were or are equally distant both from communism and from American liberalism, who are in a void, but who found other people of the same persuasion with whom they are able to form a collectivity. There's always a sort of collective basis to the certainty one has about ideas, and ideology itself reflects that fact. So Althusser's credentials for presenting these critiques and Marx's credentials for analyzing all of capitalism will, in a sense, refer him to the notion of science, but, on the other hand, there is also this collective sense that there is a human population or reality that you are somehow in solidarity with. That is why the word "solidarity" has its very special meaning on the Left.

These two problems, then, are the subject-object problems. The problem of ideology is that of the subject, and the problem of mode of production is that of the object. How to connect those two? In his "Introduction" to

A Contribution to the Critique of Political Economy, Marx lays these things out in a very crude way, for the first and last time, as the base and super-structure. Base and superstructure form an opposition which has always made a lot of trouble. Perry Anderson says we should give it a decent burial. But you don't have to think of it as a dogma if you think of it instead as a problem. How does one connect the base and superstructure? What is the relationship between base and superstructure in a given historical situation? The question is posed as a two-part fractional model, in which you have a top term and a bottom term. You have a double inscription: the signifier and signified, superstructure and base.

I've already mentioned that, throughout everybody's philosophizing in this period, going back even to Sartre, there is always the question of the break. You don't want essences, which are unified, homogeneous entities. You want breaks. You want cuts. You want more than a tension. And you want breaks in time as well as breaks in an object like the subject. The subject, Lacan says, is this matter of breaks, gaps, *béances*, holes, whatever you want to call these phenomena where things don't come together. They will even find them back in the nineteenth century. Marx posits a social formation in which we have to separate out the productive base of a society from all these other superstructures. The funny thing is that, in the base itself, there is also a break between two dimensions of production. There are forces of production, and there are relations of production. Here is the subject and object, the mind and body, already in the body, in the base. Relations of production are class relations; forces of production are technology. Marxism is not a technologism, but it is also not—if you know the history and terminology of the working-class movement—a workerism. Unions can be as much obstacles to revolutionary movements as technologies can. There, in the base, you get that problem all over again, and these breaks are going to multiply themselves. This is why I keep coming back to this model of homologies, analogies, and levels, because the older way of thinking about all of this was to assume that the base is the ultimately determining instance. You had all these levels—culture, philosophy, the state, law—and then, underneath the bar, you have the ultimately determining instance, the base, production. They're supposed to be parallel, analogous, if not identical. What Althusser is trying to say is that they're not parallel. Each one has a semi-autonomous development, and you can't just put them in relationships of similarity to one another. Doing it Althusser's way still involves the contradiction of what he calls an "expressive causality." That means that an element of every level will be related to an element of every other level. I gave you the example of the Baroque the other day, but you can find this search for the common style of a society in all kinds of historical periods—and among the Marxists, a homogeneity with what is going on in the base.

Engels, who took a much more common-sense view of all this, wrote some letters in his old age which are very important for theory. You understand that Marxism was not an invention of Marx. Alongside every prophet is an ideologue; the prophet says something incomprehensible, and the ideologue turns it into a system with a slogan and a politics. This is true for statesmen as well. Sometimes they're the same, I suppose, but very rarely. So Marx, as I said, is not a founder of Marxism. Indeed, there's a famous moment when Marx gets very annoyed with all of his followers and says he is not a Marxist. "If you all are Marxists then I'm not one." So it is Engels who turns Marx's writings into a system. His late letters are very useful in making a little more precise what he found in Marx, and in one of them he finds a "zigzag relationship" (his term) between base and superstructure. Sometimes, the base does not cause the superstructure. It could be the other way around. Maybe the superstructure has an effect on the base, produces new kinds of scientific discoveries which then enter into production and modify it.

For those of you who are interested in music, there is a very interesting book by a French thinker, which would be on our list if we had had more time. Althusser wrote his essays on art and on painting, on Cremonini and on Brecht, and all our other people wrote on art as well. The same was true of this thinker, although he was an economist. He was an advisor to François Mitterrand as president. Indeed, the only time I was allowed into the Élysée Palace was when I interviewed him there. We were asking him questions, and he says, "Keep it down! Le président is right next door; he hears everything we're saying." Anyway, this is Jacques Attali, who wrote a book called Bruits, translated as Noise, on music. He tried to show it the other way around. It isn't the base that causes the superstructure. The superstructure anticipates the base. So the music of every period, in its organization, its problems, anticipates the economic development of the next period. These are the two most abstract forms of knowledge, music and economics, and they meet in some weird, circular way here.

So there is that problem, which Althusser tries to get rid of by saying the lonely hour of the last instance never comes. There is no such thing as the pure base that you could experience. Rather, there is a structural relationship of difference between all these things. Now that is hard to think, because when you say "difference," you tend to think there is no connection. These are things which are profoundly connected structurally, but which are different from each other. Each one is autonomous. I have tried to express the logic of this by a slogan, which is that, in these cases, difference relates.[2] Difference is a form of relationship, and not a form of separation and absolute disjunction; and, if you know your Hegel, you know that the law of identity and difference is such that they are the same in a dialectical way. You define the identity of something by insisting on what makes it different from everything else. And, when you try to show a difference, you're going to end up defining its identity. So there is a constant movement back and forth between identity and difference that you can never get away from which is at work in this attempt of Althusser to put these things together.

Now let's go a little further. What would be the conditions under which the superstructure somehow appears to be the "dominant." Well, everywhere in history! Capitalism is the only system in which the base is dominant, in which it is clear that economics runs society. And even that's probably not true, because a lot of non-economic features of capitalism come into our conception of economics and the market. So, in a way, it even seems possible to say that socialism would be the only system in which the base is truly the dominant. We're already using two terms that Althusser invents: the dominant and the determinant. As I said, Marx describes, in the *Grundrisse*, all the various determinants of the modes of production. In *Capital*, he says that the determinant is always economic, but it's not the same economics.[3] Baudrillard will say this is crazy, because

2 Fredric Jameson, *Valences of the Dialectic* (London: Verso, 2009), 540; Fredric Jameson, "Postmodernism, or The Cultural Logic of Late Capitalism," *New Left Review* I, no. 146 (July/August, 1984), 75.

3 See Karl Marx, *Capital, Vol. I*, trans. Ben Fowkes (New York: Penguin, 1990), 175–6, fn. 35. Quoting his own Preface to *A Contribution to the Critique of Political Economy*, Marx writes, "My view is that each particular mode of production, and the relations of production corresponding to it at each given moment, in short the 'economic structure of society,' is 'the real foundation, on which arises a legal and political superstructure and to which correspond definite forms of social consciousness,' and that 'the mode of production of material life conditions the general process of social, political and intellectual life.' In the opinion of [a] German-American publication this is all very true for our own times, in which material interests are preponderant, but not true for the Middle Ages, dominated by Catholicism, nor for Athens and Rome, dominated by politics. [. . .] One

you can't talk about economics before a society that effectively invents economics. If you import it into other societies, you are distorting their reality. Well, even if he won't say so, here we find the dialectic again, when these terms—which should be different in every historical moment—are nonetheless used across them all as if they were the same. But, in all these other societies, it's not clear that the organizing principle of the society is economic, so other organizing principles have to be used. For feudalism, for the Middle Ages, to take one example, the dominant is not economic; it is the church, religion. For the Greek polis, the city-state, the dominant is—if you limit it very strictly—the political, "democracy," and slavery.

Someone asked a question about pre-power societies, and this is going to be a popular topic in the '60s. As we say, after Lévi-Strauss, suddenly everyone is looking at utopian societies and the question about power. What is power? How can you have a society without power? Where does the state come from? If you don't like that line of questioning, then you ask what form the superstructure takes in a simple society in which you wouldn't think there were superstructures. Well, it takes the form of kinship. Kinship is then the dominant organizing principle of many of these earlier societies. If you had a real society of hunters and gatherers, one assumes that the dominant principle would be the notion of nature itself as an enemy force, as a huge danger, under which everything is subsumed. You can still see it if you read *The Forest People* of Colin Turnbull. The forest is nature. The forest is what we would call religion, except, if you don't like us using the word "economics," then we can't use the word religion either, because that's a later product as well. So we have societies with different dominants, and then we have societies with . . . the same determinants? Not quite, because, obviously, there's a tremendous difference in production between hunting and gathering, serfs working the land in medieval societies, and other forms of production. Baudrillard will tell us you can't use the word "production" for all of these societies, because they're all different. Yes, of course they're different, but they have a structural base, nonetheless.

All of these different productions must, therefore, somehow be thought of as forms of the base. That is a very fundamental idea of Althusser, and it takes several forms in his work. Raymond Williams has refined it in

thing is clear: the Middle Ages could not live on Catholicism, nor could the ancient world on politics. On the contrary, it is the manner in which they gained their livelihood which explains why in one case politics, in the other case Catholicism, played the chief part."

an interesting way. He says, looking at culture, that we should talk about residual and emergent forces in a society. Residual forces are old ones, institutions that are still in place, attitudes and opinions. England and Poland are societies in which older feudal notions of social hierarchy and aristocracy still survive in some form and influence people. Not so much here in America. Emergent: these are new kinds of thinking, new social organizations, new subjectivities that haven't found their place in society. And then he adopts the Gramscian terminology: the hegemonic (the dominant). That is the ideology in force in a given society. So you have several ways of looking at these things from different perspectives.

Now we can see why Mao Zedong should be so interesting for Althusser. "On Contradiction" is the famous essay, and his point there would seem to us to be a very obvious and simple one: there are antagonistic contradictions and there are non-antagonistic contradictions. Suddenly, from a revolutionary point of view, that changes everything. Mao Zedong can say in 1949 that socialist positions are in contradiction with these businessmen on our side who are nonetheless our allies. You can see how a notion of non-antagonistic contradictions could make alliances possible in an almost Gramscian way. Gramsci describes hegemony as a system of alliances between the groups that have some shared interest in keeping things the way they are, and, of course, the other side has its own alliances formed around a desire for change. This framework allows Gramsci to be such a marvelous analyst both of superstructures and of the base. He takes various pieces of culture and shows how all the differences of the classes and the class factions come together in strategic ways. That would be similar to Mao's notion of non-contradiction. Contradiction, then, is, of course, class struggle itself. It is all class struggle, but there are two varieties. Lenin's political, strategic, and tactical genius was to see, unlike Stalin and others, that in 1917 there was a profound relationship between two forces in Russian Tsarist society that were absolutely interested in getting rid of the old system: the peasants and the soldiers. Land and peace. That is a non-antagonistic contradiction between the city and the countryside, because both groups share a desire to end the war and Tsarism. But, ten years later, it will become an antagonistic contradiction, because many of the peasants will not want to give up their products to supply the cities, even though the cities are starving, and therefore you get what I think is really the second Soviet revolution. It is the famous Stalinist one, the collectivization of the countryside. Whatever you want to think about it,

I think one has to confront the fact that the interest of the peasants is not the interest of the city anymore.

This is all always changing, but what I really want to point out to you—because we aren't looking at classes right now—is that contradiction and non-contradiction turn out to be our old friends condensation and displacement. The antagonistic contradiction means the union of both these forces. You know that revolutions operate by dichotomization. Little by little, as a revolution progresses, everybody has to take sides, even the people who don't want to. You're forced into a position. Either you're for the revolution or you go to Miami. You can't finally get out of this increasingly polarized situation. So, in that sense, this polarization, this condensation, is going to make up what's called an antagonistic contradiction, whereas the non-antagonistic contradictions emerge side by side, like in metonymy, entering into relationships. Here again, we find our old friends metaphor and metonymy, condensation and displacement, but here we have them operating at the very heart of both Maoism and Althusserianism. I think it is one of the original characteristics of this thought.

I want to get on to ideology because it's terribly important and we haven't done anything with it yet. I discovered, to my amazement, in rereading this marvelous book of Warren Montag from a Spinozan perspective, so to speak, that there are really two interpretations of this matter of ideology. There are already two meanings of ideology. Ideology in the Marxist tradition is false consciousness, so it is opposed to science and truth. You can see how somebody lives in false consciousness and bad faith. But how do you live in science? Musil's *Man Without Qualities* presents one vision of this. Could you somehow live within science and be completely transparent? The one thing that's absolutely repressed in Althusserianism—I quoted it the other day in that letter of his—is the lived, what's experienced and felt, the existential. This is somehow rigorously expelled here. It's all thought to be part of humanism and must be eradicated alongside all of Sartre, who was supposed to be working with some kind of idealistic, humanist, existential Marxism. Get rid of that and go back to the true Marxism. But when he comes to ideology, Althusser still has to do something with subjectivity.

Science is not a feasible answer, so we have to invent something else which will make the connection between the individual subject and society, which is again another relationship of mind and body. Society is the body to which we belong, but what do we do with that? Even before all this, there are two meanings of ideology, as I said. Yes, it can be your opinions, your nasty, unconscious, racist, or sexist opinions. But there's a positive form of ideology that you find once in a while in all kinds of places, and that would be the ideology of a practice, of a kind of work. For example, all serious doctors are bound to have some kind of common ideology, which is their practice, their relationship to patients, to the body, the things they have to confront. That will be something common to them, that unifies them, and it will be different for laypersons. One supposes, when you go back in time, that the first lay intellectuals of the Middle Ages are the shoemakers. The shoemaker is always this suspicious character. People gather in his shop and talk ideas. Why? Is there an ideology of shoemaking? Because you use bits, putting things together, leather, string? After all, the blacksmith is not the intellectual of tribal society, but he is the magician, the most powerful, maybe even physically; working with fire gives not just a status but a way of thinking about the world that other people don't have. So each profession—we teachers, of course, have our own—can be a positive uniting force, but how does it work here?

I have a Lacanian view of this, but then I find—Montag doesn't hold much with Lacan—that there is a Spinozan reading of this as well. Althusser's famous statement is this: "Ideology represents the imaginary relationship of individuals to their real conditions of existence."[4] Now, anybody coming to this from Lacan, as we have, will recognize these terms "imaginary" and "real," and then will better ask themselves where the Symbolic is in all of this. Even without the Symbolic, what you can see here is a very sensible new version of ideology where ideology is not a false thought of reality. It is a picture of ourselves within reality. It is a proto-narrative thing, a fantasy thing. It is a view of how we, as an image of our self—remember selves are imaginary things, right?—fit into this image of reality we have. Both are imaginary. *Weltanschauung* or world-view seems to be a metaphysical way we think about the world as a whole, but Althusser's ideology doesn't work like that. *Weltanschauung* is a purely intellectual picture of the whole, one without the self, pseudo-objective, but the Althusserian view is one which includes our self, the way we represent our self in this world, if you understand self to be this imaginary picture

---

4   Louis Althusser, "Ideology and Ideological State Apparatuses," in *Lenin and Philosophy and Other Essays*, trans. Ben Brewster (New York: Monthly Review Press, 1971), 109.

of ourselves, following Sartre and Lacan in some very general way. The self is always there in this picture we have of the world which is ideology.

And this will be why ideology is eternal. Everybody thinks this is the weirdest thing you can imagine. Why does ideology have no history? Or, better still, a very annoying question for the Communist Party: Why will there always be ideology? In a socialist utopia, we're still going to have a self, and there is still going to be a reality out there. So the human animal is always going to have to imagine this self in a web of connections and to map its relationship to society. It's not going to have a transparent picture of society, however transparent everything else may be. Maybe we will have a more transparent view of the self. But ideology will mean we have to know where we are. We have to project a picture of the self out there, and that is going to be a narrative picture, because it tells us what to do. That is where interpellation comes in.

Somebody asked about race and interpellation. An ordinary reader, following Althusser's own illustration, will understand interpellation as indicating the presence of the police. Montag reminds us that this is the moment of the great demonstrations in the '60s and '70s, so, of course, the police are going to ask for your papers, and the policeman is going to identify you and offer you a categorization. That categorization is going to be as a worker, as an immigrant, a Black person, a woman, and so on. A whole set of ideological classifications on which our society is based is going to be a part of that interpellation. He seems to say we accept that. Of course, we don't have to accept that. I can say, "No, in my classification you're a pig and I am a culture worker, not an idle intellectual." But, I think the point would be that you're caught inside a system of classifications. You can resist one, but then you have to find another place for yourself. There is a certain asphyxiation to this classification system. Society has its various tasks and niches, and you have to fit into your own, even if you think you don't. Of course, the free-floating intellectuals don't want to think they're a part of classes, but, if you extend classes to classification, you can see why you can't get out of this system. It is your being-for-others, your visibility. You are a being-for-others, and that means that others have a name for you and a word for you. I think that's what interpellation really is. I am a so-and-so, and that means, yes, that's how other people see me. That is my classification. Now what do I do in the middle of that? That is, then, a situation, and, there, you can take various positions within it.

The difference of this account from Althusser's own would be that this classification system operates with the Symbolic, and, therefore, the Symbolic order enters ideology only insofar as ideology specifies this classification system. And we all know, by now, from Lévi-Strauss how closely bound up the Symbolic order is with classification systems of all kinds. So now we see that ideology is placing us within this system. Maybe we can become aware of that classification system, recognize where we're supposed to fit as an imaginary self, and transform our relationship to that position. We can see that there are conditions of existence, but that there could be an explosion of the Real in those conditions, which would be a very different situation from a simple acceptance of the system. All those things can come into play, but Montag doesn't take that route. He claims that it's ideology itself which is interpellating us, and he bases that on a Spinozan reading. I don't think those two readings are so far apart, but his is a dimension of all this that I have never really been aware of and that I think is an interesting one.

This is the sense in which there will always be ideology, because society will always have a classification system. This is why people were so annoyed with the Althusserians, because they would say, "Oh, you're a petty-bourgeois so-and-so," and that sounds like an attack. The problem here is that everybody assumes that being ideological is a bad thing, because whenever you classify somebody, you're attacking them. In a certain sense, that's what language always does. Language reifies people. So there are constant attempts to find euphemisms to suggest some way of relating to people and groups that escape what is already operative in language, and this is why in identity politics—going back to Hegel—there is also a politics of difference. The two are the same politically, and in either case the political problem revolves around secession. If you insist on the difference of a group through the Sartrean affirmation of that group, as in *Black Orpheus* or in Fanon, then, in a sense, you are also separating them off. The great political problem then becomes: what are the connections between those different kinds of identities? Is there a kind of liberal tolerance in which all these identities can work together? I think, in practice, it doesn't always work that way.

But this is all part of the matter of interpellation, which I think should be also thought of in terms of language and in terms of reification. All these things are present in Althusser's notion of ideology. But his point would be that you're never going to get out of those problems. Is the answer assimilation? Marx's answer was assimilation. He said if you don't want to be caught in this anti-Semitic politics, then, he says, Judaism has to disappear, just as Christianity and all other religious distinctions have to disappear in a revolutionary civil society. Of course, people have said this is a profoundly anti-Semitic point in Marx, that Marx is a self-hating Jew, an anti-Semitic Jew. I prefer to leave it as a profound ambiguity which is in the very nature of Marx's thought, but, of course, it gets talked about.

So this is where the question of the superstructure and state apparatuses comes in. Who is doing the interpellation? Remember that, for Althusser, that is to be a materialist question, and so, clearly, the answer is the institutions (I won't use the word "apparatus" now). They are installed in society in such a way that they tell you where you belong. They are producing a classification system. The point is that, among these institutions, besides the educational system—and, remember, there are all kinds of versions of educational discipline, yes, in a very centralized country like France, but also in England where kids are classified when they're eleven or twelve through exams, when they're picked out and put on their educational track—there are plenty of other ones. Religion, for example. I suppose, a few years ago, people would not have insisted on that so much, but, if you look at Ireland and the Troubles, if you look at evangelicals here or in South America, then you know that religion is a powerful force for ideological reproduction. And, finally, the family. Sartre's Freudian idea is that you first learn about classes and the outside world through the family. Class comes in through the practices of the family, just as sexism, patriarchy, the position of sex and gender in the family. All of those things are going to be apparatuses that reproduce ideology in new forms, no doubt, because each generational renewal will modify this preexisting ideological material.

Now, in a certain sense, as people have always said, the repressive state apparatuses are not unrelated to this ideological realm. Both Pascal and Rousseau say your relationship to the police begins as soon as you learn to recognize their uniform. They don't have to do anything. They don't even have to take out their truncheon, because the uniform reminds you that they have the monopoly of physical force, as Max Weber said, and that's enough. Now does that refer us to superstructure or base, body or mind? Obviously, much of this has to do with the superstructure, and the bigger question one wants to ask is, in that case, how one can think of the state as a superstructure. How can one consider law and power as a superstructure? Shouldn't that be a material thing in the base? As soon as you ask that question, we're going to get into functionalism. Everybody thinks functionalism is bad. I don't quite see why, because, in some fundamental way, the superstructure is defined as what perpetuates the base. I prefer my own illustration in terms of immune systems. Here is the immune system. The superstructure is part of that. The minute the base gets a disease or virus, the superstructure is going to work overtime to try to save the base. It doesn't want the base to be changed in some deeper way. So all of these things are, I think, functional in the sense that they are all in some organic—although nobody would like that word either—solidarity with each other, much like the way parts of the body are in organic solidarity with each other.

As I have suggested, Althusser is here providing his version of what Gramsci calls hegemony. Althusser will have a real problem here, because he has to respect Gramsci as one of the great theoreticians of the communist movement, since Gramsci occupies this commanding position for any communist. But, nonetheless, he has to be nervous about Gramscian humanism and about dialectical tendencies in Gramsci. Nonetheless, both meditate on how ideology—culture, let's say—functions to reproduce the system and to keep it in being, both right now and across generations, something which I may say the socialist societies were not really able to do very well, but maybe this society hasn't truly figured it out either. You would want to know, from our perspective, where commodification and consumerism fit into this. What kind of a superstructure do those phenomena produce? At this point, we can go back to the fact of individuation itself. I said that the very structure of society has formed you as a separate individual with your own destiny, or your own death, Heidegger would say. Is that ideological? Yes, of course, because it produces a notion of the self as separate from everybody else. It is a force of destruction of the communal. But consumerism has another kind of relationship to the self which may even involve Freudian attachments—acquiring objects and so on. These are things that would have to be included in any newer elaborations of all this.

These are then Althusser's two great contributions. Now there is also the work of art, on which an Althusserian position is articulated in Macherey's essay on Lenin and Tolstoy.[5] On that point, let me just say one thing. Remember that one of the great enemies for many of these poststructuralists, beginning with Lacan and Althusser, is unity or unification. They

---

5   Pierre Macherey, "Lenin, Critic of Tolstoy," in *A Theory of Literary Production*, trans. Geoffrey Wall (London: Routledge & Kegan Paul, 1978), 105–51.

have to have their breaks and gaps. What Macherey and Althusser are attacking in the work of art is its unification. New Criticism taught us from the very beginning that the work is a unified whole; criticism would then be about demonstrating that wholeness. Macherey's and the Althusserian view of art is that art is a bundle of different raw materials. It is pieced together out of all those things and marked with a kind of unity which will reflect back our illusion of unity as a subject, which extends out onto the unity of experience and social unity. So this notion of unification is the ideological point in art. Heidegger wanted the destruction of metaphysics, while Derrida wants its deconstruction. What Althusser and Macherey propose for art is literally an unconstruction. Let's take all that apart in its turn and see why we have this notion of unification of the work. Maybe we'll have time to come back to that on another occasion.

March 4, 2021

14

How to Avoid Meaning

{Derrida}

Many of your questions were concerned with definitional problems that we can easily resolve. There are no definitions. This was Nietzsche's idea, and you could expand it by saying one of two things. Either the person who asked you for definitions is hostile and wishes to throw a monkey wrench in your ideas, or they're asking you not for the meaning of the term but for its use. This second idea will be very important for us in reading Derrida and Deleuze, for example, who assert that, even though meaning is a will-o'-the-wisp, you can show how terms are used; you can show their effects. Anyway, so much for definitions.

Then there are philosophical questions—we can deal with those—and, finally, the questions that can't be answered, or at least problems to which I have no solution. I think the most fruitful question was put to me roughly as follows. We go to one writer—let's say Sartre—and we find out what Sartre is saying, and in some sense we have to appreciate the truth of Sartre. That is, if we don't see the use of Sartre's thought, then there's not much point in messing with it. But then we go on to another stage—Lacan, for example—where we may find some Sartrean motifs, but where we also find something radically different from Sartre. So which is true? Or is this a Hegelian system in which we have stages, and if so, are the stages going anywhere? In our case, they are going somewhere in time, but I don't think they are going to reach any ultimate truth like they do in Hegel. So we are left with a problem we can call "historicism." That is to say, we're in a situation where there aren't any absolutes anymore. We're not going to reach a stage of ultimate truth. That is the precondition of the so-called post-structuralist thought that we are entering now, and perhaps even in Lacan or Althusser. Is Marxism the ultimate truth in Althusser? Yes, but he is trying to work out what exactly it is! What can he do with the ultimately determining instance? And is psychoanalysis an ultimate truth for Lacan? With the Real, we never know what it is until it overwhelms us, and, therefore, only when we are blinded by it do we ever reach it. Is that a truth, an absolute? What about linguistics for each of them? Can there be a science of linguistics? Can there be *science*? Or is that not yet another illusory concept? So, in the absence of any absolute, we are left to figure out, for each of these stages, what their local truth is. One of you observed quite appropriately that we are always using this expression: "the truth of such-and-such." The truth of the ontic is ontological. The truth of the Sartrean taste for skiing is the will to glide over being. Is that not relativistic? Yes, but we need a new notion of relativism. Each of these historical moments has its truth. Many German thinkers, at least in the Frankfurt School, use the idea of the "moment of truth" of an idea or position. The entirety of a system may be illusory, but under the right circumstances it lets off a glimpse of truth. Of course, that still presupposes that you are going to fit it into another, ultimately true system, which conflicts with the anti-systematic aims of this period.

Therefore, we have to approach a notion of theory. Theory is going to tell us what is wrong. It is going to question whether language can say anything or not. If it is going to say something, don't we have to submit it to radical critiques, as Althusser did in the letter I read you, telling people "don't use that word" and "don't use this word"? Be very careful to ward off the ideological misunderstandings that certain words carry. Words are baggage. They carry ideology around in them. So you have to be careful that you use the right words in the right situation and indeed that you put them together in the right way. So, yes, to say that the truth of something is something else, maybe that's a bad way of putting it after all. Maybe that should be submitted to critique.

But I would say that there is no answer to this question of historicism. I mentioned Ranke's idea in the early nineteenth century that all ages are immediate to God, meaning that each age has its own truth, its own absolute. The absolute of the Babylonians is not ours anymore. But there is Babylonian art. Marx even comes to this. At the very end of the introduction to the *Grundrisse*, he breaks off with the question of Greek art. He says that Ancient Greece is the eternal childhood of the human race, but why is it that, in full capitalism, we still find the Greeks attractive? What can be their value for us, since we're not in the Greek world anymore? What is their truth for us? Gramsci called Marxism an absolute historicism, and I subscribe to that idea. We get the truths of these other systems—these other moments of time, of history—by way of notions of production, of class, of struggle, of history. We have to have a certain relativism, but it must be an absolute relativism. Otherwise, we just throw out the rest of history. The most distressing thing about common language philosophy and Anglo-American philosophy, for example, is that they decided to start philosophy afresh to rid the discipline of its false problems. They wanted to look at how we're thinking today, and in that case the rest of thought is irrelevant. It is irrelevant what mistakes Hobbes or Hume or Plato made. We don't need the history of philosophy. I don't believe that, but of course I'm an intellectual and I have a commitment to these older things. So it goes back to your situation. I can't answer this question any more than that.

Then there were questions about the construction of subjectivity. I don't know that we have gotten there yet. I would say that, in the structuralist period, the major thought was that language produces us, that what we think of as our identity and our subjectivity is an effect of language. There is a line of poetry I quoted in an old chapter on structuralism: "I was word among the letters."[1] So, in a funny kind of way, the "I," the "me," subjectivity, is produced out of the categories of language. I don't think anybody would go that far today. So is it a nothingness, as Sartre thinks? Is it produced by language? Whatever answer you give to that question will be a political answer, because it's going to have something to do with subjectivity. If you think subjectivity is not to be unified, then you have a political duty to destroy the illusions of unification. In a sense, that would be the politics of much of poststructuralism. The One is an illusion, but it is an illusion that has effects. It is an objective appearance; and the people who believe in it want unification. Let's take it further: they want purity.

---

1   "*J'ai été mot parmi les lettres.*" Denis Roche, quoted in Marcelin Pleynet, "*La Poésie doit avoir pour but . . .*" in *Tel Quel: Théorie d'ensemble* (Paris: Seuil, 1968), 106. See Fredric Jameson, *The Prison-House of Language*, 138.

Does that mean racial purity? Well, yes, of course! Then we have Nazism and fascism. So these thinkers see unification as a noxious political ideal.

Now I want to go on to Derrida, simply because we have to make some progress here. I don't see how you could write a good book on Derrida. You could write Derridean books about other things, but how could you write a Derridean book on Derrida? Geoffrey Bennington tried to write a little intellectual biography of Derrida, but he collaborated with Derrida himself, so you can't tell who's speaking most of the time.[2] You are never going to find all of Derrida in any one of his works. There is no masterpiece or basic work, and he doesn't write in that genre anymore. So I would say that above all I would recommend this late work called *A Derrida Reader: Between the Blinds*, edited by Peggy Kamuf, who was a close disciple of his and knows this stuff very well. Derrida collaborated on this as well. The extracts are excellently chosen, although it only goes up to 1991, so it would have been better for it to be published a little later. As it turns out, in the later years, there's a kind of turning in Derrida. Is it a *Kehre* in Heidegger's sense? I'm not sure. But something emerges called "positive deconstruction." That is, it isn't negative anymore. It is saying something, and there Derrida is dealing with—although it isn't as immediate as a book of political science—topics like justice, violence, immigration, citizenship, the other. In our own journal, which is *South Atlantic Quarterly*, which Michael Hardt edits, there is the Spring 2007 issue, edited by Ian Balfour, called "Late Derrida." This will give you a number of essays on the kind of things he did in that period, which we won't really be dealing with here.

There were a number of questions on Derrida, beginning with the crucial question: What is deconstruction? First, I have to go back and tell you a little bit of biography. What I want you to understand is that none of these people had so many enemies as Derrida. Derrida would drive people crazy. When he first came to Yale, everybody wanted to hear Derrida. His lecture lasted for three hours, so, after an hour and a half, you saw dinosaurs going crazy and trying to get out of there as fast as they could. But, with Derrida and with the Derrideans—he had an American follow-ing—you can't say anything which cannot be deconstructed, so you could imagine the kind of annoyance that people felt with this and the kinds of

---

2 Geoffrey Bennington and Jacques Derrida, *Jacques Derrida*, trans. Geoffrey Bennington (Chicago: University of Chicago Press), 1999.

reproaches it garnered. "It's nihilism. They say that there are no meanings. It's terrible and it's destroying education and culture, destroying the minds of our students, and we should get rid of it." In France, Derrida used to say, every time Heidegger comes up in the newspapers—some new revelation about his Nazism—it's merely a pretense for attacking deconstruction. I think that's probably true, but I'm using it only to illustrate the force of the hatred of deconstruction before he becomes a grand figure.

In a sense, his first following is American. He doesn't have the right French degrees. He doesn't go through the system in the same way. I don't know if I've told you this anecdote before, but I do always think it's funny. In the 1830s, Hegel was already in Berlin. There was a brilliant but very arrogant young man who thought that Hegel was terrible and that he himself had discovered the meaning of life. That was the young Schopenhauer, and as he began to teach, he scheduled his seminars at exactly the same time as Hegel's, because, if anybody was going to Hegel's seminars then he didn't want any part of them. Well, he got no students. That was the end of Schopenhauer's teaching, leaving him the time to live off his personal fortune and to write the things we now all read. He was a genius, but the truth of his work was not for the 1830s but for the 1850s. Suddenly, with the rediscovery of ancient materialism in Lange's *History of Materialism*—very important for everybody at the time, especially Nietzsche—changes occur in the whole temperature of intellectual life and in this musical pessimism that begins with Wagner. So I see Derrida, with a lot of differences here, like Schopenhauer. I imagine Althusser up there in the auditorium of the École teaching his Marxist students, hundreds of them, while, down in the basement, Derrida is giving a little seminar on Husserl. As he said, if people had an interest in Husserl then those are the students he wanted to work with. Far from hating Althusser, however, the two of them got along very well, and as I said before, he was the only one to visit Althusser in his last years.

So there was not really any place for Derrida at the beginning of his career in France. These trips to the United States, to Yale, then Irvine, earned him an American following which then reverberated back into France. A whole school of American Derrideans forms around him and his work. I think it's easier to illustrate what is going on here if you take a very quick glance at his collaborator Paul de Man, who is the one who finally brought him to Yale. De Man had a much clearer *Weltanschauung*, so to speak, and it was simply that—several of these people believed this, and I have vaguely illustrated it in science-fictional ways—language is inhuman. Humanism is simply for people who believe that human life is meaningful and central. Freud talked about his Copernican revolution. The Earth used to be the center of the universe, and the sun turned around the Earth. Copernicus changes that. Freud's Copernican revolution is that human life used to turn around consciousness. Now, suddenly, human consciousness turns around the unconscious. It is radically displaced and decentered. "Decentering" is your best concept for understanding this kind of thought. Derrida doesn't get rid of the subject, but he radically decenters it, as do other thinkers in their own ways. But the notion that it is bad for human consciousness to be in the center is already in Sartre. Sartre's idea is that the bourgeois person wants to believe that bourgeois order is the center of the world. Therefore, to be at the center, you have to have margins and marginals; the respectable bourgeoisie has to have criminals and deviants in order to exist as a center, a subject. So you can see that there is a political dimension to this decentering, too, and we'll shortly get that demonstrated in Foucault. There is a political basis for this.

So Derrida's work will perform a decentering in some way, but it will also be a linguistic operation in the Althusserian sense. Derrida doesn't use an expression like ideology, but the kind of things the Althusserians did with the language of the humanist or the non-Marxist, tracking down the ideology at work inside of language, resembles what Derrida is doing, except he doesn't need Marxism anymore. He had a relationship to Marx, but that's not crucial and certainly not absolute. Derrida doesn't have any absolutes. So what is it that you're doing if you're tracking down all these things going on in language, which you used to be able to call ideological, but which you now want to get rid of? *Do* you want to get rid of them? *Can* you get rid of them? What are you going to call that process? He begins with Husserl, but, if you begin with Husserl, you end up sliding down into Heidegger. Much of Derrida's work is a commentary on Heidegger, and this is why he took the attacks on Heidegger personally. Not that he was an anti-Semite or Nazi—far from it—but he understood that you could get at him through Heidegger. Why is he talking about Heidegger so much? And, besides, that's Germanic; maybe he's not really French, because he's Jewish. The attacks would go in this direction.

People asked about Heidegger's relationship to history. I don't know if he has a relation to history, but he has a vision of the history of philosophy, which he called the history of metaphysics. For Heidegger, at a certain moment, there was a Fall; we lost the sense of Being. Now, in Heidegger, the sense of Being is not what you might think. Heidegger's work has religious overtones. There can be no doubt about that. He was raised a Catholic, and, on his deathbed, he asked for a Catholic funeral. But, on the other hand, for Heidegger, the proper approach to thought is not to believe in Being. No, it's to ask the question of Being, and the question of Being is very simple: Why is there something rather than nothing at all? And if you answer that question, you're in metaphysics, because what you should be doing is raising the question, opening the question, Heidegger might say. It would be the same with personal identity. What is human nature? What is the being of *Dasein*? With *Dasein*, you can at least add up the symptoms, but with Being, the point is that the question about Being is the same as Being. It's only when you glimpse this question that you have some contact with Being. So, clearly, a philosophy that had all the answers, a philosophy that, by deciding what Being was, got rid of the question of Being, is already metaphysical, and philosophy will be metaphysical up until . . . Nietzsche? Not quite, he says. Nietzsche thought he was getting rid of metaphysics, Heidegger says in his long lectures on Nietzsche, but he was still tied up in its resolution (the will to power), whereas I, Heidegger, am finally eliminating such resolutions. What do we do with metaphysics? It is an operation Heidegger calls, a little alarmingly, *Destruktion*, destruction. We must destroy the history of metaphysics. We must destroy metaphysics itself. It sounds very violent for someone whose work is so much thought of as a quasi-religious meditation.

Derrida believes in something analogous. "Metaphysical" would be a bad word for him. But, if you alter Heidegger's word just a little bit, and instead of *Destruktion* you say *deconstruction*, then we're in a similar relationship to metaphysics. We are seeing that metaphysics is providing a ground, a belief system, on which various concepts are built, and we are examining the building blocks of that metaphysical structure. Can we destroy them? Heidegger thinks that we could go back to the old, pre-Socratic relationship to the question of Being—or maybe it's too late. In his last, posthumous interview he famously said: "Only a god can save us now." In Derrida, I don't think there is a utopian element. He doesn't think we can get rid of metaphysics, but we can become aware of its actions, its effects, and we can track them down. That would be something like ideology for Marx and the Marxist tradition, although Althusser has another use for that word.

So what does this business of deconstruction result in? I think Derrida understands that we're not going to get out of metaphysics, at least not that easily. He finds, then, in postwar Heidegger, an odd thing. Heidegger is asked about humanism, because Sartre wrote this infamous essay, "Existentialism Is a Humanism," which I think gave rise to a lot of misunderstandings. At the end of the war, Germany is divided. The Red Army is right on the edge of the occupation zones of the French, American, and English occupying armies. Berlin is still this open place. This is the situation in which Heidegger offers his essay on humanism, the one place he talks about Marx. He says that the theory of alienation in the early Marx could offer a relationship to Being. He could allow a certain Marx, the Marx of alienation, to be a meditation on Being. That doesn't come back very much in Heidegger, but you can see the situation in the mid-forties, where, having just gone through World War II, the Soviets could very easily overrun Western Europe if they wanted to. Heidegger is thinking: "I didn't quite get to be the philosopher of Nazism, because after all there were a lot of other claimants, and they didn't like me much, just tolerated me, but could I survive under Soviet occupation? Could I become the philosopher of Marxism? Could I invent an ontology of Marxism? But," Heidegger says, "I don't like the word 'alienation.' I'm not going to use that word—and even the word 'Being'"—because Heidegger begins by being suspicious of language. If you don't understand what he means by Being, then using the word is going to be worse than bad. So he proposes to draw an X through it. You can see in these early essays of Heidegger words with an X through them. "Being" with an X, "humanism" with an X. You tell people you're not humanist. Well, then, especially in that context, for God's sake, they think you want to kill people. You're not humanist? You don't believe in human life? What do we call it now in American foreign policy? Human values? You're thought to be immoral. That would be like Nietzsche, beyond good and evil. Does beyond good and evil mean everything is permitted? In Dostoyevsky, sort of, as a narrative experiment, but I don't think Nietzsche meant that if everything is permitted then you're going to go out and kill people. So, in Heidegger, you have to go on using these words. Derrida will make that into a concept he calls "under erasure." We have to go on using this old metaphysical, ideological language, but now we're going to use it under erasure, X'd out, and, that way, we are going to know that it isn't the right word, a metaphysical word, but we have to go on using it. This is what Gayatri Spivak ingeniously calls "strategic essentialism." It

is a position Derrida shares with Heidegger, but, in a way, it also determines the whole movement of his philosophy, which we're going to look
at now.

Is it a philosophy? It is not a system. He was always saying that deconstruction is not a method. Did I tell you this other anecdote? It's one of
my favorites. A distinguished modern theologian, Paul Tillich, is giving an
elaborate philosophical speech, and, at the end of it, somebody stands up
and says: "That's all very well and good, all that complicated philosophy.
But I just want to ask you one question. Do you believe in God?" And
Tillich says, "If you have to put it that way, I don't." As with Derrida, God
is under erasure. I would call this an aesthetic of deconstruction. That
isn't a word that Derrida would have liked, because he didn't like people
to think of this as a literary endeavor, but I would say that a Derrida essay
of the earlier period follows a rule. The rule is that you are not to make a
philosophical proposition. You are not to make a pronouncement. You are
not to have a system. You are not to emit any metaphysical propositions.
The whole of the work must be analytical and negative, and that's why
Derrida always—as I say, his work is related to commentaries—works
with a text, and it is generally a fragment, because you cannot comment
on things much beyond that. It is always a fragment of a text. So, instead
of doing Rousseau's Second Discourse, he does a fragment of what was a
note for the Second Discourse, which is called "The Origins of Language."
Instead of doing Marx, he does a little fragment from *The German Ideology*
on Stirner. Instead of doing Freud, you get a few sentences of Freud. The
whole point of the commentary is the deconstruction, the unraveling of
this text which thought it said something, but which finally doesn't say
anything at all that is not full of metaphysical assumptions. What it says
has to be under erasure.

The reason I mention Paul de Man is that this is much clearer in his
work. De Man thinks that the meaning of language is tropological, figures
of speech, metaphor, metonymy, and all the rest. But, most of the time,
the people who believe in meaning, the scientists and the philosophers,
don't think that this is the case. They think they're reasoning in a language
that means something. I would say they believe in literal language, that
you could name a concept and use words as names, whereas, he says, in
fact, only literary writing is really truthful, because what it shows is that
it is entirely a matter of tropes. It is aware of itself as tropological. So he
is another nihilist.

The first contact between de Man and Derrida is when de Man writes an essay characteristically attacking Derrida's *Grammatology* for its analysis of Rousseau. He says, yes, what you say about Rousseau is all true, but Rousseau knew it already, because Rousseau was a literary writer, if one wants to put it that way—it sounds horrible—and his writing was aware of itself as tropes. He knew that he wasn't saying something in the way in which the philosophers were saying something. So de Man would be a nice caricature—my caricature, of course—of what Derrida is doing on a larger and more philosophical scale; and, of course, the result of something like that is that finally there isn't any literal language. All language is figurative. How can you say anything? In a sense, the first target of all this is meaning as such, and that is very distressing to a lot of people, clearly.

So what happens in a Derrida essay? First, I'll give you a materialist analysis of Derrida. In the places he had to teach, most often the École, he spends the year preparing students for the basic exam. The topics of these exams are given in advance every year. Let's say it's life and death. Then Derrida has an assignment: to prepare his students for life and death. So he has to pick his texts. What's he going to choose? A text from vitalism, Bergson. Freud, of course, on the death wish. Heidegger on death. So Derrida is constrained by his professional system to work on certain texts. But that suits him perfectly, because his work each year will be an analysis of certain crucial texts which he can work with very closely. The deconstruction of those texts will be his production for the year: his seminars and then the essays that come from the seminars. So that would be a materialist explanation of why his work takes the form it does. It could not take the form of his own philosophy, as in someone like Schopenhauer. He can't have a philosophy. He is a commentator, an exegete, but a philosophical exegete who is going to take philosophy apart.

Will nothing positive come of this? The other side of this negative procedure is the set of neologisms. He is going to invent a series of new words. Remember, the old ones are useless. You have to use them with a cross through them, an X. So he will find himself obliged to invent new ones. "Logocentrism," for example. We don't have an old word for that. That's a diagnostic term which is going to tell us something about a certain kind of thought—not necessarily even a philosophical one—a kind of thought which believes that, in language and particularly in spoken language, there's an idea of a certain kind of presence. Although not quite a neologism, "presence" will be another one of these keywords.

What do you do when you have a keyword like that? Clearly one of the crucial themes here—in all of this, really—is the word "difference." Suppose I took *différence* and I changed the third vowel: *différance*. In French it's pronounced the same! But the writing is different. So I have made this common word into a neologism, and it will now begin to have a diagnostic meaning. It will mean something in space and something in time. He uses *espacement*. He gets it from English 'spacing.' It is also supposed to mean something temporally, namely deferral, an incompleteness in time. The present is not complete, nor are you centered in the present. Deferral means putting it off. In spacing, you're never in the center either. You are at a certain distance. So *différance* with an *a* will be an ingenious way of saying something without saying something. We don't have to use erasure anymore. We don't need the X, because the word is telling us this is not your usual meaning of difference. This is a special kind of difference. This is a two-step thing. We have the text trying to say one thing, and now I'm going to show that what's going on here is not quite what we think. It needs to be rectified. On the other hand, it can't be rectified. The neologism is going to present my philosophy, but I don't have a philosophy. So it is going to present you a way of thinking through this deconstructed text.

In a sense, that means that all of Derrida is the same. He's going to do the same thing with everything. He's going to do it for linguistics, psychoanalysis, eventually, Marxism—all kinds of texts, because the topics that the École has to deal with are going to be immensely varied, meaning his work is immensely varied, yet the operation is the same. Is grammatology a method? That doesn't really catch on, but deconstruction does. We forget that that's another of his neologisms. It's the great success, in a sense, of Derrideanism, although any "-ism" is of course a reification, the thought of the university as Lacan might put it.

I want to point out to you that my mode of dealing with these problems is in terms of reification. What he is coming up against here is reification. Every meaning that you put into words is going to slowly congeal like grease in a pan; it's going to become an object. If anything "means," we would have to put "mean" under erasure. In French, "to mean" could be *signifier*, but that's caught up in semiotics; the more common expression is *vouloir dire*, literally, "to want to say." That is a very suspicious way of translating meaning, because meaning, we thought, was somehow objectively established. The philosopher establishes a meaning, a position. But if it's just *vouloir dire*, just what he wanted to say, then it could be anything! Meaning falls to pieces. So you can see how, via the French, the very notion of meaning that Husserl was after, and the notion of a living present and some ultimate stability of things, is going to fall apart under this kind of examination.

Next time, we will actually look at some of these texts and see how he does this, especially in the little section of the *Grammatology* in which all of the major themes of this early period come through: presence, origin, ontology itself, trace, difference, logocentrism. It's all there in that little section.

March 11, 2021

15

Linguistic Politics of the Third Way

{Derrida}

To begin, there are five strands of contemporary French theory that I want simply to mention to show what has come out of all this. This means that the course ought, at some point, to deal with the question of what theory is, something I'm very willing to do, but not so much today. It will also have to deal with a question of whether theory exists anymore. Is there a death of theory, along with the death of the author, the end of art, and all the rest of it? There is certainly a regression in philosophy in general, very much in France, a regression to the standard philosophical disciplines. Theory was always a revolt against disciplines; I think you found this revolt in Derrida, where it's clear that he wants to undermine the philosophical tradition. Heidegger, as I told you last time, uses the word "destroy," *Destruktion*, which, of course, he didn't mean, because his whole work is a set of commentaries on the classics. If he was anything, Heidegger was a great classicist, and I think his commentaries on the Platonic dialogues are always interesting and full of insights. At any rate, theory, if it meant revolting against a philosophical system, can be said to have waned in an era when everybody is returning to a system. And I would add that many people are turning all these systems into various versions of aesthetics, that our period is a period of aestheticization—a word I borrow from Benjamin—although I won't be able to take it any further than that at the moment. But that is where we're heading. I think somebody like Rancière is a perfect example of someone who started out with Althusser and ended up in the arts. Visuality, commodification, all those things today fall under aesthetics. Anyway, that is not the issue.

I provided the Stiegler article as an approximation of the future, more as an announcement or promise of something than an actual thing, although I think it is very important for you to understand how it could be such a promise.[1] I don't think you could say that Stiegler was a Derridean in any strict sense, but Derrida was very good to him and made a lot of things possible for him that would not have been possible otherwise. I wanted you to see how a renewed meditation on media could come out of a Derridean category like "supplement." That's the way I see Stiegler. Derrida would never produce a study of media. But out of Derrideanism comes something which is absolutely current today, a certain version of media theory; I won't say it is the only one. So that was the point of the Stiegler article: to anticipate some of those questions which we find in Derrida about memory.

As we turn now to feminism, maybe I should go back to this business of the relationship to foreign countries in philosophy. I've noted that philosophy today, whether we're talking about Germany, France, America, or some other place, has become a nationalist thing. The Americans want to go back to William James and Peirce. The Germans don't have to go back, really, because they're still in Husserl, Heidegger, Nietzsche, and Hegel. And the French, oddly, with Deleuze, will go back to their one great modern philosopher, because their tradition has been, until Sartre, much more mechanical and academic, and that one great philosopher is, of course, Bergson. We will find Bergson's work on time behind a lot of this stuff. But, as far as the international connections, I want to mark two of them very mechanically. Husserl came to Paris in 1929 and lectured at the Sorbonne. He gave—it is appropriate, since he is in France—what he would call his *Cartesian Meditations*. Of course, there is a longstanding relationship between Descartes's *cogito* and phenomenology. So this is one link between Husserl's problematics and those which will preoccupy both French phenomenology and those attacking it. There we are back to Derrida.

---

1 Bernard Stiegler, "Memory," in *Critical Terms for Media Studies*, eds. W. J. T. Mitchell and Mark Hansen (Chicago: University of Chicago Press, 2010), 64–87.

But then, in the 1930s, a Russian arrives in Paris: Alexandre Kojève. He gives a series of lectures on Hegel, and, in particular, on the master-slave dialectic. Kojève is a very interesting character. He fled the Revolution; however, in a sense, he remained a believer and a Stalinist. He equates Stalin to Napoleon in Hegel, for whom Napoleon is the world spirit on horseback. But Kojève ultimately dies as a bureaucrat, in the service of the European Community in Brussels, so his life follows an interesting trajectory. But these lectures on Hegel are the massive reintroduction of Hegel in France, and his intervention functions a little like that of Parmenides in ancient Greece. Everybody attends: the young Sartre, the young Merleau-Ponty, the young Lacan, everybody is listening to these lectures in the mid-thirties, including people I haven't mentioned in these lectures yet: Georges Bataille, Raymond Queneau, people I want to touch on a little bit this morning, just very briefly. So there is a connection with German philosophy, and that is what, in a sense, Badiou was talking about in the first essay we read together.

Now what about America? You have seen the love-hate relationship of Beauvoir and Sartre with America. I have told you that Derrida's following was essentially American in the beginning, although he has some French disciples, but I think he was never quite as popular in France as over here. So, when it comes to feminism, I think you also have to know that there is a lot of tension between what we call feminism in the United States and French feminism. Americans have felt that French feminists are far too theoretical and abstract.

The first question about feminism is: Who can be a feminist? Is Beauvoir really a feminist? She ends up joining women's groups after they are formed; she doesn't take part in founding them. Beauvoir's relationship to feminism is like something that is so obvious that you don't even think of it for a moment until somebody points it out. She came to write *The Second Sex* after somebody approached her and said some things to her which suddenly made her realize that she, Beauvoir, is also a woman, and that this is a weird category to be a part of. There are very special things and problems involved in this that she never thought of, because she feels completely certain of herself, and she doesn't feel oppressed, coming from a well-to-do family. She has been successful all her life, but, suddenly, she realizes that there are many things about women's condition which are unique. This is like the outsider principle: let's say you have a mathematical problem or a theatrical problem in staging; the professionals knock their heads over it and can't figure out a way out, until somebody wanders in who has nothing to do with the profession who says, "Oh, you just have to put this together with that," and, suddenly, the whole thing is solved. The outsider sees things which the professional, trained in their blinders, can't see. That is sort of Beauvoir's relationship to her description of women. In a sense, she comes from outside the condition of women. I don't say she thinks she is a man, but she never thought about her femininity, and, suddenly, she realizes: I have to describe this strange thing! Suddenly men and women come to find out that this condition is strange.

So, Beauvoir, a feminist? What about Kristeva? She has written on feminism; she would certainly not object to it. But, on the other hand, I think that there is a great tension between American feminism, and, indeed, maybe much of the world, but especially France. And it is important, in this respect, that we be careful, because French sexism is not the same as American sexism. Yes, of course, if you want "sexism" or "patriarchy" to be huge categories of that kind, of course, all these things fit together, as they do with racism across the world. But, if you want to be specific in the modes in which these things operate, you have to understand that they are different in France, and you have to be sensitive to that difference, or else you aren't going to understand what these women are talking about. All right, so much for that. We'll come back to it next time.

While we're jumping ahead, I also want to jump back in time to mention two people from the pre-war period who were behind the scenes here, both of whom were very prestigious. I haven't included them because, in a sense, they belong to the prehistory of this period, and it would be difficult to pick things for you to read, but you should know about their existence. One is Maurice Blanchot, who has a very rigorous, almost Mallarméan reflection on literature and death; literature and death are two themes of his work that entangle each other in all kinds of strange ways. The writer of unique kinds of essays, Blanchot was not a leftist; he was actually a royalist and a reactionary in the '30s. If you had student movements in the '30s, they were right-wing student movements. I wanted to say that also because it occurred to me that, with the events of January 6 at the Capitol, you should keep in mind a larger understanding of French history where we can find something analogous. In 1934, when Hitler is in power in Germany, countries are still sealed off from each other. This is far from the EU. These are really foreign countries, and it is completely unlike the kind of travel before World War I, where you didn't even need a passport.

Nonetheless, people know what is happening in Germany. There are right-wing groups which range from monarchism to outright fascism in France. Some of these groups have a great demonstration in 1934; they march on the National Assembly, and the whole thing is dispersed by police and opposed by left-wing groups, including the Communist Party. And it is from that anti-fascist demonstration that the Popular Front emerges as a reaction. That is, in a classical Sartrean scenario, it is the demonstration of fascism that awakens the countermovement of the Left. Before that, in the so-called Third Period, the Communist Party brandished a very stupid slogan about "social fascists," a hostility to the Socialist Party. That gets dropped completely in this period. Meanwhile, of course, the Spanish Civil War is in the background after '36. Suddenly, there forms a unity on the Left, which, indeed, comes to power in France. France swings back and forth. The next counterrevolution will be, of course, World War II and the zone of Vichy, the counterrevolution against the Popular Front. Then you have the *Libération*, the liberation of Paris, which is this upswing of leftist utopianism. Then a bourgeois moment, the return of General de Gaulle to power, which is a different General de Gaulle, in a way, but that's another question. So Blanchot began as a monarchist, but not a Hitlerite, because you understand that, if you're for the return of the French monarchy, as with the *Action Française* of Charles Maurras—and this is a very powerful thing in the politics of that period—you're not going to be pro-German. If you're a French nationalist, you don't want the Germans whether they're fascists or not. Until the Occupation, it's as complicated for the Right as it is for the Left.

Anyway, Blanchot separates himself from that. He is a very mysterious figure. After the war, he becomes more and more sympathetic to the student movement, and like everybody else is overwhelmed by May '68. So he becomes something of a left-wing, if esoteric, literary figure. Mallarmé plays a role in all of that, as in Derrida and in Badiou, who calls himself a Mallarméan. What emerges from Blanchot is not exactly an avant garde. It's not Surrealism, but it's a more esoteric relationship of writing itself to being in some way, although it's not Derridean, either. All right, so much for Blanchot.

The other person I want to mention is Georges Bataille, a renegade Surrealist who starts his own movement, the *Collège de sociologie*, a kind of secret society. There are a number of people involved, some foreigners; Walter Benjamin is a part of that. What is it? Well, to this day, we don't really know. Did it involve all kinds of secret meetings, orgies, things like that, rituals? They were all interested in occult things. Bataille wrote, as did some of the others, philosophical pornographic novels, so to speak—that is, novels in which sexuality is mixed up with mysticism and philosophy. But his major idea, I would say, is the notion of excess, what exceeds forms by breaking out of them, what resists form in the name of what he called *l'informe*, the formless. Rosalind Krauss, one of our great art critics, has demonstrated the omnipresence of this underlying raw material, what Kristeva will call *chora*, a kind of magma that is underneath art and that bursts out of it; that is a very Bataille-type idea. All of these people, the imitations of the Surrealist movement around Kristeva, for example, will draw a lot of inspiration from Bataille, and I have a special use I want to make of him today, which is why I'm mentioning him.

There is an essay by Derrida on Bataille in *Writing and Difference*, which is, I would say, his most elegant collection of essays, essays that haven't blossomed into the excesses of the three-hour seminar, but which still keep the essay form. Foucault was very angry at the essay on his *Folie et Déraison*. Other essays are on Lévi-Strauss, Jabès, Bataille, Artaud, Levinas.

So there is a lot of interest in this collection, *Writing and Difference*, and it is a much more measured introduction to Derrida's . . . thought? Does Derrida think? I tried to make the point the other day that there aren't thoughts in Derrida, or, at least, that they're not produced like little objects. I would rather call it his "cognitive performance." These are performances, performances of reading and writing. They are to be experienced, but one must avoid—and I always come back to this notion of reification—reifying them into ideas. People take logocentrism or deconstruction to be thoughts, the philosophical positions of Derrida. No, I think they are names for moments in a performance, and Derrida's misfortune is, first, that he started with writing, got associated with ideas of writing, *écriture*, and then that stuck, so he is known as the philosopher of *écriture*. Well, that doesn't make any sense. He isn't a philosopher of writing. Then he himself had the brilliance to coin this phrase "deconstruction," and then it's all over, because he is stuck with this forever. But maybe there is some-thing good about this business of reification. Maybe we have to first reify things like ideas, to give them names, before we can then break them up and understand that the names don't work. I have tried to insist on the way in which language is central for all these people, not because it's an instrument of communication, but because it is always a problem. These people have decided that it is a problem. Already this is true of existentialism itself. If you look back at Pascal, there is a constant meditation on why language doesn't work. In fact, Heidegger, of all people, quotes a "*pensée*" of Pascal at the beginning of *Being and Time*.[2] But these are all, in some sense, language pessimists, anti-language people.

Derrida's neologisms are attempts to break up language, but language is a wound that seals itself over immediately, and these become the names of his thoughts, when, as I have insisted, he doesn't have any thoughts. Do we really think? If so, is it something that happens in the head? When are we thinking? Maybe you know that the word "invention" comes from the word "discovery." An invention is something you discover. So an invention, if it is inventing at all, is inventing a problem, and the discovery is discovering the problem, which is the same as solving it in some way. But actual thinking? When do we do that? Probably only in crisis situations when we have to think our way out of something. You remember that, in *Ulysses*, Mr. Bloom thinks in words, and people have called that his telegraphic style. We probably don't think that way either, but it would be just as appropriate to take that version of thinking as our usual one.

So much for that. Before we get back to the supplement in Derrida, I want to tell you a bit more about the resistance to what was called at the time "the philosophy of the subject." A young mathematician of genius, Jean Cavaillès, who was killed by the Gestapo in the Resistance, had a very interesting position on this. He held out for something which would be not a philosophy of thoughts, consciousness, or the subject. But what is consciousness? Nobody knows what it is, and it's not an adequate basis for anything. So then what is? Objects, materialism? Well, that's a little harder to make a real philosophy out of. As I said, Democritus and the ancient materialists are rediscovered in the mid-nineteenth century, a period when in the sciences things like energy and thermodynamics are being explored, so there is some kind of materialism to be found there. But, more generally, you would have to say that materialism is simply anti-idealism. Idealism is probably anti-something, but maybe not anti-materialism. Anyway, you

---

2 "On ne peut entreprendre de définir l'être sans tomber dans cette absurdité: car on ne peut définir un mot sans commencer par celui-ci, c'est, soit qu'on l'exprime ou qu'on le sous-entende. Donc pour définir l'être, il faudrait dire c'est, et ainsi employer le mot défini dans sa définition." Pascal, *Pensées et Opuscules* (Paris, 1912), 169; quoted in Martin Heidegger, *Being and Time*, trans. John Macquarrie and Edward Robinson (Malden, MA: Blackwell, 1962), 23, fn. 4.

can see when you're working with this opposition it becomes political in some sense. The Left is materialist, or at least it wants to be. The Right thus must be, if not idealist, then spiritualist. Why not?

But, in this kind of situation, there's always the illusion of the third way. This is a moment when I want to alert you to a very annoying but seemingly perpetual misunderstanding. A lot of these people will declare themselves anti-dialectical. Deleuze is very clear about that. Derrida is, of course, a much more measured and polite philosopher, but you will see he wants to distinguish oppositions from dialectics. People also define dialectics in all kinds of other ways. I have my own way of doing it. Hegel generally avoids the term. Hegel isn't busy talking about dialectics. It is very rare. And, in Kant or in Plato, it means something completely different, so forget about their dialectics. But some people do still think, no matter how often you tell them, that Hegel is all about thesis, antithesis, and then synthesis. Dialectics, then, seems to be some kind of a third way, a synthesis, but there is no such thing. There is no tripartite scheme in Hegel. Slavoj Žižek has said it very well: There are many oppositions in the *Logic*, but the moment of synthesis is always a failure. It doesn't solve anything. It doesn't unite two opposites. It simply leads you on to propose a new opposition. Yes, two opposing terms can turn into each other; after all, one of the great ways of understanding Hegel's dialectic is that it is the identity of the identical and the non-identical, or, on the other hand, the non-identity of the identical and the non-identical. So you might be tempted to go back and forth, and to see how these oppositions ruin themselves.

But this problem of the third term also becomes a political allegory, because France, after the war, is caught between the two superpowers. This is one interpretation; some historians accept it, some don't: It seems to me not unlikely that Hitler, already in his second, never-published manuscript of *Mein Kampf*, understood that the future belonged to the superstate. There were two superstates, and Germany was not one of them. His plans for the postwar were to kill off all the non-German speakers. He tried it in the East. He seemed to have a much more tolerant relationship to France and to the Scandinavian peoples, but that was probably just temporary. The whole project was to create a German superstate. And this is today an interesting political question; it's the only political question, if you're talking about geopolitics: the difference between a superstate and a nation-state, or, with the Europeans, a "member-state." So the third way in this postwar period comes from a rejection of two alternatives. Part of the Left in France looks to the Soviet Union; everybody knows that they had, at that stage, the purge trials and the Stalin-Hitler pact, but they don't really know much about the gulags. Nonetheless, the Soviet Union is supposed to be progressive. Some admire the Americans, but, on the other hand, they know that the Americans have their aggressive plans, as with NATO.

So, right after the war, the temptation is to find some third way. Sartre tries to start a party based on the third way. It doesn't work. Gaullism is preeminently a third way, and, indeed, I think de Gaulle managed—in a period of dichotomization and the reduction of Europe to client states of one or the other superpower—to preserve a certain uniqueness of France from which we benefit, because we would not have these writers without some sense of the uniqueness of what they're doing as Parisians. One of these people, Régis Debray, who was an ally of Che Guevara, arrested and imprisoned by the South American dictatorships, finally became a Gaullist, which is probably, in some sense, if you're in a capitalist world, an intelligent position. But we'll leave all of that aside. This is just to tell you that this third way business is an ideology that you mustn't attribute to Hegel. But they do, they do.

So what I want to try to show you now is the way I wish to deal with Derrida, which you don't all have to accept, and I want to do that in the framework of the "supplement." I told you about the origin points of these early works—obviously, Husserl was very important to him—but, presumably, at some point, he was also asked to teach something about writing. So we get this plethora of writings. *Grammatology* is not a major work; it's a collection of different studies, one on semiotics, an attack on Saussure, an attack on structuralism (although I suppose that attacking structuralism is one way of defining a structuralist). Then, you have a long section on a fragment of Rousseau called "The Origin of Language." Of course, Rousseau takes us back to natural man, and, therefore, we turn to some anthropology, the origins of humanity and language, in a very influential anthropological work by André Leroi-Gourhan called *Gesture and Speech*. It has to do with evolution, standing upright, coming out of the trees into these deforested veldts that the early hominids had to live in, and the emergence of the face as well as of the hand. You know that animals don't have faces. There's a marvelous chapter in Deleuze on "faceness," *visagéité*, in which he asks: what is faceness? How is it we recognize faces? Whatever it is, it's obviously the result of standing upright. For the ancients, this was because we now look at the sky, whereas the animals are always looking down at their feet.

So *Grammatology* is a collection of these studies, but it has a certain unity in what it pursues and what it finds as its mission in pursuing. It is not a method. Grammatology seems to mean the study of alphabets, characters, earlier forms of writings, marks. That is, I suppose, a special taste, but that certainly is not what Derrida is proposing. So this is more the study of the relationship of writing to language and why there would be such a thing as "arche-writing." I think this was one of his jokes, which got to be very famous and much admired and ridiculed. That's *archē*, meaning origin or essence in Greek, but we know this from our ontic-ontological distinction. Writing is an ontic phenomenon, what we do on pieces of paper. But would there be an ontological version of writing? Certainly, writing is an existent, but what does it have to do with being? Well, if Derrida were an ontologist, then you could say, yes, *archi-écriture* is a phenomenon of Being, and all Being is like writing. But he is not an ontologist, and he reminds us that Heidegger himself gave up this concept mid-career, as a not very useful term. But his discussion of voice has its equivalent in Heidegger, because in *Sein und Zeit* he talks about the *Ruf des Gewissens*, the "call of conscience." What does he mean by that? I think it is the sense that we're wasting our lives. We're wasting our being. He was a Catholic, anyway; it isn't a Protestant idea of conscience, not the inner light, but it is understood as a call. Derrida never mentions Althusser's famous interpellation, but, there too, you have a voice telling you something. So this has its role in our thinking. Is Derrida just criticizing ideas like the presence of the voice? Logocentrism means believing that the voice is foremost. Socrates tells us in the *Phaedrus*: yes, the best use of language is when you have a teacher like me, Socrates, telling you the truth. What is funny is that Socrates never tells anyone anything. He asks them. He makes them find out themselves.

So all of this is going to turn on the way in which, in all these philosophers from time immemorial, all the way up through Rousseau and Saussure, writing is considered the poor cousin of speaking. Speech comes first, *la parole*. After that, yes, you can write it down, Saussure thinks, but it is a memory-saving device. The revival of this in structuralism is, of course, to say that writing is associated with power, as in the chapter in the *Tristes Tropiques* where Lévi-Strauss is seen scribbling something on his pad, writing his notes, by the chief of this tribe. In a sense, that is to say, you have sacred books. Those are authoritative, if we want to say that, from an economic point of view as well. The state only comes into existence with the surplus, and the earliest samples of writing are to be found on little baked squares on which little marks were made to catalog the surplus, because once you start a granary and fill it with your riches, you have to keep track of it. The cataloging of the surplus allows the chief to hire a bodyguard and to establish a priesthood, all of whom are going to serve him. So, in a sense, counting the surplus is a first version of writing.

People wanted to know what the political content of Derrida is. I think it has to do with norms. This is radically against norms. I think these people want to show that rules are contradictory, and that norms are always there and to be resisted. Later on, Derrida will have a big argument, a kind of great academic scandal, with the linguistic philosopher John Searle, who will make this attack on Derrida as completely meaningless theoretical jargon, an attack Derrida will counter-reply with an essay called "Limited Inc." There the point turns on what is called the felicitous sentence, which comes out of Chomsky. Let's say, as a general rule, "Mary tends to sleep heavily." Okay, that's a perfectly grammatical sentence, right? It has a meaning; we don't have to elaborately deconstruct it. But then suppose you said—and this is the famous example of Chomsky—"Green ideas sleep furiously." This is the archetypal model of a perfect sentence which also doesn't mean anything. It isn't even proper nonsense. I don't know what Deleuze would make of it, or Lewis Carroll for that matter.

So Derrida is out to destroy this idea of a norm in language, any form of regularity of that sort, and this is the point where I think Derrida is political. He also took up lots of political causes in his life. He was very accessible, like Sartre. In the earlier period, he would sign petitions, and he eventually got arrested by the government in Czechoslovakia because he was meeting with some so-called dissidents in a study group in one of their apartments. There was a great outcry, "Free Derrida," so he was let loose the next day. At any rate, he did other things of a quite valuable nature, including a defense of Marx. I assigned the *Specters of Marx* review by Moishe Postone, whom I consider one of the most notable contemporary Marxist theorists.[3] That's a very interesting review. I don't consider *Specters* one of the more valuable or probing contributions to Marxist

---

3   Moishe Postone, "Deconstruction as Social Critique: Derrida on Marx and the New World Order," *History and Theory* 37, no. 3 (October 1998): 370–387.

theory, but it was certainly a gesture, a very important gesture of support for people who were being attacked in the late '70s and early '80s in France for their Marxist background. There was a great wave of what I would call "de-Marxification" in France. A certain group began in the Communist Party, then became Maoists, then leftists, and finally anti-communists when they read Solzhenitsyn, who was translated in the late '70s. But, just as the United States and Britain with Reagan and Thatcher, France moved into neoliberal politics, and so also did the intellectuals begin to dissociate themselves systematically from their Marxist background, so that by the end of it, as somebody said, the only Marxists left were the Communists. So Derrida's *Specters of Marx* has to be understood in that context, as a rebuke to these young philosophers, the *nouveaux philosophes*, who are busy attacking Marxism. (Deleuze also planned a book on Marx in that same spirit called *Gloire de Marx* but never got around to writing it.)

My own point of view on this—not just on Derrida but on all the things we are studying—is that of a kind of formalism. "Dialectical formalism," do you want to call it? I don't know. That is to say, I'm not so much interested in the content of what they say but in the operations of this philosophy. Here, in this sequence of things, you get the discovery of a word, "supplement," which is a clue or a symptom. It is taken out of fragmentary quotes—Plato's myth, this rather inconclusive fragment in Rousseau—and it proves to mean several things. It means writing is to be opposed to the voice. The voice is thought to be the true, natural thing, the norm, full, meaningful, whereas writing has to be followed through; there is the hermeneutic circle, in which you are not always sure what you are reading, and meanwhile, of course, it does all these illusory things. So writing is, then, the supplement, and, in the *pharmakon*, it becomes like a medicine which turns out to be a poison. It's supposed to augment your memory, but on the contrary, as we know very well today, it causes you to forget everything. I had an acquaintance who traveled a lot and would tell you all about his wonderful experiences. He went to Turkey one year, which he liked a lot, but he had just bought a camera and learned how to take photographs, and he photographed everything, and when he came back, he had nothing more to say, couldn't even remember it, because it was in the supplement. Everything was registered and copied, and, therefore, you don't have to remember it anymore. Žižek used to like to tell this story. There were still in those days VCRs and copy machines. In Yugoslavia, in those days, the great Hollywood epics like *Cleopatra* would be exported and flown over to Belgrade, where they were copied *in the plane*, so that, the minute the plane landed, all these phony copies were circulating in the streets of Belgrade. You could buy them for a dollar, the way you still can in China. So, as Žižek said—I think he was trying to define *jouissance*—you get this movie, and you want to see it very much, so you copy it. Then, he says, you don't have to see it anymore. The machine has had the *jouissance*. The point is that, as far as *jouissance* is concerned—and this is why pleasure is a stupid idea—you don't need to have pleasure yourself. It's enough that *jouissance* exists somewhere. Life is meaningful again.

So this is a dialectic of supplementarity, if you like, that you can add on to the Derridean motif, but this is a supplement whose character is also undecidable. The point about these supplements is that their oppositions can turn around. And this would be a different way of defining Derrida's project: not just an attack on the norm, but also on centrality. If you can't make a rule out of it, then you make it central. So the voice is central and writing is subsidiary. Men are central and women are subsidiary. You have a whole dialectic of power—at least I would call it a dialectic—involved in all these operations. Every opposition is secretly asymmetrical. The linguists call them "marked" and "unmarked," because you can't have two equal parts. What would equality be in this situation? Can't you just say, yes, voice is important, but so is writing? Not really. Derrida's is a critique of categories. It isn't about the content; it doesn't matter whether it's language or medicines. He seems to be talking about writing in Plato's pharmacology, but the content is indifferent. You know that Rousseau's *Confessions* is truly confessional in an amazing way, and when Rousseau uses the word "supplement," this dangerous supplement, he is talking about masturbation. So, all of a sudden, it turns out that these categories of original and supplement don't have a content. They are to be found in everything. It is, perhaps we can say, a category of the mind, and that's why it's so difficult to name it, because it is never just one thing.

So we come back to this notion of differences without positive terms. That is the sense in which I think structuralism again kicks off what I would call a meditation on the dialectic. I think this analysis of supplements is dialectical, but for immediate reasons, contextual reasons in France, that is not the word you would use. The dialecticians would be very annoyed with you, so you don't say it. But it seems to me the point is that you have to have oppositions. This is the teaching of Saussure, but it goes back to Hegel. You must also at the same time deconstruct these oppositions. Deconstructing an opposition in a dialectical way means finding a contradiction. Derrida wants to be a lot more formal than that, and he also wants, he says, to do it from the inside. That means you're not running around denouncing people as idealists. You're not running around claiming you're a materialist or looking for some third way. You're not doing this from the outside. It is a politics, but it is an internal politics. It is seeing how everything you are saying is carrying contradictions within itself, regardless of what it actually is.

What else can we deduce from this? If the voice is not central, that doesn't mean that writing is central. It means the relationship has to be invented, but it also means that you have to somehow register your aware-ness in a new category, and that category will be called "the text." So the text will be this interplay in which you never know whether the thing is central or decentered. Even if you try to decenter it, you can't get out of it. The text is the perpetual problem of all of deconstruction. This is the place of *différance*. What are we going to call this whole thing? We could call it "history," he says, but the word has been so abused that we can't use it anymore.[4] So it is history, but, even more so, it is another abused word: time. And this is why *différance* must mean both "difference" and "deferral," why this language of linearity—I don't like that very much—but why linearity is dragged into this critique, because its objects are things that have to move in time. Any kind of meaning is going to move in time. And this is why, in a funny way, Derrida will refuse Lacan. In Lacan, it is the movement of the signifiers that projects some illusion of the signified, of meaning. For Derrida, no, it is the signified which is the fundamental ideology, the so-called transcendental signified, the absolute, like God, and the signifiers are just an appearance of movement on its surface.

One of the places where you can see that the most clearly, this contra-diction in time itself, is the trace. People asked what that word meant. The point about the trace is that it ought not to exist. The trace is supposed to mark something from the past, right? I want to take as my example the theory of photography. This has interested people, yet, from Benjamin to Sontag to Barthes, the point has been that there can be no theory of pho-tography. Why? Because the photograph is a trace. If you are an ontologist, what you want to know is: Where is it? A photograph is a picture of the

---

4 Jacques Derrida, "Differance," in *Margins of Philosophy*, trans. Alan Bass (Chicago: University of Chicago Press, 1982), 11.

past, but the past doesn't exist. The photograph exists, but not as the past. It just exists as a thing. Is it a memory? It is a thing, and a thing itself can't be a memory. Is it an image? But what's an image? I don't think there can be a theory of the image either, if you want me to be completely frank with you. In philosophy, imagination is often taken as a faculty. It is a place in which one wrestles with problems, but not ontological problems. They are ontological contradictions, because the past is not, and the present is. So what can the photograph be? It has no ontological status. It can't possibly have the status of registering the past, because the past doesn't exist, and it can't possibly be a thing in the present, because it's nothing in the present.

So that is why the trace embodies everything contradictory. The trace is an *écriture* of the temporal contradiction, the contradiction of time itself, the fact that time is not an object of ontological contemplation. There are always two times: the present and the sequence of present, past, and future. Those are not the same. Kierkegaard says that the present is not a temporal concept.[5] What does that mean? That is a very strange idea. We thought the present was time itself. It isn't a temporal concept? But, of course, he has another word in reserve which the religious tradition is keeping warm for him, and that's "eternal," because the present is, of course, eternal. It is always there, so it isn't temporal. Anyway, all of this is in the background of the trace, since the present can't be something that contains the trace as a marker of temporality.

Actually, I wanted to begin with this, but I'll end with it instead. I mentioned Jean Cavaillès. His book came out after the war, and what it proposed, to return to our earlier discussion, was a third way. He was a philosopher as well as a mathematician. It proposes not idealism, not a philosophy of the subject, not a philosophy of Being, or the thing, or matter, but a philosophy of the concept. This is the crucial way out for many of these philosophers. *Begriff*, in German, comes from *begreifen*, "to grip," "to grab"; when you suddenly understand something, you have a *Begriff*. It is the major Hegelian word, *Begriff*. In the older translations, they sometimes translate it—it's very quaint, I think—as "the Notion." So, if you see Hegelians talking about "the Notion," it's the *Begriff*.

---

5 "The present, however, is not a concept of time, except precisely as something infinitely contentless, which again is the infinite vanishing. If this is not kept in mind, no matter how quickly it may disappear, the present is posited, and being posited it again appears in the categories: the past and the future." Søren Kierkegaard, *The Concept of Anxiety*, trans. Reidar Thomte (Princeton, NJ: Princeton University Press, 1980), 86.

So, if philosophy is busy analyzing the concept, then you don't have to talk about consciousness and you don't have to talk about things. You don't have to be either idealist or materialist, because you have concepts of both those things. And this is a bit like Althusser's weird epistemology in which the scientific ideas are never corresponding to reality. This is not even Lenin's reflection theory, although I think he would not like one to say so. But you're caught up in this self-analyzing, self-criticizing realm in which you are not really referring to things or images or anything. You are dealing exclusively with concepts and their movement. Then you're in a funny kind of zone with this philosophy of the concept. In Deleuze, it's not just for philosophers. Everybody is dealing with the concept. Film has its own conceptuality, the concepts that are awakened in film. Music as well is a kind of thinking, but it's not abstract, not verbal. Concepts don't necessarily have to deal with words. But, if you're going to deal with words the way these philosophers do, then you have to realize that they're completely contradictory. So this is what Derrida means by the famous saying, *il n'y a pas de hors-texte*. The French is much stronger. "There is nothing outside of the text."[6] There is no exterior to the text.

Does that mean everything is writing? For us intellectuals, of course, this would be delightful, because it means that everything belongs to us, the people of the text, but it doesn't mean that. It means that anything we are thinking of, or doing, is already text in some sense. It is already this difference and deferral. It is life in time. That's what life in time is. That's why we can't have ontology. That is why we can't have meaning in the vulgar sense of meaning: because we are always in this process. So everything you think of as external to this is really inside of it, and that's what Hegel means a little by positing. When asking about the *Ding-an-sich* in Kant, he says we have the phenomenon, but we can't see it; we don't know what it is. Is there this ultimate reality of the thing-in-itself? No, he says, you are *positing* a thing-in-itself that would be outside of your experience. That's also going on in your mind. There isn't any thing-in-itself. It's part of your way of thinking about phenomena which must, to be thought, posit a thing beyond itself. But he would not say that's going on in your mind. Rather, it's going on in the Hegelian logic of the concept. Now you can think what you want about that. You can think for example

6   Jacques Derrida, *Of Grammatology*, trans. Gayatri Spivak (Baltimore, MD: Johns Hopkins University Press, 1974), 158.

about its political consequences. Are they good? Are they bad? I think that there is a political contestation in Derrida, as I've tried to show you, but this initial insight is what he always pursued. If you think that that's worthless as a project, so be it, but on the other hand, people have also thought this was an enormous insight. This is why it's very difficult. This is not a philosophy. It only defines what philosophy ought to be doing, namely deconstructing.

Maybe we'll pursue a few of these things the next time, and we'll go on to what should not be called "French feminism." That was why I brought up America in the first place, because the French say there is no such thing as poststructuralism; you Americans invented that. Just because we received all these people at once—Derrida, Foucault, and Deleuze translated all at once—you decided to call it "poststructuralism," because it isn't Lévi-Strauss. So this is an American invention. Obviously, Foucault and Foucauldians don't like to be associated with these other people. The same is true with so-called French feminisms. That is considered to be an invention by American feminists, especially the ones who don't like all this theoretical stuff, whether they think it is pernicious or ought to be going in a different direction. Whether or not that is true, we will go on to it next time.

March 16, 2021

16

Feminism as Transgression

{Beauvoir, Wittig, Irigaray}

Since we're working on keywords, I want to return to Georges Bataille to discuss his notions of "excess" and "transgression." Most of the people we will now be looking at are interested in the notion of transgression. If you have a law, a norm, a regularity which is often conceived to be or supposed to be natural, these people are interested in how you can subvert it, weaken its authority, overthrow it, replace it with something, or transgress it. Maybe it momentarily falls back in place. Maybe you don't have the power to change it all together. But all of these things are at stake in the notion of transgression.

Bataille's reputation is that of a heretic. He is the outsider. He is the heretic to the Surrealist group. He gets thrown out, so he starts his own group. He is surrounded by other people who are traditional outsiders, in a way. Did I share any anecdotes about Bataille? I don't believe so. I just wanted to tell this one. In real life—that is to say, professionally—he was actually a librarian. It's very odd to have a librarian—those are respectable people—with all this secret interest in transgression, orgies, primitive and modern. He did a book on Lascaux when it was first discovered.[1] Anything heretical or underground interested him. Anyway, he was a

---

1 Georges Bataille, *Lascaux, or, the Birth of Art: Prehistoric Painting*, trans. Austryn Wainhouse (Milan: Skira, 1955).

librarian, and he started a very important critical journal, *Critique*, which is still around, one of the basic theoretical journals in France. Many of the most important philosophical articles have appeared there. He also rose to be the librarian of the Bibliothèque Nationale of France, which is like the Library of Congress. He had a relationship with Walter Benjamin. Benjamin died on the Spanish border trying to flee France. There's now a little monument to him there. He was carrying a briefcase full of notes, which were lost. The presence of these things has always been an interest and a worry for people. Anyway, after the war, Paris was not destroyed, but the rest of Europe was. Adorno, who was a disciple of Benjamin and then a close friend, makes a first trip back to Europe. I might as well embed that anecdote in the larger one about Bataille. You know that Thomas Mann was, of course, the great German novelist in America, because he was the one who was translated, one of the great figures of modern literature. He had just published *Doctor Faustus*, his great book on contemporary music, and Adorno was a close collaborator, so he remained in touch. Later, Adorno writes a letter back to Thomas Mann, who is delighted with it and shows it to his family. Adorno writes from Germany, "*Lieber Herr Doktor*," or whatever he called him, "I have some remarkable news to tell you. I've just gotten back to Germany." (He left Germany in the mid-thirties.) "The astonishing thing is, here in Germany today, there are no Nazis! I ask everyone and they say, 'Well, of course, *I* was not a Nazi, but I know all these *other* people who were.'" That's a quick Adorno story. But, meanwhile, Adorno had been in correspondence with Benjamin in Paris. Benjamin had been working on a long project on nineteenth-century France called the *Arcades Project*, for which he assembled all this material. After he committed suicide, nobody knew where it was. So Adorno goes to Paris as Benjamin's executor, trying to find whatever papers might be left there. He goes to Bataille in the Bibliothèque Nationale and says, "You were close to Walter in the '30s. Do you have any idea where he might have left some of these things?" And Bataille says, "Yes of course! They're right here." He takes him up a few floors. Whenever you want to hide a book in a library, take it off the shelves and stick it somewhere high up so that nobody can ever find it again. Bataille takes down off the stacks an enormous package of papers. It is the *Arcades Project*. Benjamin has left a complete copy of it. So, suddenly, by the intermediary of Bataille, this thing is saved and published. This just demonstrates how Bataille is secretly central to so much that was happening at the time.

Enough of that. Our work today and next time faces a specific kind of problem, which is that both of our topics—French feminism and film studies—have become disciplines. That means not only that they have enormous bibliographies, but also that they have developed certain norms. Indeed, I think many of you have been or are being trained in one or the other of these disciplines. So we're going to try to take a somewhat different approach to this, since we can't possibly entertain here the idea of a history of French women's studies or a history of French film studies. This is a historical course in the framework of what I guess we have to call "the history of ideas." Foucault hated that expression, because, of course, it was always applied to him, and rightly so, because he invented his own version of the history of ideas. So we need to look at this in historical terms, especially in terms of French history, as opposed to our American background. I've already alluded to the fact that there is a tension between the French tradition, at least in our period of women's studies, and that of the United States.

I would say that, for American feminists, French feminism has, at its worst, been a nuisance and an overly theoretical dead end, whose most revolutionary idea is that of women's writing, which we'll get to at some point today. I haven't given you any of her work, but one of the leading proponents of the idea that there is a specific kind of women's writing, and that women writers should cultivate this kind of writing, is Hélène Cixous. For American feminists, that idea has never been very attractive. But let me put this difference a little more strongly, if you like: French feminism has been concerned with theory, in one way or another, while American feminism, I would say, has tended to be more concerned with practice. But let me put this another way that I think will be even more striking for you. American feminism, as it develops, evolved into a study of what we call "gender." There was no idea of gender in French feminism. Why is that? That's a very interesting matter, it seems to me. First of all, *genre* in French includes gender, kind, literary genres, anything you like, so it's not a very marked term, whereas "gender," in English, has a sexual component.

Let me raise this as a proposition for you. Gender was most successfully popularized as a theoretical concept by Judith Butler. I think gender is something which can include both sexual norms—that is, heterosexuality—and other things that are non-normative. It can put all those things together in a way which may or may not tend to obscure the differences between all those phenomena. So the study of gender in the United States, which is then followed by queer theory, often produces an alliance politics, in which a whole set of different sexual politics are covered as in some kind of big tent. In France that's not so, and clearly that has something to do with the kind of sexism that is unique to France. The politics of intellectuals will also leave its mark on these movements as much as on anything else.

There, I want to interrupt myself and quote Régis Debray, whose most famous book, besides the one he wrote about Cuba, Fidel, and Che Guavara, is called *Teachers, Writers, Celebrities*. It's a book that goes back to 1979. It's a history of intellectuals and where their authority comes from, sort of from the mid-nineteenth century on. It points out the role of the universities and of authority as it was vested in the famous professors, the founders of all these disciplines. Then he goes on to writers. Suddenly, in France, you get a prestige of writers in the modernist period, people like Proust, even the Surrealists, an enormous prestige. And, after that, with TV, you start to get a different kind of prestige. The French had a program that began around 1975 called *Apostrophes*, in which the interviewer got all kinds of philosophers, teachers, and writers to discuss highly intellectual topics. It was on primetime, and I think it was the most widely viewed program in France for about fifteen years. You might want to compare it to something like Oprah, because the differences would be equally revealing. But what happens in that period is that these former authorities who were teachers and writers have now mutated into television celebrities. People have told me that the late Michel Serres, whom I'll say something about later on, was on these shows every week, not only *Apostrophes* but all the other talk-show programs. So the announcers would have to say, "Well, this is an unusual week because Michel Serres will not be with us." And he is a very scholarly theorist indeed, with a wide variety of theories on everything. So you have a mutation in the very nature of the intellectuals.

I've pointed out several times that, in America, we have to contend as intellectuals with an anti-intellectual climate, a tradition. No one wants to be called an intellectual, and all intellectuals are accusing each other of being nothing but intellectuals. I think it goes back to something which is related to our topic today, which is puritanism and its various traces. At any rate, nobody thinks that being a teacher or being an intellectual is really much of an achievement in the United States. Once, during the Vietnam War, I was over in France. There were lots of manifestos in those days because of this stupid, endless war. One was from Norman Mailer and a few other writers who sent President Johnson a manifesto asking him to leave Vietnam. So I pointed out to this friend of mine that this is an absolutely pointless piece of writing. Nobody in the United States would pay any attention to a letter from Norman Mailer to Lyndon Johnson demanding that the war be ended and our troops be withdrawn, even though it got coverage in *Le Monde*, the whole second page reviewing this absolutely insignificant document and its signatories. So he said to me, "No, that's not the point. We know that your intellectuals don't have any power. But we in France are interested in what your intellectuals say." Suddenly, I realized that he's right. We Americans are not interested in what our intellectuals have to say, because it's worthless and it has no power. So you have to take that into account in understanding what French theory means. Intellectuals have a role. I would compare it to the role of the exegete in the course of the Jewish tradition. The other place in the world in which intellectuals have had a power and an existence is China. In any case, I would say it's very important for us to keep that in mind, especially because, in the United States, it's not something we think about.

So we are in the philosophy of the concept and we are talking about action, praxis, as it is conceived by intellectuals. One should say several things about that. I think Beauvoir is absolutely right in saying—and anybody involved in any kind of politics would understand this—that politics is spatial and that you have to have some kind of common space. The reason for the lack of women's political power is that women have "lack[ed] concrete means for organizing themselves into a unit which can stand face to face with the correlative unit"—that is, the men.

> They have no past, no history, no religion of their own; and they have no such solidarity of work and interest as that of the proletariat. They are not even promiscuously herded together in the way that creates community feeling among the American Negroes, the ghetto Jews, the workers of Saint-Denis, or the factory hands of Renault. They live dispersed among the males, attached to residence, housework, economic conditions, social standing, to certain men—fathers or husbands—more firmly than they are to other women. If they belong to the bourgeoisie, they feel solidarity with men of that class, not with proletarian women; if they are white, their allegiance is to white men, not to Negro women. The proletariat could propose to massacre the ruling class and

a sufficiently fanatical Jew or Negro might dream of getting sole possession of the atomic bomb and making humanity wholly Jewish or black;
but women cannot even dream of exterminating the males.[2]

Now, to be sure, there are fantasies. I hope you know of the major
breakthrough in American science fiction, Joanna Russ's *The Female
Man*, for example. This is a path-breaking, all-woman utopia. But we can
understand what Beauvoir is saying by asking why the Revolution would
take place in the old Russia of the Tsarist days. Well, besides the war
and the peasantry, which we discussed earlier, because there were huge
factories concentrated in the city. That is, you didn't have separate little
factories all over the landscape; there was a proletariat which was spatially
concentrated in certain places and thereby had a power which it wouldn't
have had. So space must also be taken into account in these things.

Beauvoir points out a practical historical fact. Why have women played
a role in French history rather more predominant than in other European
countries? In France, the women of the revolutionary salons played a large
role, she says, because of legalities. In the history of French law, women
can inherit property. I don't say this as an outright thing but look at what
she says in *The Second Sex*. The possibility of inheriting property is crucial
for power. If you're in a system in which only the male heir inherits power,
and the women are secondary, that's a very different situation. People
would be tempted to call that process the formation of identity. If that's
identity, then you have to include a lot of other kinds of things. There
you are interpellated by the law, and the law says: "you're a woman, but
you are legally an heiress, and that's included in this identity with which
I interpellate you as a woman." People have asked about the role of race
and gender in some of the things we've read earlier in the semester.
Althusser's interpellation can include these identities, right? When the
policeman stops you, when he asks for your papers, he knows that you're
an Arab. He knows that you're of Algerian descent. *The Invisible Man*:
he certainly knows you're Black. He knows you're a woman. These are
all parts of interpellation, of what the outside is doing to you and how it
is classifying you. So these problems have certainly been present in our
other readings.

---

2   Simone de Beauvoir, *The Second Sex*, trans. H. M. Parshley (London: Vintage
Books, 1989), 18–19.

This is the other thing I'll say about identity. The reason identity politics has been so strong here and not so strong in Europe is not only because of tensions within the working class. In the United States, in 1955, there was the union of the AFL and the CIO. That represented a pact with business and with government. It was the beginning of the welfare state, in some sense. It secured pensions, all kinds of workers' rights, on one condition: no more strikes, general or otherwise. So, from 1955, you can really date what the French call *les trente glorieuses*, that is, the golden age of capitalism, which is, not surprisingly, also the golden age of social democracy. It is the most prosperous era, because there are no strikes. The proletariat is integrated into the system in a way it wasn't before. Before then, unionizing was a heroic act of the type that is still happening in the South and in some industries right now, but, in the '30s, unionizing was a big thing. Now the unions are there; they have their power, and they are integrated into the system. I also want to point out that in France the big union is communist. The Party has power through the unions—or did. But the other major difference with the United States has to do with race. It's a little different to be of Algerian descent or Turkish descent than to be the inheritor of slavery, to have slavery as your history. The fact of the population of African Americans in this country has meant that there was a considerable mass of people behind questions of identity, behind a politics that we would today be considered as that of identity, which is not the same in Europe, even though it's much stronger than it used to be, particularly with immigration crises.

I mentioned that the student groups in the '30s in France were fascist. I should put it this way: the student groups in France are political. Maybe it was a fascist politics in the '30s, and maybe it was a leftist politics in the postwar period, but they were political. Our youth culture is quite different from that. Régis Debray—just to quote him one last time—wrote a wonderful sentence, which unfortunately I'm having to reconstruct from memory, so it isn't quite as eloquent as he writes it. But talking about May '68 and the great student revolt in France, he says something like this: these Columbuses of revolution, the students, setting forth for China—China in those days meant the Cultural Revolution—found instead that they had landed in California—that is, sex, drugs, and rock and roll. Instead of arriving at the Maoist revolution, they arrived at the youth movement of the United States. So that just dramatizes for you some of the differences through which all these things are happening.

I want to go back then to our questions. Today, the abstract question is again that of oppositions. We've talked about the dialectic. I pointed out my feeling that, although the poststructuralists may claim to be anti-Hegelian and anti-dialectical, structuralism really was the beginning of a reinvention of the dialectic for modern thought by way of the binary opposition and by way of the role of negativity. Sometimes, that comes out as the dialectic and sometimes it doesn't. But opposition and negation, these are basic to the dialectic, and they are reintroduced by the odd, roundabout side trip of linguistics. Foucault has a wonderful expression for this kind of opposition. I have said it over and over again: It is the old mind-body split. Are those two dimensions, as Spinoza thought? Is there a mediation between them? Foucault calls this—running through history but particularly since Kant and in the nineteenth century—the transcendental-empirical doublet.[3] Kant called the transcendental all those categories that we couldn't think. The rest of it was empirical: the measurement of this, what these two chemicals do together. Matters are deterministic in Kant, whereas the transcendental is the realm of freedom. So there is always this back and forth between these two things. It is the mind-body split, and all these people in this period want to get over it. Now I want you to understand that the fantasy of getting over these two things will get a name with Deleuze. It's going to be called "immanence." The plane of immanence in Deleuze is where there is no longer a division between matter and mind. This is the very notion of a philosophy of the concept: there is a place which is neither consciousness nor bodies; it is a realm of the categories, and it is the philosophy of the concept. When Hegel unrolls his *Logic*—all these categories one after the other—it is the philosophy of the concept. They don't like to say that Hegel invented it, but he did. That's what immanence is, but immanence can also be a very embarrassing thing. There is no metalanguage: that means immanence in Lacan. You have your language, and you think you can get outside of it and talk about it? No, there's nothing outside of it. You want to do something to the text? *Il n'y a pas de hors-texte.* There is nothing outside of the text, because, in Derrida, the concept is text. Sartre reads the world as a text, interprets it. Our tastes, our bodies, everything is interpretable. So we don't need to get out of it. How could we ever get out of it, unless

---

3 Michel Foucault, *The Order of Things: An Archaeology of the Human Sciences* (New York: Vintage, 1994).

it is a question of some god behind all this, like *The Truman Show* or the *Wizard of Oz*? That would be an *hors-texte*.

But think of our other problems here: race and gender. Can we find a place outside of those things to talk about them? Am I not implicated in race? Where can I find a language that is outside my own situation? Can anyone talk about sexual difference when we all belong to it? Are we not somehow in this immanence in such a way that we're implicated in it? I think the most dramatic form of this problem is going to be found in the psychoanalytic idea of transference. How can I, lying on the couch, with the master—Lacan, Freud, or somebody else—sitting behind me, drop out of my life for an hour? How can this human being, with his own interests, passions, sex, everything else, say anything to me about that which is not part of this session? Well, the transference is precisely that. Everything that the analyst says is going to be tugged back by me inside of my own neuroses and used within it. It's the famous falling in love with the doctor—or hating the doctor, as far as that's concerned. But there can't be a place outside this world of the psychoanalytic session in which everything is suspended, both for the doctor and for the patient. So transference is a very odd thing. It poses the question of immanence in psychoanalysis. We have both the ideal of this immanence in which everything means something, and yet, if everything means something, we mean something; we're inside of it and therefore we can't get outside of it to talk about it. This would be at least one of the things that is going to be at stake in French feminism.

The other historical reference I would like to make for understanding French feminism brings us back to Hegel's master and slave. Hegel's first version, we're told, was the battle of the sexes. It's not the two men fighting over who is going to be master and who the slave. It's the man and the woman. That sheds a very interesting light on all this. The first form then of the sexual relationship—and we'll get to the various versions of this in a minute—would be this agon between masculine and feminine. How could you solve that? Well, somebody wins. Then you have hierarchy and domination. The person who wins has, presumably, been the man. But, if the woman were to win, then maybe we could imagine something like matriarchy, where the woman rules. And this is the constant temptation, a particularly leftist temptation—I don't think fascists are tempted by matriarchy—but the Left has always had a thought that, if women ran things, then maybe everything would be better. But this is still caught in this agon. The point of the matriarchy is that there never has been one, because the anthropologists tell us that still the categories of male and female are present, and the person who has the power in a matriarchy is typically not the woman; it's the woman's brother. So there goes that idea. All right, what else could we have? Could we have—because Hegel uses the word recognition, which a lot of people have picked up—mutual recognition, in which there was equality? That's certainly not the Sartrean view of this, and I think it isn't really Hegel's view either, because after all power remains. You can say, "Yes, I recognize you; you can have the vote and inherit property, but we're still going to control everything." But, on the contrary, is it possible that women can be absolutely equal to men? This has certainly been the position in the arsenal of liberals and social democrats, for whom it is preferable to strive for a society of pure equality in which everybody has the same rights. Is that possible? Maybe, but it's better to ask what this kind of equality would mean.

So what else is there? There could be secession. One whole group—women—moves off into another society, meaning the men have to do so as well. Secession is always an interesting logical alternative. In the history of Black politics, Marcus Garvey's great movement, Garveyism, was really the kick-off for many African independence movements. He was a leader so committed to this idea that he even bought a ship to sail back to Africa. All the great African revolutionaries read his book. Jomo Kenyatta read Garvey's work and knew it well. This was a powerful secessionist idea, which already informed the Communist Party's position on race in the 1930s: Black people would have the South as their separate, autonomous soviet republic, so to speak.

That's not impossible, of course, and, in the stuff we're reading today, it is advocated, or it is implied. It looks like it is being implied in the form of lesbian separatism. Lesbian separatism is the position that fits that logical solution to the struggle. There are two different ways of abolishing this agon. Just as the solution to the class struggle is not workerism but the abolition of classes, so too we find a desire to exit sex altogether. So what about Monique Wittig's position, the abolition of what we call sexuality? That doesn't mean sexual practices, but it does mean a place in which sexual difference doesn't exist as a category. That's the upshot of Wittig's view that the struggle of the sexes is to be read as a form of class struggle, because you can't say that this is a Marxist feminism or a feminist Marxism. This is Marxism in the realm of "the woman question," so to speak. She views sex as a form of class, and what is desirable with respect to class, as I say, is not to bring one class up to the other or to make them equal, but to abolish the concept itself. Well, what would abolishing the concept of sex mean? Wittig, as you may know, was a novelist as well. She has her utopian novel, *Les Guérillères*, in which there is a battle between men and women; women triumph alongside their ally, young boys, young men who haven't gone through this patriarchal system. It's an interesting attempt to imagine something which is beyond the imagination, but which is very different from anything else being pushed in France or America. As I tried to convey, Wittig's proposal for the transcendence or elimination of sexual difference as a classification is utterly different than what gender studies has tended to propose, in which all of these differences remain. They don't remain for Wittig.

Is this a purely intellectual exercise? In any case, I'm afraid what it meant was that Wittig became an outcast. She came to the United States. She wouldn't really find a following here. Whereas American theories of non-heterosexual sexuality are all over the place, hers really didn't gain purchase, and she is often not counted among the pantheon of the discipline. Probably the same is true of Guy Hocquenghem with respect to male homosexuality. He died of AIDS very young, but his work was the furthest out in a position on gay politics. He disagreed with everybody the way Wittig attacks everything: difference, certainly gender, the myth of woman, the idea that there is such a thing as woman.

All of these people, for her, are collaborating with the enemy by pushing the idea, for example, of women's writing, the idea that you're going to find an essence of women's condition to which corresponds a certain kind of language. Now that's rather interesting, especially when it's connected to Irigaray and other aberrant forms of writing like schizophrenia. I believe that Irigaray began her clinical work on the language of schizophrenics, and Kristeva, who has become an analyst, was interested in that as well. So the aberrant forms of language would be of theoretical interest for them, but, for somebody like Wittig, it's not. So, finally, she is against what she calls universalization, which I would call the reification of language. I can just read you a little bit here: "I can only underline the oppressive character that the straight mind is clothed in in its tendency to immediately universalize its production of concepts into general laws that claim to hold true for all societies, all epochs, and all individuals." I would wish to talk there in terms of the reification of language: that you have an idea; it turns into a word and a slogan and is then perpetuated. I continue with Wittig: "Thus one speaks of *the* exchange of women"—Lévi-Strauss—"of *the* difference between the sexes"—that's anybody—"*the* symbolic order"—that's Lacan—"*the* Unconscious"—psychoanalysis—"Desire, Jouissance, Culture, History, giving an absolute meaning to these concepts when they are only categories founded upon heterosexuality, or thought which produces the difference between the sexes as a political and philosophical dogma."[4] And she goes on with that in the next page. And she also attacks the universal proliferation of the theme of otherness. When Sartre develops his theory of otherness, it is a very painful thing to think of all relations with the other as being ontologically antagonistic in their very being. Another philosopher who has been important but who has now been taken to be religious in character, Emmanuel Levinas, then takes this and turns it into a theory of otherness in general. Obviously, the big Other, as Kristeva puts it, who has also gotten into this religious stuff, is God. But then, as every kind of other is to be respected in a kind of absolute theoretical non-violence, the whole notion of otherness loses its specificity. But this is already denounced by Wittig.

Now I want to spend a little bit of our remaining time on Irigaray, because I think she would certainly fall under many of these critiques of Wittig. She is actually an analyst, and her position is that Freud's whole theory, being founded on castration, is thus obviously lopsided. There is apparently nothing in Freud that corresponds to this, except in penis envy. So what she says is that women lack a position in the symbolic order. She is following Lacan here. The passage from the Imaginary to the Symbolic is the moment of castration. Okay, from out of that come notions and positions of manhood, but the woman has nothing like that. So the father continues even after the father is killed by the primal horde or by Oedipus or whoever, and the father forms the ideal image of what the human is to become. But the human female, what does she have? What she has is the myth, the legend, the story of Oresteia. Clytemnestra kills Agamemnon and then is killed by her son. So this is a murder of the mother that doesn't, as in Freud, come back as the ego image of the dead father, but is, instead, repressed. Irigaray insists, as does Kristeva, on the absence of the maternal figure in our patriarchal culture. She proposes

---

4   Monique Wittig, "The Straight Mind," *French Feminism Reader*, ed. Kelly Oliver (Lanham, MD: Rowman and Littlefield, 2000), 140.

a way of somehow finding a position for this archetype of the mother in the symbolic order. The mother has no place in this order. It is a kind of psychoanalytic solution and revision.

> The maternal-feminine remains the *place separated from 'its' own place*, deprived of 'its' place. She is or ceaselessly becomes the place of the other who cannot separate himself from it. Without her knowing or willing it, she is then threatening because of what she lacks: a 'proper' place. She would have to re-envelope herself with herself, and do so at least twice: as a woman and as a mother. Which would presuppose a change in the whole economy of space, time.[5]

Now the other analyst whom we haven't mentioned—she is not French, but she has become a very important figure in the psychoanalytic tradition, very important to Lacan—is Melanie Klein. Melanie Klein's work turns very much around the position of the mother, and, in a sense, Irigaray's work comes out of that tradition, since she, as with Kristeva, somehow introduces myths of the mother, a culture of the mother, an ideal of the matriarchy, which would somehow give women a new place in the symbolic order. We'll talk more about her later on.

So I suppose you could say Irigaray is proposing something which is gradually happening now, because we have women prime ministers, women in authority, women governors and bureaucrats and so on. Maybe the glass ceiling is not completely broken. But the symbolic order is going to invent places for those women, and, in a sense, maybe Irigaray is right that what she thinks should be done is itself happening in this kind of society, the late-capitalist, globalized consumer society that we have. It's an interesting development. So you see how the whole question of sex and gender is here being reorganized through contradictions or problems in the concept around these problems of opposition and of the logical possibilities for restructuring this opposition or even getting rid of it.

We'll go on with Kristeva a little bit next time, because Kristeva has an immense body of work, and she is a remarkable figure in her own right. She has a distance from this since she is from a country of actually existing socialism, Bulgaria; she is an outlier in the Parisian community

---

5   Luce Irigaray, "An Ethics of Sexual Difference," in *French Feminism Reader*, ed. Kelly Oliver (Lanham, MD: Rowman and Littlefield, 2000), 230.

of intellectuals. Of course, most of the time, she is trying to weasel her way around her political ambiguities. When she meets these intellectuals in *Tel Quel* in the '60s, they're all in the Communist Party. They stay in it until they visit China, but they're secretly Maoists. It's the story of *Tel Quel*, which I've alluded to before, and of which she gives you a partial version, but you will see that there's some wriggling going on in her story here. Nonetheless, it illustrates a very unusual trajectory. She begins in linguistics, drawing on Russian stuff, Bakhtin, for example. She is the first to translate Bakhtin into French. Then semiotic theory. She works with Benveniste. Her thesis, which is published, is an immense book. I won't frighten you with it. It's 600 pages long, this huge thing, *The Revolution in Poetic Language*, quite remarkable for somebody in her late twenties. It has her own theory of language as applied to art, something that the French didn't quite have a notion of, something she doesn't call it here but that we would call "modernism." It's about her theory of language and an analysis of two great modernist breakthroughs or revolutions, namely those of Mallarmé and Lautréamont, a heretical modernist in a lot of ways. So, she gradually works her way via this group of *Tel Quel*, who represent a kind of avant garde, into a combination of psychoanalysis and religion, finally ending up with a weird position for religion, like the Communist Party's position for Maoism, a behind-the-scenes place in which all kinds of interesting psychic developments can be practiced and observed. She is an analyst—she is probably retired by now—and her current procedure is one in which there is a value given to religion in the psychic sense. She also is concerned to restore the maternal and the mother to analytic practice.

Let me say, also, that her theory of language implies two levels, which are vaguely familiar to you. We have the double inscription. We have the level of phonetics or phonetic oppositions, and then we have the level of word formations and meaning, if you like, the signifier and the signified. She is going to convert those into something called the symbolic—that will be the top level, the level of meaning, of the social—and this bottom level, which she is going to call—it's very annoying—a semiotic. It should not be confused with the semiotics that people like Greimas were trying to organize as a field of study. It comes from *semiosis*, the Greek word for "sign," but she uses it in an almost bodily sense. She connects it to an idea of Plato in the *Timaeus* when he is talking about the creation of the world, the *chora*, the raw material of the universe. Lacan called the physical nature of language *lalangue*, all as one word (the French of course is *language*, but since you always use an article with a French noun, it is *la langue*). So *lalangue* will be this physical dimension of language, the sound dimension, the bodily dimension. In English, how would we translate that? Well, here the translator really got inspired—I think it's quite wonderful—and he calls it "llanguage," with two "l"s.

You know that Joyce's daughter was schizophrenic. Of course, Lacan as a young man had seen Joyce around Paris, where he lived. He could be seen in the Sylvia Beach bookstore or in the bars, probably because, like Faulkner, he was an alcoholic. At any rate, his daughter was a schizophrenic, and Lacan imagines that *Finnegans Wake* is sort of Joyce's adoption of his daughter's schizophrenic language into his own language, the adoption of *lalangue*, of what Kristeva calls the semiotic dimension, the nighttime dimension, into the daytime world of words and sentences and language. I think that is a little too psychoanalytic for what Joyce was trying to do in *Finnegans Wake*, which was the book of the world, the integration of all languages into this book. Since we mentioned him before: I know some anthropologists who are crazy about *Finnegans Wake*—people get crazy about *Finnegans Wake*—and they carry it around with them and read it all the time. These people knew something about Black history, and they noticed something that nobody had ever seen in Joyce: it's full of references to Marcus Garvey! Who would have thought! But none of the academic or literary readers of *Finnegans Wake* ever knew anything about the Pan-African side of it. There is a little bit of everything in there. Everything that Joyce could put into it, he put into it. However, *Finnegans Wake* would have been an appropriate illustration for Kristeva. For her, there is a choice: if you don't fit into the symbolic order—that is, society—then your language can either veer into madness or into modernism. So Mallarmé, Lautréament, and Joyce—and, later on, Céline—are all, in some sense, eruptions of the Symbolic. They are—so I end up where I began—transgressions. This is what Bataille claims to give you, the instrument for understanding this eruption of the unconscious, the perverse, the insane, into civilized life, which we are called upon to live in our so-called symbolic order, in our daily lives in capitalism.

At any rate, we will come back to Kristeva next time, and we will go on to film theory as a different kind of semiotics than that of French feminism.

March 18, 2021

17

Mothers and Moving Images

{Kristeva, Comolli, Baudry}

We are still talking about French feminism, but it may seem that we're just picking up a few loose ends today. One half an hour on cinema does not seem very promising either. Actually, I think you're going to find that a lot of the themes from the earlier part of this course will continue through this work as well, and I think one interesting feature of these readings is that they have similar thematics, but in different forms. I will illustrate this through Kristeva's work. She has been called one of the worst words in the critical vocabulary of those days—"eclectic"—because she puts together all these different languages of the period. You move from linguistics to psychoanalysis to religion. And, yet, there is a profound unity in her work that I want to bring out. After all, I'm not sure that it *is* eclectic, at least in the sense that these are themes that do run through all these different languages and codes. Yet her work presents not so much a synthesis of these codes as much as—would one want to call it a bricolage, as in Lévi-Strauss? I don't think that's exactly right, but it is a new configuration of these themes. For example, I would like to point out that Kristeva has written on one of the crucial themes of affect theory, namely depression, in a book called *Black Sun*. That's a familiar topic even from antiquity and the Middle Ages, melancholy being a term of the humors; and it will be central in that feminism which I think passes over into affect theory. Her work on this is very interesting, but I would say it is not decisive, whereas I think she has really discovered something untheorized with the idea of the abject in her book called *Powers of Horror*.[1] She has invented what I would like to call a new signifier. This will give you an idea of the power of this word and what it means in Lacan's symbolic order. I think I told you about his reflections on whether day and night could emerge as new signifiers. Kristeva is dealing with something like that. In other words, this is more than an idea. It is a little different from a new word. She does take this word "abject" and do all kinds of things with it, before which it was not a particularly marked psychoanalytic term; and she has made it into this cluster of named ideas which is called a signifier. So that is a very remarkable thing, I think, and it doesn't happen very often, but I consider it the most interesting part of her work.

Anyway, we will start back a little further. Let me begin by reiterating something about the influence of Melanie Klein. We don't have time to go into details, and, in any case, I'm certainly not the historian of psychoanalysis who is equipped to lay this out. Melanie Klein was an immigrant to England. Somehow, she managed to have a practice there, which is quite unusual, because she didn't have any degrees, although she had been trained in Vienna and Budapest. She was an analyst of children, and that put her in a very special position, because Freud did not often analyze children. As far as the emphasis on the mother, I can't think of any moment when the role of the mother is of any great significance in the Freudian myths, whereas, for Klein, it's quite central. The official inheritor of Freudian doctrine in the West was Freud's daughter, Anna Freud, the inventor of something called "Ego therapy," which posited a strengthening of the bonds of the ego. That line passes over into the United States, and much of American analysis, in the old days at least, was brought by German immigrant psychoanalysts who were part of the heritage of Anna Freud.

With Melanie Klein, it is rather different. She is the source, if you like, of a properly English tradition which has to do with object relations, though I think that is a very misleading term. She invented the notion of the splitting of good and bad objects. But you can see that this emphasis on the other—on the moment when the child begins to smile at the mother instead of crying and yelling—inaugurates a very different notion of the

---

1   Julia Kristeva, *Powers of Horror: An Essay on Abjection*, trans. Leon S. Roudiez (New York: Columbia University Press, 1982).

psyche, one which will eventually include what Lacan calls the big Other, that is, the idea that the psyche is not this ego fortress all by itself, some kind of Cartesian unconscious, but, rather, has the other inside of it and is structured by a relationship to the other. In this case, of course, it's not just the father. Deleuze and Guattari, as you will see, write a book called *Anti-Oedipus* in which they denounce Freudian reductionism. What they mean is that Freud wanted to reduce everything to the notion of the Oedipus complex: the father, the family. I think their attack is a little bit hysterical, but it's certain that the Freudian story of development really only has two characters. It has the child and the father. To be sure, the child desires the mother and is therefore punished by the fear of castration, but, somehow, the father is the essential figure in this mythic story. Later, Freud will develop this in the anthropological visions of *Totem and Taboo*, the primal horde, the murder of the Ur-father, the primal father. The minute you put a character like the mother in there, then something interesting begins to happen, because, as we'll see, there's something that corresponds to the Oedipus complex: the Electra complex. You remember the myth of Electra, who is Agamemnon and Clytemnestra's daughter. Electra is, in most of the great dramatizations from the Greeks up to Richard Strauss and Hofmannsthal, up to Sartre's *Flies*, the figure of abjection, having been turned into a chambermaid by her mother. She hates her mother. In this story, there is a moment in which the child must be separated from the mother, weaned, and this is the moment in which the child's identity is somehow formed. So the mother is both life-enhancing and life-producing, unlike the father, but she is also that from which you must extricate yourself. You are somehow part of this thing which is the mother and which seems to want to drown you in itself and hold onto you, and therefore you must separate yourself from it. So this is a second myth that doesn't exclude the father but that becomes another interesting event for the psychoanalytic drama, so to speak.

In Lacan, there is a weird idea called *das Ding*, in German, "the thing." Nobody really knows what it means, but it seems to be somewhere in the place of the Real in Lacan. So you're not aware of it, except every so often when it breaks through in a moment of trauma and horror. Is it the unconscious personified? We know that, for Lacan, the unconscious isn't really a force in that sense. He gets this idea of *das Ding* from one word in Freud's early, unpublished paper for a scientific psychotherapy, which uses all these energy categories and which posits a moment when the child feels the other like a kind of thing, *ein Ding*.[2] So *das Ding* is this warm presence that the child has no categories for. As you remember, this is one of the problems that is underscored in Irigaray's system, that is, the problem that there has not been developed a symbolic category, a signifier, for the mother. So, if *das Ding* is this warm presence, why would its breakthrough be horrible later on? Well, that belongs to the mysteries of Lacanianism that we can't explore any further. But it's clear, in this analysis, that *das Ding* is the mother! Lacan gets a lot of this from Melanie Klein, so it makes sense that his enemies would be her enemies, namely Anna Freud and the psychoanalytic establishment. And the idea of the object relation—that is, the relationship to the other—as a crucial part of the psychic apparatus is very consistent with the Kleinian tradition, even if it isn't the immediate reference here.

So how does this get into Kristeva's work? Other feminists had a single dominant theme, although I would say that what characterizes Wittig is that there isn't really any great emphasis on psychoanalysis in her work. Irigaray, on the other hand, who is a clinically trained psychoanalyst, has a single problematic that her work turns on. Kristeva, meanwhile, has gone through all these different formations, and, therefore, this problem will evolve and take on all kinds of different forms, which is why this is especially interesting. Hers is one of the great modern theoretical oeuvres. I don't doubt that for a minute. One must have immense admiration for the variety of things she has accomplished. At any rate, you have read her autobiographical story, which is fraught, as I told you the last time, with a lot of political evasions.[3] And then we assigned an excellent essay by myself, if I do say so—which I can do because I've completely forgotten writing it and wouldn't have been capable of doing any of it today—a review of a number of histories of the journal *Tel Quel*, in which she played a part, and whose founder, Philippe Sollers, she married.[4]

Although I don't mention Kristeva much in this essay, it gives you an important piece of background for understanding her, and it fits today's

2 Sigmund Freud, *Project for a Scientific Psychology*, in *Standard Edition of the Complete Psychological Works of Sigmund Freud, Vol. I*, trans. James Strachey (London: Hogarth Press, 1966 [1895]).
3 Julia Kristeva, "My Mother's Hyperbole," *The Portable Kristeva*, ed. Kelly Oliver (New York: Columbia University Press, 2002 [1984]), 3–23.
4 Fredric Jameson, "Après the Avant Garde," *New Left Review* 18, no. 24 (December, 1996).

work in an unexpected way, because it is the story of a journal, just as the film theory I gave you also forms part of the story of a journal, *Cahiers du Cinéma*. These journals will be very significant in the '60s. There was an old literary journal founded by André Gide, the *Nouvelle Revue Française*, the *NRF*, which fell into the hands of collaborationists in the war in Vichy; when it subsequently was revived, they had to call it the *Nouvelle Nouvelle Revue Française*, *NNRF*, and it remained a fundamental place for traditional modernism, if you want to call it that. These journals publish the most important writers of the period. Then you have Sartre's journal, *Les Temps Modernes*, which becomes one of the dominant journals. And, finally, you have a series of journals that emerge in the '60s, of which *Tel Quel* is the noisiest one, the one that involves our people the most, since Foucault, Barthes, and Derrida all publish in it at a certain moment and are connected with it. These journals are all in competition with each other. There is a fight going on with the dominant film journal, *Cahiers du Cinéma*, which is the organ of the *Nouvelle Vague*, just as *Tel Quel* is the organ of a certain literary avant garde. So both of these things turn around journals. Someone—I forget who—said that what we learned in the '60s is that the most important organization in a revolutionary movement is not the party but the journal. The journal is what unites people around a common cause. It has to become a common cause in order for a journal really to function like an avant garde, and this is certainly the case here. One may say that, if the way one could characterize the contemporary period is as the end of the avant garde, then it entails the end of avant-garde journals. But *Cahiers du Cinéma*, coming out of Bazin, with its various tendencies, is fighting with other journals as well, some of which are connected to *Tel Quel*. So this piece gives you the background of all of these polemics that are going on in Paris around these movements.

Now Kristeva arrives in Paris as a linguist, and her first big book will be her *Revolution in Poetic Language*, a huge book of which there is a theoretical part and then a study of two writers, Mallarmé and Lautréamont, whom I mentioned last time. France has never had the idea of modernism as a movement as it has been elaborated in the Anglophone world. The word "modern" does go back to Baudelaire, but French experiments begin with Mallarmé, in a sense, and go on with individual writers and occasional avant-garde movements like Surrealism or *Tel Quel*. It is, in a sense, as though Kristeva wanted to invent "modernism" for French literature. That is one way of conceiving this enormous thesis of hers. We don't have to look at the other writers involved, but, as you can imagine, Bataille plays a big part. Later on, she becomes concerned with Céline, one of the most notorious collaborators, a doctor who ended up being picked as Pétain's personal physician, and who fled with the rest of them into Germany at the end of the war, and managed to conceal himself somehow either in Belgium or Holland. (He himself tells the story in one of his best novels, *Nord*.) There are all kinds of stories about him. One story goes like this. He was the most notorious of all collaborators, and since some of them were shot at the liberation, certainly they would have shot him if they had been able to get their hands on him. You know that capital cities—it's very interesting that Washington D.C. is under consideration for statehood— have traditionally not had self-government. The function of the mayor has often been appointed by the government, because the one place you don't want to have elections is in the capital city, so it has to be under the control of the central authority. If you have a mayor who is from a different party, then all kinds of different things could happen. In France, at that time, the prefect of police was in fact the mayor of Paris. A friend of his goes to see him in the '50s and says: "Look, things are dying down now. I have a friend who's had to live abroad because he had some connection with Vichy, but it's time for him to come home. He would really appreciate it if you could just sign this paper and allow him to return to France." So, the prefect says, "Sure, if he didn't do anything too bad. What's his name?" "Louis Ferdinand Destouches," which is of course Céline's given name; but the prefect didn't know that. So he signs the paper, which allows Céline scandalously to return to Paris. They say he lived in a house surrounded by walls and dogs, all kinds of defenses. There was an underground passage between the house and his favorite restaurant, so he could go out and have a good dinner. His books are very famous. *Journey to the End of Night* was thought both by the Left and the Right to be a masterpiece. He was invited to Moscow. They wanted him to become a great communist writer. He was a doctor in the poor areas. There's much pity for the underclasses in Céline. The second book, *Death on Credit, Mort à crédit*, is, to my mind, just extraordinary, a more autobiographical text. Then it all goes crazy. An insane anti-Semitism rages through his work. In the postwar stuff, there is a little bit of a reprieve. Some people like those the best. These are delirious works composed of a very special kind of language, so you could see why Kristeva, besides wishing to make a rather scandalous mark on the then-existing French canon, would find these to be very much a revolution in language, an undermining of language of a very different kind from Mallarmé or Lautréamont.

Anyway, if you look at her book *Black Sun* on melancholy, you will see she has chapters on all of her candidates, so to speak, for a modernist or Kristevan canon. At any rate, as we've seen, she proposes a certain theory in her books. We're back to the double inscription: the symbolic order and the semiotic one, by which she means an underlying, unconscious mass of linguistic material that every so often breaks through into the symbolic order. Here is your revolution of symbolic language. There is this moment in which this unconscious magma explodes into ordinary daytime speech. Now that will take two forms, and we've already seen how that works in the interrogations of women's language in Irigaray and others. This is psychotic language, but, for Kristeva—and I think this tallies well with the underlying tendency here—there is also an opposition detectable in the results of this semiotic breakthrough. It can result either in symptoms or in sublimation. So this revolution can either lead to the language of schizophrenia, the language of what Lacan calls a *forclusion*, a foreclosure of language, a casting of language outside the self, or to this artistic transformation of symbolic language, which is the semiotic work of what will become poetry or modernist literature, if we want to use those terms.

What is semiotics for Kristeva? She describes it in terms she borrows from the ancient Greeks. In Plato, the great cosmology is laid out in the *Timaeus*, which is a very strange dialogue, in which Plato describes the making of the world and all the parts of it, which are almost geometrical and Pythagorean. For people who only know of Plato's traditionally famous dialogues, this is a real eye-opener. The point here is: where does the world come from? The world, says Timaeus, who is the primary narrator of this text—Socrates is there, but as listener—has four elements: fire, earth, water, and air. Everything is made up of them. But where do they come from? They are in perpetual transformation. Look at fire: it's always different, taking different forms. The pre-Socratics, of course, began that way. They said everything is made out of certain elements. Plato builds on that idea in a new way by saying, no, the elements must themselves all be made out of some primal element, but we can't ever see that primal element because it has already become fire, air, water, or earth. He calls that primal element *chora*, which, in Greek, means "space," but it's translated as "receptacle," which is not a good word, unless you take it to mean a receptacle of form, a womb; this is a very traditional, even sexist version of form and content, and I would say it is Plato's anticipation of the whole dynamic of materialism.

So what is the *chora*? It's the mother, of course. For each of us, this primal matter is the mother. And this is what will explode, this *chora*, this semiotic or presymbolic meaning, into the daytime world of symbolic—indeed, paternal—meaning and transform language. So here, at the very beginning of her career, we have the notion that the mother is somehow the category of this ultimate matter of the universe. Can this be understood as space? Well, yes, I think space becomes very interesting if you think of it as a kind of matter before form, but that takes us too far. Derrida was also interested in this, and, in his collaboration with the architect Peter Eisenman in *Le Parc de la Villette*, he tried to imagine how you would do an architectural representation of this notion of the *chora*, of the ultimate reality. It's not terribly successful, but you can see where the fascination comes from. In any case, what the *chora* actually *is* has remained a complete mystery in classical studies. There are any number of proposals about what Plato could possibly have meant by this. But it is clear what Kristeva thinks it means: the maternal *Ding* of "llanguage," if you like.

So you can see how a lot of our earlier themes have already emerged at the very beginning of Kristeva's work. From here, she moves on to the *Tel Quel* period, the avant garde and modernism. It's clear that her work has already been a kind of manifesto for *Tel Quel*. At that point, after this political adventure of *Tel Quel* that you will read about in my article, she, like the rest of them, withdraws from that scene. She becomes an analyst. If you take an analytic view on these problems, you can see that all of this obviously has some connection with Bataille, this notion of excess that's pouring through language and transforming it. It's also going to have something to do with religion, "the sacred," as they called it in Bataille's terms. It doesn't mean any established religion, although in each era, for each great religion, there is a specific type of abjection, let's say. The sacred will be what you have recourse to after the end of the official religions. That's the religion of art. So, if psychoanalysis is the talking cure, you can almost say that Kristeva foresees the "writing cure," that is to say, the production of the poetic out of this excess and transgression either in schizophrenia and psychosis or in writing. So you can see how this fits into all the preoccupations of the era and in a way she kind of represents all of them.

Now I want to quickly move on to what the abject means for Kristeva. I consider it to be very closely related to what in this country has become affect theory. Affect theory, I think, has a deeper connection to melancholy and to depression, but Kristeva's notion of abjection gives you a different handle on that kind of thinking. Sadness, she says, is a way of integrating the ego. Abjection is the falling apart of identity. The basic operating theme of her description is the boundary: inside and outside. In the abject, which is a matter of disgust and revulsion, you can see how the body is reacting to the various substances of the outside and imagining itself as incorporating them.

Where does her idea of the abject come from? Her essay is quite interesting for tracing its ideas back to phenomenology. Consider it as her way of laying down some parameters. To understand this concept, you have to project yourself into some other place where you can see that you have taken care of these various parameters. I'm not altogether sure that I fully grasp what she has in mind, but, in any case, it describes a kind of writing which is an incentive to recreate this state either in one's self or as a literary production. That's the moment of discovery from which all of this comes, starting with Sartre and phenomenology, where the boundary between literature and philosophical analysis breaks down and you move between the ontic and the ontological as you begin to describe these various relationships to being. Well, this is another one of those relationships, but it is described in psychoanalytic language, something that Lacan did not do, or didn't have the patience to do. She gives you a whole set of indications of how that kind of relationship is related to identity, and ultimately how it's related to the mother. This is, in a sense, a moment when the mother is flowing back into the separated identity and beginning to destroy the boundaries which were created when the child separated itself from the maternal and affirmed its own identity. It is the abject because it no longer has an object. To have an object, you have to have a boundary that separates the object and makes it external. The object is outside of yourself, perhaps as an object of desire.

The abject is more than just the opposite of desire. It's the breakdown of the whole system in which desire functions, and that's the sense in which the abject can be thought of, if you like, as a very powerful, primal affect. It's more than just depression, which has its own dynamic, which was analyzed by Kristeva in *Black Sun*, and by Freud himself in the famous essay "Mourning and Melancholia." It is very interesting that Kristeva should also connect it with the sublime as an aesthetic category, which also has no object and which is this feeling of worldness, if you like, because this is somehow the tonality of the whole world, this kind of abjection, this breakdown of the ego, which demands then, she seems to indicate, some kind of purification ritual. That is, you must somehow be purified of this disgusting thing which is abjection, a purification that would be both therapeutic and aesthetic. At any rate, I think the next book, *Powers of Horror*, is one of the furthest poles, if you like, of the experimentation of this whole period, and it is a kind of marker for a truly remarkable discovery, but we've only just tapped the surface of it.

With that, we must leave Kristeva and move on to cinema—although, God knows, Kristeva has something to say about that, as with everything else. She does work on painting, in particular on Bellini's use of blue in her work on the maternal, so she certainly knows something about the visual. In any case, we move into something else, which is the realm of visuality. Comolli gives you an idea of what these critics are trying to do, especially with this desperate attempt to pin down what political or revolutionary art is.[5] And, yes, these people are filmmakers too, unlike in the United States, where you have filmmakers who were only filmmakers. But the French all started as theorists, the earliest of whom—the disciples of André Bazin, the great origin-figure of cinema theory during the war and a little later—are named François Truffaut, Éric Rohmer, and Jean-Luc Godard. Out of their film criticism comes a whole cinematographic movement.

This is the moment of the Nouvelle Vague. Its first films appear in the late '50s; Godard's *Breathless* or Truffaut's *Les quatre cents coups* are the kick-off films. There are others, and I would particularly refer you to *Last Year at Marienbad*, written by a novelist, Alain Robbe-Grillet, because that film makes the connection between filmic language and the experiments of the so-called New Novel, of which Barthes was an apologist. That is the moment when this intellectual and creative impulse is turned toward language as a medium. The point that it arrives at is not that language is a medium in the sense that it "means," but rather in the sense that it is matter. Sartre described language as a rug. It has a surface, which is decorated with all kinds of patterns, its meanings. Then you turn it over and you have all the loose ends of the material that the rug is made from. Poetry, he says, is like this rug: it directs our attention to the materiality of language. We can also find this play with language in Robbe-Grillet's

5   Jean-Louis Comolli and Jean Narboni, "Cinema/Ideology/Criticism," in *Movies and Methods, Vol. I*, ed. Bill Nichols (Berkeley: University of California Press, 1976), 22–30.

novels, the most famous of which is called *La Jalousie*, 'jealousy' being both a state of mind and, in French, the slats of a blind; when you talk about film noir in English or French, it always brings to mind the shadows of blinds on somebody's face. But I would refer you either to his novel *Le voyeur*, or, later on, *Project for a Revolution in New York*. Robbe-Grillet, however, is not supposed to be read, because his work is profoundly sexist. It's nothing but women's naked bodies, torture, and all the rest of it. In my own opinion, it isn't that this is morally evil; it's just that it's stupid. One gets very tired of it. Robbe-Grillet finally was attacked for the content of these novels, but these are the pieces, the raw material that makes up the operation of his novels.

Look at it this way. The narrator describes a torture, obviously of a woman, because that's what he always does. Then you begin to see that, no, the words have not told you enough, because this is visual description. In fact, you realize you're looking at this whole scene through a keyhole. So, suddenly, it is a different matter than what you had imagined. Finally, at the end, you discover that it isn't an act of torture at all; it's the cover of a pornographic magazine. So you see how the limits of the words that we use to describe things are being cunningly exploited. We're being made to think that we're looking at one referent, but, owing to the material defects of language and its abstractions, it turns into something else, such that the novel has turned on itself and made you look at its process of representation, rather than its content.

So this becomes, in a way, analogous to what the filmmakers of the New Wave are doing. This work is making you think you're following a representation, but then it gradually reveals the structure of the representation and the materiality of the process whereby the representation is made. *Last Year at Marienbad* is an example of that, because it is a film in which you never know where you are, the representations taking you one direction, the flashback taking you another; nobody knows exactly what's happened. You could say that it is a rather mechanical product. Yes, but it has a real mystery and beauty to it, and I think one can't deny its success.

So this is what is going on in literature and in cinema. Godard is certainly one of the great figures of the age. Whatever you think of his films, he has produced a prodigious oeuvre, and it is certainly as great as any of the writers or poets of the period. If you've never seen any Godard, I would recommend first the political film about May '68, *Tout Va Bien*, starring Jane Fonda and Yves Montand in the middle of the strikes and crises of the

'60s. An early work, one that I really like, is called *Weekend*, in which the world ends in a traffic jam. Then there is the political period of the Dziga Vertov Group, whose films are overtly political and exploratory, dealing especially with the wars of national liberation. After that, later films like *Passion* and *Carmen*, and, finally, a return to politics, where the struggles of the Palestinian people are transferred to the Balkans and the horrors of civil war. So Godard spans all these periods and becomes the filmmaker of History itself, which predictably he identifies with the history of cinema (the four parts of *Histoire(s) du Cinéma*).

All of the theoretical work of these filmmakers and groups like *Tel Quel* is being produced against the background of the great explosion of May '68 and the reaction against it in the '70s, when the parties have broken down into *groupuscules*, small tendency groups; meanwhile, in Germany and Italy, these small groups will become—I don't like this word, but it is the word people use—so-called terrorist groups, one of which will end in the kidnapping and death of Aldo Moro. A little more short lived here was The Weathermen, and in Canada the Front de libération du Québec. All over the world, there are sequels to the failure of May '68.

Film has a special presence in this moment. I would put the problem of revolutionary film this way: If you represent your oppressed population as being too weak, then what the film projects is that they're incapable of making revolution. If they are shown as the victim, in the long run, the more you succeed, the more you fail, because the more you succeed in showing how miserable and oppressed they are, the less capable they seem of making any kind of revolution. On the other hand, if you try to show the political possibilities, the heroism of these classes, then, of course, that is false as well, because why would they have to revolt if they were that powerful? So, in between, you get the temptation of the leader, of political heroism, which also becomes a kind of fairy tale. It is a very delicate balance that one must find to show revolution in the content. Here, I would be very old-fashioned and insist on a distinction between form and content, which you're getting in Comolli in his various categorizations, because he understands that you don't want to throw out the window all the old films that show revolutionary activity in a style of traditional filmmaking, because why should you abandon those to the enemy? Even if the enemy is traditional, realistic representation, Hollywood, nonetheless these are films with tremendous power. And I would say the greatest of those is called *Burn!* by the filmmaker, Pontecorvo, who made *The Battle of Algiers*. It is in English, and the star is Marlon Brando; I think it is also his greatest movie. It is about the liberation of a colonial island called Queimada ("burnt"). I highly recommend it to you.

On the other hand, these theorists have talked themselves into a system where the great activity is not to be found in the content of the works but in the revolution of filmic language itself. So which is more revolutionary: a film about revolution or a film in which the very forms of narrative are revolutionized and in which the attention is given to the cinematographic revolution in the forms, like Eisenstein, maybe (although the cultural hero of all this is Dziga Vertov)? On the other hand, if you're a political militant and you're working with workers and radical groups, these esoteric films about the making of film are not likely to arouse much interest in their self-conscious revolutionary technique. So you have a problem. I think Comolli is here trying to respect these various categories and to recognize them all in their various ways of doing things. But, of course, that is not really a solution.

Jean-Louis Baudry is doing something else, and here we're coming back to visuality with a vengeance. You will see when we get to Foucault next time that this problematic of the visual doesn't go away if we leave behind the explicit concern with film. It is this nagging problem that begins with Sartre's notion of the look, goes through Lacan and the object gaze, and then comes back in these filmmakers. In Baudry, the interesting thing is the emergence of a different kind of theme, one that we've also insisted on here. So far, we have called it "humanism." We don't have to keep that word, but it is the same that Foucault is attacking when talks about the death of the author. We'll look at that next time.

But, with Baudry, film itself is enlisted in this campaign for the death of the subject. Of course, the subject doesn't die; it's only decentered. We're to see with Sartre personal identity as an object of consciousness and not the constitution of consciousness. With Lacan, we are to see how, in the mirror stage, the subject produces itself as a visual unity. But we are also to understand how the very idea of unity is itself an ideological theme, because you don't have a centered bourgeois subject without an entire society being unified around it. Now, suddenly, in this new and tremendously influential cinematographic theory, we have the notion of an object as ideology, and that object is the apparatus, or, in other words, the camera. Suddenly, something has happened to the bourgeois subject. It goes into the theater. It is no longer bodily active. Another one of the

great cinema theorists of this period, Christian Metz, has been very interested in analyzing the attraction of film, the desire called film. (I say "film"
despite the whole shift to digital because it's just the word we've come to
use.) What is it that we find in the theater in this abandonment of self?
A phenomenological *epoché*, a bracketing of the world? Or something
psychoanalytic? Is the screen not like the mother's breast? Is this not a
regression to some passivity of the child, where you can somehow simply
take all this in? You can see how many paths this thinking could pursue.
One of the most interesting—and the great American book on this is
Stanley Cavell's *The World Viewed*—is that cinema is our chance to see
the world without ourselves. Cinema would have us think we're not in
this picture. Of course, we really are. That's its ideology. Ideology means
that our presence is masked and that we are made to think that what we
see is the *Ding-an-sich*, that we're seeing the world without our categories,
without our own personal subjectivity. Film is proving to us that the world
exists, and it's doing so at a very slight price: the cost of the ticket and the
cost of sitting still for two hours. You're abandoning your body. You're
abandoning action, so to speak, and allowing everything to pass through
this profoundly ideological realm, which is the visual.

How is this done, according to Baudry? Here, we go back to the ideology
of Western painting, of perspective, which is discovered in the Quattro-
cento, in the fifteenth century, when oil paint is imported into Italy from
the Netherlands. Of course, perspective is ideological; perspective assumes
one eye which is going to organize the world around itself in this fan-like
map of space, of which the final line is a slight curvature of the horizon.
Perspective will then make the world our own and make us the center
of it. And remember that this is the basis of Ptolemaic centrality, against
which the Copernican revolution and Freud and all modern theory is
directed. We are not the center of our world, they say. The unconscious
is the center of our world. We are a satellite to our own unconscious, or,
with the linguists, we are not the center of our language, because we are
spoken by our language. Our intentionality, our freedom, is not the source
of everything. So, here again, film, like perspectival painting, is persuading
us—literally in action—that we are the center of our world, and this unity
that's given to us in painting, and then on the film screen, is the unity of
the world itself. It has ratified us as its center and the vanishing point as
our symptom, so to speak. So you see why the young Sartre, coming out
of the movie theater, would rediscover the medieval idea of contingency:

When you're watching a movie, you're at the center of everything, but, when you come out into the street, there isn't a center anymore. The world is not centered around you, but film is so enticing because it persuades you that you are.

Someone had the genius to mention *Rear Window*—they were crazy about Hitchcock in those days—which is the great dramatization of this whole process. Jimmy Stewart is the center of the world, and suddenly, in a kind of Foucauldian turn, when the world looks back at him, he is immobilized, paralyzed, just the same way we are in the movie theater. So, if you're a film critic like them, you might like to say that this is the film making an ideological analysis of itself. This is film reflecting on itself. Now you see the revolutionary, political problem here, because you're not going to take *Rear Window* around and show it to revolutionary groups as your energizing work of art, and, yet, it does many of the things that a revolutionary art might like to do. In general, Hitchcock was fascinating to all these people, despite what they thought of Hollywood, because he shows you all the hidden traps of visuality. Hitchcock was like the god of the era, and if you're interested, Truffaut had a week-long conversation with Hitchcock, which is quite fascinating and gives you a sense of his importance.[6]

So that is the great discovery of Baudry: It is the very materiality of the operation of film which is ideological.[7] One might even like to say that visuality itself is somehow profoundly ideological. What do we do with that? In one of your papers, someone discussed the relationship of all this to science and scientific visuality, because, of course, visuality comes to us in experiment. Now, if you want an almost Kristevan turn on this relationship, you should look ahead—we'll mention him much later on—to Bruno Latour's first work, which proves that scientific truth is an effect of writing. He says that something isn't accepted as truth unless it's been mentioned in an increasing plurality of published scientific papers. Verification in science is not really an action or operation in the real world; it's just the number of papers written to prove something. So here, in Latour, scientific truth and its mode of visuality are suddenly turned back into the great obsession of the period, which is writing. But, so far, this is still

6   See François Truffaut with Helen G. Scott, *Hitchcock* (New York: Simon & Schuster, 1984).

7   Jean-Louis Baudry, "Ideological Effects of the Basic Cinematographic Apparatus," trans. Alan Williams, *Film Quarterly* 28, no. 2 (1974), 39–47.

wrapped up in questions of sight and visibility. In *Rear Window*, Jimmy Stewart suddenly gets his comeuppance because he is visible. He is the object of the gaze, not only the source of the gaze. Film, too, shows that the look is a double-edged sword, as it was in Sartre and Lacan.

So these things all inscribe themselves in the anti-humanist struggle, so to speak, the struggle against the centrality of the subject and of consciousness, which, of course, begins way back with Freud and Marx, to the degree that it is the bourgeois subject that is at stake here, since it is the bourgeoisie whose very triumph is the construction of this notion of individualism. Individualism is the centered subject, the idea that our lives have a biographical unity, that we have selves, that we have identities. All of this is the rich, civilized heritage of the bourgeois revolution as it affirms our individual freedoms against the hierarchies of earlier kinds of societies. So, in that sense, yes, they are inscribing themselves in a revolutionary tradition, but it's easy after the fact to turn that into a kind of mocking reflection on the powerlessness of the intellectuals. In light of all this, I think you can begin to sense the reaction that follows this great intellectual ferment and this revolutionary moment. In film theory, it's followed in this country by Bordwell and Thompson, their versions of Hollywood normality and their affirmation that, finally, the only real kind of film is Hollywood's, that Hollywood realistic representation has finally reabsorbed all the movements around the world that affirmed the possibility of a different kind of experimental film, and that it is the destiny of all of these countries, not just France. One of you mentioned Third Cinema, but Bordwell and Thompson say—it's a very depressing and dramatic moment of their work—no, Hollywood is sufficiently elastic to draw back into itself all those experiments and to absorb them into the essential practices of bourgeois representation. So Hollywood film and realism, the enemy, so to speak, the very center of this whole process, has finished by assimilating not only its competitors but also its critics and its transgressors or revolutionaries. And that process provides an allegory of the disappearance of politics from the globalized world. But we must take account of an interesting irony, because this is happening at the very moment that all of these theorists are telling us that Hollywood is over and film is over. These people were working before several revolutions. One is the digital revolution. What does that do to the notion of the cinematic apparatus, when you don't really have an apparatus of the analog or "filmic" type? Several of you mentioned television, and I would add video games, a whole different set of representations that begin to take the place of films and maybe of filmic stories. Do we want filmic stories, narrative, anymore? Don't we want, even in the blockbusters, just a series of thrills? We don't really want a story anymore. But don't these replacements undermine traditional narratives and the idea of the destiny of the centered subject? A story is about the destiny of the centered subject, of the personality, but if there is no personality, identity, or center, what can a story be about? If it's a schizophrenic flux, as in Deleuze, then there's nothing to tell anymore, maybe just the flood of images. There is no narrative. So all these institutions begin to collapse, and as some of these film critics have said, you can only tell this story at the moment when its central object is dying or has disappeared, but that's a later matter, and it certainly doesn't concern us at this stage where filmmaking is still going on and there is still somebody like Godard constantly innovating and transforming the very material of film.

Next time, we will trace this business of visuality into Foucault and take a closer look at his place within this moment.

March 23, 2021

18

"Moi, Michel Foucault..."

{Foucault}

Today, we arrive at one of the centers of this class, one of the great thinkers of French theory. Foucault is certainly the most dramatic of all our theorists. But, before we get to him, I want to add a few things to our previous discussion of visuality.

We haven't read anything on the philosophy of photography in this class, but that's a very interesting problem, because photography presents us with an antinomy. Barthes will write a whole book on photography, which we won't have time to read. But the problem about thinking photography is epitomized by the Derridean concept of the trace. The point is that the photograph belongs to the past, but the past doesn't exist. In the present the photo is nothing but an image. The point to arrive at is one in which you question the whole notion of the image and whether it means anything. I think that's a very important question for understanding visuality. In some sense, film solves the problem of the trace, because the photographic image is somehow a trace of the past whose ontology is ... what? What is its being? Is it a piece of paper? Is it a piece of the past? Does the past exist? Does it have a being in the present, and what would it be to have a being in the present? These philosophers have arrived at the moment when they are challenging ontology itself and the consistency of the present. Okay, but if you take that photograph and you reproduce it twenty-four times per second, then, suddenly, the past is projected into the future, into a narrative of something happening in time, which may or may not have been latent in the single photograph. So film will take the contradictions of photography, and by adding the future and movement to it, it will change the ontological structure of the image. Does that mean one can have an ontology of film but not of the photograph? I don't know. I simply wanted to bring this question to your attention.

The other thing I wanted to say brings us to Foucault. In 1970, almost ten years before his death, he began to give lectures at the Collège de France—a unique kind of institution—which are now published. He wrote books, lots of articles, and he gave plenty of interviews, for reasons we'll look at in a minute. In French, everything except the books was collected in four immense volumes. The Americans have done that much better, I think, so we have a three-volume Foucault now, which is published by The New Press in New York. So that's another resource you should know about.

Now Velázquez. Alois Riegl was a very interesting art historian who died young in the late nineteenth century and had an underground influence on a lot of people. He wrote a book on the Dutch collective portrait.[1] Why is that of importance? Holland had the first bourgeois revolution. England had a Thermidor of sorts with the death of Cromwell and constructed a class compromise. In Holland, things turn out a little bit differently. Holland really precedes France as the great bourgeois nation; it is also the first Northern capitalist center and the first center of imperialism. The Dutch colonized East Asia before the British land in India, eventually fighting with the Dutch to acquire this for themselves. So one would expect Holland to have some very special symptoms of all this to show us, and, of course, they do, especially in painting. We have the painting, the so-called greatest painter in the world, Rembrandt—or Vermeer, if you prefer—and we have then that collective painting which is *The Night Watch*. I don't know how many of you have been to Holland, but this painting is a stunning experience. It's huge. There is nothing else in the room. You come in, and this thing is there. It feels life-sized and depicts a patrol; all these men in the patrol are looking at you, about to arrest you, no doubt. It is not the Rembrandt of chiaroscuro and the portraits. This is a very powerful and militant thing, this Spinozan multitude which is

---

1   Alois Riegl, *The Group Portraiture of Holland* (Oxford: Oxford University Press, 1999).

addressing you out of this frame—because Spinoza is another part of the Dutch revolutionary spirit.

So we have this collectivity which is *The Night Watch*. In other periods, there are different kinds of great collective paintings. There is *The Raft of the Medusa* by Géricault, in the early nineteenth century, a raft on which all these starving people are going to die. It's another enormous thing with all these starving people staring at you. Finally, what would be the equivalent in a modern period where we don't have collectives of these earlier types? If you wanted to be semi-humorous, I suppose you could say *Les Demoiselles d'Avignon* by Picasso, five prostitutes looking at you, of a very strange nature.

Velázquez's *Meninas* is another of these collective paintings. It is the collective painting of the court of the Spanish empire, which, at that moment, is the greatest empire in the world, leaving Qing China out of it, no doubt. And let's say it: Rembrandt and Michelangelo, sure, but Velázquez is the greatest painter in the world. If you look at this thing and you see it in reality, you will understand this as much as you will understand this moment of Spanish hegemony. Is that what Foucault's talking about here? He is very methodical in his analysis. This is probably one of the most famous set-pieces in French theory, this description of *Las Meninas*, the *infanta*, this little girl, and the people who take care of her. But we'll leave that for later.

First, let's go back and think a little bit more about how this business of schizophrenia is infecting everything we're reading. We saw how feminist theory ends up having something to do with language; feminist theory is moving into some place in which women's writing will seem to take on value as a solution, but the people who are pushing women's writing as a unique kind of writing are also people who are very interested in the language of schizophrenia. And where do these psychic classifications come from? They're not in the Bible. A huge handbook, the DSM, had to be created that name all of these states that are supposed to be diseases; then, if the physician sees somebody acting strangely, they leaf through their handbook and find out what they're called and have them dealt with. In an earlier society—let's think of the Middle Ages—there are agricultural villages and there is the church. So you don't need shamans anymore, who were once those people who happened to behave and think differently. In medieval towns, some of these people are now wandering loose. This being understood, as I would claim, that, in a sense, everybody is neurotic; there isn't any true normality. Sartre really pioneered this notion that, if everybody is neurotic, there is no need for that category, and, therefore, there is a kind of democracy about this; there aren't any fixed mental identities that can be compared, except in the sense that one identity functions, whereas another is found to be abnormal. So, suddenly, everybody is alike. In the early modern, however, you have people wandering around the streets of the older cities, where there are no safe places. These are muddy openings, unlit streets, marauders. What do you do? At a certain moment, the city fathers, workman's guilds, round up these people who are a nuisance—they don't know what dangers they present—and stick them on a boat. Medieval cities are founded on rivers, because rivers were the most convenient mechanism for travel; the roads are much too difficult. So you send them to your neighbor, because you don't want them in your town. The next town can deal with them. These are the famous "the ships of fools" ("fools" being of course the insane, *folie* being the French word from which "fool" comes and which means "insanity").

So Foucault will begin his first great book with a study of the ways in which the cities and towns get rid of these people who are wandering around. They do so by excluding them, and as he says, the first great example of this is leprosy. You exclude lepers, you make a special place for them sometimes—the *leproserie*. The lepers are excluded from normal everyday life, and they roam these waterways in their ships; who knows what happens to them or where they end up? But this is an image of freedom in a way. And you're going to see that what Foucault is interested in, besides the history of these things, is really the mechanisms by which they happen. Do they have classifications? We can see how this works in his analysis of these populations. At this point, what the towns want to do is get rid of them. They don't want to study them or understand them. This doesn't need to turn into any kind of power. You just need to exclude. These are matters of exclusion. But, centuries later, there will happen something which he calls "the great confinement." All of a sudden, as the city grows in importance and as the country emerges in the seventeenth century from the chaos of the religious wars, as there develops an absolute monarchy, you do something else with them: you lock them up. You take all the people on those boats and you build a structure in which to confine them.

So from exclusion there is a transition to confinement, and it turns out, if I remember correctly, and nothing guarantees that I do, this is more or less contemporarily happening all over the place in Europe at this time. It's as though something in the atmosphere changed, and this is now what you do with these oddballs. It happens more or less at the same time as Descartes is publishing his paper on reason, *Discourse on Method*, in 1637—the first great statement on the *cogito*. Can one make a connection here? Well, Foucault will make a connection, obviously. You don't really have the modern notion of reason in medieval theology, but, all the sudden, with Descartes, it is here. Once you have the notion of reason, what else do you have? You have its opposite, the notion of the irrational, the notion of madness. Until you have reason, you can't have a notion of madness. In a sense, one would say, if you wanted to follow our model, that once you have reason you can have two kinds of negatives. You can have the irrational and the non-rational. So the irrational will turn out to be, in the next century or so, the people who contest the notion of reason in a kind of politics of non-reason. Of course, what the first rationalists are really going to end up contesting is religion, which is for them the supreme form of the non-rational, of superstition. Even yesterday and still with Habermas, the politics of the Right is called the politics of irrationality. I think we're no longer in a period where that is a useful designation, but some people still think so. And, certainly, while you still have a conception of reason, you can have a philosophy of the irrational, even of the unconscious, and then you can have non-reason, insanity.

So, suddenly, we reach a turning point, in which one strategy for handling the unwanted, the strategy of exclusion, is no longer possible for all kinds of reasons, and Foucault would be delighted to list all these various factors in the momentous change that will give us a new period. Foucault is interested in history in the sense of periodization. When we get to *The Order of Things*, the book which is simultaneous with everything happening in 1966–1967—Lacan, Derrida, the big explosion of this so-called poststructuralist moment—he will give us a history, his only real history, and that will be a history based on four periods. Each of these periods will be ordered by a dominant, so to speak, a mode of understanding that he calls an *episteme*. This is his way of classifying periods (cultures, some people used to call them).

Foucault would deny all of this. His temperament, I think, is essentially perverse, which is quite in keeping with the dialectics of sight and visibility. You try to characterize him one way and he will tell you, "No, that's wrong. This is structuralist. No, I'm not a structuralist. This is a history of ideas. No, it isn't." So you always have to take Foucault with a grain of salt, and indeed I think this is the first thing to understand about Foucault's writings. It is also why there are so many interviews. Some of the philosophers at the time said he was not really a philosopher but rather a historian. Well, that is why we have the word "theory." We don't have to decide. It is clear that his histories, unlike most histories, are theoretical. Are they philosophical? Well, if you think philosophy is what they teach in academic philosophy departments, then maybe not, but certainly for us they work on concepts, and we've begun to see what that work comprises. But what you find in Foucault's work is that there is a historical basis for this thinking. He goes to the Bibliothèque Nationale and finds all these volumes about madness, written in Latin in the seventeenth century or earlier, and he is going to go through them and write that up. And then he will tell you that's one kind of activity. If it is true, as Deleuze says, that a painting expresses a concept but in a language of painting, then we can say that Foucault expresses a concept in the form of historiography. But it is a concept, and your normal historian will not wish to be associated with a concept, because a historian is supposed to be writing and arguing about the empirical facts. That's not what Foucault is doing here.

So that is one side of his work. The other side is telling you what it means or what its consequences are. There are all kinds of empty, abstract speculations on Foucault's part about what this means, to what it is a contribution, what he is going to do with this, and so on. The interviews are full of that. It gets into these books a little bit, because he suggests, with each new study, that it will only be a little part of something that leads to something else. For example, here, at the end of *Discipline and Punish*: "At this point I end a book that must serve as a historical background to various studies of the power of normalization and the formation of knowledge in modern society."[2] More research needs to be done; I'm going to go on and write more on the sequel to this. This is just an introduction. But there are all kinds of other ways of framing his work, and I would single out this notion, which he often articulates himself: his main thrust is in describing the situation—a Sartrean language which he would reject, but it doesn't matter—in which subjectivity is formed, or to which it is a response.

So let's look at the origin of this word "subject." Everybody at this time is talking about the subject. They mean consciousness, right? But we can't

---

2   Michel Foucault, *Discipline and Punish*, trans. Alan Sheridan (New York: Vintage, 1995), 308.

talk about consciousness anymore, because it isn't anything. Still, the place of consciousness is part of all these theoretical problems, so we have to call it something. Maybe we'll call it the subject and reject these precursors, whom we call philosophers of the subject, and we'll try to do something else. In that case, what is this subject? There can be a subject of a sentence. Nietzsche said very famously that, if you want to get rid of God, but you still have the sentence, the subject of the sentence, you haven't gotten rid of God. That's a very interesting reflection. That's a kind of motto for all of these people, in a way. How to get rid of the subject? But why would you want to get rid of the subject? Maybe that's a better question.

What is Foucault doing here? Look at the word "subject." It comes from the Latin *subjectum*, that which underlies something. But the dictionary says of the etymology: "a person under the control of another." The king's subjects. So, while we thought that the subject was the subject of the sentences, that the subject was consciousness, that we're the center of the world, it isn't that at all. It's somebody who's subject to something. Foucault is interested, he says—but it isn't always easy to see that he is doing it—in subjectification and individualization. How is the individual formed? If you can't figure out what to do with consciousness, at least you can figure out how it is formed. All these people want to know where consciousness came from and how we are different from other creatures. But suddenly there's another word that imposes itself: "subjection." We're going to find that the Foucauldian idea of the subject is what forms your mode of subjection.

Nothing irritates Foucault politically more than the leftist philosophies of liberation in this period. The name with which we associate all of those is Marcuse, I think. The utopian thought of the Left, the liberation of subjectivities as well as of peoples, colonial peoples, oppressed peoples. Foucault uses the word "liberation" every once in a while, but, at the end of this essay on Kant's essay on the Enlightenment—in which Foucault tries to come to terms with modernity—he says: "I do not know whether it must be said today that the critical task still entails faith in the Enlightenment; I continue to think that this task requires work on our limits"—the limits of Enlightenment—"that is, a patient labor giving form to our impatience for liberty."[3] Does that mean that we're never going to be liberated? Or does it simply mean that we're always impatient for a liberation that we'll

---

3 Michel Foucault, "What Is Enlightenment?," trans. Catherine Porter, *The Foucault Reader*, ed. Paul Rabinow (New York: Pantheon Books, 1984), 50.

never get to? I think it means subjection, and I think each form of these periods that we're going to look at is going to be a different form of subjection. Each will presuppose a different kind of subject.

I'll jump ahead to the end. Foucault works through all these things on power, as we see, and suddenly, we're told, he has some mysterious revelation in Death Valley; I don't know if this is so. He has been working with one of the great historians of the early Christian era, a biographer of Saint Augustine and the author of books on Christian asceticism, Peter Brown, and suddenly he changes his direction entirely. He begins to write about an early period in which stoicism and the self-mastery of the Romans gives way to Christian asceticism. Is this work completely different from what preceded it? There's certainly a break. And you can read all kinds of things about how this fits perfectly into his project on the spirit of rationalization, which is the other part of his writing, if not his research. In a way, yes, of course, because asceticism and Roman virtue are all forms of your own subjection of yourself. It's your control of yourself, in some way. So, if before there is a subjection from the state, maybe in modern times there is a subjection of yourself by yourself in a situation in which the old feudal state doesn't exist anymore, as we'll see in a moment.

I think that is true, and I would go even further. I would like to say that, although Foucault has been associated with a whole set of watchwords, "power" among them, I think he is really interested in imprisonment, not power. Power is what imprisons you. If one were to imagine a psychoanalysis of Foucault, one would say that his main obsession is what is done to you in confinement. The ship of fools—is that confinement? At one point, we thought it was a kind of freedom, but, ultimately, it is confinement, because it means you are excluded, and in the old days, exclusion, banishment—that's the end of it. You're being thrown out of your world. You have no home. Sometimes, famous Greeks would go to the Persian emperor and work in his service. We know these stories. But Socrates, you remember, preferred to die rather than to be banished. So exclusion is a very powerful punishment. It removes you from one form of subjection but leaves you in another.

Now we can see how each of Foucault's preoccupations is going to return to the imprisonment of the self. And, in a way, his later work—we're not going to look at it very much—also deals with imprisonment. You are imprisoned in a set of self-imposed rules and norms. Since I mention norms, I want you to notice that this is really all about normalization. In a sense, you can say that, not just Sartre, but all the previous literature we have read is about bourgeois norms and how horrible they are. When we arrived at Derrida, I tried to show you that, in a way, everything he is deconstructing is a norm. When he gets to linguistics, the idea of a sentence is the norm, the rule. Derrida undoes that. He shows that rules and norms are somehow contradictory, not a word he would use. Now, with Foucault, I think it is very clear that the history he is writing is the history of normalization. The consequence of the norm is then that it establishes those who are normal and those who are not, that which is central and that which is excluded or marginal. That is its politics.

Speaking of politics, although Foucault certainly had the reputation of being a political figure, the one great thing that he was involved in was the prison movement. He happened to be teaching in upstate New York when Attica happened. Foucault was very struck by this, and he sponsored prison movements all over France, and not just for the reform of prisons but for a deeper look into this thing itself which is imprisonment. As we well know in this country, where we have the largest imprisoned population in the world, prisons are how you exclude people, and Foucault will be concerned with the history of this process, at least in the major part of his career, the one we're looking at.

So we have a turning point here, in which the Renaissance institution of the "ship of fools" is suddenly abolished; now the abnormals are registered as such and are stuck into a place of confinement. What else resembles that process? It turns out that this concept of confinement is a spatial idea, an architectural idea. All kinds of interesting architecture appears in this period, and we get various spatial versions of confinement. They don't all have to seem negative. There are schools. There are monasteries, although the monastery begins much earlier; Weber says the monastery is the first form of what we call capitalism, the first form in which production is organized and counted. Then there are the clinics. His second book will be called *The Birth of the Clinic*. People will take it as a critique of psychoanalysis, but it's also about how the very notion of medicality has changed. So hospitals can be seen as another form of the prison. We're talking about forms, now, the reorganization of the world in such a way as to correspond to this new period, this new episteme, which is organized around some kind of normalization and the isolation, the enclosure of certain populations. And "population" will be an important word in Foucault, because in a way, as for Marx in some ways, it is the pressure of population that springs all these things open at crucial moments when you have to deal with larger and larger numbers of people. The old methods don't work anymore. If you have a growing city, there's a point at which there are too many people running around who have to be gotten rid of, and not enough ships for all of them, so you build an insane asylum. Too many criminals—you can't execute them all, so you build prisons, asylums, clinics. With his study of the clinics comes also this new idea, a new slogan, which the Foucauldians attach to him but which I think is not useful anymore: "power-knowledge," the idea that the development of knowledge is connected to the development of power. Foucault himself makes fun of that later on in some of his interviews. It's stupid: Power is not knowledge, and knowledge is not power, but they do develop side by side. You need to have certain kinds of knowledge as power expands. So what he is saying, in effect, to the university system is that you are, all in one way or another, in the service of this new administered world. He will call that "governmentality." The state is not just a few powerful figures who give orders. It is a whole network—we sometimes call it a bureaucracy, but that then elides all the differences too. It is a new set of mechanisms which produces a new way of administering society. (The Frankfurt School also spoke of "the administered society," *verwaltete Gesellschaft*.)

One could go on about the clinic. There was this expression in American psychotherapy: "non-directive." The analyst wasn't supposed to say anything. Just repeat what you said. "I'm very unhappy." "You're very unhappy?" And then you have to make your own decisions, and maybe that strengthens the ego. But Freud was not non-directive at all. He indoctrinated these people. He said, "Look, what you have here I call an Oedipus complex. You're in love with your mother. You hate your father." If you want to find the most scandalous moment in the relationship between feminism and Freudianism, you come to the famous analysis of Dora. Freud is intent on trying to prove to Dora that she is in love with her father, but she doesn't want to hear that. She says this is a lot of bullshit. "I'm not in love with my father." And, finally, she walks out on him and thus becomes a failed case. Especially in American feminism, but in France too, Dora has become the quintessential case . . . against Freudianism? Not exactly, but her case shows its limits. Remember that Freud has no concept of the mother. As for women, the famous phrase in Freud is *Was will das Weib?* "What does woman want?" In Lacan, that's an interesting question as well. Women psychoanalysts will want to show that they know something more, but Lacan is even going to offer you a view of women's sexuality. *Was will das Weib?*

So Freud is shaping his patients' subjectivity as a doctor, and, in a sense, all these doctors are enforcing medicalization. I mentioned this big dictionary of medical terms, the DSM. Nowadays, don't we have a thing called self-diagnosis? This is a pharmaceutical world, after all, and today's doctors—I hope nobody hears this—don't really know anything about the body anymore. They just know what pills do. You have a little iPad or smartphone, and you can consult all the pharmaceutical products and see what their effects are, what they can go with and not with, what they're good for. So, in effect, diagnosis moves away from the patient, and in our new individualism, we learn to diagnose ourselves. I look at the symptoms and decide what I'm feeling here, what kind of pill I should take. So how do you impose medicality on the individual? You make them become aware of their pains, perhaps. I take it as a given that the more aware you are of your pains, the more pains you are going to have. You're trying to see why it is you have this ache, and then you concentrate on the ache, and then you're going to discover some more, maybe some connections between them. And, then, if you're in the proper spirit of things, you begin to name those pains, or you find out that medicine got there first and already named them. This is an invasion, a penetration, a colonization of the body. It's like an unexplored realm. That was, of course, Africa for the Europeans in the nineteenth century. What are the sources of the Nile? Nobody knew. So European explorers had to go down into Africa and map out the various pieces of Africa. The sources of the Nile are not known to the Europeans until the 1870s in the expedition of Stanley. The approach to the body is like that at a certain point. There is a history of the body, and it's a history of how you little by little come to know bits of the body; DNA is only the most recent discovery. So the birth of the clinic, in short, involves all those things. Of course, it is in great interest to us to see how *Discipline and Punishment* ends but also how it begins—with the plague. It begins with exactly what we're in the middle of now in our COVID-19 isolation. It begins with the great scourges and it ends with a very different view of the body as something to be ... "controlled" is not the right word. The last paper that we have of Deleuze's is called "Societies of Control," which does not mean the English "control," but rather "testing" and "monitoring." It has been thought that this paper is a new Foucauldian theory that would describe recent times. I don't think it's very useful for us.

So there is a period in which people begin to be locked up more system-atically. Ah, but what about liberation from confinement? The first thing you want to do when you're locked up is to be freed, right? It is sometimes said—and it is a nice idea—that Marquis de Sade was imprisoned in the Bastille by a *lettre de cachet*. The family of his wife, who found him, with some justice, to be an irregular and untrustworthy character, asked the king for a *lettre de cachet*. A *lettre de cachet* is a blank letter; you write the person's name, and they're stuck into a dungeon for the rest of their life. The Marquis de Sade was stuck into a dungeon, and the dungeon happened to be called the Bastille. It's said that, as dissatisfaction was building up in the early months of 1789, as the people began to make noise, Marquis de Sade wrote all kinds of little notes—"Take power!" "Free yourself!"—threw them out the window, and this inspired the taking of the Bastille. Well, that's a nice story. Later, the Marquis de Sade became a mayor. Paris was divided during the Revolution into different *arrondissements*, as it still is today. Each one of those had a mayor. He was a *Girondin*, I think, and, if you know anything about the Marquis de Sade—which all the writers in this course do, by the way; Barthes is very interested—you will be astonished to learn that he was against capital punishment. Very strange, right? Killing people was a part of his literature, but, in politics, he was a moderate. Well, he got arrested and would have been guillotined, if the Thermidor had not arrived. He was released, and then reimprisoned by Napoleon, who really didn't like this stuff at all. Napoleon, like all the rest of them, had written his literature; he wrote a novel once. But it was more than literature, in the case of the Marquis de Sade. It is exemplary for us. Where does Napoleon put him? Not in a dungeon, but in an insane asylum. So, suddenly, there is a transformation. Something is happening to imprisonment. Meanwhile, in the asylum, Sade continues to write and puts on plays, as you can see in Peter Weiss's *Marat/Sade*.

Let's follow the path of this transformation, which will provide Foucault's next great dividing line, his next great period. It is the arrival of philanthropy and humanitarianism, brought by the new bourgeois state and its revolution. We have a word for this: "humanism." These people are humane, supposedly. The great innovators in the clinic, the treatment of the insane, are people who want to reform the system, who considered these things not physical aberrations but illnesses. They bring into being what become our modern clinics, a whole new form of treat-ment. Imprisonment—what was it before this period? I talked about enclosures, but, with criminals, a typical practice was public execution. As you may know, in the eighteenth century, in England, a dog was hanged for stealing something. You could be executed for theft. And these were great popular festivals, following the cart of the prisoner. It's not just a revolutionary guillotine at stake here; it's this tremendous carnival flavor of these things where the last words of the criminal are listened to avidly. There are ballads of the great criminals, and they are written up. Highwaymen, for example, are great heroes who, like Robin Hood, often give to the poor. So people flock around these executions and the ballads are handed out. Foucault begins this book with one of the most disgusting of all these public executions. Arnold Bennett—he has some opprobrium resulting from Virginia Woolf's essay on him called "Mr. Bennett and Mrs. Brown"—wrote a great novel called *The Old Wives' Tale*, in which there is a representation of some English travelers who see the last public execution in France, and it is, as you can imagine, very disgusting. This execution that Foucault is describing is the execution of the assassin who tried to kill Louis XV, and it is one of the most spectacular of all the executions. Why drag us through this? Well, precisely because those executions are going to be succeeded in the Romantic period by the great prisoners. All the revolutionary literature is on the prisoners for life, the Russians who are locked up in the Peter and Paul Fortress in Petersburg, later sent to Siberia. Each country has its famous prisoners, locked up forever in these dungeons. But, before that, in the eighteenth century, it is this capital execution in which the multitude witnesses what happens to a human body when it's drawn and quartered. Why? There's a book that they all draw on, Foucault in particular, by a German refugee, a member of the George-Kreis, named Ernst Kantorowicz, called *The King's Two Bodies*. Obviously, the king just has a normal human body. In Japan, when Hirohito was dying, it was illegal to publish anything about his illness in the newspapers, and the Japanese right wing, which is very active in nationalist emperor-worship, would beat people up who dared talk about Hirohito's illness, which, in another place, would be the object of endless articles and news conferences every day. In the Middle Ages, it was clear that there were two bodies. The king had an ordinary body, but also an ideal body, and any kind of crime is something done to the ideal body of the king. Any of these crimes—theft, murder—are offenses not to the victim—who cares about the victim?—but to the body of the king, and therefore it must be expiated by the body of the criminal.

What happens with this turn away from public execution and spectacle to imprisonment and bourgeois humanity? It seems to me that a first reading of *Discipline and Punish* will convince you that Foucault prefers the old regime and has nothing but contempt for this humane bourgeoisie. I think this is not quite so, but it can feel that way. At any rate, we're still in that period. We believe in humane punishments, to the point where we don't want capital punishment; we want better conditions for the prisoners. So he is, in effect, undermining our bourgeois ideology as it was formed in the great period of the bourgeois revolution in France and in the turn of the nineteenth century. Now something else will be involved here, and we will have to deal with it at some point, and it is history, because the other thing that we discover with the French Revolution is history: people can change society, and there is a story to be told of social transformation. But, at any rate, we can identify this new period with humanism, and here you get one of the great sentences of Foucault. It is the ending of *The Order of Things*, which came out in 1966. He is talking about Man. In French, humanism always concerned *l'homme*. So already you can see that there's something the matter with this humanism. But, anyway, here it is: "As the archaeology of our thought easily shows, man is an invention of recent date." Now we know: It is an invention of the French Revolution, of the end of feudalism. "If these dispositions were to disappear"—the things that produced humanism—"as they appeared, if some event"—of which we can only guess at the possibility—"without knowing either what its form will be or what it promises, were to cause them to crumble, as the ground of Classical thought did, at the end of the eighteenth century, then one can certainly wager that man would be erased, like a face drawn in sand at the edge of the sea."[4] So that notion of the disappearance of the human, the sea wiping away the human face, is Foucault's vision of this new non- or post-human future, of this new emergence of some other period, of which we cannot even foresee the shape. If one wants to take that as prophetic, what would one say? I would say maybe this names the new institutionalization of globalization itself, the immense new population of globalization as opposed to the population growths of earlier periods. Who knows? Antihumanism doesn't mean being bad or killing people or anything like that. It means the disappearance of the centeredness of consciousness. It is the Copernican revolution in subjectivity, so

---

4   Michel Foucault, *The Order of Things*, 386.

to speak. It is the completion of the Nietzschean project or the Freudian project or even the Sartrean project, and the realization that we are no longer the center of the world, that this human face which was once the icon of bourgeois humanism is now disappearing. Something new takes its place. What would this new thing be? We'll go on with this next time.

March 25, 2021

19

The Prison-House of Subjectification

{Foucault}

Today I'm going to dwell on the problem of the break in Foucault, but first let's take a step back and return to Althusser's philosophical doctrines. You remember that Althusser said ideology has no history. Why? Because ideology, in the later formulation, is the relationship of the individual self to the social order, since there will always be a social order, and there will always be some kind of self; there will also always be something that has the function of ideology. Then he says philosophy has no history either. Well, that's even stranger, because all these other people are busy working away at the history of philosophy. Not so much Sartre, but Heidegger, for example, is very intent on rewriting, or rather, as he says, destroying the history of philosophy—*Destruktion*—and rediscovering Being, finding those philosophers who, like the pre-Socratics, had a real confrontation not with the meaning of Being but with the question of Being. So the question is: What to do with all these philosophies? In any case, a history of philosophy is involved. With Derrida, it is the history of metaphysics. He is not going to write or rewrite that history, but, somehow, he remains a disciple of Heidegger. But, in the case of Althusser, there aren't any such reflections, only a history of science and its breaks. There are moments in which science is, so to speak, pre-scientific. *Science*, in French, means "knowledge," a much more specific idea than the English word, "science."

Barthes points out somewhere that "savor"—he wants the savor of words—and "science" have the same root: *saveur* and *savoir*. All of this is different in English, where science is thought of as a separate, specialized domain.

So, for Althusser, science *does* have a history. You have a break with the past. Alchemy is superstitious; then there's a break, and alchemy is transformed into chemistry, which itself will evolve. Now, to be sure, it evolves discontinuously, and that will be important, but it implies a question of knowledge, which has a history. So how is philosophy involved in this history, if it doesn't itself have a history? Well, there are several answers, each of which is articulated in a formula. First: Philosophy is class struggle in thought. So what is philosophy doing with science? What philosophy is doing—and this is the reason it has no history—is always the same: It is distinguishing between idealism and materialism. Idealism includes an ideological—not in Althusser's special sense, but in the ordinary sense—view of science, and this is a view which even the natural scientists can share—Galileo was a Platonist, for example. For Althusser, this ideology of certain sciences is necessarily distinct from real scientific practice, which is always materialist. So the philosopher has to do the same thing over and over again. The philosopher has to try to divest thought of idealism, to bring things back to materialism. So there you have a fairly clear notion of this constant process philosophy is engaged in, which is not so different from what Wittgenstein proposed: getting rid of all the false problems, all the verbiage, and going back to the things that matter, transparent or common language. It is at least analogous.

This means that materialism and idealism are going to reflect this ancient problem of the mind and the body. How to deal with that? Apparently, for Althusser, Spinoza is a shining example of the materialist solution, insofar as he poses a parallelism of the two modes of being, the body and the mind. Plato, on the other hand, is the great enemy, and Hegel will seem to be another adversary, although for different reasons, because there is actually plenty of Hegelianism in Althusser. Now the problem is that the contemporary philosophers identified one powerful, influential idealism in their midst, and it is the very idealism that all this newer French philosophy and theory comes out of, namely phenomenology. Phenomenology is, in some way, Cartesian. It is based on and limited by consciousness. The Althusserians need to get rid of phenomenology somehow. But, on the other hand, most of these people, certainly Foucault, are not working-class people, so to speak, and they don't much like the versions of materialism that are offered to them. Althusser tries to make it palatable, but the arguments you find in Lenin's *Materialism and Empirio-criticism*, the old reflection theory of knowledge, are not very attractive to these people. Actually, it is Sartre who finds the best way out of this impasse; there is a long essay earlier in his postwar period called "Materialism and Revolution," where he demonstrates that what these people call materialism is really idealist, that most materialisms are really idealisms in disguise. Well, that's another way of getting rid of that old materialism. That materialism is associated with the Communist Party, and none of these people wish to be identified with the PCF. This is not a McCarthyite period. This is a period in which the Communist Party has great power, but, nonetheless, it does not offer the philosophical solution that these bourgeois philosophers want, and therefore a third way is worked out through mathematics: Cavaillès and the so-called philosophy of the concept. So we won't have subjectivity in some Cartesian sense, but we won't have a crass, deterministic materialism either, which, by the way, has come back in the form of neuroscience and all that contemporary phrenology; there are even anticipations of that in Lévi-Strauss.

So they don't want to identify with the Communist Party's materialism, and, instead, there emerges another space, which they will not call ideal-ism, a space in which the Pythagorean theorem is true for all time, in which mathematics is true for all eternity, and which has no connection whatso-ever to subjectivity. It doesn't rely on people's thinking. It is merely there in some other place, which is neither subjective nor objective. How does that fit into Foucault? For one thing, as we have seen, Foucault is resolutely anti-humanist. One of the great driving forces of his philosophy is not just to attack humanism; no, that's much too crude. Rather, it is to show the individual subjectivity (subjection) from which humanism came, why it remains contradictory, and why it will disappear. We see that in *The Order of Things*. So that is one of his missions, but the other area he is going to explore—Foucault is a historian as much as he is a philosopher—is history and the question of how you can think history. It is clear that, except for the history of science (and the notion of overdetermination) Althusser is not much interested in history. Derrida deconstructs historical statements; as he says, *différance* could be a word for history, if the word "history" weren't already so tainted, but Derrida is not really interested in history either. Foucault, on the other hand, is preoccupied with history. So where is idealism in history? Ah! There's the first important matter, and, in fact, we have been discussing it all along: it is in the question of continuities and breaks. For Foucault, idealistic history is a history of continuities. Let me read you a bit from the Nietzsche essay: "The traditional devices for constructing a comprehensive view of history and for retracing the past as a patient and continuous development must be systematically dismantled." No more continuities. "History becomes 'effective'"—the German word he is referencing is *Wirkungsgeschichte*, in other words, when history is more than telling stories, when it has to do with what Hegel called *die Sache selbst*—"to the degree that it introduces discontinuity into our very being—as it divides our emotions, dramatizes our instincts, multiplies our body and sets it against itself. 'Effective' history deprives the self of the reassuring stability of life in nature, and it will not permit itself to be transported by a voiceless obstinacy toward a millennial ending." That is the telos. Althusser said that history may be going somewhere, but it does not have a telos or a subject. So here is this idea again. History will not "be transported toward a millennial ending. It will uproot its foundations and relentlessly disrupt its pretended continuity. This is because knowledge is not made for understanding; it is made for cutting."[1] Montage in film is also a kind of cutting, a cutting up of continuities. In a sense, there aren't any continuities here. This is Hume's critique of causality. Causality establishes a connection between that event over there in the past and this one right here. How could there be such a connection? How could something in the past be continuous with the present, except insofar as we understand it that way? So all of those things are involved in Foucault's critique of continuity.

I should note, in passing, that Foucault refuses the word "modernity." He was once invited to a conference with Habermas on modernity. "These Germans," he says, "keep talking about modernity, but I don't know what it is. I only know what Baudelaire means by it." Baudelaire's essay, "The Painter of Modern Life," goes on a great deal about modernity, but he is the only one in the French tradition who does so. I suppose there is Le Corbusier and *l'architecture moderne*, but, otherwise, this word is not used in France, I think, until after World War II—certainly not "modernism," an Americanism which is imported only very recently into France. We would need a real lexical history of modernism and modernity in the various languages to deal with this properly. But, in that sense, Foucault is following

---

1   Michel Foucault, "Nietzsche, Genealogy, History," in *The Foucault Reader*, ed. Paul Rabinow (New York: Pantheon, 1984), 88.

a French tradition, insofar as France invents modern literature too early to have any need for a word for it. As for modernity in daily life, France wasn't really modern until de Gaulle, so, in that sense, also it doesn't need the word. But Foucault's real objection is that he doesn't like generalities of that kind. Modernity doesn't mean anything to him. I suppose if you showed him various studies of the steam engine or the combustion engine, he would look at the disciplines and the places in which those knowledges appeared, and he would allow a history of those forms of knowledge. But modernity as a whole? That is not an idea Foucault will entertain.

Let me give you a better example from M. H. Abrams' work on Romanticism.[2] I always use this because it's a nice example. Abrams asks: What is modernism and modern literature? He says, yes, modern literature is fine, but we already had that in Romanticism. Modernism really comes out of Romanticism. So where does Romanticism come from? It comes out of the Christian tradition, he says. So, all of the sudden, these great breaks in history and in cultural history disappear, and we have an uninterrupted continuity between Luther, Christianity, spiritualism and its innovations, through Romanticism, and up into . . . into what? Joyce? Modern literature and painting? That's the kind of continuity that Foucault is against, those generalities in writing history. This is a history that wants to be a microhistory. But, on the other hand, it is not a static history. He wants to show changes, a history of breaks. As for Deleuze, I would say that he is the very philosopher of the new. Deleuze wants the new. He wants to know when something appeared that was new and fresh. I don't think Foucault was as excited by that moment as he was by the moment when things disappeared. When did things fall apart? When did this nice functioning system begin to break down? So his histories will be histories of breaks, as we're going to see.

It will be important for Foucault to stress the temporal level, the interruptions and the breaks. But you will remember that we already had those breaks on the synchronic level. We have Lacan showing that what we call the subject is nothing but breaks, gaps, cuts. There is a whole vocabulary of these things. Derrida doesn't use those words so much, but he wants to show that what we think is a meaningful whole is nothing of the kind; it begins to break down upon closer inspection. So deconstruction means that, if you think there can be a full meaning, or you think there is a full

---

2   M. H. Abrams, *Natural Supernaturalism: Tradition and Revolution in Romantic Literature* (New York: W. W. Norton, 1973).

334 The Years of Theory

present of time, to use his first long-term philosophical example, just look at language: the present is never there. It is partly there, but partly it isn't there yet. So, finally, that fullness of completion breaks down. On the temporal level, it is continuity that is breaking down, as in Foucault. And that breakdown will be related to what he has mysteriously called "representation." Representation means a full and meaningful picture of something. I wouldn't call it mimesis, but it is a little like representational art. You see a painting. You recognize everything in it, and it makes sense, so you believe the world is like that, just as Sartre did in the movies as a small child. Everything in this artificial picture is meaningful. Then you turn away from it, and nothing is meaningful. Everything breaks up. So, if we wanted to find, as I said last time, the greatest representational painter, who would we look to? Well, we look to Velázquez, and we'll see that Velázquez is not creating a representation; he is undermining representation. This set-piece at the beginning of *The Order of Things*, this bravura piece, is an analysis of Velázquez's painting, but, eventually, you ask yourself: This is dazzling, but what is it doing here? It's the beginning of a book on the order of things, a history of knowledge, so why are we spending so much time with this painting from 1656? Well, much later, in *The Order of Things*, this set piece reemerges at a crucial moment when he comes to the critique of representation. Deleuze would use Kant in a similar way.

So, along with continuities, we have three conceptual enemies: representation, meaning, and then this other thing, idealism, consciousness, or phenomenology, the idea that every act of consciousness is an act of positing meaning, that it poses meaning in some sense, and that it is somehow a foundation of meaning. Hold onto those enemies for a moment, because we will come back to them soon.

For now, we can't dwell much longer on *Discipline and Punish*, but I do want to point out that some people have connected its initial description of the plague with our modern situation. I don't think Foucault ever intended it to be relevant in that way, though, of course, he didn't live through this pandemic. For our moment, perhaps Deleuze's "Societies of Control" is more relevant, in the French sense of *contrôler*, 'to check,' as in to check a thermometer or a gas meter. That would be a little closer to what the plague is for us. In the scene that Foucault is giving us at the beginning of *Discipline and Punish*, the question is how to get the plague patients out of the way, to close them up, like the leper colony. With us, yes, people are confined, but, if we drew on all the resources of our wonderful technology, we would be testing everybody in confinement, and they would be testing themselves. All this testing would feed into some central bank of information. Everything would be known. We would know who you had contact with. We would know what happened to them. So far from being analogous, our moment is quite different. Foucault died in 1984, and remember that the personal computer only emerged in the early '80s, neoliberalism around 1980; the whole of the contemporary world had yet to appear when Foucault died. In any case, I think he made it up through the nineteenth century; he had a vision of something, as we saw, in the future, a future in which the human face would have been effaced from the shores of the sea, in which humanism would be gone and something else would be happening. But that's a vision of the posthuman. The posthuman as a kind of utopia—what kind could it be? I don't know. But in any case, he never seemed terribly interested in the present; the minute he reaches it in his histories, he suddenly reverses course and goes all the way back to early Christianity, asceticism, the desert fathers, the Roman stoics, and we're back in the distant past. In May '68, for example, was he participating? No, Foucault was obviously not somebody who participated in stuff like that. He was on sabbatical in Tunisia. He did salute the Iranian Revolution, in retrospect a rather ambiguous gesture. And, of course, he was instrumental in forming these prison reform groups. But his reputation is, nonetheless, as a politically engaged figure. But he said that you can't become an "organic intellectual," à la Gramsci, if you aren't already one. You can be a "specific intellectual" of some sort. To be an intellectual in general, to sign all these manifestos and engage in every kind of activity like Sartre—no, we can't do that, but in your immediate sphere you can be an intellectual demonstrating for prison reform, for example. So I think his participation in the modern world was carefully limited.

To summarize this business about *Discipline and Punish*, at one point he says: here is the difference between the panopticon and the great scenes of public execution: under the *ancien* régime, if you damage the body of the sovereign—that is to say, if you murder somebody or steal something—your body must be publicly tortured. Here we have a single spectacle viewed by masses of people; that is the nature of punishment under this period that he calls "sovereignty," a word that has many ramifications. When this new disciplinary break occurs—and this is the history of a break, a break with this abominable public torture and execution passing over into the disciplinary practices of the bourgeoisie—what do we get? What is it that arrives with the panopticon, for example, if we see it as the summit of bourgeois discipline? Well, the reverse. The multiplicity once viewed the single execution, but, here, we have a single consciousness observing, disciplining the multitude, each of whom internalizes this observation. So the whole situation of punishment has been transformed.

Over and over again in his later lectures on governmentality and bio-power, Foucault makes the point that these changes have to do with population, not so much democracy. Is this taking place during the French Revolution, when the people emerge onto the stage of history? Well, yes, the people emerge onto the stage of history, but the point is that it is lots of people. I won't say it is a Malthusian moment, but it is certainly a moment when numbers play an important role, and, increasingly, everything in modern society, right up to our own time, is dependent on population. That is, the population is getting bigger and bigger. There is less and less space. The climate is changing; people are being driven out of their countryside by a climatological change that makes it impossible to live there anymore. So population is a crucial feature of this transformation. And this was also true for Marx's notion of modes of production. When the hunters and gatherers grow too large, they must break up, because only a certain number can really occupy a terrain and exist within that mode of production. Each new mode of production will come into being in part because of a combination of geography and population. In Foucault, we might think this transformation has to do with the bourgeoisie bringing a humane view of things into the world. "No, no," he says, with his customary perversity. "That has nothing to do with it. It has to do with population. It isn't class either. It is something else." This is part of his potshot at Marxism. So that is one break: between the older forms of punishment and the newer discipline.

Now let's look at the much more dramatic unveiling of history in *The Order of Things*. It is a marvelous book, I think, very unlike Foucault's other work, in the sense that it really does attempt to be something of a synthesis. But if he is against synthesis, these big order histories, how can he write a thing like this? How does he do it? Is this not a history of a progression? No, because he will limit himself to three disciplinary areas. One is what we call biology, another is what we call linguistics, and a third is what we call economics. The contradictory nature of the enterprise is that we read these as though they are all analogous to each other, as though the developments of each one were parallel. So we're going to get out of this a more general notion of historical transformation, which we will see at work in each of these domains. He doesn't really want us to read it that way, even though that is what he has given us, because he believes that we must limit ourselves to—the current word for this is "singularity"— the singularity of the discipline. In a sense, all of this is against his own doctrine, but it is also his way of satisfying its deficiencies.

There are going to be three forms of knowledge—four, if you include the prophecies—that is, three distinct forms in which people have thought that they could know the world. In the interview that you may have read, he talks about how his whole work is about how people have established their truth.[3] Well, I don't know—maybe that's another line or theme—but I would say his emphasis is rather on how people have *thought* they knew. For example, he takes Isidore of Seville from the seventh century, who produced an immense encyclopedia in which all these different things are stuck together. "No, no," he says, "readers didn't think that all these things that Isidore of Seville was compiling were real. What interested them was what people all over had said about all these things, the weirdest and most superstitious alongside the most reasonable, because what was important to them was the kind of knowledge that had accumulated around a given object." This will be the relativism of this form of study of the epistemes, and, in a sense, it presupposes that none of the epistemes is right, that these are local truths, but that there really is not going to be any kind of permanent truth. Or, if there is in modern times, would he have posited a new episteme based on computers and so forth? I don't know, but that wouldn't have been right either, for reasons we're going to find out.

So these three or four moments go something like this. The first one is the Renaissance episteme, and, for that, he begins with France. He doesn't go back into the Middle Ages until much later. He sticks to French history. That's perfectly permissible, I think, given the kinds of restrictions on his research. He calls it "the prose of the world." That's Hegel's expression, and I think it's not what Hegel means, but it doesn't matter. This is a kind of knowledge which is based on resemblance and analogy. That is, you can say that this first Foucauldian period is a utopian world in which things that resemble each other are related somehow. Let me give you an example

---

3   Gérard Raulet, "Structuralism and Post-Structuralism: An Interview with Michel Foucault," in *Telos* (April, 1983), 195–211.

of a kind of magical medicine of the period. I don't know if you know what aconite is. It's a stone that looks like the eye. Therefore, in this period, there is a relationship between aconite and the eyes. If someone has a disease of the eyes, you can treat it by applying the stone to the eye, because they have hidden analogies and kinship. So this whole period is turning on these affinities, but it will gradually change, and, in a way, the climax is the *Quixote*, where everything seems to resemble everything else. But this moment is going to come apart, because there is always an unevenness in resemblance. One thing resembles another, rather than the latter resembling the former. There is a principle of unevenness where, little by little, there emerges a major and a minor side to these resemblances. There is also the question of language, since this is a period when etymologies of words are based on onomatopoeia. Meanwhile, language is also creating these resemblances, so it is always a little bit in excess of these things. And, finally, there is the economic stuff, which I won't bother even to try to unravel. But what will happen—and here is our first big question—is that a big system will emerge and then disintegrate. To what degree is this system the precursor of what follows it? What comes next is what the French call the classical period; we call it neoclassicism. For them, it is their great cultural period; for us it is the counterrevolution that followed the great cultural period of Shakespeare, the Elizabethans, and then the Civil War. So there is a change from the late ancien régime—enlightened despotism, so to speak—that immediately precedes the revolutionary period —the Enlightenment, Diderot, the encyclopedia. What is then this new system? It is based on classifications. It will be a kind of static system in which taxonomies and classifications establish knowledge. We no longer pick out things that resemble each other, like aconite for the eyes. Instead, we create a taxonomy of stones. If we are performing a comparison—Descartes already used a cow's eye to investigate optics—maybe, we'll do a comparison of the eyes of different animals. So, instead of this marvelous world of resemblances, we get a world of order, in which things will be reduced to these plates of the species, of the natural. Now we're beginning to get our three disciplines. Natural history will be based on these taxonomies. Language will be based on the so-called *grammaire générale* and its notion of the philosophical meaning of grammatical positionality and syntax. And as for economics, this is the moment which is dominated by the idea of riches, in particular natural riches. So you don't balance the books, but you figure up how much wealth a country can accumulate, how much a person can accumulate. This preoccupies the various economic schools.

Yes, you may not believe, someone said, any of Foucault's facts. I tend to share the belief that, whenever Foucault drags out some Latin book to quote, he is usually making this stuff up. But it doesn't really matter, because it is the overall movement of these things that will ultimately be important. Yes, this history has content, but the content is absorbed by the forms of the epistemes.

So this is a period of great order in the way in which knowledge has been assembled, but it will finally break down in several ways. Obviously, it breaks down with the French Revolution, with a different kind of history. He follows that model, but that isn't the break that interests him. What interests him is the emergence of some kind of history within each of these disciplines. Is it a kind of history that requires a notion of causality? It seems to me that what's happening at these moments of transition, from Renaissance to classicism, from classicism to what he will call the era of representation as such, is a tectonic shift—I've used this analogy before—in which the old system breaks down and leaves scattered parts, and then the survivors come along and they put those parts together in new ways, adding new parts, creating a new system which has very little to do with the old system. So you cannot write a continuous history. You are not writing how this kind of thinking turned into another kind of thinking. Instead, you are showing how this kind of thinking reached certain kinds of limits. We might call them contradictions, but he wouldn't. What they are, finally, are broken spaces. One can almost see this as a geographical exploration. You remember that Althusser talks about Marx as representing the discovery of the new continent of history. Here is a place that is unknown in classical thought. Suddenly, the explorers land in this new continent. They've never even suspected that it existed before. In Foucault, it's more like the blank spaces on the map of the new continent. The episteme covers a certain amount, and then, suddenly, it runs into things that it had never thought about before.

And that idea will provide Foucault's other explanation of his work: *l'impensé*. I mentioned immanence and the unconscious last time. Foucault does not want an unconscious. An unconscious is implied by our hermeneutic paradigm of the double inscription, which distinguishes between one line of things, and the unconscious underneath it. The unconscious will, maybe, as with Kristeva, burst into consciousness, even into language at certain points, or with the scientists, like Freud, its various features can be excavated. But Foucault doesn't think that any of this is possible. In his paradigm, what we have been calling the unconscious is "the non-thought." I think it was Donald Rumsfeld who popularized the idea that there is a known-known, an unknown-known, known-unknown, and an unknown-unknown. The unconscious is the known-unknown. Freud showed us that it was there. Everybody nowadays knows that there is an unconscious. But, by definition, we can't know it. What Foucault is interested in is the unknown-unknown. Not only have we not thought it, but it never occurred to us to think it. We have no means for thinking it. It is beyond the boundaries in which this episteme works, and therefore it remains a blank, the non-thought. To jump ahead: one of the forms that *impensé* will take—because there's also a problem with language running through this—is what he calls literature. He thinks literature emerges in the late eighteenth century; the Marquis de Sade provides his example of a language which takes on the unthought, the unthinkable. The modern literature he admires—and, here, we get Blanchot and Bataille again—is the one that has allowed us to somehow grasp this realm of the non-thinkable in ways that the normal language of knowledge cannot.

What will happen now with this disintegration of classical thought? It will mutate, and for economics and riches, there will emerge a thought of labor and value. Someone was asking about Foucault's relationship to Marx. Of course, he was against the Communist Party. He was thrown out and had a very bad experience with the party, and, in any case, it's clearly not for him. I think there is a certain antipathy—I would call him an anarchist—to the then-established forms of either the extra-parliamentary Left or the Communist Party. So he will every so often shoot potshots at them. Otherwise, Marx is present. You can see, for example, that much of *Discipline and Punish* is based on a work on penality by Otto Kirchheimer and Georg Rusche, who were related to the Frankfurt School. He said he had no connection with the Frankfurt School, but, of course, he did. These authors were the fundamental explorers of penality. Theirs is the great book on this theme.[4] Foucault says we must acknowledge this fundamental work, but, he says, since they already did it, we have to go on and do something different. Marx's are also fundamental works that are

---

4   Georg Rusche and Otto Kirchheimer, *Punishment and Social Structure* (London: Routledge, 2003).

already done. And here he will say—a very famous moment—that it is Ricardo who is important in the development of economics; Marx is just a minor Ricardian. These are the potshots. Foucault is in a world in which Marxism exists, clearly, and he is dealing with the same problems. In that sense, he could not be anti-Marxist, but he doesn't have to acknowledge Marx either. I think at best you would say he is doing things that are not already in Marx. Well, that's okay.

So, in the place of riches in classical economic thought will come different kinds of concepts: those of labor and value. In the place of life in natural history will come questions about the species and time, namely evolution. And, suddenly, there will be a historical study of life and its forms, which, of course, includes questions about how to control life, as in Foucault's famous concept of biopower. In the case of language, moving from grammar and syntax, there arrives the history of languages, Grimm's law, great evolutionary theories of the ways in which some primal Indo-European took its form in Sanskrit, in Ancient Greek, evolves toward other things, Latin, German, Slavic, the Celtic languages, and so on. All of those great theories are examples of nineteenth-century laws, which are particularly useful for us because we know that, in the realm of linguistics, there was another break later on, the break of Saussure, the moment when, having produced his great work on some Indo-European evolutionary problems, he suddenly stops and says, "Enough! This kind of thinking has nothing to do with language." So he invents a new way of thinking about language, which we will call structural linguistics, the study of the synchronic, because the nineteenth century, after all, was the conquest of the diachronic.

In all those ways, the nineteenth century will be governed by a historical representation of the world. Now this is where the interesting things begin to happen, and we can go back to *Las Meninas*. This is a little like when you're going to rob a bank and you have to figure out where the lasers are running through this space; if you trip them, you set off the alarms. In *Las Meninas*, these invisible lines are the lines of sight, of the eyes. We have a picture in which all kinds of people are looking in various places, but a lot of them seem to be looking out of the painting toward us. Who are they looking at? There is a mirror in the back, and in the mirror are two figures: the king and queen. So everyone is looking at them, but they're not in the picture. We are occupying that place of the king and queen. And, meanwhile, a third matter: We see the painter, but he has painted himself, and, in fact, the painter is standing here as he is painting the picture. So there are three positions outside of this painting, which are both occupied and not occupied. On them the painting depends. The king and queen must be there, because the whole thing is about them, and we see them reflected in the mirror. Velázquez himself is, somehow, standing here in phantasmatic form, because he has painted this. Meanwhile, we're standing here in the Prado, looking at this room crisscrossed by gazes. Without these three positions of the subject, there would be no painting. But there are three of them; they're not the same. In other words, the subject position is all important, but it's not here. It is contradictory. It is multiple. So this painting, which is a fullness of representation, also marks the place of the absence which makes it cohere. That place of absence is the place of the subject, and the place of the subject is multiple, and we cannot identify it. So making visible to us the place of the subject is the ultimate critique of representation.

All of representation is going to depend on this absent subject, and this is how he or she sees the nineteenth century, the century of representation. The whole thing depends on a subject of consciousness, this phenomenological subject, and yet the phenomenological subject is unanalyzable. It is unthought, unthinkable. How is it going to emerge? Literature will give it a certain voice, or will, at least, point to the place where it is, like an unconscious, but, of course, he doesn't use this language. Meanwhile, what we're seeing emerge here is what he calls the transcendental-empirical doublet. This is the ultimate contradiction of nineteenth-century representation. In previous philosophy, consciousness was typically called l'âme ('the soul'), but all the sudden, in the works of Victor Cousin, who was the principal French philosopher of the period and knew Hegel personally, the word "soul" disappears and gets replaced by "spirit" and "consciousness," thereby giving us a crucial marker, like all of these lexical markers. In Kant, either we have the area of values, of consciousness, the soul, or the empirical world of knowledge, determinism, and science. This transcendental world of value we simply posit. We can't know any of these things-in-themselves, but the two things are related in a kind of a double bind, a binary opposition. All empirical thought will finally depend on some presupposition of the transcendental, and the transcendental will be posited in some relationship to the empirical. What contemporary thought is going to call "correlationism," the notion that, if you have the mind and the body, you have to somehow put them together, and because you don't know how to put them together you continually switch back and forth between these languages. As we've seen in Althusser, these languages are those of materialism and idealism, but materialism and idealism go hand in hand. They're inseparable. Kant already made the connection, but it is a double bind. We can't get out of it. That's because the subject is inaccessible to the episteme of the nineteenth century, the episteme of representation. How to represent the subject? Is it a person? Well, it's empirical and transcendental. You can't represent it. And that's humanism, because, in that empty space, which is the absence of the subject, there will emerge *Geistesgeschichte*, the humanities, so to speak: history, literature, sometimes linguistics, and so on. Those will all be humanistic disciplines, because they're organized around some idea of the subject which is however not there, because the subject is supposed to be absent. So they're all somehow contradictory, and the whole edifice of this nineteenth-century episteme, very rich, full of detail and discovery, is fissured at its very base, because the very thing on which it depends, the subject, is not present, just as the place of the king is not present, not available, whereas, in the older system, you had the two bodies of the king. That worked for a time, but something else had to take its place.

Indeed, Foucault gives you thorough accounts of these disciplines—the economics, the linguistics of the period. Whether they're right or not is another matter. But he is keeping to his program, which obligates him only to the individual things, not the totality, because for him there is no totality. And all these individual things resemble each other and are telling the same story; these are all historical representations, and they are all therefore somehow flawed. So how do we get out of that problem? At that point, he says, two new kinds of things are going to emerge: psychoanalysis and ethnography. Psychoanalysis is going to show us that this consciousness, this subject that we thought was unified, is nothing of the sort. It will perform its Copernican revolution, and the subject will suddenly be outside. And ethnology will do the same. This bourgeois culture that we think is human is only one form of society, culture, consciousness, and all the rest of it, but there are many others. We will necessarily deal with them in some unsatisfactory way, but we at least have to acknowledge that there is an otherness in the world which is not ours.

So these disciplines, if we can call them that, form the prelude to the contestation of humanism and phenomenology as the disciplines that can complete this kind of knowledge. These will be the emergent things—like fossils in the eighteenth century, or, for Einstein, the orbit of Mercury, which wobbles at a certain point that can't be explained—that break into the formerly stable picture and that break it up. In that regard, they are like Barthes's punctum. When you look at a photograph, you notice this funny little thing. What is that doing there? We have no idea what it's doing there. It constitutes a part of the *impensé* of this picture. A part of its unconscious? Well, it is at least something that doesn't fit into our preestablished ways of thinking. Then what will happen? Foucault says we have no idea what kinds of events can precipitate this transformation, but someday this human face on the seashore will be effaced by the waves, and humanism itself will disappear.

As I say, he died in 1984. He no longer was entertaining those thoughts, but, of course, today we have the posthuman, as in Katherine Hayles's important book, which is a post-Foucauldian contribution in a way.[5] We have the questions of technology, media, AI. So, in an unexpected sense, maybe Foucault is right about the arrival of the posthuman, and even if it no longer can really give us a guide to the present, at least it is a very effective map of the past and the contradictoriness of a humanism which he is not content simply to denounce, but whose very evolution and inner contradictions he unravels.

Now I want to say one thing about the business of repression. With repression, Foucault takes another sort of potshot, this one at Freud. The first volume of *The History of Sexuality* is like a short pamphlet in which he wants to denounce the notion of the unconscious. He says there is no such thing as repression. It will be important to note that he and Deleuze were close in this period. He never wants to judge Deleuze. Their friendship broke up on a political question, the question of Palestine. But, nonetheless, you can see there is a sort of ideal of immanence here, reminiscent of Deleuze. The unconscious, the notion of repression, would be different from a model of immanence. Repression means pushing something down or not letting something emerge into consciousness. Foucault's *impensé* does not work that way. In the *impensé*, everything is in the same plane of immanence, but we haven't gotten there yet. It's something which is not thought, and for that very reason cannot be thought by your episteme, but it's not the same as repression. What about all this business of sexual

---

5   N. Katherine Hayles, *How We Became Posthuman: Virtual Bodies in Cybernetics, Literature, and Informatics* (Chicago: University of Chicago Press, 1999).

repression? Does that work in the same way? He says: Yes, people say that with the Puritans, Luther, Protestantism and so on, sexuality was suddenly repressed from its happy days in Mediterranean Catholicism, where sexuality was this natural thing like food, but no, that's not right. You make a mistake in thinking that sexuality has been repressed and nobody can talk about it. On the contrary, they do nothing but talk about it. If you want to say it has been repressed, then it was repressed by talking about it. Because people talk so much about sexuality, it's repressed and is not there anymore (a very Mallarméan phenomenon). Then he comes up with something which I think is a very interesting contribution both to the Althusserian model and to others. Althusser has interpellation; Foucault talks about the confession: the way we repress things is by talking about them. The confession is a key element in all this, because that's how I create myself and produce myself, by talking. It operates not by interiorization, but by exteriorization. It is a kind of reverse interpellation. Language becomes this vehicle precisely for repression and the perpetuation of the process. Anyway, it's an interesting idea that I don't think he really develops in the later volumes, so it stands out from the rest of this work.

Next time we will make something of a change, although, as I've pointed out, language is everywhere in this work of Foucault, but in a very different way from its central place in Barthes. So we'll have a look at questions of language next time.

March 30, 2021

20
Nominalism of the Photograph

{Barthes}

I want to point out that the Foucault discussion still turns around one of the most basic problems of structuralism: synchrony and diachrony. It goes back to the Russian Formalists. Jakobson and Tynianov wrote an important paper in which they try to show that there is no real incompatibility, that you can have a diachrony of synchronies or a synchrony of diachronies.[1] That may or may not be a real solution, but it is certainly the problem that has been raised with *The Order of Things* and with Foucault's global history that doesn't want to be a global history. I would suggest that the way he *thinks* that he is solving this problem—and we may well think so too—is that there is not a diachrony of states, only a diachrony of breaks. You can tell the story of the breaks, but not of the relationship of each period to other. I sometimes exaggerate the philosophical problem involved in these breaks. I think we should give him the benefit of the doubt and say that they are not simply volcanic eruptions or catastrophic landslides or something, although they are in part that, but that, in each of these breaks, in an older paradigm, leaves substantial fragments of itself behind. When a landscape is undergoing an earthquake, all kinds of things break up. Let's

---

1 Roman Jakobson and Jurij Tynjanov, "Problems in the Study of Language and Literature," trans. H. Eagle, *Poetics Today* 2, no. 1 (1980), 29–31.

say it happens in Rome. So Rome collapses. It declines and it falls, and it leaves all kinds of broken columns, statues, and ruins behind. Then you are to imagine some other civilization coming along and putting all those things together in a new way, leaving some out, certainly refunctioning others. Brecht had a word for this: *Umfunktionierung*. You take what you have, but you put it together in a new way, and indeed I think that is the way this kind of historical evolution proceeds. In evolutionary theory, there is a word for some kind of organ which is developed for one function, and then later on is used in the service of another function: exaptation. Something like that could very well be involved, but he doesn't want a theory of it, because each of these things is inaccessible, presumably, to what it produces, to each of these moments of production. But, of course, that is the problem, and we don't have a modern concept of it, which he suggests, in a very un-Foucault-like way, is building up under the surface. Of course, his answer—and it confirms what many of you have thought about all of this, that it is a kind of aesthetics—is that it's moving toward literature in his specific meaning of it, which is, I would say, not only modernism but a condemned modernism, an underside of modernism, the modernism of Sade and Bataille and the transgressors, not the high modernism of Proust and Joyce, although you could certainly argue that it also relates to that other tradition. So it is the place of an unconscious—which, of course, he doesn't believe in—which is going to be the new episteme. But he is perfectly frank in saying again that we don't know what events precipitate this, and we don't know what is to come of it, except that the human will disappear.

Now I see two themes running through all of this stuff that we've looked at. One is language and the other is visuality—and maybe meaning, that is, meaning in the sense of having a theory of something, claiming that you know the truth of something or that you know the essence of something—and I think those things are linked together. It seems to me that most of these people have associated language and seeing—to name a thing is to see a thing, and to see a thing is to name a thing—because, to isolate something from what William James called the "blooming, buzzing confusion"—a landscape of sensation before perception, before you could separate different things out—you mark it, and to mark it is already language, a naming.[2] But we need to go further than that, and I

2   William James, *The Principles of Psychology*, Vol. I (New York: Henry Holt and Co., 1890), 488.

would say that what these people don't deal with is modern technology and computation. How does differentiation bring with it the regression from language to mathematics? I don't know. But, at any rate, most of these theorists disappear in the '80s. Deleuze, it's true, lived until '95. But the '80s are the moment of what I conceive as some kind of fundamental break, in which I would include the personal computer, which only becomes widely available in 1982 or so; I would include the change from Keynesianism to neoliberalism; and there are plenty of other changes you could fit in here. So these thinkers are not able to witness or conceptualize these changes, these historical breaks. We will only have a brief moment to look at these new propositions. But, of course, you see that, moving from the theme of language to computation, you are able to get out of language, into something else which is really not a language, I think. But what do you want to call it? You're getting out of humanism and into what Kate Hayles calls "the posthuman." Anyway, that gives you another framework for what we have been looking at here.

Barthes is perhaps the fourth member of the big three. You know that, in the Second World War, the big three were Roosevelt, Stalin, and Churchill, but there was always somebody else who wanted to get in on these meetings. Chiang Kai-shek, for example, insisted on meeting with them, as did de Gaulle. Barthes is another fourth for us. I don't say he insists on being a part of this, but the unity of his career is amazing, if you look at something like this *Barthes Reader* that Susan Sontag has put together; I think it's not necessarily the best way of doing this, and I don't like some of the choices, but what is amazing is the stability of his themes. He begins with language, journals, *how* to keep a journal, and it ends with language, *whether* I can keep a journal. At the very end, Barthes was asking himself not only this question of whether we should keep a journal, but whether he should write a novel. I think the big problem there is that Barthes is somehow concerned with the synchronic rather than the diachronic. When he looks at a story like "Sarrasine," he doesn't look at the overall thing and movement of it; it's point by point. He breaks it up into different sections, separate unities, the same way his disciple Metz will break up a film into film stills. But there really is a kind of contradiction there, because if you are dealing with the film still, you can't really do much with what Metz also called *la grande syntagmatique*, that is, the movement of the whole thing which is like a giant sentence, according to them. So there is really a dual attention there, something which was always pointed out by the people whom he liked to write about. First Barthes was the champion of the new novel, Robbe-Grillet, in which there is a focus on these acts of language. But Robbe-Grillet said, "Listen, I'm glad he writes about me, but he's a great liar, and what he really likes to read is the old-fashioned stuff, Zola and Balzac." Robbe-Grillet calls that cheating. It's as though you wrote about Boulez and Stockhausen, and then you went home and listened to Schubert. And I think that went on throughout his life.

In that spirit, I think his relationship to film is very interesting. Of course, like the rest of them, he saw films all the time. You probably don't understand what a film culture is anymore, but these people went out at least two or three times a week to see movies, and, in Paris, you could see movies at 9:00 in the morning if you wanted. There were little theaters all over the place where you could even see all kinds of older, historical films. So they were all always going out to see films, from Sartre and Beauvoir to the last of them. The same was true of the Germans. Adorno and Horkheimer in Los Angeles; they may have denounced Hollywood, but they saw Hollywood films two or three times a week, and the ones they really liked were the Marx Brothers. I find it interesting that, although one of Barthes's legacies was the film theory of Metz and others, I don't recall anything on individual films as such. What we find are film stills. Yes, but reading a film still is like reading a little bit of a text, something that Derrida does. So the overall diachrony of all of these things is eluded in favor of the individual—I don't like to call them "fragments," but, in this case, maybe we can. This theme of language does become visual in Barthes as well, because Barthes is obsessed with the photograph. And, of course, his film analysis is precisely that: turning a film back into the various photographs, stills, from which it is made, whereas the great advantage of film was to have taken the dead past of the photograph and projected it into the future and made it move. So we have these two sides of an opposition, and we'll come to them later on.

The first thing that one wants to note is that the sign under which one looks at this work is the pessimism of language philosophy. Barthes is obsessed with language, his great life-long passion, but he is very negative about it. The final pronouncement does not really come as a surprise, but it is certainly fairly shocking: language is fascist. One can then make the usual objections: fascism is an easy word to use and maybe we shouldn't be using a word like that for some of these things. But Barthes will substantiate this claim, and what this means is that Barthes is fundamentally a language pessimist. But he does not begin that way, I think. In Sartre, there are the materials for language pessimism, but there isn't one as such, because what is energizing in Sartre is that you can say everything; and this is what Deleuze claims Sartre did for all these people: he opens thought up to a language of the outside, and he lets the outside in. It is no longer restricted by academic discourse, the political correctness of only being able to say one particular thing in this respectability of bourgeois language, but now you can talk about everything. If you look at *Nausea,* it would certainly give you some materials for claiming that language can only go so far, but, on the other hand, I suppose that, with Sartre, and maybe Foucault, too, the unknown-unknown you can talk about by saying precisely that. That is, you can talk about what language cannot do by saying that it can't do it. You can tell people what you would have said had you been able to say it. You can designate a kind of language that you would have used, had language really worked. But, nonetheless, there is a feeling that you can say anything. But Barthes and Sartre, at least at the beginning, share the same linguistics, so to speak. In Sartre, it comes in the image of the rug, in Barthes, the image of the windowpane: you look through the windowpane and you can see the meanings, and then, if you shift your eyes a little bit, you find that you are looking at the windowpane itself, which sometimes you can see and sometimes you can't. This windowpane is dirty, so you see the dirt on the windowpane, or it imposes itself, because it has these discolorations, but nonetheless, it has become a thing. Of course, what Barthes really liked in the new novel was that it lead you blindly down the path of meaning, and you think it is telling you a story, but, suddenly, it isn't telling you a story at all; it ends up doing something with words that have become objects, and therefore it is somehow turning language into a materiality which is no longer linguistic.

That is, I think, the reason for the other final statement of Barthes, which is also in the inaugural lecture, which has to do with the taste of language and the knowledge inherent in language. But, as he points out, these are from the same root in French: *saveur* and *savoir.* Why is this important? Because *saveur*, the flavor of language, is its materiality. Where would that lead us? Well, it would lead us to the body, because the body is the sensorium that is going to experience this savor of language, and this is what he appreciates. When he reads a novel of Zola, do you suppose he really follows what's going on? Surely, he is reading the words and the sentences, but, if you start looking at the words and sentences too closely, you're not really going to know what's going on in the larger novel. It's a different kind of reading. All those who see Flaubert as the beginning of modernity in the novel are going to point out that everything in Flaubert depends on speed. If you read *Madame Bovary* at a certain speed, then you're reading a story. If you slow down, then you're reading a modernist text, because each of these paragraphs is constructed in a certain way. Flaubert had a room he called the *gueuloir*, the place where you can yell and make noise and nobody cares. He would declaim these things aloud, and sometimes only write one paragraph per week, like Joyce, and, at that point, you have a very different notion of language. If you want to go even further into the postmodern, there's a wonderful essay by Nathalie Sarraute on Flaubert that points this out: If you read Flaubert closely, what you come to are the silences between the sentences.[3] Flaubert wrote the gaps. The sentences he let go and he let them be printed, but the crucial thing is that, finally, the truth of this language, and of modern language, is the break. You can't get from one sentence to the next without it. So Flaubert is a prototype of all these different attitudes toward the break within language. It is a machine which you can recalibrate according to each of these aesthetics.

Now I want to point out one more thing about that: the final stage in this suspicion of language is going to be nominalism, that is, an absolute linguistic pessimism, because, in nominalism, the word is disconnected from the thing. If you have to connect a word to a thing, it will only be connected to that one thing and not anything else. So, suddenly, universalism is disappearing and language is narrowing down to a set of unique names. Names are supposed to be absolutely individual. As we've seen with Lévi-Strauss, they're not. But that is the claim of naming, that it will give you your own personal identity, although a lot of other people have the same name as you, so it doesn't really work that way. Nominalism is finally the road to silence, the road to the end of language. And, as far as the diachronic is concerned, it's a bit the same. If you begin challenging the notion of the event, suddenly you're going to work yourself back into a position where only the present of time exists, and how can you write a history of that? History then disappears. So there are two kinds of time:

3   Nathalie Sarraute, *Paul Valéry et l'Enfant d'Éléphant / Flaubert le précurseur* (Paris: Gallimard, 1986).

continuity, that of the plot, and a different time, that of the breaks. One of the most interesting moments in antiquity is when Heraclitus said that you can't step into the same stream twice. This is a certain notion of total change, which you would think would be the endpoint of nominalism, but not quite, because somebody else came along—Cratylus, I think—and said, no, you can't even step into the same river once, because there isn't any single river. How can there be a river if you can't step into it twice? If an event only happens once, it has no repercussions and there is no river of time, no time. So, really, the whole figure undoes itself and you're left with this position, toward which, I think, all the things that we're looking at tend, and, if they don't, then they're not terribly interesting for us, or at least for the age, for the *Zeitgeist*. This age is very energetic, huge piles of work and writing, but it all seems to come down to something absolutely negative.

In Barthes's own career, all kinds of things are turned into language problems. He starts out writing on theater. He is a Brechtian. Brecht arrives in Paris in '53 or '54. They had an international festival; of course, East Germany was shut out of most Western cultural activities as a pariah, but, in Paris, the East Germans were invited. Brecht brought *Mother Courage*, and it was a sensation. That is the moment when Brecht becomes, for a while, the greatest dramatist in the world. So Barthes begins as a Brechtian and a Sartrean. I don't think he ever really disavows his formation under Sartre, which would be perfectly natural for anybody of his age, because that is his period and it's absolutely formative. What he begins doing under the influence of both of them, in various ways, is what we would call "cultural studies." *Mythologies*, his first collection, is one of the foundational works of cultural studies, adopted by the Birmingham School and sent around the world. What do you do with this new culture of the media and its formative influence? These first little articles are published in a left-wing journal, the old *Observateur*, anti-American, very left. These were little articles, and they were contributions to a consciousness-raising of the French about the new kinds of journalism that are infiltrating their cultural space.

Now, to show you what's interesting about those essays, I must read you a footnote that is all about the connotations of their objects, their political effectivity, what they claim to be doing, these objects of culture—many of them photographs by the way, ending with a photograph and this photographic series, *The Family of Man*, in which you have photographs from all over the world, a UN-type liberal celebration of the unity of mankind; you can't get more humanist than that, and insofar as the UN would act as a kind of American hegemony, you can't get more American than that, which is part of what he is denouncing. Here, in the very last footnote of this collection, he says: "Even here, in these mythologies, I have used trickery: finding it painful constantly to work on the evaporation of reality"—and, someplace else, he talks about the nausea of these cultural texts; they're trying to put a false, excessive meaning back into things; it's nauseating the way some kind of excess of food would be nauseating, but here he uses the opposite figure, reality's evaporation—"I've started to make it excessively dense, and to discover in it a surprising compactness which I savored with delight, and I've given a few examples of 'substantial psycho-analysis' about some mythical objects."[4] He is talking about Bachelard and Sartre and the psychoanalysis of things and of sensations. In other words, what he has set out to do was to break these things down, and to show that they were artificial constructs of a phony or ideological kind of meaning. But, every so often, he got tired of that, and he tried to show the ontological thickness of being in some of these things. This is when he talks about wood versus plastic in children's toys, wine versus milk in French politics, steak and French fries as the French national dish—it was horse steak, I believe, mostly—and wrestling versus boxing. So, suddenly, it's about bodies, the physical, ontological meaning, the being of these things, their quality, their savor, rather than this "artificial connotation," which is his term. At that point, there is a very interesting hesitation, and I think nowadays, where maybe we know a lot more about how the public sphere operates, we're not too surprised; we see through most of these things, even as they invade our lives all the more thoroughly. For example, you have the Black soldier from Senegal who salutes the French flag. Okay, well, this obviously conveys the idea that France is a Republic that has no racial divisions, that it offers its universalism to the whole world. It's a little like American ads today, where whenever you have a family, it is a multiracial family, children of mixed heritage. So, whatever else these ads are doing, selling you insurance or some kind of dietary food, they're also saying, "Look, America is the land of absolute equality; we have no racial problems here." Or, if you were a white supremacist, I suppose you would

---

4 Roland Barthes, *Mythologies*, trans. Annette Lavers (New York: Noonday Press, 1991), 164.

think that it's all a conspiracy and that all these advertising agencies have been given this *consigne* to use the word "diversity," as it is called now, and to dramatize it in every ad.

Anyway, that should give you a sense of what Barthes was pioneering in those days. He was pioneering a certain use of visual language for the transmission of a second meaning. There is a literal meaning, and then there is this connotation. Later, he will abandon the notion of connotation, I suppose because it seems too close to ideology, another word that nobody wants to use, which has its own problems, but maybe not the same ones as "connotation." So the ads are denotative, but, then, in a second degree, they are used for transmitting this illicit meaning, which is social or political. They have a connotation. And, here, I also wanted, in the spirit of completeness, to add that this is something that has been analyzed by Pierre Bourdieu at a much greater degree of sociological complexity, for example in his book *Distinction*, which means not distinction in the sense of "difference" but in the sense of "distinguished," as in "distinguished table manners," and it provides a critique of the connotations of culture. So you like to listen to classical music? Okay, then you are a little more *distingué(e)* than people who just listen to popular songs. Okay, but among the people who listen to classical music—a horrible term, as Adorno says—the people who listen to Stravinsky are much more *distingué(e)s* than those who listen to Tchaikovsky. Each of these cultural practices is going to send off all kinds of class messages, and the book called *Distinction* is an enormous comparison between peasant and worker aesthetics, everyday practices, and those of this new middle class. So Bourdieu's sociology—it has more implications than that—is nonetheless in the line of Barthes, and you can thus take this as compensating in some small way for Bourdieu's absence from this seminar.

Well, where does Barthes go on from there? Does he have any histories to tell? In the next collection—and, oddly, these very dense texts will also first be published in this same little left-wing weekly—in a book called *Writing Zero Degree*, he will propose a whole history of something which is neither literature nor language but some third thing. It is one of the most formative things that I have read, and I think remains one of his greatest books. We'll come back to that, but it is a sharpening and a philosophical intensification of that idea of connotation, but throwing it on a new plane now, because he will say that something which he calls writing, *écriture*, not to be confused with Derrida and all the rest of them, is a second degree meaning which is projected by literary style. And, here, he somehow gives us a notion of a modern break.

After that, there is already the period of structuralism. He will then seem to find his homeland in linguistics and semiotics. You have seen a little bit of his semiotic analysis of narrative. He will construct all kinds of systems of the sign from a structural point of view. He will go back—and it's very important, because everybody is moving in that direction—from structural linguistics to what preceded all this, what preceded modern linguistics: rhetoric. The last treatise of rhetoric, everybody points out, is Fontanier's, in the early nineteenth century; after that, it is a dead science. Suddenly, after the war, rhetoric makes a comeback, and everybody is going to be talking about tropes and rhetorical this and that. Barthes will himself undertake—because he gives himself some really serious tasks here—a whole seminar on the history of rhetoric from Quintilian onward, to see what is in some ways different from the modern sign. So, here again, we get certain kinds of linguistic epistemes. It's a similar historical process, but, obviously, of a very different nature. He is trying to make the study of language into a science.

And then, suddenly, Barthes decides it's a failure; or worse yet, it's boring. He gives it up. He decides not to make language a science anymore, or he gets tired of it, or he realizes that it's a dead end, and he turns back to the hedonism of language, the pleasure of the text, its savor. In a sense, he pursues that to the end of his career. He is still interested in classification systems. I think one of the most interesting Barthesian works is his book on Fourier, Loyola, and Sade: the founder of the Jesuit order with his spiritual exercises, the Marquis de Sade with his panoramas of all kinds of sexual positions, and Fourier, the great utopian, with his notion that we don't have to have a new subjectivity, that we take all subjectivities as they are given and combine them. Some people like to have quarrels with others. Some people are very finicky. Some get along. We just sort them out, Fourier says, and we give them different tasks in this super-utopia. We don't have to change people. We will group and harness all their peculiarities to the immense task of the utopia. This has fascinated people, including Marx and Engels. Fourier is the one who put an advertisement in the paper every week that said, "If you want to finance my utopian system, the phalanstery, meet me at 11 o'clock in my rooms." Nobody ever showed up. By profession, he was really a traveling salesman. Fourier is one of the most fascinating figures of the nineteenth century. But Barthes's essays are on these three people's manias for classification schemes. I think it's one of his most characteristic works, but it shows that this is all a game for him now. Where is the break? Maybe it is the elevation to the Collège de France. You understand that when he says, "Thank you for bringing me to this place without power," he means: When named to the Collège de France, you give one lecture a week, open to the public, for however many weeks, with no formal students, and you publish these lectures.[5] The joke used to be that Bergson's lectures were famous because bums would come in off the street in the winter time to get warm and take in these free philosophical lectures as they sat and dozed. I think that Barthes's lectures are not so interesting, but the seminars of Foucault are very different from what he writes; that's where we get biopower and governmentality, and those are all published, but none of them are anything like Lacan's seminars.

Barthes had his political connections. He was part of the *Tel Quel* group. He went to China with them. Kristeva worked with him. But he took his distances, and he was certainly not a political activist, except in this early period with the *Mythologies*. He died in a stupid accident. He came out of the Collège de France after a lecture and got hit by a milk truck. People said his injuries weren't that serious, but he let himself die. His mother had died a year or two before, and he had lived with her his whole life. Who knows? That's as plausible as anything. At any rate, it wasn't necessarily the end of something, because he had constantly done this work of commentary, of the searching out of language in all kinds of forms. He had reached the end of that, I think.

Let's go back then to the business of *Writing Zero Degree*, this early work, because I think it's important to see how he establishes a dividing line, and since this is France, that dividing line is the French Revolution. Germany used to have a national myth of that kind, but of course in Germany it

---

5   "Another kind of joy, more sober because more responsible, is mine today as well: that of entry into a place that we can strictly term *outside the bounds of power*. For if I may, in turn, interpret the Collège, I shall say that it is, as institutions go, one of History's last stratagems. Honour is usually a diminution of power; here it is a subtraction, power's untouched portion. [. . .] To teach or even to speak outside the limits of institutional sanction is certainly not to be rightfully and totally uncorrupted by power; power (the *libido dominandi*) is there, hidden in any discourse, even when uttered in a place outside the bounds of power. Therefore, the freer such teaching, the further we must enquire into the conditions and processes by which discourse can be disengaged from all will-to-possess." Roland Barthes, "In Inauguration of the Chair of Literary Semiology, Collège de France, January 7, 1977," trans. Richard Howard, *Oxford Literary Review* (Autumn 1979), 32.

comes with Luther and Protestantism. Do we have a myth like that in the
United States? I suppose it depends on the parties. The conservatives are
still talking about the constitution and the Founding Fathers. Maybe now
the Left is moving toward the recognition of the Civil War as the foundation. Of course, this is not a nation-state, but most nation-states have this
fetish of a national beginning, something like an "axial moment," as Ricœur
calls it, and, certainly, the French have that as much as anyone else.[6] The
French Revolution has been the center of French politics, even when it
is attacked. Is there a French politics anymore? I don't know. One of the
influential counterrevolutionary moves of the de-Marxification of the '80s
and '90s was François Furet's attack on the very idea of the Revolution:
maybe there never was such a thing. A similar attack has been made on
the English Revolution and Cromwell. So history gets ideologically reorganized in various ways.

But, here, the break is between, of course, the ancien régime and the
bourgeoisie, and it involves the opposition of rhetoric versus style. What's
the difference? In rhetoric, you want to reproduce eloquence. You want to
reproduce the classics of the past. You are in rivalry with the great orators.
So it is with Demosthenes that Cicero is in rivalry, and it is with Cicero that
Edmund Burke is in rivalry. Meanwhile, what you quote in essays like those
of Montaigne are pieces of beautiful style. So you select a bit of Horace,
a bit of Virgil, because it is a sample of elegance. With the nineteenth-
century view of language, suddenly, you don't want to reproduce the same
any longer. You want to be different. But, more than that—and this is the
part I wanted to draw your attention to—are Barthes's remarks on style.
This is one of the great examples of early Barthes. There is language and
literature, but there is also style. Style is beyond these boundaries, where

> imagery, delivery, vocabulary spring from the body and the past of the
> writer and gradually become the very reflexes of his art. Thus a self-
> sufficient language has evolved [. . .] which has its roots only in the
> depths of the author's personal and secret mythology, that subnature
> of expression where the first coition of words and things takes place,
> where once and for all the great verbal themes of his existence come
> to be installed.[7]

6   Paul Ricœur, *From Text to Action*, trans. Kathleen Blamey and John B. Thompson
(Evanston, IL: Northwestern University Press, 1991), 214.
7   Roland Barthes, *Writing Degree Zero*, in *A Barthes Reader,* ed. Susan Sontag (New
York: Hill and Wang, 1982), 32.

And he talks about how, in the great poets, there's also this bell-like echo of crucial words that come back again and again—in Valéry, for example, the word *pur*. "[Style] is the decorative voice of hidden secret flesh; it works as does Necessity, as if, in this kind of floral growth, style were no more than the outcome of a blind and stubborn metamorphosis starting with the sub-language elaborated where flesh and external reality come together."[8] There are a couple pages here that are of great interest, and one of their interests is to be completely contemporary in this sense: that it seems possible one might challenge this notion of style or use it by asking whether it has disappeared, and whether the kind of profound originality of the idiolect, of the private language—Wittgenstein says it doesn't exist, but it does exist in poetry and in style itself—has also come to an end. The great practitioners of style studies were German, and they were from Romance language philologists—Spitzer, Auerbach, and so forth. Spitzer always said that what you look for is whatever is weird in a writer, these expressions that come back like a facial tic, and then you start with those and follow them into the very core of the thing. Spitzer's *Linguistics and Literary History* will give you samples of this kind of analysis and the great manifesto of how one does it, the method, and I think that is very close to the kinds of things that interest Barthes.

So what would the end of style be? Now we might call it the postmodern, the end of the modern. Style characterizes the modern, modernism, and it begins, as Abrams might tell us, with Romanticism, but it ends with the stylelessness of anonymity. Barthes will prophetically foresee this in the last chapter of this book and in its title, *Writing Degree Zero*. It is an attempt to imagine what a styleless language would be. But why? Because writing, in Barthes's sense, is a very specific property, which is the relationship of the text to the institution of literature. So just like his other example in *Mythologies*—"I am an example of Latin grammar"—the writing is saying to you, regardless of whatever it's about, "I am an example of fine writing, of rhetoric." Or, later on, "I am an example of style." So, for example, if you read some of these political biographies, you understand that there is a kind of novelistic writing that is employed in these things every so often, and it makes of the historical or political commentary a relationship to novelistic language. All these things are at work in the notion of *écriture*. *Écriture* is where the text designates its relationship to the institution, or else it says, "I am an anti-institution. I am *not* literature. I'm something

---

8   Roland Barthes, *Writing Degree Zero*, 33.

else." But, in any case, it gives off this supplementary message, and, for Barthes, then, its zero degree would be the point at which the text is somehow not giving off a relationship to anything. I would contend, rather, that it is announcing its relationship to the absence of literature. He talks about guilt. Literature is guilty, because it's an institution among other institutions. It's supposed to be a diversion. This is a business society. Literature has no value in the business sense. The text says, "Wait a minute. I don't have to have value, because I'm outside all of that." So it takes its distance from the literary, academic, or philosophical institution, and we've seen how Sartre is, in a sense, the explosion out of those institutions. Sartre stops teaching. He has no relationship to the academy. He writes about all kinds of marginal figures, sexuality, stuff you're not supposed to write about, but it ends up, like everything else, becoming literature in spite of itself. So Barthes's utopia is not altogether uncontradictory. What he calls all that is "connotation." Well, connotation can be taken as the relationship to the institution. It connotes the institution. "I wish to be different. I'm not a novelist or a poet like all those other people. I don't do that kind of stuff. I don't have that view of the world"—and yet the meaning of all this is: "I'm also a poet, a part of great literature," and so on. "I refuse all the past of literature to replace it with *Finnegan's Wake*, but what I'm replacing it with is still literature. I have now written the book of the world and you don't need any other books."

Now I wanted slowly to get back to the business of visuality, and maybe also meaning. The Eiffel Tower, for example, gives us a wonderful solution to nominalism, because, as Barthes says, you can't get away from it. It's everywhere, but it is unique. It's a sign, maybe, but it's the only sign in the world like this. Do you know the expression *hapax legomenon*? It is a word or a thing that has only been used once, of which only one version exists. I can't think of any words like this. Mallarmé made one up—*ptyx*—as a rhyme in one of his sonnets.[9] This word doesn't exist, but it now exists as a piece of Mallarmé's vocabulary which was used only once ever. So it is a *hapax legomenon*, and of course in the history of philology there are a lot of these things. For example, Lukács's view of Flaubert's *Sentimental Education* as the supreme example of the ironic novel is immediately amended with the claim that it is the only one. But how can it be the

---

9   Stéphane Mallarmé, *Collected Poems*, trans. E. H. and A. M. Blackmore (Oxford: Oxford World Classics, 2006), 70.

supreme example of something of which it is the only exemplar? In any case, the Eiffel Tower is a *hapax legomenon*. There is nothing like it in the world. It has a unique meaning of a unique thing—Paris, France. It serves absolutely no purpose. There's a wonderful story of Frank Lloyd Wright visiting the Yale campus. They say to him, "Well, Mr. Wright, where would you like to live if you were at Yale?" He says, "I'd like to live in the Harkness Tower. That way I wouldn't have to look at it." The only way you can get away from the Eiffel Tower is by getting inside of it. Otherwise, you're seeing it, and it's seeing you, like a panopticon. The panopticon is also a unique place. There is only one—here's nominalism again—subject of the look. You don't even know what it is. Maybe nobody is up there, but it is looking at everything else. The Eiffel Tower is also this unique center of everything, which is not a center, because it is nothing and it serves no purpose. In a way, that essay is one climax of this whole search for the mechanisms of language.

I want to mention three more things in Barthes's work, because we are running out of time. First, what do the mythologies do? That is, what is their political purpose? Their general effect—and this is Barthes's Brechtian side—is to show how what seems natural is in fact historical. Brecht's estrangement effect was always supposed to work this way. He takes something you might think is natural and shows that it is historically produced and therefore political. People made it, so they can change it, whereas, if it is natural, it is simply there, and you can't change it. So the function of the mythologies calls for Brechtian estrangement, and *Mythologies* is an exercise in Brecht's estrangement effect, in showing how all these things are historical, have been made, have their history. He quotes Marx on the cherry tree. Marx's lesson to Feuerbach is this: So you think the cherry tree is so beautiful? You wouldn't think that if it hadn't been brought to Europe in such-and-such century. Now you think it's natural to look out your window at it, but it's a result of history, and everything else in nature is like that. I think the important passage for us is where the natural becomes the normative, and so the attack of all these people on norms and normativity—Foucault and Derrida say this explicitly—is also an attack on the natural and the universal, because these are the instruments whereby norms are created. If there is a human nature, then it must be the same and changeless, and people who don't conform must be excluded or killed.

I wanted to end with what Barthes does with photography. What I'm doing is filling you in on the famous things about Barthes. Ask any schoolchild what they know about Barthes, and the answer will be: "studium" and "punctum." The photograph has a subject—that is, it is *about* something—and then, somewhere in this photograph, if you look at it long enough, you find something weird. For example, I was watching a symphony concert. There are lots of nice videos of concerts, and they show the orchestra close up, and, if they're well done, they will follow the score. Suddenly, as I watch, I notice a cello player has a band-aid on his finger. That has nothing to do with Brahms, and it has nothing to do with the orchestra, but it is certainly strange. What the hell is that band-aid doing there! Doesn't the cello player know he is being filmed? Is he wearing it deliberately? How did he hurt his hand? That's the punctum. The punctum is this weird little thing that disturbs order. It is meaningless. Barthes's other famous essay, "The Effect of the Real," is about how, if you want to show reality, you have to include all these things that are meaningless. I think his example is a barometer, one among a whole set of objects in a bourgeois home. Overstuffed chairs, appliances—they don't mean anything. It's not like Poe, where, if you have an object, it will come back at the end of the story. The pearly white teeth—oh no, something horrible is going to happen to them! No, these objects mean nothing, except insofar as they connote reality. All these bourgeois objects prove to you that this is really a story about bourgeois reality. I have to list them all so that you understand that this is real. So these are the tricks of the realist novelist. Now, by the time you get to Zola, he will know that this is the case, so he will just give you a list, and then you realize: that is Zola, not reality. Anyway, this is a very crucial thing in Barthes. It's the center of his analysis of the still photograph.

The other thing I wanted to tell you about is something that brings us back to Foucault's denunciation of history and continuity. "An entire historical tradition (theological or rationalistic) aims at dissolving the singular event into an ideal continuity [. . .]."[10] Okay, there you have one way of expressing all these oppositions that have come out in Barthes as much as anybody else. Continuity, generality, universality, the functioning of language versus the singular event or—because this has become a buzzword—singularity itself. Singularity is not a particularity. No, a particularity is on its way to nominalism, but it can never get there. So this means that effective history "shortens its vision to those things nearest

10 Michel Foucault, "Nietzsche, Genealogy, History," 88.

to it—the body, the nervous system, nutrition, digestion, and energies; it unearths the periods of decadence, and if it chances upon lofty epochs, it is with the suspicion—not vindictive but joyous"—a Deleuzean word—"of finding a barbarous and shameful confusion."[11] So that's the approach to absolute contingency and singularity, but, once you get there, meaning itself, it seems to me, is going to dissolve. Barthes's relationship to language takes him back and forth between these different positions. I didn't read you the stuff about wood and plastic, but you see why he would celebrate wooden toys as opposed to flimsy plastic toys. What is implied here as a method of defamiliarization will always work through an opposition, because you must have something more natural to show that something else is unnatural, and so we find ourselves caught in the same dilemma with which we began.

April 1, 2021

---

11   Michel Foucault, "Nietzsche, Genealogy, History," 89.

21

Philosophy's Postmodern Theater

{Deleuze}

We didn't get around to saying why Barthes thought language was fascist, so it seems to me we should settle that problem before going on to anything else. It is quite unusual in Barthes's work for him to make that kind of political statement. Obviously, there were a lot of people concerned with fascism in the '60s, but that kind of political language is alien to Barthes, even though we've certainly seen that his work has effective political significance. One thing he could mean by this statement is that there is a disjunction between language and experience. We saw that already in existentialism and in the mystics, the idea that language can't really express these things. You get another version of this in Lacan's famous phrase: The Real is "what resists symbolisation absolutely," where symbolization means language, linguistic expression.[1] The Real can never be put into words. Why not? If language gets ahold of something, it will distort it. Why? Because language is reification; it abounds with generalities and universals, whereas for all these theories, it is important to recognize that things are always singular. We are already, with them, and almost by definition, in a kind of nominalism.

---

1   Jacques Lacan, *The Seminar of Jacques Lacan, Book I: Freud's Papers on Technique, 1953–1954*, 66.

I don't think Barthes means anything too metaphysical by this, because he is not really a metaphysician, but, certainly, the work in *Mythologies* has a different answer for us, namely that language, generalities, and universals are always stereotypes in one way or another. A universal is a stereotype. If you believed the other way around—maybe that would be a kind of idealism—you would say that the singularities are just examples. So you get a dialectic here: either side is bad. If you make the object of language an example, then it's not much. If you make the language in which you discuss an object a stereotype, then that is just as bad. Out of stereotypes comes various racisms, sexisms, and specific forms of fascism. But they can just as well take good forms. That is, everything in language has to be a stereotype, because that's what a universal is. I'm thinking of an experiment of Leibniz. He taught at a court in one of the principalities of early eighteenth-century Germany. He took the court ladies out into the garden, and said, "Find me one leaf which is absolutely unique." Well, then the word "leaf" would not apply. That's what Barthes means. He is, in effect, returning to his earliest insights that he practiced in terms of mythologies, the connotations of mass culture. There is much more to be said about that, but we have to leave it there.

On to Deleuze now. His is an immense work, very popular nowadays, some of it quite difficult. I'm going to try to do this in terms of what I promised for the course as a whole—I don't know if I have really done it this way—that is to say, in terms of keywords. Here would be just a few of Deleuze's keywords that I picked at random: "rhizome," "assemblage," "molar/molecular," "overcoding," "intensity," "body without organs," "schizo," "line of flight," "territorialization," "plane of consistency," "plane of immanence." I think it would be good to go through Deleuze term by term, because, in my opinion, this is not a systematic philosophy. This raises another topic that should be central for us, even if it hasn't always been central to our discussions: the difference between theory and philosophy. I would like to say that Deleuze is both, but that there is a fundamental discontinuity or even contradiction between these things. I think that philosophy, or, as Heidegger and Derrida like to call it, "metaphysics," always has a system or is aiming to create a system, and that system will— as Derrida showed—always have a center, or, if you like more elaborate language, an absolute. What happens if we follow the lesson of Nietzsche and decide there aren't any absolutes? Then the process of making a system is going to fall to pieces. What do we do then? Well, we have to take on something like a Socratic position as a sniper. We have to make unrelated raids on this or that field, as Socrates did with his various objects of critique, or as Nietzsche did, although he was no admirer of Socrates, with his various forms of attack. I think that theory does something similar, in the sense that its absolutes become themes. For example, for Paul Virilio, whom we haven't looked at yet, you could say that his basic theme is speed. We find speed in machinery, photography, but also all kinds of other things, some of them social. Speed would not be an absolute, exactly; it's a center of his discourse, not a metaphysic, I think. But you can see how it could easily slip into a metaphysic, so that out of it could emerge some image of the world as nothing but momentum and various rates of velocity. So theory is always very close to slipping into systematicity, but, on the other hand, theory is, for that very reason, always going to insist on language and on the linguistic construction of these various themes, which are no longer to be seen as realities, metaphysical or otherwise, but rather as pure constructions.

So those are the things, I think, that characterize theory. It is an attempt to do something that philosophy used to do, but in a situation in which philosophy no longer seems possible. Now, in Deleuze, we get both of these things at once, because he is a professional philosopher. Some of the people we've looked at were not: Lévi-Strauss was an anthropologist; Barthes was—what is he?—a literary critic, a semiotician, not a philosopher. But Deleuze is a professional philosopher, so he has written books of technical philosophy, studies of various philosophers. He has also written all kinds of other things, and I want to look at those, but I want to look at them from a particular point of view, which may astound you. The beginning and the end of his work complement each other; they are two rigorously philosophical texts: *Difference and Repetition*, which was published a little later, but it was his thesis, and *What Is Philosophy?* at the end of his career, written with Guattari, about whom we'll have occasion to say a word. Those seem to be systematic, but if you look closely at them, *Difference and Repetition* is, for example, a terribly difficult book to read, because you want to find a system in it, and yet, in a way, each chapter is disjoined from every other one. I believe—though there are certainly experts who have tried and probably succeeded more than I have—that it cannot be made into a system, but you can ransack it for a series of themes, if you like. Each of its chapters is a kind of book in itself.

I was quite intrigued by a remark of his in an interview. He says that, after he writes something, he never tries to remember it. Hegel had various things he had to write: He had to have a study of nature, a study of human nature, then he had to have a study of the categories of nature, a logic, an aesthetics, a politics, and so each of these is a separate task. It's like the branches of a tree, as we'll see. Something grows out of this root, which is the Hegelian notion of the Absolute, I suppose, and then branches come off it, and they have to have their own individual elaborations. If this is the case, then Hegel has to remember what he said, and he either has to qualify it or to be true to it and to keep the same vocabulary while he enriches it. All the more so for Aristotle, or for Thomas Aquinus, since those are rather similar system-builders. If not, then there may be a break. Maybe you say you're going to have a *Kehre* now, a turn, and you're not going to talk about *Dasein* anymore; you're not going to profess existentialism, in Heidegger's case.

Deleuze is telling you that he doesn't have a single, ongoing project. "I want to forget about the thing that I just wrote," he says. "I'm going to start completely afresh, and I'm going to do something new." And there are people like that, as you know. He was a thinking machine, one of the great thinking machines. Deleuze is one of the most marvelous thinkers of the twentieth century. No matter how you classify him, Deleuzean scholars will tell you that's not quite right; it isn't this and it isn't that. But you can say that, nonetheless, there is an affiliation between this concept and that concept, this is a newer version of that one. Deleuze himself has nothing to do with that. Each thing is a separate project, or a separate problem, and I'll get to the business of problem-solving later on, which is, I think, one of the less interesting parts of Deleuze.

How do we deal with the uniqueness of each Deleuzean project? My method, for example, will have some obvious objections: I have established some continuities, but you can say all of them are fictive, if you like; other people would have done it another way, and in any case, these continuities are abusive. I'm going to say, for example, shortly, that the body without organs is a Deleuzean word for the synchronic. This is very abusive, in the sense that any Deleuzean will tell you it's not the synchronic and that it doesn't mean the same thing at all. Why not? Well, it's just something else, the Deleuzean might respond. Besides, we know what the synchronic is: It's old, almost traditional now; it's boring. We want something new. The body without organs is certainly completely different from that.

Any attempt to translate these new and unknown things into the terms we know is going to have that effect. If you say, for example, that Gramsci's notion of hegemony is a new version of ideology, then the Gramscians are going to tell you that it's completely different; it's a whole set of new inventions. Yes, but the minute you translate something into something else, it acquires its own autonomy. It floats off in a different direction. It gets a new kind of consistency, although I don't want to abuse that word. Translating the new into the old, postulating the emergence of the new from the old, is always abusive, and we can and should denounce it; but on the other hand, it is a way into this very complicated stuff, and I don't really know any other way of doing this in a satisfactory way.

But now there is something else we must take into account. I've characterized Foucault as perverse, in the sense that he is busy figuring out what you think you know already, and then telling you not to think like that. What Deleuze is doing is not exactly like that. This is not the history of ideas, and it's not structuralism. Deleuze is going to write on a series of not only traditional, but classical philosophers: David Hume, Bergson, the Stoics, Leibniz. Nietzsche, Foucault, and Spinoza as well, but these are a little bit different from introductions or treatises. What does he do with all those philosophies? Well, he takes them and turns them into versions of himself. So all these philosophers become what Deleuze has done with them. They are Deleuzean. That is not the way we were taught the history of philosophy, and it really is not somehow plausible that they were all Deleuzean thinkers. Of course, he has his enemies, Hegel and Plato, and they're not Deleuzean, but the very fact that they're not Deleuzean itself becomes an interesting transformation. In the old days, everybody was very excited by masks. That was a predominant theme of modernism, as in Pirandello. We could say Deleuze is putting on these masks, so we have a kind of carnival in which suddenly Kant or Spinoza or Hume pop up, but suddenly we find—no, no—it's not them. It's Deleuze wearing a mask.

That could be one way of looking at it, but I don't like that very much. I think it's a little more active than that. Sometimes he can be a very useful guide to these people. He has incredible ideas about them, all kinds of new ideas. Sometimes you might think it would be better to find out what the traditional philosophers think of this, since this is not really Kant or Hume. But I do think of it this way: these are, in some sense, stagings, or better still, performances. This idea of performativity comes out of J. L. Austin's linguistics. Derrida, de Man, Judith Butler, and others have adopted it for other purposes, and I mean something like what they mean. But these are performances in the sense of postmodern stagings of the classics. I'm going to give you a familiar example, because there are all kinds of things one could choose that might not be in your frame of reference. People used to talk about *Hamlet* without the prince. What do they mean by that? Well, that could be a bad performance, in which the Hamlet figure is weak, but other actors are very good. It could be a version or interpretation of Shakespeare, where Hamlet plays no role at all. Or, let's say you rewrote *Hamlet*, and you decided to put in the foreground what has always been understood to be marginal, in the background. That could be, for example, these two rich but officious schoolmates of his, who are quite repulsive in their spying, and who have an unhappy ending, Rosencrantz and Guildenstern. Then you could write a play which you could call *Rosencrantz and Guildenstern Are Dead*, and it would be about these two minor characters, and it would be a *Hamlet* from a new vantage. That's what I mean by postmodern staging, and I think that's what Deleuze does with all these philosophers. Yes, he gives you the dates of their major books, but suddenly we're not in that kind of philosophy at all. They are all recognizable figures and thoughts, but they have been completely turned around. Deleuze is a great director, as a director of the theater or the opera, and he has completely redone all of this in a modern—I prefer to say a postmodern—form, because, in the modern, you might do that with Shakespeare, but, later on, you do it with everything. Many postmodern stagings are quite good, actually, and effective versions of their originals. I consider that the theoretical Deleuze is doing that with his philosophers. Meanwhile, the philosophical Deleuze is denying it and trying to do technical philosophy. So you yourself have a choice: You can read it like the one or like the other. But if you want the full impact, I think you have to understand this business of staging.

Yes, I'll talk about what this philosophical system is—sometimes it's not terribly original—but my purpose here would be to get you to enjoy reading it. He is a great writer, and this is a marvelous experience. I don't care how true or false it is. Some people have, I think, hijacked Deleuze in the direction of the virtual and of virtuality, an idea which I don't think plays such an important part here, although you can certainly drag him in all kinds of directions. That's fine, but that is not the Deleuze I want you to understand. I would like you to feel the excitement of this stuff, even when you don't necessarily understand it.

He himself occasionally branches out and writes literary or artistic commentaries. So here we get two very important books, one on Proust, one on Kafka. Both of these are really sensational. The Proust book completely transforms the tradition of Proust interpretation, which had been, for the previous fifty years, largely based on the function of involuntary memory. Yes, we know that Proust was the cousin of Bergson. Is his work Bergsonian or not? It is at least about temporality. Well, enough is enough, Deleuze says, and he drops the whole matter of temporality to show that Proust is working with a hermeneutics of perception. Far from having anything to do with this mystical business of the past coming alive, it has to do with systems of signs and percepts. That inversion in *Proust and Signs* completely changed the orientation of Proust scholarship. With Kafka, I would say that it was not so much the interpretation but rather the introduction of the concepts of minor literature and minor language, and the idea that Kafka is making a certain proto-political use of the languages with which he had some familiarity, German and Yiddish. Kafka says in his diaries that the biggest decision he had to make is whether to write in German or in Yiddish. Yes, he writes in German, but not official German. Kafka takes official German and makes a weird sort of idiolect out of it which is no longer German in any strict sense, but which isn't Yiddish either. The minor language is like a parasite inside the major language. It's not a dialect, exactly. Some dialects are minor versions, or some of them are actual languages, but they're still dialects. You know the linguists have always had a problem with the definition of "dialect." I think Chomsky was the one who said there isn't any such thing as a dialect; a language is a dialect that has an airline, a prison, and a flag. So the major language is the state, and the dialect, the minor language, is this thing existing in the interstices of the state which uses bits of it for alternate purposes.

Then Deleuze writes a wonderful book on Sacher-Masoch and on masochism. There are some things I do want to mention to you. There are some smaller articles, a famous one on "Bartleby" of Melville. Now everybody is talking about "Bartleby," politically and otherwise, and I think this comes out of Deleuze's essay. Another is on a French novelist whom you may not know, Michel Tournier. It is a version—here are these versions again—or rather a staging of *Robinson Crusoe* called *Friday*, a book of delirium, visions, relationships to the other. It is a marvelous book by a classmate of Deleuze, a great writer, and it's a pity he isn't better known. Deleuze was also very interested in American literature, which he saw in the same way that Sartre and Beauvoir saw American literature, as this on-the-road liberatory set of expressions, written against the law and against the state. So all of those are very interesting, but the major thing that comes out of that is his work on the painter Francis Bacon, which I think is a monumental contribution to a whole new set of categories to work with. But that shows you that when Deleuze sets himself to something like that, he completely reinvents it. And I suppose you could list under that side of Deleuze his two books on film, *Cinema 1* and *2*, which are an extraordinary rewriting of the whole canon of films from the silent era onward and a reorganization of them in a way which ought to completely transform film studies, if it were allowed to be part of academic film studies, which has not always, I think, been on the cards.

Each of these things is going to involve a new vocabulary. So these separate works should be kept separate, and yet each one has its own vocabulary, its own set of neologisms, its own new terminology. He doesn't forget each completely; he will use some of an earlier vocabulary later on, and some of it he will discard, which is also very interesting, when a term fails to reappear in Deleuze. So each work is a field in its own right, a terminological field, and demands a separate reading and apprenticeship.

In the interview, when he says he forgets about everything he has written, he still seems to be a modernist, in the sense that he is pursuing the new. The new is the great category in Deleuze. Why bother if you can't make something new out of it? In that sense, he would probably refuse the idea of a postmodern staging by saying that he is making each of these philosophers new. At any rate, the one allegiance that he holds throughout all of these things is to Spinoza. He wrote two books on Spinoza: one is a technical work, *Expressionism in Philosophy*; another is a popular work called *Spinoza: Practical Philosophy*. You can say that Bergson and Nietzsche are also constants, but I think not quite so much. So that's something we have to take into account. The constantly returning part of Spinoza has to do with his notion of the body and of the relationship of bodies to each other. Its appeal is partly based on this drive toward materialism that is present in all these philosophies, but it is a drive toward expression, since everything in the body has its equivalent. For Spinoza, God has several modes of appearance, and you can call them "attributes." One is bodies, and the other is thought. Extension and thought are very Cartesian categories, but in Spinoza they are the same, even as they remain different in some way. So our thoughts are like bodies, our bodies like thoughts, but there is no relationship to them except insofar as they are the same. And then there are modes of these various things, the objects, the thoughts. There is also a doctrine of affects that I'll get to later. But I think Deleuze saw in Spinoza a way of keeping his practice of philosophical distinctions while understanding it as a bodily matter.

What is Deleuze's philosophy all about? I think that, ultimately, there is a classic politics of subversion or anarchism in Deleuze, if you want to put it that way. All these people, in one way or another, are obsessed with transgression. I don't think that Deleuze ever wrote much on Bataille. He would have been capable of it, but I don't think he did. One philosopher he never wrote much about—thank goodness—is Heidegger. There are all kinds of references to Heidegger in *Difference and Repetition*, but Heidegger, this obsession with Heidegger in France at the time, this absolute necessity to quote him on every page, to come back over and over to these rather simple thoughts, is completely absent from Deleuze, so we don't have to worry about that. But subversion, in the Kristevan sense of the semiotic bursting into the symbolic and transgressing it and transforming it, is at work here in a different form. The late form is this: it is a historical form, the historical myth of the state and the nomads. This is the fundamental political vision of Deleuze. You have the state, the establishment, so to speak. The establishment will be assailed by groups of nomads. Sometimes, they conquer the state, as in China, and they become the state. When they are the state, others become nomads. Sometimes, they are repulsed, sometimes destroyed, but new ones emerge, and this is—as I think it is for anarchism more generally—a cyclical, never-ending process. There never is an ultimate revolution. The anarchists don't want to produce a new state, and they don't want to produce a new society. They just want some kind of freedom against this social order, and they want to destroy it. I remember that, toward the end of his life, Hayden White was very interested in the anarchists. He says that when you have all these uprisings, the state then finally asks them what they want. "What is your program? What can we give you?" And they respond, "Oh, we don't want anything! We just want to destroy everything." In a sense, that's the spirit of the nomads.

But the point about a nomad is that a nomad has no place. Do the nomads have their own laws? Well, the minute they do, the state emerges again. So here we have the whole problem of power that we saw emerging in anthropology at an earlier moment. There is a question of power in

Deleuze, the question of establishment, normalization, just as it concerned everybody else, Barthes, Foucault. Yet, here, it takes a mythic form in two books that I haven't mentioned yet, which are part of his collaboration with Guattari, *Anti-Oedipus* and *A Thousand Plateaus*. These two books belong together, but they are quite different in some ways. It's always hard to know how the psychology of collaboration works; it's an interesting but rare thing. Sometimes, when novelists collaborate, one writes the plot, the other writes the dialogue. One never knows what form this takes with Deleuze and Guattari. What we're told is that they would meet and each bring stuff they had read—all kinds of stuff, from student papers all the way to obscure articles on linguistics or zoology—and they would share all these things with each other. Then they go away, read some more, and come back together. And, finally, at one point, Deleuze says, *Ça suffit comme ça.* "Stop." And he sits down and writes it all up.

I used to think you could always tell them apart. There are great tirades against Freud in the *Anti-Oedipus*; I used to think, "Oh, that must be Guattari." Guattari was a so-called anti-psychiatrist. In the '60s, there was a whole group of these people who drew on things like Foucault's notion of the clinic as an institution for normalization. Ronald Laing was the name of the most famous English anti-psychiatrist who rebelled against all this stuff and who, interestingly for us, among his other works, produced an abridgement, if that's possible for a book of 800 very difficult pages, of Sartre's *Critique of Dialectical Reason*, a 200-page summary of it. What was Sartre doing in the middle of all this? In a sense, Sartre's *Critique* is also a theory of anarchism, of small groups, of nomads. Sartre's groups-in-fusion are nomads. Seriality is not exactly the state, which is presumed to be around there somewhere, but doesn't require a theory, because it just comes into being all by itself. But the groups that resist it, groups-in-fusion, are nomads already in Sartre, and he doesn't get beyond that, really, any more than he gets beyond individual consciousness, that is, the limits of phenomenology and the *cogito*, so we never get really to capitalism; we only get to Stalin, who represents the transformation of the nomads into the state. So Laing's intuition that this is a study of a collective way of resisting the state was an appropriate one.

Anyway, Guattari is one of those anti-psychiatrists. He works in a clinic. He is a psychiatrist, or an analyst who deals with sick people, but with all kinds of other resistances, attempts to transform the institution, to transform the teachings of psychoanalysis. But, obviously, Guattari was also a political activist, something Deleuze was not. You know that Kant never set foot outside of Königsberg. He never traveled anywhere outside that Prussian city in the far east. Deleuze went back and forth to his seminars, huge seminars at the end, but one has the sense that he never left his apartment. I mean that Deleuze has a closed space in which he is separate from everybody else, and the point has been made over and over again that he was a real outsider. Because he taught philosophy for a living, he had to be part of an academic institution and have a student public of sorts—Foucault was a great help to him in his promotions, his academic assignments—but, in a sense, he was outside of all that. He didn't want to belong to anything, certainly not to politics.

You know the famous remark of Oscar Wilde. Wilde wrote one of the great works on socialism, "The Soul of Man under Socialism," in which he evolved a theory, which is quite wonderful: "I'm not a socialist because I feel sorry for the poor. In fact," he says, "I don't *want* to feel sorry for the poor! It's a horrible feeling. I want to get rid of the situation in which I have to feel sorry for the poor. I want to make a situation in which I don't have to feel sorry for anybody, and this is why I'm a socialist." In any case, Guattari was a militant in that sense. I don't say he brought Marx to Deleuze, but soon there will be a very important intervention of Deleuze into Marxism. We're told that at the end of his life—as with Derrida's book on Marx in an atmosphere of French de-Marxification and the utter end of the Left in France—Deleuze also was planning to write a book on Marx, but I think we have no trace of that, unless that one essay, "Societies of Control," was supposed to be a chapter, as some of his disciples have said.

So Guattari brought a lot of things to Deleuze, including an engagement with psychoanalysis, and he brought an activist's relationship to the world that I think Deleuze, purely as a philosopher or as an aesthetician, didn't have. We have some notes on their collaboration now, and they're interesting, biographically, but it was, for Deleuze, obviously a very great, very important experience to have run into Guattari and in a sense to have meshed in this dualism. You notice how often they say "we." That is not an impersonal "we," not the royal "we." It's the collaborative "we." So Guattari made it possible, I think, for Deleuze to solve this problem of individual consciousness and authorship, and to make it somehow an impersonal thing which was neither the one subjectivity or the other, but something else.

So these two books are where I'm going to start with Deleuze, because I think that most of the terms that we get from Deleuze come from the first of the two. The dual work is called *Capitalism and Schizophrenia*, but nobody really uses that title, even if they choose to read them together. They are very different in spirit. *A Thousand Plateaus* is much more popular, because it's divided, as some of you know, into chapters to which fantastic dates have been attached. So a chapter on semiotics will include "587 BC" in its title. What does it mean? Does it have any significance? It certainly has a significance for what it implies about history and historical narrative. But anything else? I haven't found any study—I'm sure people have tried to do it—which accounts for all these dates, but it would be interesting to do.

I'll take *A Thousand Plateaus* first, because it seems to be a stand-alone book. It has an opening piece on the rhizome. One of you said it was not a good idea to start this set of readings with the rhizome. I agree, but it was there. Everybody knows about it. I think we have to take it into account. It may be a false methodology, but it is certainly interesting. Then there is a long, mythic narrative in which Deleuze—for convenience, from now on, I'll simply call the collaborators "Deleuze"—borrows a character from Arthur Conan Doyle, Professor Challenger, and attributes to him a whole new set of ideas about stratification that are extremely complex. And, after that, we get into a series of different monographs on all kinds of topics. We talked about literature and painting. There is one on music, on the ritornello, or the refrain. One on face-ness. And then, finally, at the very end, we get to the myth of nomads and the state, the Nomadology, as that section is called. But those can be read separately, which, in part, has made it the more popular book.

Anti-Oedipus, however, the first volume of *Capitalism and Schizophrenia*, seems to have a more focused intent, if you like, and that is the critique of psychoanalysis. It is certainly very interesting that *Anti-Oedipus* should come out in '72. It partakes of all the disillusioned energies of its moment, and as its title suggests, it is against Oedipus. Œdipe, in French theoretical jargon, means the Oedipus complex. So this work is really against the Oedipus complex, "anti-" in the famous sense of the *Anti-Dühring* of Engels. Why is this against the Oedipus complex? Because, as I told you, Freud indoctrinated his patients and taught them that all the things they felt could be traced back to this original trauma with the father and the mother, the fear of castration, and all the rest of it. I don't like the word "reductive," because it's used all the time in stupid ways, but, in this case, it is absolutely what they mean: Freudian psychoanalysis is reductive of your experience. It reduces everything to the family triangle: mommy, daddy, and the child. It makes you rewrite all your own experience in terms of that triangle.

After all, remember that Freudian analysis is one long rewriting of your biography, of your identity as you see it. This and that happened to you, which is why you are the way you are, and you hold it against so-and-so, your mother or your father, and you carry that resentment through your life. Soon, we will see what that means for Deleuze and for Spinoza. But, for now, you are impoverishing your life by this form of what Spinoza calls "the sad passions." That means you spend your whole life in this effectively infantile situation. Remember Dora. Dora said simply, "No, I'm not in love with my father, and goodbye," and walked out of Freud's office. So Freud is, in this book, caricatured as the villain who tries to take away everything about our experience except this infantile drama. With Lacan they're a little more circumspect, because they admire Lacan, but they are also a little nervous, because you don't quite attack Lacan in the same way, at least not in that period. In a way, they hang onto everything that Freud discovered, but by getting rid of Freud. It is *Hamlet* without the prince, psychoanalysis without Freud. Wilhelm Reich is also a major figure in this work, the great champion of an early Freudo-Marxism, in which, like Fanon later, neurosis is connected to the social situation and social oppression, so in a sense, those parts are preserved. But the attempt is to sort of loosen up this connection, which is, for them, a kind of interpretation.

Okay, in that sense, *Anti-Oedipus* is against interpretation, very much, I think, along the lines of Susan Sontag's famous essay, in which she says that people are always interpreting things that ought to be taken aesthetically, as objects, as language. I think that's something very close to Deleuze, for whom interpretation always means to substitute one thing for another. There is a surface of things and then something behind it, the true meaning or essence of the work, which requires substituting that true essence for the false one. This is the model of the dual surfaces, the dual hermeneutics, the signifier and the signified, which reintroduces what Derrida calls "the transcendental signified," namely, a signifier in the sense of meaning, the meaning hidden behind the work; it reintroduces a bad kind of herme-neutics, which can also be considered reductive. As they say in a famous passage—I think I quote it somewhere—they don't want to know what a thing means; they want to know how it works.[2]

So that leads us to this famous "plane of immanence." The plane of immanence is a space in which nothing is hidden, in which the meanings are in the things themselves. It sounds like phenomenology, actually, and I think Husserl was certainly after immanence as much as anybody. But they refuse his imprisonment in a Cartesian kind of consciousness, a philosophy of the subject. At that point, we get a new set of heroes. What would ethical existence be if you weren't caught up in reductivism, if you somehow used these psychiatric classifications, schizophrenia or paranoia? Here, they raise the question of fascism. Fascism is paranoia. In the '60s, there was a whole return of the problem of fascism, in the sense that I think no one had realized the degree to which fascism was an ongoing reality. Nazism, perhaps not. As Adorno's famous letter said, there are no Nazis left in Germany. But in Italy, and, of course, in Spain, fascist political forms were certainly not dead. So-called terrorism came out of this too. It became clear that something about Nazism really appealed to the working classes, that is, that it was not only the fault of the Communist Party, the failure of socialism in Germany, but it was a positive appeal of fascism to the masses that made the first years of Hitler's rule almost a unanimous

---

2   "The unconscious poses no problem of meaning, solely problems of use. The question posed by desire is not 'What does it mean?' but rather '*How does it work?*' . . . [The unconscious] represents nothing, but it produces. It means nothing, but it works. Desire makes its entry with the general collapse of the question 'What does it mean?' No one has been able to pose the problem of language except to the extent that linguists and logicians have first eliminated meaning; and the greatest force of language was only discovered once a *work* was viewed as a machine, producing certain effects, amenable to a certain use. Malcolm Lowry says of his work: it's anything you want it to be, so long as it works—'It works too, believe me, as I have found out'—a machinery. But on condition that meaning be nothing other than use, that it become a firm principle only if we have at our disposal *immanent criteria* capable of determining the legitimate uses, as opposed to the illegitimate ones that relate use instead to a hypothetical meaning and re-establish a kind of transcendence." Gilles Deleuze and Félix Guattari, *Anti-Oedipus*, trans. Robert Hurley, Mark Seem, and Helen R. Lane (New York: Viking, 1977), 109; quoted in Fredric Jameson, *The Political Unconscious: Narrative as a Socially Symbolic Act* (Ithaca, NY: Cornell University Press, 1981), 22. "From our present standpoint, however, the ideal of an immanent analysis of the text, of a dismantling or deconstruction of its parts and a description of its functioning and malfunctioning, amounts less to a wholesale nullification of all interpretive activity than to a demand for the construction of some new and more adequate, immanent or anti-transcendent hermeneutic model, which it will be the task of the following pages to propose." Fredric Jameson, *The Political Unconscious*, 23.

adherence of the society to Hitlerism. So it needed to be explained in other ways, and psychoanalysis needed to be harnessed to this explanation of fascism, and, in fact, a whole flock of different books arose on this subject. Adorno pioneered this book on the authoritarian personality; I somehow feel that it was not his greatest effort. It was a collective effort, in any case. But there were other ones. This is also Deleuze and Guattari's intervention: the appeal of paranoia. But it's very Sartrean, too, in the sense that, in Sartre, even though freedom is an ideal, everything that you choose, you choose completely and are completely responsible for, and therefore each of these choices is an absolute: there is an absolute of fascism, like an absolute of the Left or an absolute of anarchism, which is to be acknowledged in its own way.

So we have paranoia as a projective fascism, perversion as the creation of a "secret garden" of your own, so to speak, and then we have schizophrenia, which is extremely important for Deleuze and Guattari. What is schizophrenia? It is a breakdown of the signifying chain. Lacan saw it as the projection of language outside of the psyche—not a word he would have used—a *forclusion*, a foreclosure within your world as a projection outside of your world. It is a breakdown of identity and of continuity, so that, as we'll see a little later, Nietzsche in his final, delirious letters, he will say, "I am all the names of history. I'm Heliogabalus. I'm Julius Caesar. I'm Christ," because, after all, what we call our identity is molded by the past, by the way we see ourselves in a certain continuity of development, the way we attach our childhood to our present. If historical continuities break down, then there is nothing but an absolute present.

In this first volume of Deleuze and Guattari, the hero is the ideal schizophrenic who lives completely in the present. He gives some examples, literary illustrations of how "the schizo," as he says, fulfills this absolute ideal of living completely in the present, of being hampered neither by a past, some Freudian version of what your family did to you, nor by a future that could be tainted by utilitarianism, or in other words, questions of why to do certain things and what their consequences would be. Instead, there is a complete identification with the present. Deleuze later regretted their choice of this psychiatric language, because he saw what was happening to his students, not just with drugs, with all kinds of other things. But, for the moment, the schizo represents a certain kind of freedom in Deleuze, the utopian figure against whom you would judge all these other political and personal situations. At that point, having established this alternative norm—because it is a kind of ideal norm—the opposition of the schizo versus the paranoiac will become the nomad versus the state. The nomad is a collective category, maybe like a collective schizophrenia, but that idea only emerges in *A Thousand Plateaus*. Yet the idea is not dissimilar, particularly if you factor the business of the oppression of the clinical institutions into this language. Then you get something quite congenial to Guattari as an anti-psychiatrist.

This is the moment in which, all of a sudden, they stop to reconstruct a version of Marx's pre-capitalist forms. This is, I think, their great contribution to Marxism, in which the three areas—tribal society, or hunters and gatherers, oriental despotism, or the empire, and finally capitalism—are all re-read in terms of the language of the *Anti-Oedipus*. You have already read "How Do We Recognize Structuralism?" which was very important to Althusser, at least in the beginning. This section on pre-capitalist forms is similar in its analysis of capitalism, and I thought that we would save these more diachronic stories for next time, that series of modes of production in which Deleuze, very uncharacteristically, deals with change and writes what we would call a historical narrative of some kind. It's not that these things are non-narrative, but they are somehow distinct, since the point of view of the schizo is that of the absolute present. So there is change, but it is change in the present. You remember that one of the basic moments in *A Thousand Plateaus* is what Deleuze calls "becoming-animal." That is this perpetual set of changes. In a sense, the heroism of the schizo is replaced by the becoming of the becoming-animal, the becoming of anything else.

I should say that, if you wanted to see Deleuze in action, there is a marvelous, quite long interview conducted by his students and collaborators. It's called *L'Abécédaire de Gilles Deleuze*, in which the students pick out themes for him to perform, from *animal*, A; *boisson* is B, "drink," in which he talks about F. Scott Fitzgerald and alcoholism. It is subtitled now in English, and it's quite a wonderful, interesting experience. But it is segmentary and not a continuous argument. You can see that his work is segmentary, in that sense, and we'll see what that is when we come back to the *Anti-Oedipus*. Maybe we should do that right now.

The most enigmatic of all Deleuzean categories is the body without organs. This is one of the principal concepts that emerges from the language of the *Anti-Oedipus*, and it will linger around. He draws the idea from another writer who has been especially important in this book, an actor named Antonin Artaud, whom you can see in the great silent epic of

Abel Gance on Napoleon. He became very famous. He left Europe, went
to Mexico, lived with the Tarahumara Tribe, took all kinds of *stupéfiants*.
He was in a clinic in Rodez where Van Gogh lived and died. Then he
came back to Paris. He had a whole theory of the theater that he called
"the theater of cruelty," the return to the body in staging. He gave a very
famous talk called *Pour en finir avec le jugement de Dieu*, "Let's Finish
Off the Idea of God," a great, delirious monologue, of which there exists
a recording. The body without organs was a delirious idea from this talk
of Artaud's, and there is a great deal of disagreement about what it means,
whether it always means the same thing, or whether it means anything at
all. I want to see it as another version of the synchronic, in the sense that
it has to do with relationships, inscriptions, in a kind of present of time.
Normally, we're not even aware of our organs unless we're sick or we have
a pain. This pain is the outsider, the organ, the code. The clinicians have
made a map of the body and its normality. That is a different kind of body,
a blank body, one with no organs, but it is a space, he will say—and this
is also the language of the *Anti-Oedipus*—a space of inscription, in which
all kinds of things get coded or inscribed. The codes are the paths of the
hunters and gatherers, the places animals come to drink, the thickets
where we can find rare plants for healing.

Now I'm going to jump to a different figure. In many ways, the body
without organs is like a rhizome in which all kinds of unlikely things
come together as in the relationship of signifiers. All these weird things
come together—the flower and the bee. Some of you quoted that passage;
it comes from Proust, actually, where, somehow, one order of the world,
the order of plants, has something to do with another order, the order of
entomology and the evolution of bees.[3] What is that? What are these
connections between all these random things? Isn't the fly connected
to the spider and the web? And what is the relationship of these things
to each other? This is another term, this one Guattari's: transversality.
Normally, you think of some bunch of things over there as an academic
specialty, and this bunch of things over here as a separate one, and so on.
"Transversality" means some unexpected crossing in which those things
get connected, in which something proves to be a bee and something else
proves to be a flower.

---

3   "The orchid does not reproduce the tracing of the wasp; it forms a map with the
wasp, in a rhizome." Gilles Deleuze and Félix Guattari, *A Thousand Plateaus*, trans. Brian
Massumi (Minneapolis, MN: University of Minnesota Press, 1987), 12.

And, here, arises something called the "desiring-machines." It is certainly very interesting how it doesn't matter to him whether he uses a mechanical term or an organic image like a rhizome, itself opposed to the tree, which has normally been thought to be the very image of the Aristotelian order of progression from the universal to the particular, whereas the rhizome is like a potato that just sends its roots out in all directions. I don't know if you know what a Rube Goldberg machine is. These are crazy machines that have various parts attached to them that have nothing to do with each other but that grow in all directions. That is an image of the desiring-machine. It has parts. One thing leads to another, but very improbably. There is nothing normative in the connections. Here, you have something rather different from the normal idea of desire. In the desiring-machine, a whole cluster of things are stuck together—a little notion of something from the Aztecs, for example, and then some modern medicine that you know something about, and you tie all these things together so that they become your private chain of signifiers, as Lacan might call it.

But the best way of understanding the desiring-machine is to understand it in the context of Deleuze's polemic, which is that desire is not based on lack. It is not negative. At this point, I want to come back to dualisms in Deleuze. He is supposed to be against dualisms, and yet he is profoundly dualistic. How do we deal with that? After all, *Difference and Repetition* is one long attack on Plato, Hegel, idealism, the negative, and negativity. Evidently, Deleuze always likes to have an other. Deleuze is the philosopher of differentiation. You think you see one idea here? No, no. Two ideas. He is always cutting apart, hairsplitting these cognitive objects and leading you in all kinds of directions. So he practices differentiation in a dualistic, binary way, and yet he wants to get rid of binarism, to get out of it through a constant movement toward the new. I think we'll have to come back to that next time.

April 6, 2021

22

Joyousness of Gilles Deleuze

{Deleuze}

What I want to do today is to put some content into these discussions of Deleuze, but, first, it is important to get a few things straight. I have said I am very reluctant to turn this into a system, but, obviously, he has something systematic to say. Some of you claim this philosophical language is metaphorical. Yes, in a way, but, in another way, his notion of strata, or plateaus, is not exactly one of homology. Is it allegorical? In a way, yes, if we reintroduce into allegory Guattari's notion of transversality, which is a way of shooting across these different levels or strata. In any case, once he gets going with strata, which you find in the third chapter, "The Geology of Morals"—not "genealogy"—there is a horrendously complicated account of strata and how they double and redouble, a brilliant set-piece that we don't necessarily have to worry about. But the main reason this is not metaphorical is that metaphor requires a system of language, a system of reality, and the ability to shift from one to the other. The nice thing about this stage in French philosophy is that everybody has understood what will come to be called correlationism: we have the subject and the object, and we can't talk about the one without the other. At any rate, modern philosophy has been caught on the horns of this dilemma: idealism and materialism. Now it seems to me that the choice being made in modern French theory, once it comes up against phenomenology—which is the final, strongest statement of a way of posing consciousness as a center without making it into an object and thereby imprisoning it within its own limits—is to account for a movement in which it is necessary to stop talking about the subject and the object and to start talking about movements which are common to both.

In Deleuze, for example, there is a dualism of the smooth and the striated. Those concepts expand until they become general rhythms of the universe. It is immaterial whether they pertain to human consciousness or to the world of things. At that point, they are beyond any question of the metaphorical. This shows that in Deleuze you are dealing with a fluid matter where you can never rely on this distinction between subject and object. One or the other could be there or could not be there. This is why these statements are not metaphorical. That is to say, this philosophical language may be an object or may be a thought in subjectivity, whereas metaphor, on the other hand, implies a rigid or fixed categorization of the relationship of language to reality, such that there must be a literal language which is separate from a language of the tropes or the deformations, one of which is metaphor. That would entail doing something to literal language, which is at one with things. No, that kind of language has no place in this Heraclitean world of becoming of Deleuze and Guattari. And that's why, unlike a lot of very metaphorical writers, this really is about reality. You really cannot discard these connections because they are mere tropological decorations that can be stripped away to find out what is really going on, as in Wittgenstein. You can't do that. This is sometimes about forms of thought, sometimes about reality. Anyway, that would be an answer to the question of whether this work is metaphorical.

So we are in a world beyond the subject-object distinction, because any distinction for Deleuze must be made within this area which he calls "the plane of immanence." What is the plane of immanence? Immanence in philosophy, if we're using it technically, is the opposite of transcendence. The transcendent, as Kant says, are the things that are beyond the categories of the understanding, some ultimate reality that we can't reach. There is always a question about what is transcendent. Remember the Sartrean distinction: to transcend, in the older language of Sartre, is simply to be an object of consciousness; everything transcends consciousness because consciousness isn't anything. But, for Deleuze, transcendence means something which is set outside of immediacy or experience. For example, interpretation would imply transcendence. I have a text here, and I'm going to say what it means. The meaning isn't there in the text, so it is transcendent to the text. To be immanent to the text might imply so-called surface reading. Immanence is only what is there. But for them, everything is there.

The illustration I've wanted to use is a film by Nicholas Ray. I don't know if any of you still see Nicholas Ray's films, but they are quite delirious. In this one, a character goes berserk and is yelling all kinds of things, racist rants. He is the father of one of the other characters. How do we understand this? This is obviously a mishmash of attitudes. We get the Oedipus complex, racism, sexism, and each of them is a separate cause that feeds into this delirium. For Deleuze and Guattari, no, there aren't any external causes; it is all there on the surface, on the plane of immanence.[1] We don't want to reduce it the way the Freudians do. Hume is the one who challenges causality. He says that there is something in the here and now, but other philosophers are saying that the cause is something that was in this world ten minutes ago but is no longer in this world, or only in the form of this effect. No, he says, that is imaginary. The notion of a cause is imaginary, and that is why the word "effect" will be a keyword, not only in Deleuze but also in Althusser. Effects include causes. Otherwise, the cause is transcendent to the effect. Deleuze will call his Humeanism "transcendental empiricism," which refers to Kant's transcendental, rather than the transcendent. So the word "effect," which is also a Spinozan word, is going to soak up all those transcendences and try to be complete in itself.

I think the great motto of Deleuze's project can be found in Pascal's religious meditation, where he has Jesus say, "You wouldn't look for me if you hadn't already found me." If you want to believe, that is the sign

---

1   The film that they and Jameson refer to is Nicholas Ray's *Bigger Than Life* (1956). "Perhaps cinema is able to capture the movement of madness, precisely because it is not analytical and regressive, but explores a global field of coexistence. Witness a film by [Nicholas] Ray, supposedly representing the formation of a cortisone delirium: an overworked father, a high-school teacher who works overtime for a radio-taxi service and is being treated for heart trouble. He begins to rave about the educational system *in general*, the need to restore a pure *race*, the salvation of the social and moral *order*, then he passes to *religion*, the timeliness of a return to the Bible, Abraham. But what in fact did Abraham do? Well now, he killed or wanted to kill his son, and perhaps God's only error lies in having stayed his hand. But doesn't this man, the film's protagonist, have a son of his own? Hmm . . . What the film shows so well, to the shame of psychiatrists, is that every delirium is first of all the investment of a field that is social, economic, political, cultural, racial and racist, pedagogical, and religious: the delirious person applies a delirium to his family and his son that overreaches them on all sides" (Deleuze and Guattari, *Anti-Oedipus*, 274).

that you already believe. This is Deleuze's notion of desire. He says that desire is not a lack. It is not something you feel here because you want this absent object over there. No, it is complete in itself. The notion of lack is bad, just as negativity itself is bad. All of this is contained in desire. That could make one think of the Sartrean notion of immanence, in which what you want in desire is not an object; you want the *desire* for the object. In other words, desire has its own meaning and rationale, and it has its own satisfaction, and that may be a satisfaction which does not include what one would normally call the satisfaction of desire. It doesn't mean you attain the desired object, because what you actually want is to desire that object. So Deleuze has an immanent notion of desire, and, in a sense, that could also be considered as a body without organs, if you like, because the object and its connections are no longer external to desire. When Hemingway writes, he must first sharpen a dozen pencils. Is this a phallic symbol? No, Deleuze says, there is something special for him in the pencil, the productive instrument. It is a part of writing even though it hasn't written anything yet. It is part of that world, that particular plane of immanence, which is Hemingway's satisfaction, although Deleuze doesn't use that Hegelian term.

For Deleuze, this notion of desire entails either Nietzschean force or Spinozan feeling, so we move from the plane of immanence to a certain kind of ethics. Why is Spinoza's book called the *Ethics*? It is all about cosmology, God, human feelings. Why ethics? Because he tells us how to live. In a way, so does Deleuze. Over and over again he tells you, "Don't do this. That's a bad concept. Do it this way. We believe in this." The "we," remember, is the place of abolished individuality. There is a nice story—"nice"—about the purge trials that I feel I must include here. In the purge trials in the '30s in the Soviet Union, all kinds of people are being arrested. One of Stalin's old friends comes to see him and says, "Koba, what's going on? This is crazy. They just arrested my nephew." And Stalin says, "What can I do about this? They're doing this to my family too! It's the will of Stalin." "But you're Stalin," says Stalin's friend. "I'm not Stalin," says Stalin. "The will of Stalin is up above all of us." And, of course, that was the great phrase in the Soviet Union. Whenever anything happens in the Soviet Union, it's the will of Stalin. So Stalin is not a person; the will of Stalin is impersonal, just as the "we" is impersonal, even as it is telling you what to do. In that sense, since I have been talking about dualism—I apologize for making so many interconnections among these ideas, but it is certainly Deleuzean in spirit—that's why the binary is so important. You have to start with it to get out of it. Deleuze is the great differentiator, I said. But he needs something to begin with. So you begin with the binary. Smooth and striated. Molar and molecular. Any number of binaries run through this work, and the whole thing is unthinkable without them, because his next move is to say that one of these binaries is itself composed of a binary, and so on. Suddenly, we find ourselves in something much more complicated than a static opposition. We must begin with the binary to overcome it, although that is a rather dialectical way of saying it, and he wouldn't like us to use such a dialectical expression.

Let's go back to ethics. I think, for Nietzsche, the main point of ethics cannot turn on a master-slave relationship, which could turn out to be fascist. Rather, it must be a question of power, which could also be fascist. In French, you have two words for "power": *pouvoir* and *puissance*. It is a distinction Foucault makes all the time, but it has been pointed out that he only uses the one word, *pouvoir*. In Deleuze, this works a little bit differently. *Pouvoir* implies the state, laws, the police, and so on. *Puissance* is the feeling of power, of centrality. This is what Nietzsche means by "strength": Your decisions irradiate from you and are *active*, whereas, if you don't have this strength, everything you do is *reactive* and is based on your way of dealing with power, *puissance*. You don't have *puissance*. You define yourself as having no *puissance*. Could we use the terms of center and margin again? Yes, in some sense. I am the center of my being as someone strong, whereas, if I'm weak, I have to think about these people whom I hate, who are above me; I have to constantly react to everybody else and what they're doing. For Nietzsche, the exemplar of the reactive personality is the person of *ressentiment*. *Ressentiment* is the feeling of reaction.

So Deleuze is going to combine that idea—or to discover that Nietzsche has already done so—with Spinoza's system, which is very similar. In Spinoza, you must start with the reactive personality, but Spinoza's idea of reaction is much broader. It includes what he calls the "sad passions." These are the passions of what I think one could call the negative, although that's not a very Deleuzean term, and they include *ressentiment*. Is *ressentiment* then to be identified with sadness itself? I think certain depressions could be forms of *ressentiment*. Let's take the most dramatic example: suicides that are committed as a way of getting back at somebody else. That is the ultimate sad passion and the height of Nietzschean *ressentiment*. Often, in

Spinoza, "sad" means the reaction of Spinoza, of the wise person, to these passions. Why are people wasting their lives doing this to themselves?

What is the opposite of the sad passions? It is joy. You find throughout Deleuze that joy means the sense of *puissance*, of being the center of my feelings. Spinoza wouldn't talk in quite those terms, and he doesn't use the language of strength and weakness, but joy would be what I feel when I'm liberated from the sad passions. So there is a gamut here of what is today called "affects," but it ends in a different place. I think affect theory has emerged, at least in the United States, around notions of depression and trauma. What is the opposite of those? Somehow, melancholy becomes its own opposite. There isn't any way out of it, because, if you are not melancholy, then you are smug or somehow oblivious to your condition. Your optimism is worthless. But, in Spinoza, optimism and pessimism are not the significant measures of feeling. It would be the joyous relationship to the world or to God, which is nature, as opposed to this constant *ressentiment*, which informs the sad passions.

So it is important to understand the way in which, for Deleuze, this is meant to affirm a certain kind of ethics or a certain kind of being. "In Nietzsche's terminology the reversal of values means the active in place of the reactive (strictly speaking, it is the reversal of a reversal, since the reactive began by taking the place of action). But [the transvaluation] of values"—that's Nietzsche's slogan, beyond good and evil—"means affirmation instead of negation—negation transformed into a power of affirmation, the supreme Dionysian metamorphosis."[2] This is a part of the doctrine of the eternal return. What is the eternal return in Nietzsche? It is a kind of law, like the categorical imperative: you must act as though this present were going to return and return and return forever. You must choose this present, in a sense. This is, then, the affirmation of the present or of life. As opposed to what most of us would think about the eternal return, namely how boring it would be, as in the *Groundhog Day* phenomenon. That's the opposite of what Nietzsche had in mind, but it would certainly bring us to the question of repetition—very complicated in Deleuze—and I'm afraid we don't have time for that, because I want to get on to notions of history in Deleuze.

After all, this work is all about becoming. None of these states is permanent. It is the opposite of the eternal return. Everything is to be new.

---

2   Gilles Deleuze, *Nietzsche and Philosophy*, trans. Hugh Tomlinson, in *The Deleuze Reader*, ed. Constantin V. Boundas (Columbia University Press, NY: 1993), 93.

We want to produce new concepts, new images, new sounds, new philosophies. So that is becoming. Is it a becoming which is just "one damn thing after another," as in Henry Ford's definition of history? On the contrary, it is what he will come to call "continuous variation," and it will define his thoughts on the theater, which turn on an Italian actor and director named Carmelo Bene. He talks about all the arts in one of the books of interviews. We'll come to music in a moment, but of course one of the great theories of modern music involves continuous variation, variation without an original, namely Schoenberg's. Variations without an original: this could very well identify the position of Deleuze. Everything is becoming, variation. What Deleuze provides for us are not copies or variations on a given philosophical theme.

Some of you thought that the notion of becoming-animal was metaphorical, because we don't become animals. In contemporary culture, I suppose it isn't the werewolf so much as the vampire or the zombie that has interested people. But the theme of becoming is present in popular culture, particularly in a situation in which nobody becomes anything and everybody is imprisoned in their identities in our rigidly organized societies. But some of you objected to the language in which becoming is expressed. "Particles," for example. No, of course this doesn't mean that you turn into a dog. You could turn into an insect, as in Kafka, but you're not going to become a dog. Rather, some of the particles of dogness will infiltrate your particles, and you mingle with them. Isn't that a metaphor? Simply think of the physiological analysis of the sense of smell. It really does involve physical particles, although it's horrible to think so. A beautiful perfume, a horrible smell—each of them means that little particles are going into your nose. Maybe it's not quite so metaphorical after all.

You could say that the whole of Deleuze is about these becomings. Is history then just this constant set of becomings or flows (I prefer the translation "flux," but it doesn't have a good plural in English)? At certain points, Deleuze says that history is the temporal mark of power. There are several remarks which resemble Sartre's last notes to the *Critique*, which argue that History isn't something we want; it's something we want to get out of. History is horrible. Lévi-Strauss says we need never have had history. We could have stayed in the state of tribal societies. Capitalism was an accident that need not have happened. Some of us use History in a very positive way, looking for the historical connections with things, but this is a condemnation of History. It means that the histories we learn are the histories of defeats. If you take this minoritarian view of Deleuze, which is always against power, disciplines, or rigid institution, then, of course, history is a collection of defeats, because the institutional forms have always won out, and they have always organized contingencies into various forms of oppression.

But, nonetheless, there are histories in Deleuze. Shall we say they are local histories? Not exactly. Some of the most obvious of these histories, dualist still, are the film books, *Cinema 1* and *Cinema 2*. The first is about the movement-image, and the second is about the time-image. I think these books represent what in literature we used to call the realist novel and the modernist novel. Realism is the movement-image, because its content is recognizable actions. The time-image, on the other hand, is not actions. It is, somehow, an image. The first kind of film is there to project an action and its destiny. The second one, the modernist one, is there to bring us face to face with something that isn't really an object, namely time itself. This would be like Heidegger saying we meet ontic existence all the time in daily life, and then every so often, behind them, we see their ontological dimension, which is Being itself. So, in a sense, for Deleuze, the time-image is something that is capable of bringing us up against time itself, fleetingly. It will also clearly be Deleuze's plane of immanence. It will be all these strange things that are connected together and will somehow produce this . . . vision? It is not a vision, nor is it a thought. Is it a concept of the film? Film is thinking, Deleuze argues. It is thinking its own kind of concepts.

He goes through hundreds of very interesting but uniquely contingent kinds of films. But, if the second moment of film is so interesting for him, why does he need the first part? It is a binary opposition: Something has to be opposed to it. You might think that if the time-image is good, then the image-movement is not good, right? After all, this is a binary opposition. That's the old, bad, traditional storytelling, representational, realist film. This is the new, good, modernist self-referential film. But Deleuze is never that way, even with Hegel and Plato. He can use them in a polemic, but when he turns his attention to something which is supposed to be bad, this process of differentiation goes to work on it, and it becomes something very interesting. So, in the first volume of the film books, all the great traditional filmmakers are there: Ford, Renoir. Welles is a transitional figure. All the greats are analyzed with impressive results. So it doesn't exactly become good versus bad, but it does operate by differentiation.

How is he going to move from one to the other? This really does seem to be a historical way of approaching film. We used to make films that way; now we make them this way. The watershed is World War II. Sure, but how? Deleuze does not like schemes like this. It is clear that he would react to the language of modernism the same as I've quoted to you from Foucault's reaction. What is this modernism? He doesn't know what it means. This is a vague, worthless historical concept, a "bad concept." Realist film? What is that? Deleuze can't have any theory of realism as such. He deals with what we call realism, but when he is done with it, it doesn't look like our traditional uses of these empty, abstract kinds of universal words. And I think he would be capable of taking all the filmmakers in the first part, the realistic ones, and turning them into modernists, but that's a different matter. The one moment when he has to justify the historical and conceptual passage from one to the other is very interesting.[3] He says that this is the breakdown of action, that we no longer are able to

---

3   "These are the five apparent characteristics of the new image: *the dispersive situation, the deliberately weak links, the* ballade *form, the consciousness of clichés, the condemnation of plot.* It is the crisis of both the action-image and of the American Dream. Everywhere there is a reexamination of the sensory-motor schema; and the Actors Studio becomes the object of severe criticism, at the same time as it undergoes an evolution and internal splits. But how can the cinema attack the dark organisation of clichés, when it participates in their fabrication and propagation, as much as magazines or television? Perhaps the special conditions under which it produces and reproduces clichés allow certain directors to attain a critical reflection which they would not have had at their disposal elsewhere. It is the organisation of the cinema which means that, however great the controls which bear upon him, the creator has at his disposal at least a certain time to 'commit' the irreversible. He has the chance to extract an Image from all the clichés and to set it up against them. On the condition, however, of there being an aesthetic and political project capable of constituting a positive enterprise. Now, it is here that the American cinema finds its limits. All the aesthetic or even political qualities that it can have remain narrowly critical and in this way even less 'dangerous' than if they were being made use of in a project of positive creation. [. . .] As Lawrence said about painting, the rage against clichés, does not lead to much if it is content only to parody them; maltreated, mutilated, destroyed, a cliché is not slow to be reborn from its ashes. In fact, what gave the American cinema its advantage, the fact of being born without a previous tradition to suffocate it, now rebounded against it. For the cinema of the action-image had itself engendered a tradition from which it could now only, in the majority of cases, extricate itself negatively. The great genres of this cinema, the psycho-social film, the *film noir*, the Western, the American comedy, collapse and yet maintain their empty frame. For great creators the path of emigration was thus reversed, for reasons which were not just related to McCarthyism. In fact, Europe had more freedom in this respect; and it is first of all in Italy that the great crisis of the action-image took place. The timing is something like: around 1948, Italy; about 1958 France; about 1968, Germany." Gilles Deleuze, *Cinema 1,*

The Years of Theory

film actions as though they were complete things. Now action is breaking down, and actions become cliches. Here is his Barthesian side. Actions become what in French are called *balades*. *Balade* must be related to our "ballad." It means "stroll," as in aimless wandering, like the *flâneur* in Benjamin. So the film image is no longer about the movements that make up part of an action. They're about wandering around, and what you see as you wander around. Okay, so that's an example, but it situates what has become a very important part of Deleuze's work for you in this whole framework. Otherwise you ask yourself: Why is a philosopher of Kant and Hume going on about film?

Now we move on to the second major historical story that Deleuze tells us, namely the rewriting of Marx's modes of production. If all of these Deleuzian things are commentaries and replays of other philosophers but with masks or maybe even new stagings, then the section of *Anti-Oedipus* on modes of production is his version of Marx, and, in particular, the section of the *Grundrisse* on social formations that precede capitalism. So this section is concerned with older modes of production, and, therefore, it begins with the primitive or the tribal mode of production, hunters and gatherers; then the Asiatic mode of production, which is that of the great empires and the despot. In Marx, the tribal mode of production, "primitive communism," as he calls it, works on the body of the earth. The hunters and gatherers have to somehow make something of their terrain, which is the body of the earth. When we come to the despot, the body of the despot usurps this importance. In Foucault's rendition of the great executions, the criminal has done something to that second body of the king, which is the state. Therefore, the criminal's body must be sacrificed. So the body of the despot is now the center of this empire. Then, in Marx, there is feudalism. People have proposed other modes of production.

In the '60s we saw the anthropologists trying to figure out what power is. Where did power come from? We have power societies, and then somewhere beyond them, more than power, is capitalism, a strange formation of its own. It has plenty of power in it, but it is not feudalism. Marx works with some other formations. But here in Deleuze it is reduced to three forms, which he derives, via Marx, from Lewis Morgan's *Ancient Society*. They are going to be differentiated, I suppose, with respect to the body

trans. Hugh Tomlinson and Barbara Habberjam (Minneapolis, MN: University of Minnesota Press, 1986), 210–211; translation altered.

without organs, because on each there will be an inscription. This is all from the section of *Anti-Oedipus* called "Savagery, Barbarism, Civilization," "civilized" being used, if you like, in an ironic way. *Anti-Oedipus* comes out in '72, appropriately enough. It has its individual doctrine, which opposes the schizo to the paranoid. But what will be the collective equivalent of the schizophrenic? It ought to be, presumably, hunters and gatherers. These other modes of production will be the despotic ones, and then we have capitalism, which is really a decentered mode of production, because in capitalism there is no powerful individual who organizes things or around whom things are organized, but rather it is organized by these weird abstractions, value, circulation, and exchange. Exchange is present in all of them, but in capitalism it becomes absolutely central as a mechanism that no longer needs violence. Hegel's idea of the proper kind of society was a constitutional monarchy with a written constitution and a monarch. But the monarch is an empty place in Hegel. The monarch's only purpose is to exist as a central point. This might sound very Derridean: There has to be a center, but an empty center, because nobody cares who the monarch is. The monarch—but it could be anybody—is going to occupy that central space, and then society will go on its way around it.

This is, as I say, the last book of Deleuze in which this old '60s obsession with writing will play a role. Inscription is still the mechanism through which these changes are measured. It can be found in Lévi-Strauss: tattoos, inscriptions on the body. The hunters and gatherers make inscriptions on the body of the earth, itself a kind of super-body without organs. So what are these inscriptions that constantly appear in *Anti-Oedipus*? Inscription is what Deleuze calls "coding." Initially, to code is to use the primal identities of the earth to produce a contingent, particular form. In Lévi-Strauss's *pensée sauvage*, inscription is something that almost undoes the separation of codes and things, as when there is no abstract word for "leaves" in *pensée sauvage*, so that of the many different kinds of leaves, from fig leaves to poison ivy, one of them—let's say oak leaves—will come to name the set of which it is a set. There are no abstractions in this *pensée sauvage*. The code, like inscription, is something that has no abstraction and that signifies itself. That can be difficult to understand, but once we get to power, it becomes much clearer, because there we see how power society *overcodes* what preceded it. In power society, all these different codes *se rabattent*, fold back into one fundamental language, a sacred language, which is the language of despotism.

So coding begets overcoding. Now what happens with capitalism? Ah! There we shift from codes to axiomatics, another difficult thing to understand. An axiomatic is a code without an original. Let's say all of the codes are borrowed from the natural world. So we could do this in terms of the elements, in terms of water, fire, air, or earth, and those would be the various ways in which the body without organs is coded. In despotism, they all become levels of the same substance. They become forces. Axiomatics, on the other hand, are just given, like numbers. They don't have any symbolic content. The codes and the overcodes seem to have natural foundations, but when you get to the axiomatic, it's like machinery. They have no meaningful essence. Gödel showed that there was no ultimate foundation for Euclidean geometry, for any of these series of axioms in mathematics or physics. They are all open. None of them can finally be founded on anything. That is the disturbing revelation of Gödel's theorem, and it reveals what the axiomatic is. The point about the axiomatic, unlike the codes, is that you can add to it all the time. It's like a law with a codicil. I have a law about something—oops! I've forgotten to include dogs. So I add another axiom having to do with dogs. But I don't want dogs that bite, so I include another axiom saying this does not apply to dogs that bite. So axiomatics become infinitely multiple, but they have no ultimate basis. Capitalism functions this way. It doesn't use codes anymore. It abolishes nature. There aren't any natural elements.

Consider the origins of capitalism. Where does profit come from? It's very funny that, when Locke is trying to set up his bourgeois notions of freedom and representation, his politics, he says that originally everybody owned their own work, but, the minute exchange and money were introduced into society, that original ownership goes out the window. Property supplants all of that. In a way, that is the basis for capitalism to emerge. Property is an axiom that has no meaning in terms of the codes. The despot owned everything, and therefore there wasn't any such notion as property. Property was the emanation of the despot's body, and nothing else in the world is comparable to it, whereas private property began to operate by separating the code from the body. I made this and I own it. You own that. Different individuals own things, but in the axiomatic, the axiom is arbitrary. Here is the return of the arbitrariness of the sign that the structuralists were so fond of. The codes are not arbitrary in the Saussurean sense. They are part and parcel of the things that they are trying to express. As in Cratylus or Heidegger, the words include their own etymologies, their own meanings. But, once we get to capitalism, we're in the realm of the arbitrariness of the sign, which is in constant expansion. You know the rest of it.

To understand this whole new way of thinking about things, Deleuze says, we need a new concept. I think this one comes from Guattari, but it doesn't matter. It is the concept of "territoriality." What is territoriality? Again, I can't completely define it, because its real uses will be its negations and reformulations, but we can begin to see how it is used. It is followed by "deterritorialization" and "reterritorialization." The usefulness of the adjunct concepts will only become apparent when we get that far, but let's start with territoriality. Deleuze has discussed literature, painting, biology, many other things—seemingly everything—but what about music? For music, we turn to the chapter on the refrain. What is the refrain in music? It is a territorializing operation. Imagine the infant coming into the world. There is no center. It simply exists in an unorganized space. It must make a home for yourself in this space. Its first identity is to organize these things around itself so that it feels at home. The first page of Proust: I woke up, and I never knew in the beginning where I was, so I went through all the bedrooms of my life. The way I think of it is like a Disney film. First, you think it was better when you were seven years old, and furniture looked a certain way. Then you think, no, it was best when you were twelve, so all the chairs dance around and restructure themselves into the bedroom you had when you were twelve. Finally, you reach your current age, and, here, they find their places in yet a different arrangement. Territorialization works in this way. In music, the refrain is making that home for yourself in music by territorializing sound through repetition.

What does it mean to have a home? I don't know whether any of you have seen bullfights; maybe you think they are horrible, or maybe you are interested in death, like Hemingway. In a bullfight, the bull emerges out into a world which is completely unfamiliar. The bull must then territorialize this world, so he finds a part of the bull ring—it's arbitrary, because the space is all the same—which will be his terrain. In bullfighting language, this is called the *querencia*, from *querer*. This space belongs to the bull. None of the actors in the bullfight, and especially not the matador, will ever try to get into that place. They have to identify it, because there the bull is supreme. They have to lure it out of its *querencia* in order to fight it in some other place. All of this is in Hemingway's *Death in the Afternoon*, his book on the bullfight. As he says, he was interested in the bullfight because, as a writer, he wanted to know what death was, and the bullfight often results in the deaths of the bulls and also of the matadors. But you can see the usefulness of understanding territorialization as your *querencia*, the way you naturalize, normalize, make your own space, space being understood in the sense of the plane of immanence, that is to say, the connections of all these things. Some are interests or passions; some are objects, tasks, or habits. All that you organize into something which I guess you call your identity, but it isn't your identity; it is your territorialization, and you are caught in it. For the infant, that will be the parents. Why do you think Deleuze and Guattari attack Freud and the Oedipus complex? Who wants to be caught with their parents their whole life? You want to get away from them. Kristeva and Irigaray's description of the mother: You have to get away. You have to deterritorialize.

And now another crucial Deleuzean expression: the line of flight. You must try to invent lines of flight out of your territory, because your territory is going to be taken over by Google, by General Motors, by Coca-Cola. It will lie in the globalized world of the great corporations. It doesn't belong to you anymore. You can try to make a little space that you call your own, and that will be what Deleuze calls your secret garden. That would be covered in this book by the psychiatric term of perversion. That is, it's a uniquely individual, private way of adapting desire so as to make it safe from these other territorializations. But the state is also busy territorializing. This is not just people. The state is busy annexing things and territorializing things and organizing space. If you're caught, as we all are, in these multiple territorializations, then we have to look for lines of flight. It could be interiority. It could simply be physically leaving. *À la fin tu es las de ce monde ancien* (Apollinaire). And then arises the possibility of reterritorialization. When you're out in the unknown, having escaped territoriality, the original deterritorialized space can be reassimilated or a new one territorialized. (Guattari says these distinctions originally came from Sartre's *Critique*.)

This will be the logic of this Deleuzean language, and it can be very useful. Along with these new concepts—we don't have time to talk about them—are the various kinds of logical syntheses. This is a tough part. There are three: the connective synthesis, the disjunctive synthesis, and the conjunctive synthesis. The connective synthesis is easy. It means connecting up bits of yourself with bits of the outside world, making wholes which are not temporary but somehow belong to you in some sense.

Disjunctive syntheses: Those are the things that you have to get rid of, that disgust you or that you have to break with, even though they are part of you. We saw that in Nietzsche and Spinoza: the affirmation that you are not this, not that. So the disjunctive synthesis becomes an important mode of definition as well. And finally the conjunctive synthesis, or what he calls "the nomadic synthesis," because—guess what?—the schizo is free of all this; he doesn't have a territory. He doesn't have anything. He just has the present. So, in this *balade,* this wandering, the schizo is the hero, much more than the *flâneur.* The schizo is like a positive version of Agamben's naked life. Naked life means the reduction to sheer biological existence. You have nothing else. In the Deleuzean formulation, at least in *Anti-Oedipus,* the schizo has something that the rest of us don't have, because he isn't weighed down by anything, whereas the paranoid is trying somehow to annex the world and to create enemies.

So the schizo is the individual hero of Deleuzean ethics, but the collective hero, the political hero, are the nomads that face the collective power of the state and its absolute territorialization. The nomads are able to deterritorialize in a provisional way and attack the state, even though they risk becoming the state, as when the Manchus conquer China. Other outcomes are possible: they can disappear, or they can be seduced into living in one separate enclave. Or they don't appear at all. Maybe you know the marvelous poem of Constantine Cavafy, "Waiting for the Barbarians," where they wait all day, but the barbarians don't arrive. At the end of it he says, "What are we going to do without the barbarians?" At least the barbarians opened up a line of flight, we might say. Everything was going to change with their arrival. But they don't appear. So the nomads constitute a collective level of Deleuze's heroic forces. I think we have to stop with that.

April 8, 2021

23

Return of *le Politique*

{Rancière, Balibar, Nancy}

Today we're going to talk about politics. To be sure, you may say we have always been talking about politics. But there are a few things I wanted to say about Deleuze which are political in a more direct way. First of all, the use of his terminology for understanding Marx. The crucial moment in any Marxist history of the modes of production is the transition to capitalism or the emergence of capitalism. What Deleuze's terminology allows him to say is that the codes bind—and here's a new term that I don't think we've used with Deleuze—"energies." When the codes are unbound and are replaced by the axiomatics of capitalism, certain energies are released. Of course, what he is referring to is land enclosure in England. The agriculturalists and owners at one time found that their profits would be in sheep. In Thomas More's *Utopia* you have the famous, ferocious passage about sheep eating men. At a historical moment, the lands are enclosed, and the peasants are thrown off. They eventually become a part of a generalized proletariat, wandering around very much like Foucault's "ship of fools," available for work in the new factories. As Marx says, the moment of the emergence of capitalism is the explosive meeting between all the treasure accumulated by primitive accumulation—that is to say, by the pirating of the new world, the gold and silver extracted from the great Mayan and Aztec and Incan civilizations—and this floating, deterritorialized population of workers who are made dependent on the wage.

That is one way in which the new vocabulary may or may not add something. Codes have a limit. Codes seem natural. The axiomatic has an arbitrary beginning, and then you add things on. So, if, for example, the Left comes to power and makes a law against certain labor practices, then when the Right comes to power then it adds a new axiomatic. The best axiomatic is the notion that corporations are people. If you have trouble with a legal system that is making its resolutions on behalf of individuals, then you add the new axiomatic that legally a corporation is an individual and therefore has the same rights as other, biological individuals. So the notion of axiomatic allows for this expansion which is inherent in capitalism, because capitalism is subject internally to crises. It can't be a perfect system. In fact, the whole point of it is not to be a perfect system, a system at equilibrium. But with each crisis it expands, and that's the whole point of Marx's theorization in the *Grundrisse*, that capitalism's ultimate limit is the world market, which blocks expansion; that is sort of what we're at now. Anyway, these are a couple ways in which the vocabulary of Deleuze is useful. There's a lot more. So let me put it this way: Deleuze may not be a political thinker—in fact, it may be difficult to say what kind of thinker he is or to categorize him—but there is much political thought in Deleuze.

Before I go on to the theorists I want to look at today, let me make another kind of announcement. We are approaching another historical anniversary, that of the premiere of the film called *The Matrix*, which many of you will know, and which, whatever you think of it, like *Star Wars* or *2001: A Space Odyssey*, is a film which plays a part in culture. I mention this because Baudrillard was, of course, in the minds of the Wachowskis—the film was a kind of commentary on Baudrillard—and, since we're talking about Baudrillard on Thursday, some of you may want to see whether these films are faithful to Baudrillard or whether Baudrillard is to be judged on the basis of it. I don't know whether Baudrillard himself ever commented directly on *The Matrix*. The one work about which he wrote something very striking is the rather scandalous book by J. G. Ballard called *Crash*, which the Canadian director David Cronenberg made into a film. Anyway, that's a very different kind of film. It is a film about the Real, no doubt, in this case death, but it is also about passions that have little to do with the preoccupations of *The Matrix*.

Today, I would like to touch on three or four people. I think this is a moment in which political reflection begins again, and I would say that a new periodization is therefore necessary. I think you all understand that the end of the Soviet Union and the fall of the Berlin Wall in 1989 is a marker. I hope you also understand that the end of the welfare state and the emergence of neoliberalism takes place in the early '80s. The other date that I think you have to be aware of is that of the Treaty of Maastricht, 1992. There were a number of treaties in the European Union, but Maastricht was the central one, and it has to do, as with neoliberalism in general, with the budget. There's a moment when the European nations are no longer allowed to overspend their budget, and therefore the welfare state becomes impossible insofar as it demands spending on public services. Another word for the rollback of the welfare state is "austerity." That's not just a term; it is a whole politics. It means precisely that it is prohibited to outspend one's income. And the way this is done—very cunningly, and this was the genius of Mrs. Thatcher—was to lower taxes, because, the minute the taxes can't pay for public services, then they can't be supported under the regime of austerity or neoliberalism or Maastricht. So these countries have tied themselves into knots, as everyone else did, and this produces a situation, as we will see, which has something to do with thought.

At any rate, political writing will not be the same after this dual moment of the end of the Soviet Union and the beginning of the European Union, which you could characterize as follows: There is no longer only a regime of nation-states; there is now a regime of member-states. That's a very profound transformation. There are cultures like the French culture, which has its own centrality and traditions. Now it's just a member-state. Of course, the reunification of Germany makes it weaker in a lot of ways, but there also, the fact of becoming a member state ends national history, in some sense. So, to the degree that thinkers are connected to national history and to the perpetuation of national history, these are momentous events, and they impose quite a few changes. They particularly have something to do with politics and political history, because, as with globalization—the EU can be seen as a small-scale version of the political problem of globalization in general—if you cannot control your own budget, you can't make political decisions. The EU is a system which has no central government. Its central government is the central bank. It is not an elected government. The parliament of Strasbourg is not a governing body but a place of expression—you remember how, for Clastres, the chief had no power, no function except to talk (like lots of left representatives in the European parliament!). Therefore, you have a situation in which all the economic decisions are being made without popular consent. So the issue of representative democracy no longer comes into play here, and that will also be very important for our theorists.

I think you can see this at work in the United States in one of the most scandalous moments of American political history, where, in Michigan, the elective governor takes it on himself to suspend elected city and state governments if they overspend their budgets. If they overspend, then they can't govern themselves. This is austerity in action. Politics is controlled by the budget, and, at that point, the whole notion of elective politics becomes meaningless. In a globalized framework you can see how, in some ways, this problem reproduces itself on a larger scale. Now, Deleuze thinks that, in a sense, the state can be thought of as the infrastructure, and the nation as the superstructure. Of course, he is a European, and nationalism is certainly more than just the nation; it is language, history, and so on. So there is a way in which the nation is a formation of subjectivity in a way that the state as a form of power and administration is not. So much turns around whether there is still a nation in this sense and what the nation has to do with the people, a question we'll look at shortly. Deleuze is very fond of this phrase that he borrows from the Italian director Carmelo Bene: "The people is missing." The people is not yet there. The people is to come, to be formed, and that is what we're going to talk about today.

Now there are four people to discuss. First Jean-François Lyotard, who was born in 1924, which makes him of a very different generation, closer to Deleuze and people like that than the others we are looking at today; Jean-Luc Nancy, who wrote *The Inoperative Community*; Jacques Rancière, who you may know from his aesthetic writings but who also wrote a book called *Disagreement*, which is rather important; and Étienne Balibar, who was a student of Althusser and finally broke with him; he was born in 1942. The Nancy work, one of his rare political reflections, is from 1986. Rancière's one big political work, *La Mésentente*, is from 1995. So this is another generation.

But, first, I'm going to say something in passing about Lyotard's book, *The Differend*, which is from 1983. All of these works, as you can see, are much closer to the center of what I would consider the crisis of Europe. But I want to focus for a moment on Lyotard. Maybe we can come back to him next week, because I think this is not his most interesting work, but it is emblematic of what we have to discuss today. Lyotard was very close to Deleuze at a certain point. We talked about Deleuze's unbound energies; Lyotard invented the idea of energy investment. That is, what happens to an energy? It can be invested. Of course, this is already in some of Freud's more mechanistic theories, the energy theories, which were very popular at the end of the nineteenth century, but, with Lyotard, it takes a particular form. He calls it *économie libidinale*, libido being energy in a more general sense, but on the model, I suppose, of sexual energy.

Let me give you his history, because I think it might be of use. He was in the Communist Party for a while. He did his alternate service as a teacher in Algeria. He then broke with the communists on account of their disinterest in the colonial state of Algeria and became a member of a group of oppositional, heretical Marxist theorists called Socialisme ou Barbarie. This group included Cornelius Castoriadis, the most famous. At any rate, he was with them for a long time, and then he broke with them as well. He broke with a lot of people. He had produced a more academic philosophical work on phenomenology. During this period, when he was active politically, he didn't write anything, and then he re-emerged with other essays as much on aesthetics as anything else, including the book *Discours, figure*, which is, as I said when we were talking about Kristeva, somewhat similar—though somewhat earlier than Kristeva—to the idea that figuration is a breakthrough of forms, and that a lower level of energies can break through this surface and create new forms. He will then write interesting essays on both Freud and Marx. These come together in a work called precisely *Libidinal Economy*, which is a scandal for all kinds of reasons, in 1974. He calls it "my wicked book." It was seen as almost a fascist work, a work in which every kind of libidinal investment is equivalent to every other kind, including the "wicked" ones. It is very interesting. But then, ten years later, as penance, he brings out this work that will very briefly now detain us, *The Differend*.

A differend is an impossible argument. What Lyotard wants to use this concept for is to argue against consensus. All of this is against Habermas; in Anglo-American terms, it might be against Rawls. But let's see what Lyotard objects to in Habermas, with the latter's theory of communicational praxis. *The Theory of Communicative Action* is Habermas's major contribution in this respect, and it tries to see how the democratic system is a way of settling social differences and is therefore the system that works. He began as a disciple of the Frankfurt School. He was Adorno's research assistant. His later interpretation of his teachers was that the Frankfurt School was completely wrong and must be mistrusted altogether. I don't think Adorno or Horkheimer would have approved of the direction he took their project. I would say, from an academic point of view, that his work was obviously in sync with the Bundesrepublik, and really smothered the field. The Marxists were ousted, sometimes in a literal sense, after the "German Autumn," the terrorist incidents in the West, and after the *Wende*, the East was colonized by what you could call "carpetbaggers," flown in from the West, who reorganized universities and got rid of the Marxists. So the orthodoxy in Germany became Habermasian. Within Germany, you have to say that Habermas was politically very good. That is, he was against the Social-Democratic Party when it started to de-Marxify and sell out to free enterprise. I've seen him debate Schröder in one of the elections, and he was very strong. So one can admire him in many ways, but, on the other hand, the communicational theory allows you to believe that communications can succeed, that they work. In Habermas, money is noise, in the sense ascribed to that term in informational theory. Money is like static on the radio. So you could clean it up a little bit; that is, you could institute regulations where a democratic system was not threatened by money. It seems to me that this is not an adequate way of dealing with the problems of commodification.

Anyway, it is this philosophical defense of the democratic representational form—do we want to call it liberalism anymore?—that each of these French theorists is criticizing. This is not so much the case with Nancy—we'll come back to him—but certainly with Rancière and Balibar. For Lyotard, I think this is also a matter of the critique of consensus and the notion that consensus is possible. Lyotard is pitching this at a lower level, not in terms of politics as a whole, but simply in terms of the arguments about things that you want to reach a consensus on; so the whole thing will be written in terms of logic and speech acts. In that sense, it is very different from *Libidinal Economy*, which is delirious, and not very readable, I think. The central point of *Le Différend* is simply that most of the essential problems on which you wish to reach a consensus involve—let's use this word—incommensurability, because each party is working with a different notion of the presuppositions of the speech act. Therefore, it cannot be so simple a matter as deciding how much money a firm is going to pay its workers, because the workers have a conception of the wage which has nothing to do with that of the bosses, and there can be no reconciliation on the basis of these distinct conceptions. So the attempts at the level of argument to resolve this disagreement are not able to resolve anything.

This is a first attempt to show that, in politics, there are fundamental incommensurabilities—a term that in this case I like better than contradictions. Yes, you could say that this is a basic contradiction within what are called democracies or representative systems. They have other kinds of contradictions, such as that between face-to-face Rousseauean democracy where the people is present versus representation by individuals, but, in this case, it is a question of the impossibility of reconciling these two sets of terms. The two frameworks in which this kind of difference is to be argued out are not in sync with each other and can never be. But this is not what you are arguing about. To jump ahead, I would think—and there is certainly a critique involved in this—that Rancière's idea is that politics happens precisely when there is disagreement, not when two demands on the same level are observed, as when a union bargains with an employer, but, rather, when these lower-level, deeper frameworks in which each one sees the common object are incompatible. That is the moment of politics, and therefore, according to Rancière, it is fairly rare.

In France, it became very fashionable in this period to talk about the difference between *la politique* and *le politique*. *La politique* is the noun "politics." *Le politique* is the adjective "political." Politics is the official framework, as in a political section of the newspaper or of the news, a book on politics or political theory, political figures. The political, *le politique*, however, is much more general than that. Politics is institutional, whereas the political only surfaces every so often. For example, when looking at our previous readings, I have said that Sartre's politics were essentially anti-imperialist, and that this would be a position he would share with Deleuze and Foucault. In France, I would say that, from the Revolution on, all the great writers in the French tradition are anti-bourgeois. You will say, "Well, that can't be true. What about right-wing writers? What about Catholics?" If you are talking about crazy right-wing anti-Semites like Céline, yes, he is also anti-bourgeois, and there is a way in which fascism, in some of its forms, is anti-bourgeois. If you're talking about Catholics—my God, you should read some of the great Catholic writers of the nineteenth century like Léon Bloy! They are ferociously anti-bourgeois. Flaubert was certainly anti-bourgeois, but he also thought the Commune was abominable. The things he wrote about the Commune and what they ought to do to the workers sound like Martin Luther on the peasants, who said that they should be killed, drawn and quartered—ferocious rants of this kind. But Flaubert is a quite respectable anti-bourgeois in this sense, although you can say that he was bourgeois himself. Yes, if you like, but forms of self-hatred don't affect the anti-bourgeois tradition. From the twentieth century, you might have seen Bresson's filmic versions of Georges Bernanos; Bernanos was, of course, anti-fascist, but he was a profoundly Catholic writer. So, in France, the existence of the bourgeoisie makes a political attitude possible which takes the place of any kind of real politics.

So, for politics—*la politique*—there has to be something more. Althusser is in the Communist Party, so one assumes that he is engaged in a politics of some kind, but we would have to look at what the PCF did in the years after the war. We would have to look at Althusser's activity. There is a politics within politics. As Régis Debray said, there is a revolution within the revolution. The revolution itself has to know an internal revolution against the party. That is the connection with Maoism. So it's not so clear with Althusser where politics is, but he does tell us one important thing: philosophy is class struggle in thought. What is political about those philosophical decisions? I have used myself this antithesis—another incommensurability, if you like—in historical periodization. For a long time, history is written in terms of continuities. Now, following Foucault, it's written in terms of breaks and disjunctions. Now how do you decide on those breaks? I think this is a political question. That is to say, it is a leap in the void. Politics is a leap in the void. Certainly, your political ideologies are formed that way, and there would also be psychoanalytic ways of looking at those leaps. I would say that, when religion became a leap in the void, with Pascal, with Kierkegaard, it was a political choice. Gödel's law of politics: there is no final foundation for these choices. They are absolute choices, Sartrean choices, existential choices. There is no logical ground on which to rationalize them. You can't simply conclude that loving people is some ultimate absolute, that loving people is all one must do. That is also a political choice that carries you back down institutions, subjectivity, and, finally, to yet another ultimate leap. That is why the question of political theory is full of paradoxes and impossibilities, because I would think—and frankly I think all the positions we are discussing today are in accord with this—that political theory is not possible. It is not possible to theorize politics. If politics is a leap in the void, then there is no way of theorizing it. Its foundation cannot be theorized. You cannot go back to first principles in terms of politics. Why? How do these theorists come to that impossibility?

First, I want to look at Nancy's work, which is characteristic of a lot of the thinking of the period. Nancy was very close to Derrida. Derrida wrote a book about him. He comes out of phenomenology, heavily indebted to Heidegger, but not a Derridean. He is willing to theorize things like justice and community which no true Derridean—Derrida himself may have lapsed in this sense—would venture, because deconstruction is based on the sense that there is something which you cannot resolve in questions of meaning, whereas Nancy is working at resolving those in some strange kind of way.

Nancy is close to German thought. He and his collaborator, Philippe Lacoue-Labarthe, write a book on German Romanticism, *The Literary Absolute*, which has become a central reference. German Romanticism was not well known in France, so the importation of Schlegel and other Romantics is owed to Nancy and Lacoue-Labarthe; Hölderlin as the central image of the poetic vocation is another of their great themes, but maybe due more to Heidegger. Nancy will also be a philosopher—in some relationship to Merleau-Ponty—of the body and the flesh. When you say "flesh," though, you get a different kind of sound. When you say "flesh," what do you think of next? Incarnation. This is moving toward religion. I would call it "negative theology." You get a kind of religiose sense in his book on the inoperative community, but I think it does have some interesting things to tell us.

Its title, *La Communauté désœuvrée*, as everybody says, is a problem. *Oeuvre* means work. Foucault said that madness is the absence of work, in the sense of the impossibility of producing an *oeuvre*. The point about the madman is that he can't produce. Is that too restrictive a definition? When Lacan treats a schizophrenic patient for eight years, the guy continues to go to work. He functions. Madness is not functioning. What does it mean to function? It means being productive in some sense or another. So *désœuvrée*: This kind of community does not produce, but the word can range from "idle" to "unemployed." This is very strange. It is a community without work. Is it a community of idlers? Is it a community of the unemployed? That would be very interesting. In any case, it is not a community that can be produced. It cannot be the result of work.

What is it exactly? Note that I prefer the word collectivity, because it means everybody. A community is not a collectivity for Nancy. It is the group that you identify with. So this really can go in all kinds of directions, this thing. It is not the society, but it's something that can appear within the society. So maybe we have a community of the faithful, whatever faith it is. There's a community of stamp collectors, a community of doctors, a community of teachers, of lovers of Deleuze. French citizens: Is that a community? What is a nation? "A republic," I should say, because France is a republic in which, theoretically, everybody is equal, in which, therefore, there cannot be a community. In a republic, there are no factions. This is something that our founding fathers tried to insist on and failed to bring about, because immediately, at the very beginning of our so-called republic, parties emerged. So this community—will it be factions, parties? He doesn't get that far. Should the party be a community, or shouldn't it? Or should it be a bunch of leaders and people who sign up? Those are questions on which it seems to me Nancy is trying to reflect. And that is always, I think, the way in which we have to examine politics, even though this does not really get to politics, only to community as such.

So here we have a fundamental limit on community. A lot of this, as you will have noticed, is a commentary on Bataille. I think Nancy gives us a different slant on which we can come to these ideas. What he wants to do is to show that none of these conceptions of community is really possible. There are a couple of alternatives. You can say there once was community and there isn't anymore. Choose your utopia. Was it Athens? Lots of slaves, lots of non-citizens in Athens. Let's go back to hunters and gatherers then. There's fifty or sixty people in a tribal utopia. Are they a community? I think his point would be: no, there never was a community, and therefore the appeal to nostalgia is impossible, and nostalgia for a lost community is ungrounded. What about a community to come? I think it's implicit that that also is impossible, that nostalgia for the future is not there. It's true that this is less and less at work around us, although you could almost say the disappearance of a future community is a disappearance of politics. That will be a big question for us. Is it important to have a view of community, even if it is philosophically untenable, a view of the coming community, as Agamben calls it in his reply?[1] Is it necessary to keep this idea of a future community alive in order for politics to happen? I think that is not Nancy's position, and therefore the question remains about what community is in the first place.

I think the other theme of this work is a question of individual and community, because the individual is—and this is an existential word,

1   Giorgio Agamben, *The Coming Community*, trans. Michael Hardt (Minneapolis, MN: University of Minnesota Press, 1993).

much more of a Heideggerian word than a Sartrean one, but it is the crucial word of all existentialists—finitude. The fundamental experience of the individual human being is finitude. What's that? Well, it's obviously mortality. It is the fact that you have to be in this place at this time in history. You cannot be everything, everywhere. Whatever community is, it has to deal with its members, all of whom are finite. Now, one of the visions of community that people normally have is that the community transcends these limits of the individual, that, in the community, we are somehow transcended with respect even to our own finitude, that the community will continue us in some way. You could have a version of this with the family. You can see how this notion of a collective that somehow transcends the individual is possible. I would say that the interesting thing about Nancy's thought is that the community is also finite. He uses the word "common" a great deal. You may know that, in Hardt and Negri, and in the American Left, this has become a very special term by virtue of an extension of "common" to the notion of "the commons" as a form of property or an institution. So we're getting some wordplay back and forth. This will reach its most unreadable, I would say, in Rancière, but it is a new kind of wordplay which is not the same exactly as Derridean puns, but which is also a kind of argument issuing from these words. So, to have something in common then suggests a juridical perspective in which there is such a thing as a commons and a communal form of property. Nancy does not deal with that. Balibar does deal with property in a very interesting way, and the book of his that I recommend is a book called *Masses, Classes, and Ideas*, in which there is a very wide-ranging set of topics, all the way to contemporary issues, critiques of a certain kind of Marxism, since he was obviously active in the Communist Party with Althusser, although he is not anymore. Balibar is somebody who has an extremely sharp sense of logical contradiction, who goes after what is contradictory with an unerring precision, and who then writes up these contradictions in great detail.

Now I come back to Nancy, who is not playing on the word "common" very much, but is dealing with this question of common finitude. It's as though he is asking how an existential being can project any kind of being in common with other people. Heidegger's notion of *Mitsein* is resurrected here in a way. This is a matter of others, although it's not a question of a people or anything like that. We don't have the adequate categories for community. But let me quote this sentence, which I think is crucial: "Being *in* common has nothing to do with communion, with fusion into a body, into a unique and ultimate identity which would no longer be exposed. Being *in* common means, to the contrary, *no longer having, in any form, in any empirical or ideal place, such a substantial identity and sharing this* (narcissistic) *'lack of identity.'* This is what philosophy calls 'finitude,' and the following texts are entirely and uniquely devoted to the understanding of it."[2] He is saying that not only is the individual finite, but the community is also no escape from finitude. Derrida as well can be read in that proto-existential sense as saying there is never any plenitude. We are always outside of ourselves, before and after. We're like writing in that sense, where the writing is never complete, and all your illusions of a complete presence are illusory. So there is a notion of finitude in Derrida which is not reasoned in the traditional existential forms. Those come back here, and Nancy is saying that the finitude of the individual is not subsumed by the community. Rather, the community also reflects all these finitudes. It isn't a thing, so you can't say it is also finite, nor is it able to *aufheben* or to dialectically transcend the finitude of the individual.

How to imagine this? Let's go back to Sartre: The community doesn't have an *en-soi*. The problem of the *pour-soi*, the individual, was that it was not an *en-soi*, that it was not complete, that it could not fully *be*. Ah! So now we have the notion of a community which is not a being, which can never be, in some sense. I think that what you are to understand is that the community is always formed of people who share their not-being, and what they long for in the shape of a community is a common not-being. Now that's very strange, because we often think of a communitarian ethos by imagining that if not now, then, at some future point, we will overcome our finitude. We will be saved, and we will transcend the limits of our individuality. In these terms, that's what you call fascism. Fascism promises to complete our incompleteness with a future state—not in the political sense, but in the sense of a condition—and it promises that a full community is possible for people who are not themselves full entities. I think that Nancy is saying that you have to begin with the longing for community—which is a part of our incompleteness—but it has to be the longing for a community that is itself incomplete. If you want to think that through, you are likely to arrive at some notion of religion. The community of the faithful, except

---

2 Jean-Luc Nancy, *The Inoperative Community*, trans. Peter Conner, Lisa Garbus, Michael Holland, Simona Sawhney (Minneapolis, MN: University of Minnesota Press, 1991), *xxxviii*.

in the most horrible, fanatical circumstances, is supposed to think of itself as a bunch of finite people. They are not unified by the church. The church is simply a place in which their finitudes come together in some way, but it is not itself the transcendent community.

Nancy is obviously a man of the Left, but I think this work is anti-Left. I think the Left has imagined that there is something like a utopian condition, a condition which is different from the one we live in today and which has some kind of plenitude. But the crisis of that imagination in this period will signify where the Left is virtually disappearing. This will be the political question, or at least one of them. In this work, we don't even come to the question of how communities could be related to societies. The community itself is somehow impossible, and I think that this work is a dramatization of that aporia. To use a different set of terms: how can we imagine the community as *being* when it's founded on *not-being*?

I want to get on to Rancière, because I think his is a remarkable work, one which is very difficult but very characteristic of this period. This one arrives ten years after Nancy's, after the definitive end of the Communist Party, which he went through. He is another disciple of Althusser and was a participant in this collective seminar called *Reading Capital*. Then he breaks with Althusser and goes his own way. I think a kind of Marxism is still implicit here, but one can make one's own judgment. After his break, he writes a book against Althusser in which he accuses Althusser—just as Althusser accused himself—of theoreticism. He takes a classic anti-intellectual position that identifies Althusser as elitist and claims that Marxism itself is elitism, because any notion of science naturally entails the notion that a few people know what the truth is and then diffuse it to other people. Rancière, I would like to say—but it's a word people are not now using in the same ways—is a radical populist, just as the term "workerism" might arise when somebody believes that only the workers really know what reality is and that an intellectual will always necessarily be alienated from that reality. You may know that, in France, in 1968, some of the more radical Maoists gave up their professions and worked in factories in ways that were very disabling for them, in some cases even physically.[3] It would be a more general populism that appeals to Rancière, one that would include "the people," the common people,

3   For an autobiographical account of this process, see Robert Linhart, *L'Établi* (Paris: Éditions de Minuit, 1978); translated as *The Assembly Line*, trans. Margaret Crosland (Amherst, MA: University of Massachusetts Press, 1981).

everybody. Intellectuals are judged because by definition they think that they are somehow above the people. So Althusser is an elitist. Theory itself is elitist. And, yet, Rancière will go on doing it.

He is thinking of Lenin's famous remark that the revolutionary party is formed by workers and intellectuals from outside the working class like himself. It is a combination of workers and intellectuals. Our country, as I've said many times, is an anti-intellectual country. That sounds very bad indeed. I would like us to have a more positive notion of what an intellectual is, to know why it's important to have active intellectuals, and to be proud of being an intellectual. On the other hand, everyone understands that intellectuals are—Sartre dramatizes this often—traitors, class traitors. An intellectual is somebody at odds with his social class. If he decides to identify with it, then he can become little more than a spokesperson for the people in power. If he separates himself from it and tries to join the other class —as happened in the eighteenth century with the great Revolution—he is always the object of suspicion, because he can never really be a part of that class. This has been true in workers' movements since the very beginning, the enduring suspicion of the intellectual who is not really one of you. So, in that sense, Rancière is a classic anti-intellectual, but in a country which thinks of intellectuals in a very different way than we do. I don't know that anybody has called him an anti-intellectual, because, in France, that wouldn't make a lot of sense, but his kind of populism is very strange.

Anyway, after this attack on Althusser and the break, he becomes a kind of historian. He writes on a few interesting figures. The most famous book is called *The Ignorant Schoolmaster*, in which he finds a proto-intellectual who abandons his positions and has this odd idea that people can teach themselves. To teach the people is to take an attitude of condescension. So, instead, you somehow participate in their self-production. It reminds me of Tolstoy. I don't think I've mentioned Tolstoy's period—he was a great landowner, of course—when he opens a school for peasant children on his estate and begins teaching them to write. Tolstoy himself writes a wonderful essay called "Who Should Learn Writing from Whom? Peasant Children from Us, or Us from Peasant Children?" Then he has to shut it down, because, of course, the other landowners don't like it. In American slavery, as you know, slaves were not taught to read and write. In fact, it was a crime to teach slaves to read and write. In Russia, as well, to teach these peasant children to write, let alone to read, was very dangerous.

Anyway, Rancière's book tries to square this circle. How can the people become their own intellectuals?

Then, in 1995, he writes *Disagreement*, which is his major political work. Since then, he has turned toward aesthetics, and I assume you will know him from these innumerable essays—my God!—on everything from painting and film, to literature of all kinds, to general aesthetic theory, where you will find a certain connection with his politics. At any rate, we won't get to any of that, because there is a sense in which we need to know how this theory of the political is going to move toward aestheticism. I think in the period after theory, which is the one we're gradually approaching, there is a movement toward what Benjamin would call "aesthetization," not just the revival of aesthetics as a philosophical discipline. I think some of Rancière's popularity in this country has come from the fact that, as a student told me once, he allows us to talk about works of art again. Well, okay. He does that sometimes very well, sometimes not, but he tries to make it part of his populism by using a particular term. The word "part" is very significant in this work. Let's take the aesthetic formula. It's a formula called *le partage du sensible*. What does *partage* mean? It means, like Freud's "primal words," two separate and opposing things. *Partage* can mean dividing things up, or it can mean sharing. *Partager*. You can share a meal, but you have to cut up the pie somehow. So, in this *partage du sensible*, the *sensible* is what is sensory, the sensory world. That becomes his aesthetic, but it is also, in some, sense the politics of this book.

I can only very quickly say something about this. Again, our old friends from Heidegger: the ontic and the ontological. Let me put it to you this way: everyone says there is too much inequality; we must make people equal. This is everyone, right? This is our current political problem, in the United States above all. Rancière says no. No, everyone is equal already. Inequality itself can only arise on the basis of universal equality. That is his populism: everybody is already equal. I think this goes back to a Sartrean idea of consciousness. If consciousness is nothing, then everybody has to be equal in their nothingness. Nobody is anything, whereas, in normal social thought, some people are smarter than others, some have more money than others, some more talent, such that we must arrange the world so as to mitigate this general inequality. But what about this business of the ontic and the ontological? Let me give you a different opposition from *la politique* and *le politique*: politics versus police. The original meaning of "police" is from a Renaissance word that means "government." The policing of things means governing, not just guys with tasers and uniforms and violence. It doesn't quite mean what Foucault means by governmentality. It means the social order. So you can see, in that instant, how many of the things that are considered political matters are simply matters of policing, in all the senses that you care to give the word: policing, ordering, governing. Here, we're back to Lyotard again: The question of politics therefore means bringing about a fundamental disorder in this ordering of the police. It means touching on something which is much more fundamental and which upsets all order. Again, politics is very rare. You can read this, if you like, from a Marxist perspective, from which the only real historical events are revolutions. Add in all the failed revolutions, and Rancière is saying something similar. Politics emerges only when it comes to an absolute crunch.

When does that happen? Now we get the second version of this formula having to do with the word *partage. La part,* the part: the "part of those who have no part."[4] This is a crazy formula that is repeated over and over again in Rancière's politics. The people who have no part, you know sort of who those are: the oppressed, the proletariat, whatever group is excluded from this community. His references are often to Plato and Athens, which works well, because that's supposed to be for the West the great discovery of democracy, but, of course, the only people who had a right to vote were the male aristocrats. Workers, such as they were, women, slaves, all didn't have the right to vote. Those are the people who have no part. But they do have a part, because on the level of the police, of society, they are assigned a part. They are assigned a part, but that part is of having no part, because they take no part in society, even though they are, by definition, part of a collectivity which includes everybody and in which everybody is equal. So it is on that basis of equality that they are selected out as having no part. There is no *partage* for them.

And then we get a couple new things, freedom and equality, although I suppose he would distinguish freedom from equality. Freedom takes place on the level of the struggle to have a part, but equality is there already. So what about citizenship, which supposedly involves these things? Citizenship is a constant for contemporary French political thought. Who is a citizen? Who gets the right to be a citizen? What is this right? And since

---

4   Jacques Rancière, *Dissensus: On Politics and Aesthetics,* trans. Steven Corcoran (New York: Continuum, 2010).

this is still French theory, language comes in here, because the people who don't have a part don't have a voice. Sartre already said, once upon a time, that there was a world in which there were 500 million humans and 1.5 billion *indigènes*. "The former possessed the Word, the others borrowed it."[5] The taking of a voice, having a voice, is a part of disagreement. You can't disagree with people without language. So having a voice is a part of instituting this impossible quarrel which is politics.

I think we have to leave it here. I will come back to this briefly next time, particularly because Rancière does criticize Baudrillard, and we'll see how Debord fits into all of this.

April 13, 2021

---

5   Jean-Paul Sartre, "Preface," *The Wretched of the Earth*, xliii.

24

Simulating the End of History

{Debord, Baudrillard}

As I warned, some loose ends are left over. I didn't mention Jean-Luc Nancy's interesting idea of literary communism. I won't judge it further, but I think he is welcoming the return of our old friends writing and reading. Reading is a kind of communism, in the sense that, when you are reading, you are in what I suppose Sartre might call a serial state. Other people are reading; your reading is not the only one, not central or definitive, and, therefore, your reading has a break in it, a gap, an absence, as do those of all other people, and yet you do form some kind of group with them. So this would be in line with Nancy's idea that we are in quest of a failed group. A successful group or community can be nothing other than fascism. We are failed, in the sense that, because we are split subjects, the collectivity will therefore also be split and a failure in the ontological sense, and that would be the authentic kind of group which we all vainly desire to join. I'm reading this into Nancy. I don't know how serious he is about that idea, but he is a very serious guy, and I presume he meant it, or at least that would be my interpretation.

On Rancière, I wanted to go back briefly to say that he makes a basic connection using this wordplay on *part* and *partage*, *partage* meaning making parts and dividing, "part" being the part of the part of no part. As he becomes a literary critic, so to speak, he seems to transfer all of this to art in the name of this other slogan of his, the *partage du sensible*, the sharing of this sensory world, the distribution of the sensible. Like I said, the word *partage* means separating things or sharing things, so you can't tell which. The whole point is that this comes back to the central ambiguity of *aesthesis* in Greek, which means perception. So aesthetics, when the word was invented in the eighteenth century by Alexander Baumgarten, I believe, was the study of perception, and art was then considered its major form. Art forms our senses—I don't think we would see the world in the same way had we not had modernism—in a very material sense. The commodities that are produced today—your furniture, your clothing—are dependent on a modernist revolution in forms, which was, at that time, scandalous, but is now the basis of commodity production. I don't think Rancière would read it that way. He would say, on the other hand, no: Modernism made a whole host of democratic perceptions possible, which included mass production, the mass production of a world that now many more people can inhabit than they did in the nineteenth century. Does that involve the distribution of the senses? That is what interests me. We have been very interested in visuality here out of necessity, because we stumble back over it in all these readings. We will again today. But, for visuality to emerge, it must emerge on the basis of the retreat of other senses. There is a structure to this. It is not an accident that Nancy thinks he's doing something relatively revolutionary when he advances the sense of touch rather than the sense of sight. Does Rancière mean something similar? I don't see any evidence of that.

In any case, I recommend Rancière's book *The Politics of Literature*, which has some very important essays and general statements in it, including a participation in the fight over the foundations of modernism, which is in this case Flaubert. Flaubert either is the beginning of a religion of art, or of some breakdown in the older system of hierarchical values, which entails the expansion of the content of art in a democratic way: which is, of course, Rancière's position. But he knows that Flaubert was also an elitist in politics. So he has some fancy polemics to wage on that.

For myself, I think this is not necessary. None of these people— Rancière, Nancy—really take into account mass culture. Rancière does, to an extent; he says it is the realm of what Adorno called kitsch. It confuses art with everyday life. His example, again, is Flaubert's *Madame Bovary*. She wasn't an intellectual, but she thought of everything in aesthetic terms. For Rancière, the aestheticization of life is the transfer of artistic perceptions to all of everyday life. That he condemns; art should be separate in some sense. On the other hand, I believe that this is the tendency of all these thinkers: to move toward a form of aestheticism, even when you are criticizing it. What is Debord's notion of spectacle society if it isn't the accusation that society is becoming more aesthetic, seeing things as a spectacle? I would say that, in a situation in which politics gets blocked—and with all these people it is blocked—it is all very well and good to say that politics appears when there are fights. Yes, of course. I think Debord also would say that: There is only real politics where there are basic contradictions at stake. But, if you don't any longer have an idea of social transformation, then I really don't know what we're talking about. Even Badiou, who is thought to be the most politically orthodox of all these people, evokes a fidelity to the Event: The Event means revolution, but it is in the past. And Badiou doesn't believe in the revolution anymore, I think, at least not now, not here. By definition, it isn't in the present. Badiou tries to reconcile the notion that there is not a full present, that there is not an Event in the present, which is substantial and in itself, and that, therefore, every revolution, even one that might be taking place right now somewhere, is in the past because it is objectified.

We don't have to talk about revolutions, but, in modern times, after '68, which is now understood as a failure rather than as a success, I would say there is a popular position, that of Wallerstein and Rancière, that the '60s were this immense opening up and enlargement of possibilities—who could deny that?—but, on the Left, it is also the moment of failure. Many of these transformations are happening in the '60s, certainly in the '70s, but by the '80s and '90s, the situation is quite different. When looking at this historically, you must always take into account the generational question: When were these people born? Which period are they working in? In that sense, they are not all equal. It is the generational problem. The Russians formulated it in the nineteenth century. They had the people of the '50s, '60s, '70s, each of whom were formed in these moments and had different attitudes because of the visibility of the future, let's say, in those periods, or because of its repression. But all periods are not equal. You can certainly talk about people of the '60s, but what about people of the '50s? That is not a generation of the same type as the people of the '60s. Maybe it isn't even a generation at all. Who—as Mallarmé asked—is really a contemporary of himself? In a generation, you have contemporaneity, a term that the art historians and critics are using nowadays for contemporary art, but it is a very hollow phrase, because this isn't an age in which there is contemporaneity, where all these artists feel that they're participating in the same thing. It seems to me a reaction.

We're getting off the subject. I just wanted to highlight this problem in Rancière which turns on the cunning but rather ambiguous use of the words *part, partage,* and "sensible," as though these were private properties of vision. You could go back and argue: yes, but working-class people have less time for culture and, therefore, their sensibilities are somehow limited. But none of that argument takes into account mass culture today and what it does, and I think that has to be an issue when talking about aestheticization, and Rancière is perhaps not doing that in a way that interests us.

I wanted to draw your attention, since we didn't get to talk about Balibar much, to his notion that none of these kinds of political concepts are frozen, and that the crucial political concept—in this sense he obviously does remain a Marxist—is that of property in its multiple meanings. His position is that it is not important to decide what is property and what is not, in some juridical way. He is also talking about the ownership of information, which is a new dimension of this whole matter of property. "They too"—these various techniques of ownership—"create an increasing quantity of *that which cannot be possessed or mastered*, which does not put an end to appropriation but becomes its condition. Data and methods are irresistibly 'disseminated';"—a Derridean phrase—"the paternity of the results of scientific and technological research can no longer be defined [...]."[1] In short, what he is saying is that one of the ways of defining politics—that which is truly political—is that it puts the reigning categories of property back into question. It may do this by proposing a new category of property or by undermining an old one, but the new political struggle, if it is really politics, must bring the question of property into play. Now you can say that Rancière is trying to do that by talking about *partage*, who owns what, what can be distributed, the status of your ownership of that piece as opposed to this piece. That is possible, but I think Balibar's is a useful reminder of a much more basic way of posing the question of what is political.

Baudrillard and Debord are working in a related but distinct problematic. We don't have to talk about *The Matrix*, but I like the idea of a more

---

1   Étienne Balibar, *Masses, Classes, Ideas: Studies on Politics and Philosophy Before and After Marx*, trans. James Swenson (London: Routledge, 1994), 222.

science-fictional frame of reference for some of these people, because I think it marks a shift in what we're dealing with. Both Baudrillard and Debord paint a picture of a world that is subject to certain kinds of forces. They move toward a narrative image of the world. You will say that all these philosophies or theories, whether they like it or not, imply a worldview which could be narrativized, but here it is much stronger. It certainly goes in the direction of what I would call a culture critique, which I always say is a relatively bad thing. I trace it back to anthropological "culture-and-society" stuff. On the other hand, today there is a return of interest to Boaz and his disciples, and that was maybe a democratic thing in the old days, this notion of culture being distinctive, each one being equidistant from God, as in Ranke, by way of its own kind of psychosis, as in Ruth Benedict's work. There is a paranoid culture here, but a narcissistic culture there. That does seem to me a welcome kind of relativism. But, finally, when we get to politics, we have all these rather impotent culture critiques of various kinds. If you have ever read your horoscope, this is similar to the way your daily horoscope will tell you things about your own psychology and you think, "Oh, that's absolutely true—how could they know that!" But, unfortunately, if you have read through everybody's horoscope, each different one would seem pertinent in exactly the same way. These are so general that any one of them could apply to you, or, rather, you could adapt yourself to any one of them. So also with these culture critiques, and I think this is a psychological distraction from more basic critiques of production and social structure.

These two figures are born more or less at the same time, Debord in 1931, Baudrillard in 1929. So they are roughly contemporary, but Debord's work had its influence in the '70s, Baudrillard's much later, and these societies are quite different by that time, so we have to allow for a basic change in figuration that everybody feels. Neither of these people would feel that way. Certainly, Debord would be furious at being assimilated to Baudrillard. I don't know whether Baudrillard ever mentions Debord. That is always a tell-tale absence—like Heidegger, the great philosopher of time, never mentioning his most illustrious predecessor, namely Henri Bergson, except in one footnote at the end of *Sein und Zeit* where you could easily miss it. So it is always interesting to know who they avoid mentioning. But we do feel that they have something in common, even if it could be different forms of representation, *The Matrix* versus *The Truman Show*, or something like that. At least they both seem to give us an image of an aestheticized society, which is quite nightmarish, whereas Marcuse, for example, thought that the aestheticization of work was certainly a utopian project. You want to make work aesthetic; you want to make work like play, which is, of course, a crucial political concept invented by Schiller in the immediate post-Kantian period of the French Revolution. The idea that work should no longer be alienating, that it should be play, was a great utopian motif. Does one want to accuse Marcuse of aestheticization? Well, the term would apply. But this no longer has the same feeling. Marcuse is writing in an American '50s and '60s. Politics will happen during Marcuse's American stay, but it isn't a given the way it is in Europe.[2]

The other interesting thing is that both are related to Henri Lefebvre, who was the great communist philosopher of the period, but who was a philosopher advancing beyond the traditional limits of what the Communist Party thought to be orthodoxy, and who has invented all kinds of interesting things, above all, I would say, the notion of everyday life. In wartime: that is essentially when all the great scientific discoveries are made, from Penicillin to computers. So, after the war, there is a tremendous burst of productivity, city-building, transformation of life. Lefebvre was particularly interested in the city and urbanism, where he saw these transformations. He was from the Pyrenees, and it was in his hometown there that he began to see this. So the notion of everyday life, as Lefebvre pioneered it, was a great theoretical discovery, which maybe we should have included in this course as well. The PCF wasn't interested. Nobody paid any attention, so it migrated slowly to the North, where it was rediscovered in Holland and Denmark. Around it, at the same time, a whole host of artists, utopians and the like, developed in those countries. One of the most famous and interesting is Constant Nieuwenhuys, who worked his whole life on a project he called *New Babylon*, which was a utopian city, a whole utopian world. Marcuse's work is known to them.

Meanwhile, the work of Debord hooks up with those same people, and

---

2 Herbert Marcuse, *Eros and Civilization* (Boston: Beacon Press, 1966). Marcuse's position extends that of Schiller: "It must be understood that the liberation from the reality which is here envisaged is not transcendental, 'inner,' or merely intellectual freedom (as Schiller explicitly emphasizes) but freedom *in* the reality. The reality that 'loses its seriousness' is the inhumane reality of want and need, and it loses its seriousness when wants and needs can be satisfied without alienated labor. Then, man is free to 'play' with his faculties and potentialities and with those of nature, and only by 'playing' with them is he free." (188). See Fredric Jameson, "Marcuse and Schiller," in *Marxism and Form* (Princeton, NJ: Princeton University Press, 1971), 83–115.

finally, out of that group—which is not just French or Belgian but also Scandinavian—Situationism emerges as a movement. That could be a new avant-garde. Maybe that was the last avant-garde after Surrealism. There were other attempts at avant-gardes. An avant garde is always an attempt at an avant-garde. But we know a lot more about Surrealism, so that becomes the true archetype of all avant-gardes. But we don't necessarily have to take it that way. Situationism certainly had its political program, its aesthetic program, its exchanges; it was very important in Italy. This was an underground movement in Europe when art is now dominated— because the Cold War is also an aesthetic conflict—by American abstract art. *How New York Stole the Idea of Modern Art* by Serge Guilbaut is about the triumph of abstract expressionism, as the latest and virtually the last flourish of modernism proper, and its role as anti-Soviet propaganda— because the reputation was that, whereas Russia is a place of art and the artistic, the Americans are these *nekulturny* savages. So this is very much a part of the whole rhetoric of the Cold War, where the opening exhibit of abstract expressionists in Paris right after the war was a crucial *coup* for the American side in the cultural Cold War. So it looked from that vantage point as though Europe was exhausted: no art in Europe anymore. They've done their bit and now it passes to the Americans. The Soviets did not quite pick up the challenge. But, underground, we have this movement known as *Lettrisme*, before it becomes Situationism. So Debord is in contact with Lefebvre, and their aims, for a while, are very close: utopianism, the festival as the celebration of the people, and so on. They break when Lefebvre writes a big book on the Paris Commune, a topic supposed to belong to Debord.[3] Debord was very dictatorial, like most founders of avant-garde movements. I don't think he was a student of Lefebvre. Baudrillard, on the other hand, was a pupil.

So both of them begin with Marxism. Debord remains a Marxist, although an anti-Soviet one. However, I don't think there is really anything heretical. There are certainly new ideas in *The Society of the Spectacle*.[4] I think it is in the line of Lukács—the Lukács of *History and Class Consciousness* is quoted on the first page—and if you read the sections on history, it is

3   Henri Lefebvre, *La Proclamation de la Commune, 26 Mars 1871* (Paris: La Fabrique, 2018). See "Lefebvre on the Situationists: An Interview," in Kristen Ross, *The Politics and Poetics of Everyday Life* (London: Verso, 2023), 12–34.

4   Guy Debord, *The Society of the Spectacle*, trans. Fredy Perlman (Detroit, MI: Black & Red, 2010).

one very good introduction to Marxism, if we have to pick one, but I don't think it is ever treated that way, though maybe it should be. Politically, one must say, Debord adheres to the doctrine which is called "convergence." That means Soviet society is not revolutionary anymore; the Maoists will call it "revisionist." It is a bureaucratic society. It has evolved away from the true traditions of revolution. And, in fact, the two forces in the world who were busy fighting this so-called Cold War end up being the same. They may look different in all kinds of ways, but they are all imperialist and bureaucratic societies.

Where do you go from there? If you're on the Left, you could go into Trotskyism. Debord, however, thinks that is just more Stalinism. You could go into anarchism; Debord has his critiques of that as well. He believes that the original sin was the crushing of the Kronstadt uprising by Lenin and the end of soviets and council communism. But I'm not sure that one could ever classify him in any one of those groups, and he never really ended up being a member of any party but his own. He committed suicide in 1994.

This major work of his is from 1968, after which he dissolved the Situationist International, as it was called. So we have a Lefebvrian outcome there, and an excuse for the description of everyday life. The doctrine of everyday life is going to play a formal role in encouraging you as a theorist to evolve a theory of what is happening in everyday life. We have the theory of the infrastructure. We know how capitalism functions: commodities, surplus-value, imperialism, blah, blah, blah. All those things are givens, as they still are, of course. But, for both Debord and Baudrillard, in a sense, they are to be transcended in new ways. Debord is supposed to be offering us a mode of subversion or protest, and an international one. There was an American Situationism in San Francisco in the old days. So it did have a kind of politics.

The crucial terms for the situationists were what they called *détournement* and *dérive*. *Détournement* means grabbing things out of their routine place and using them for other purposes, like Brechtian estrangement. You seize things and transform them, suddenly, by giving them new purposes. *Dérive* means running off the track. In the *dérive*, you set up new tracks for the city. They had a practice called "psychogeography," which would be a way of looking at the city which was not the standard one programmed by the authorities and by everyday life. Of course, the Surrealists had their own version of that. They had the *promenade surréaliste*, the Surrealist *balade*. They had all kinds of ways of changing the city. I always think that the problematic of the city cuts across the problematic of the economic in some way. Somehow, to theorize capitalist production—factories, distribution, markets—is different from theorizing the city, despite the fact that, in some sense, it is from the cities that capitalism emerges. I think there are several lines here, but it was the genius of the situationists to have included all of those, and their politics will be a politics of *détournement*, of trying to transform people's vision and experience.

So we are back in aesthetics. Politics is aesthetics: making people see differently, changing their share of the sensible, as Rancière might say. I think it is also understood by Debord—he says so in so many words here—that the fundamental forms of politics are precisely those that Rancière laid out, that is, the moments in which really impossible demands are made on the system. In the American New Left, there was such a theory. I don't know whether we attribute it to Marcuse or not. They said that one of the goals of capitalism is to make people buy stuff. So modern capitalism involves a stimulation of desire. It involves in its very structure a fundamental increase in everyone's desire. And the contradiction comes precisely where the economic system cannot possibly satisfy that desire, if only because, as production and automation becomes more and more sophisticated, unemployment increases, so the public that is being stimulated into desiring more will also have no means to fulfill that desire. This seems to me an original and very interesting analysis. *The Port Huron Statement* of the '60s was one of the great American left manifestos. The problem was that, although it was a revolutionary theory, a theory of contradictions, it did not create a revolution. Things happened, but they happened because of Vietnam and not because of some pre-revolutionary situation.

Baudrillard will also have something to say about all this. Via Lefebvre, he comes out of the same tradition. Daily life will return with a vengeance in his notion of simulation, but he comes out of Lefebvre's Marxism from a different branch, one which is concerned with commodities and commodification. What Baudrillard saw in his early work was that structuralism and the theory of the signifier needed to be combined with a theory of the commodity. So his system of objects led him off into a wholly new direction, that of signs and the critique of signs. It eventually led to his theories of simulation.

There is a tremendous variety of positions in Baudrillard's work that you don't get in Debord because we don't have very much; *Society of the Spectacle* is the work that he put everything into, although he was also a filmmaker. *Society of the Spectacle* is a book organized around the image. Some of his films do not have images, just a blank screen with a voiceover. I can't speak very authoritatively about them because I've never had the patience to watch one of them through, but they do exist and are available. So he was also an artist. But, essentially, the centrality of the image for him is marked by that practice of filmmaking, film being the central place in which the obsession with the image is brought to fruition in capitalism.

With Baudrillard, on the other hand, we get a critique of the sign. We touched on this a little bit back when we looked at Baudrillard in terms of symbolic exchange, which was his utopian moment, his belief that something else was possible before a system of exchange, the theoretical form of equivalence. Equivalence means the same. It means finding some way in which everything can be made the same. Commodity culture is therefore a culture of absolute sameness. Everything is judged in terms of the same, the mechanism of which is money. Clearly, there has to be a trick here, because, if you just exchange the same thing back and forth, nobody is going to make any money. So other things must be added to the theory. Derrida also came to this problem in his critique of Mauss and Malinowski in a book called *Given Time*, in which he works with the return of the gift in Mauss's framework. At the end of the *kula*, after your gift has gone through all these islands of the archipelago, finally someone gives it back to you. You cannot leave a gift unfulfilled, in a sense. Derrida says that, the minute it is exchanged back, it cannot be a gift anymore. So the gift only exists in a brief moment of non-reciprocity. In Baudrillard, that becomes an idyllic moment in which you no longer have this domination of exchange-value; you have a utopia.

All of this involves a critique of the semiotic fraction. The sign is the signifier over the signified. Lacan addresses the signifier: there is no signified, or better still, the signified is the relation of the signifiers among themselves. There are many versions of a culture of the signifier. For Deleuze, things are the same. The signifier is an absolute and therefore it is bad. Their critiques share the point that the signifier is like the phallus, one of these absolutes that we have to get rid of. But, in Derrida, it's a little more straightforward or obvious. He says that the signified is what is transcendental in this fraction. There is a transcendental signified. The signified is meaning, not the signifier. When you try to loosen the signifiers, you are trying to escape from meaning. Meaning is the basis of the exchange of signs. So you have to do something in some way with meaning.

I think the logic of a lot of these positions, Baudrillard's included, is to take this semiotic fraction and turn it around by saying that it is the signifier that produces the signified. Meaning is produced by the sign of meaning. And, for Baudrillard, this will also be true of value. Money is not the sign of value; value is the production of money itself. There is a wonderful moment in Georg Simmel, the great sociologist—you should all read the famous essays, "Metropolis and Mental Life" being the most important, important for Benjamin, for everybody really—in his book called *The Philosophy of Money*, a little long and not so readable, but there are moments, as when he discusses prostitution. The reason prostitution is scandalous, he says, is not because this sacred thing, the human body, is being soiled by money. It's quite the opposite. This sacred thing, money, is being soiled by the human body. That is the scandal of prostitution.

Here the signifier is producing itself. Baudrillard will concretize all of this in terms of Borges's fable of the map that was the same size as the territory it represents. An emperor asks that a map be produced of his land, but it wasn't ever detailed enough, because the map was always too small. So the map grew until finally it was exactly the size of the territory itself. This dramatizes, if you like, the dissolution of the signified. Where is reality? Which is reality, the territory or the map? Baudrillard used this example a few times, and then he got tired of it, but his position there was what he calls "precession." That means that it is the later thing which causes the earlier thing. So, in fact the map precedes the territory. The signifier precedes the signified. There is a bold reversal of base and superstructure in these arguments. The superstructure produces the base. Culture produces our ideas of labor and value. So Baudrillard arrives at a transformation of the notion of culture or superstructure, which becomes the basis of culture critique.

So what is the difference between Debord and Baudrillard? I think we can answer this by looking at where their critiques come from. Debord begins with the word "separation," *Trennung*, which is a very important idea in the early Marx. This is not a vague description, but a very exact way of defining the processes of capitalism that emerge in the famous manuscripts of 1844—which were not rediscovered until 1929, published among others by Lefebvre in France, creating Althusser's need to criticize the humanist Marx's theory of alienation. What is this alienation? There are four aspects of alienation.[5] The worker is separated from his tools. He doesn't own them. He is separated from the object he produces. That will not belong to him either. He is separated from his work, because he has sold his work-time for a wage. And, finally, he is separated—what is this?—from his species-being, from his very human nature. This is where the notion of humanism and human nature is most obviously a part of this theory. It would be easier to say that the worker is separated from his fellow worker, because the basis of the wage labor system is competition for jobs and wages. So you see that one basic form of the commodity is labor-power itself. Capitalism is the commodification of labor, essentially. When we talk about a world market, we mean a world in which gradually all the older forms of labor are transformed into commodities, and capitalism is absolute when that is complete, when peasant labor, for example, becomes paid and subsumed into agribusiness. That is one of the basic forms of the completion of capitalism and the total commodification of the world.

Marx's intellectual instrument for defining this unique alienation which is true of wage work and which will define the uniqueness of capitalism as such is this notion of *Trennung*, of separation. It is very clear that Debord is preoccupied with separation, but he seems not quite to be going in the same direction as Marx's initial theories. He is moving toward spectacle society. What does separation have to do with spectacle society, except in the very basic sense that you might pay for a spectacle? Spectacle society is one in which the eye is separated from the object, in which visuality becomes the definition of separation. When you see it at a distance, you are not working with it anymore.

You can find all the classics of Marxism here, but not only them. Debord was a great reader; I'm sure he was familiar with Heidegger. Heidegger was a presence at the time, but primarily the Heidegger of the first pages of *Sein und Zeit*, the so-called pragmatic Heidegger who says that there are two kinds of relationships to objects. One is *Zuhandenheit*: an object is available as an instrument to work with. The other is *Vorhandenheit*: to draw back away from the object and begin to know it. This is the break with nineteenth-century philosophy or epistemology and the turn toward pragmatism and other kinds of philosophy. In his own way, Debord

---

5   See Karl Marx, *Economic and Philosophic Manuscripts of 1844* (Moscow: Progress Publishers, 1977), 66–80.

summarizes all of that by saying that visuality comes into dominance precisely when we move away from things, when we are no longer working with them but only looking at them. This is, of course, how the bourgeois relates to objects. The bourgeois doesn't produce those things; he only consumes them or gets profit from them. Heidegger says that there are various ways of touching the absolute, but science isn't one of them. So this is an anti-scientific philosophy, and one of the things that Western Marxism has also been accused of—this doesn't include Althusser—is a critique of science. Althusser, of course, will attempt to reestablish science as the center of everything, but that will clearly create its own set of problems. At any rate, you can see how visuality would be included in theories of work, labor, and separation.

Once the object is separated from us, what is it? Here we come to another idea, a word, which is always a problem. Can it ever be settled? I don't know. I have my doubts whether you can ever get a clear and proper handle on this. It is the word "image." When you step back from things, then what you have is their image. The spectacle will characterize a society in which we don't have things anymore; we have images of things. Consumption becomes the consumption of the image, as it was for the very founders of advertising—and one of whom was, by the way, Freud's nephew, Edward Bernays, who came to the United States. If I'm not mistaken, some people have explored his relationship to Latin America, to United Fruit and the banana. Bernays, the inventor of modern advertisement, was the one who produced the banana as an idea for the American public, and thereby subjected all Central America to American domination. So a great number of important concepts are related here, and the image becomes the mode of relating them.

I have summarized Debord's work in a way which may be improper, but it seems to me that what he is saying is that the final form of commodity fetishism is the image, and thus spectacle society is a society of images. So this can also be put in connection with the problems involved in theories of photography, which are the problems of the trace that we discussed several weeks ago. What is this strange thing, the photograph? Its subject has already happened. That is to say, it doesn't exist. This is a picture of not-being. But it itself somehow exists, because I have a piece of paper depicting it. Where is the trace? What is its being? So, in a sense, the attempt to theorize photography, which disappears again with film—film will transcend that problem—involves that theoretical contradiction that we can't get over, which is the basis of the image. I would almost say it is photography which produces the problem of the image, as though we didn't have images before it, and in a sense we didn't. The photographic image is thus a different enhancement or intensification of an underlying problematic of representation.

That is the major difference with Baudrillard. Debord is coming out of the commodity and its *production*. Baudrillard will come out of the question of *reproduction*. Baudrillard will talk about the code, that which produces reality as a simulacrum, or a copy without an original. All previous theories of representation allege to have an original of some sort, as do all previous theories of art, including Debord's own theory. An image is an image *of* something, right? Once it was real—and I think they both can't get away from it: once upon a time there was reality—and now there isn't any. What happened to reality? Well, somebody took a picture of it, and ever since we haven't needed it anymore.

Something similar happens with the commodity. The commodity is produced, but then it becomes its own image, and people consume the image, rather than the thing itself, as we know from advertising. If you just turn on your television set, you will see that the car has nothing to do with mechanics anymore: the car means speed, a happy family, an exotic landscape, a wonderful vacation in a non-alienated place. That is what the car is. That is what you are buying. Much of this comes from Thorstein Veblen's idea of conspicuous consumption. Veblen has always been seen as an oddball in American sociology, but this kind of thinking comes from him, and Baudrillard would have agreed. A certain McLuhanism is also an influence.

But the main thing for Baudrillard is *le code*, the double helix. The double helix produces a thing. Yes, it is coded in the process, but it doesn't exist by itself. Everything is a copy. There is no original. It can be difficult to theorize, but fun to theorize, because every theorization is going to be not only a paradox but also a provocation. Baudrillard is both a poet and a provocateur. So too when he writes *The Gulf War Did Not Take Place*. A famous play in France, right before World War II, by Jean Giraudoux, is called *The Trojan War Will Not Take Place*. The embassies of the Trojans and the Greeks decide to make peace, until one of the crazier Trojans throws a spear, kills a Greek, and the Trojan War finally does begin. In Baudrillard, however, it doesn't take place; he will provocatively say that the Gulf War doesn't really take place because it is all on television. It is natural to immediately respond by saying that people died; this is real. The original war, George H. W. Bush's war, after Saddam invaded Kuwait, did not last very long. Saddam quickly withdrew. The later one, which was so mishandled by the American government, is a different story. There was a big fight in France about this article, because all these French intellectuals had endorsed the Gulf War. Why is that? Anti-Islam, I think. France has always had its own little piece of the Middle East. French Orientalism goes back to at least Napoleon. You can read Edward Said on this. But the intellectuals thought that it was better to crush radical Islam in whatever its form than to obey any Left ideals of anti-imperialism, so that was yet another dividing line in French de-Marxification and the deradicalization of the intellectuals. But that is another matter.

So the code means that we are losing reality, but that there was no basic reality to begin with. The language of a copy is tainted with this notion of an original, so Baudrillard calls it simulation. A simulation is, for example, the first trip to the moon. Like the Gulf War, there never was a moon landing shot; it was shot in the studio and broadcast out on television. Everybody thought that Americans had landed on the moon. No such thing. Didn't exist. That is the archetype of simulation. You act it out as though it happened.

It's very funny that we began this course with ontology, the question of being and nothingness, the nothingness of consciousness, the lack of being at the heart of *Dasein,* of human reality, and now we're back at the lack of being all over again. But this lack of being is not in us anymore, because, in a sense, there isn't any *us*—just a lot of consumers, serial consumers at that, serial in Sartre's sense. The lack of being has invaded the world of things. It has always struck me as very paradoxical that nihilism emerges not when you're confronted with nature but when you're confronted with manmade things. Increasingly in the nineteenth century, human activity, human praxis, builds up the world. The world around us becomes more and more the product of human labor in a very obvious sense. Cities and roads didn't grow like nature—and with the newer cybernetic mechanisms, even more so. A new campus was being built in La Jolla many years ago. The workers piled up a bunch of dirt, stuck a dead piece of wood in it, and then covered the whole mound with some kind of filigree of ropes, a kind of tar color, before sprinkling the whole thing with a white substance. And, in a couple weeks, all of that turned into grass and a tree. If you think nature is natural, you only have to witness something like that to see that nothing is natural in nature, at least in nature today. So why is it that when human beings have built everything, life is suddenly meaningless? Shouldn't life be much more meaningful if we made it all? Shouldn't the opposite be true? Where would nihilism come from? Why aren't people, in much more limited ecological situations, nihilists? Maybe they're too busy working to stay alive. Maybe when you get rich enough and you don't have to do very much work to perpetuate yourself, then you have nothing to do and then life becomes meaningless. But it seems to me that there is a relationship between the construction of a human society and this sudden feeling that nothing means anything.

So the science-fictional view of someone like Baudrillard is the final flower of this nihilism, at least in that period; I think it takes on other forms later. Suddenly, things are meaningless, in the sense that meaning is natural, and the natural has ceased to exist. But the big question is: can you have an idea of meaninglessness if you don't have an idea of meaning? Can it subsist on its own, or must it be the negation of something that it presupposes? If there is no idea of meaning, it wouldn't be at all surprising for things to be meaningless, because it never occurred to anybody that they had any meaning in the first place. If there was no notion of production, then the idea that things are just images would also be meaningless. These kinds of nihilism, if that is what you want to call them, presuppose the things that they cancel in some dialectical way that remains to be looked at further.

I think all the people we have been reading, with their notions of split subjects and absent causes, are trying to hang on to meaninglessness without letting it disappear completely down its own black hole. But I would say that the more interesting question related to the politics of all this is the matter of aestheticization. To what degree is the return of aesthetics not just the revival of a kind of dead branch of philosophy? Nobody was really interested in aesthetic philosophies between, let's say, Hegel and Adorno, but the extension of the aesthetic everywhere provides the discipline a quite different situation, which is also why aesthetic theory is of no interest on its own, because it isn't any longer concerned with something separate from everyday life; it's about everything. So that would be another question to leave you with.

Baudrillard says that this expansion of the aesthetic doesn't mean the end of history; it means precisely that history is never going to end. That is the problem with the end of history. In fact, he says, instead of having the end of history, all the old stuff is coming back. It is all being recycled. If you want, you could transfer the notion of the image to this notion of Baudrillard by saying that today we don't have the revival of aesthetic philosophy or ethical philosophy—all this old stuff that used to be part of philosophy departments—but rather that it had been swept away by theory and is now creeping back as a sort of regression or nostalgia. What we have is the image of all those things. We don't have real aesthetic philosophy. We have the image of aesthetic philosophy. In art, what happened with postmodern architecture was that it gave up on the aesthetics of the modern—Le Corbusier—and it began to borrow its aesthetics from any place. So you had neo-Baroque postmodernisms, Greco-Roman postmodernisms, African postmodernisms. Finally, at the end of all that, you get some properly modernist postmodernism, where postmodernism finally begins to imitate the modernism with which it broke, such that a simulation of the modern emerges within the very thing that was supposed to cancel it; it is a little like Stravinsky, who imitates others throughout his life, until, at the very end, he decides to adopt the theory of his great rival Schoenberg and to write twelve-tone music. History doesn't end, exactly, but it becomes the image of itself. Anyway, that is the Baudrillardian vision. All of this stuff I would call "postmodern," but, of course, that wasn't a word that was used in France. Next time we'll look at some more recent stuff.

April 15, 2021

Envoi: Theory after De-Marxification

{Latour, Meillassoux, Stiegler, Laruelle}

I much appreciated your comments. I would say that I learned some things from them, but it is a little too late to use them. In any case, I realized some things I should have done.

"Why France?" people asked. There are a number of reasons. I would say, for one thing, in a shrinking economic situation, intellectuals are being produced for whom there isn't enough space for employment; that energy goes into other things, sometimes into theoretical production and sometimes into politics. Additionally, in France, you have to make a place for the role of Paris, which is a unique city. It is, in a sense, the only city in France. Consider the other movements we began with. Athens, in ancient Greece. In Germany, there wasn't any central place at the time of the idealist philosophers, but you might say the aspiration toward a united Germany filled that space of provincialization that all these thinkers at the beginning of the nineteenth century felt. Berlin was never that kind of capital. Munich was the artistic capital in the twentieth century, before the war. England has no center like that. Oxford and Cambridge are quite different from London, which is not the capital of cultural scholarship of the same kind. And in the United States, New York would be a very special example. But Paris is unique. Everybody is there together. Polemics are not only possible but inevitable. I think that is over now, even as Paris remains, not just for the French but for other countries, a space in which all kinds of things can happen.

This has been a history course, and this is a question of periodization, as people have mentioned. Maybe we should reflect more on what literary or intellectual history is, but I think we don't even have enough evidence here to make those kinds of reflections. But we can at least see that these movements, these moments, whether in philosophical history or cultural history, don't last. We can date this one very specifically from 1943, the publication of *Being and Nothingness*. Where do we end it? If it is to end with the death of some of these theorists in the '80s or the '90s, then it is a fifty-year period. That is quite exceptional. What happens is not just that great discoveries are made but that you don't have the same kind of space afterwards. Intellectual spaces are filled up, spaces for innovation are filled up. Intellectuals are then busy looking for new spaces rather than actually inventing them. And you can see with somebody like Deleuze that it is an encyclopedic endeavor that swallows everything up, after which there is no more room. Are there Deleuzeans? It would seem so—everybody is talking about Deleuze—but I don't really think so, because there is not a single doctrine. There have been Derrideans. Are there any more? Maybe now in France, but not in those days.

The other thing that happens to this movement is that it gets internationalized. When do you want to date the beginning of globalization? I would say from the '80s somewhere. But that means that, suddenly, there is a great deal more internationalization of this kind of thinking. So, in that sense, French theory may be an inspiration to intellectuals in other countries, but it is no longer really French anymore. Suddenly it's all over the place, and that ends a certain kind of hegemony. The American interest in these people was certainly part of a '60s passion for new thinking which had to do with politics as much as anything else. People have connected, for example, the Derrida movement in the United States to the New Criticism, which focused our attention to small texts. I'm not sure that's quite the case.

I think Derrida made a place for a special kind of ideological analysis, and this gave people a mission. What we find in Derrida is a relentless tracking down of plenitude, the present, presentism, all kinds of norms, and this is a method that also has its aim built into it. I consider that a very important part of this: You are not just teaching some kind of method of reading; you are prolonging—and I would say this is one of the things that this class has shown us—what Althusser, in his specific mode of analysis, called class struggle in theory. In his case, this struggle is idealism versus materialism. In Derrida's case, it is difference versus whatever the enemy of difference is, identity, totalization, although also idealism in some sense. So these are all enemies whose traces you can find in the text, and we will see the final avatar of that kind of thinking in a moment when we get to contemporary thinking. But it is easy to see that this is the kind of thing that would provide a group impetus and a reason to share this commitment to a quasi-political aim, namely, I would say—going back to Heidegger, who can always serve as an example of something—the identification and extirpation of metaphysics, for example. I'm not sure whether Derrida thinks that you can get rid of these things. His followers were practitioners of that kind of search-and-destroy mission, so to speak, that kind of reading powered by a notion of ideological tendencies, and each one has a different way of saying that.

And, finally, I suppose, deconstruction goes back to Nietzsche and the death of God, in the sense that it must posit a god term of some sort. For Derrida, it could be "center" or the idea of logocentrism. For other people, it could be something else. It could be totality, maybe. But they all have as their end the search for the hidden god term which turns things into idealisms that have to be unmasked, even if they can't be destroyed. Nietzsche said that as long as you still have the first person singular in language, in sentences, God is still there in some form: the "I," personal identity, phenomenology, or the philosophy of the subject. It then became a major goal to get rid of phenomenology somehow, to identify what was wrong with phenomenology, what was wrong with the centered subject, what was wrong with humanism. And, in a sense—and I haven't talked about this much—this is also an attempt to end philosophy as such, because philosophy, in its technical form, is systematic, or at least aims toward a system that is organized around these terms. It is organized around an absolute. What do you do if there aren't any absolutes? Badiou, who still wants to be a philosopher and considers himself the writer of great works of philosophy, wants to call that anti-philosophy. So somebody like Lacan is an anti-philosopher. I'm not sure that's a good solution. What this was generally called was "theory," and theory was a kind of ideologically powered search for these elements in a text which had attempted to do away with its own center. Theory was never supposed to turn into a system; it was supposed to destroy systems in some way and to exist as a kind of local enterprise, to have a local existence which did not end up becoming a system. Now that is very hard to do, because there is such a thing as reification. There is a way in which Derrida became the philosopher of *écriture*, of writing, of difference, although he certainly changed the names of his targets all the time and fashioned new neologisms for them. So the slippage back into philosophy is a permanent danger.

Several things have to be said about that danger. What about Marxism? What about psychoanalysis? In some sense, both Freud and Marx are not philosophies; they are unities of theory and practice. Each one of them ideally posits a practice, and so it isn't complete as a thought system. The proof is simply, just to take Marxism, that you can find I don't know how many different philosophies of Marxism. There are Christian philosophies of Marxism, humanist philosophies of Marxism, materialist philosophies of Marixsm. I think the one I still admire the most still is that of Lukács, but Lukács philosophized Marxism, at least in *History and Class Consciousness*, not so much the later stuff, which is, of course, something that you can also attack. Engels philosophized Marxism. Lenin obviously created the philosophy we call Marxism-Leninism. But those are philosophies. Dialectical materialism is a philosophy; Stalin elaborated it. Historical materialism, on the other hand, is this kind of provisional theory that we are talking about. It's hard to get around that, but nonetheless I think this is so, and I think you find this to be true of the various Freudianisms, because they all have to go back and look at the original, the sacred texts, and make some new philosophical system out of them, or, if they are coming from theoreticians, to build a new theory which is fatally going to turn into a philosophy.

What does one do with that problem? I myself think there is nothing to be done, except to be aware of it. And, today, my inclination is to evoke a regression on all fronts. I think that postmodernity in this area, even in France, has been a regression to various things, and above all to the older academic disciplines. Theory was supposed to destroy the disciplines, not only philosophy but also aesthetics as a discipline, history as a discipline, ethics, of course, and even political science as a discipline. And now all of those have come back in one way or another, in the revival of ethical philosophy, aesthetic philosophy, film theory, narratology; all these things mark the institutionalization of what used to be theory and thereby the return to some kind of establishment, which certainly allows the production of all kinds of rich stuff, but the one thing it can't do is call for anything really new. And all the people we have read, out of some modernist impulse, were busy looking for the new. In Deleuze, in Lyotard, all the rest of them, it is a matter of the new.

I would like first just to recapitulate some of the things that we discovered here without really going any further with them, because we have gone as far as we can. We did stumble over this matter of visuality, the primacy of visuality. It is very interesting, and I think it does run through the whole period. I don't know how to consider it. I think the last word has not been said. If it is a part of a superstructure, an intellectual practice, then we know that there is an infrastructural reality that it corresponds to: advertising, a society of images. Somebody has calculated how many images we are bombarded with in a day. In older societies, before World War II—it's enough to go back to that—we had essentially image-poor societies, in which you were only exposed to so many images in the course of a day. The novelty of Debord was to seize on this notion of the image and to say that there is a creeping image culture which he calls spectacle. Now we live so profoundly within the spectacle that it doesn't even make any sense to say that. That is the sense in which Baudrillard follows Debord, because a culture of simulation is a culture of the generalized image, and there is nothing further to be dramatically revealed about this, although we can still try to analyze it.

Another theme which has been of importance is this business of binary oppositions. Are they good? Are they bad? How long do you hold onto them? When do they become dualisms? When do they become ideological? Do you have to start with them and move on to something else? And what about this business of double inscriptions? Is there an unconscious? Are there unconscious meanings? If you have a surface of a text, then what is going on beneath it, behind it? I have not insisted enough in this course on the importance of the critique of representation. It is too late to do that, but representation as our mental or conceptual image of some reality, which is therefore outside it, has certainly been one of our themes here, and one of the counter-themes related to it, I would say—but it has come out much more today, as we'll see—is the idea of immanence. What is the opposite of a two-term system? What is the opposite of a double inscription? It is the absence of a binary opposition. Everything is on the so-called plane of immanence. Everything is immanent. There is no unconscious. There is no hidden interpretation to be made. There is no diagnosis to be made. All of this is on the surface. In a sense, this is an old dream, the dream of immanence in philosophy. But at any rate these are formal thematics of oppositions, the use of oppositions. Does the one come out of the two? Does the two come out of the one? All of that is a part of the thematics of the binary opposition.

Then, of course, historically, there is this matter of breaks and ruptures. I think that the whole problematic of the new comes out of the notion of a break with the familiar and the past. Has that been sufficiently theorized? People indeed ask for more of the theory of history behind this kind of intellectual history that we have been doing. But this too is a part of the so-called class struggle in theory, that is to say, the driving motives of all of these theories to diagnose, to track down, and to identify areas which are supposed to be not quite "errors" but something similar. This is why the notion of ideology is so useful.

Today, there is a return of idealism. That is one of the things one can say about the aftermath of this period. I used to think that the last idealist was Bergson, that nobody would call themselves an idealist anymore, and here, suddenly, we have the Bergson revival and Badiou claiming that he is a Platonist and that he believes in the idea. Of course, it is a mathematical Idea in his case. Other people are very interested in the idealisms. So the kinds of philosophies that were interested in subjectivity have been *aufgehoben*, transformed and lifted up and turned into a new way of conceiving of idealism, perhaps—not the old, religious, spiritual way, not the psychological way, but some new third way of understanding the concept, and, somehow, this sense that we are dealing with a philosophy of the concept, that we are not looking at either subject or object but at the concept, seems again to be making its way.

Let me then look at a few of the newer things. As I say, the most difficult period to characterize, so to speak, is the present, and one of the reasons why that might be so is that the darkest part of the past is the immediate past. It is much harder to understand the last ten years than to understand anything else in history. At least the rest of that you can fight over. You know what was going on. But not only do you not know everything that was going on in the last ten years, but the shape that those events take as preludes to the present is not really comprehensible until you have a present, and you never really know what your present is. Your analysis of the present is always interested, in the bad sense. You are always pushing a certain notion of the present to advance your idea, whether optimistic or pessimistic, about where it should go and what the future should be, even in a situation, which I believe is ours, in which we don't really have an imagination of the future.

I should first mention some of the older names we never got to. I have consistently had to mention Bataille and Blanchot. Was I wrong to exclude them? Blanchot did write in this period, so maybe we should have looked at that. Bataille, though, certainly was revived. Is there a kind of revival of older works which would merit their being treated as contemporary? Would you be willing to say that Mahler was a composer of the 1970s and '80s? Would you be willing to say that Bataille was a theorist of the 1960s and '70s? Those are really important questions. They involve rereadings and they can't be completely dismissed, but we probably had enough to do without them. But a few older names I need to mention, even if we don't have time for them, because they have been at work in these things.

Georges Canguilhem was a philosopher of the life sciences, especially biology, and norms, which are important both within and outside of life philosophy, maybe an ancestor of vitalism. He was Focuault's teacher and plays an important part in Foucault.

Gilbert Simondon. Simondon was a scholar of a very limited kind. He studied machinery and objects. Okay, people were not much interested at the time. But certainly, today, there has been a tremendous revival of interest in Simondon. There is nothing in particular I would recommend. But it is one of those names that will come up in contemporary theory because people are precisely interested, after Lacan, after film theory, after Althusser, after Lyotard, after the desiring-machines, in apparatuses. So that is a name you should know.

The other name you should know is Bachelard. Those of you who have been a little more adventurous in exploring these things know that, in *Being and Nothingness*, Sartre used Bachelard's analysis of the elements of matter in his existential psychoanalysis. Bachelard wrote books entitled *The Psychoanalysis of Fire, Water and Dreams, Earth and Reveries of Will*, and so on. He was trying to investigate via literature how these elements come to have their messages, as back in pagan philosophy or even pre-Socratic, pre-pagan philosophy, when the various elements have their meaning, a certain sense that they communicate. This was one basis of Sartre's existential psychoanalysis: people's choices determine a certain sensory attraction to various kinds of matter and various kinds of sensation. So there was a whole analysis of the senses, of the sensory, which I think people have not pursued so much, except maybe in some literary studies. But at the beginning he was a historian of the sciences. Althusser's idea of the epistemological break comes from Bachelard, who posited just such a moment between paradigms, where you break from one kind of thinking to another on the basis of certain kinds of problems, and his notion of the sciences I think is still very interesting.

And, finally, very much a philosopher of the present, but very much for us also a philosopher of the past, is Badiou, who really summarizes all these theorists. He starts out as a Sartrean. He follows Althusser for a while. He becomes a disciple of Lacanianism. One of his great intellectual heroes is Mallarmé. Badiou has written some immense philosophical tomes—*Being and Event*—which have a whole ontological basis. I think we will not be going into those, except to say that he has been one of those for whom mathematics and the matheme was very important as an alternative to discursive thought, to thought in language. So his books are peppered with all kinds of equations that, unless you are a mathematician, and even if you are, you might have occasion to take issue with. I don't know. They are very off-putting. His idea is that ontology is not about being; it is about the void. Being is the void. Being is number. So number becomes this kind of other terrain for thought. His thought appeals to set theory and post-Euclidean geometries and mathematics, and it is in that sense that he is a Platonist, because he thinks that those are out of time in some sense. But there is also a political motivation, a Maoism. Still, today, in some form he has a commitment to what he calls "the Event." One assumes that that is the revolutionary event. It is in the past. He practiced all kinds of politics, tried to found new groups or parties. But, at any rate, he still believes in a kind of political event. Whether he really believes in a revolution to come is not so clear, but existential truth involves having some relationship to the Event. And I think the most interesting part is this notion of his four "truth procedures," as he calls them, and these are four kinds of existential relationships to truth. That is what I would consider the most accessible part of his philosophy. These truth procedures are: science (a commitment to mathematics), art (and he is also a poet, a dramatist, a novelist), politics (a commitment to the Event), and finally, love as an existential experience. So these are the four domains of so-called truth procedures. For him those are practices. He is trying to find an escape from the systematicity of this enormously complex philosophy of his in what are essentially modes of practice. He is quite a remarkable political figure. I've heard him give analyses of political situations that were really very pertinent. Of all the people we have seen, the ones who are the most gifted for political analysis of the situation itself were Sartre, Lyotard, and Badiou. As for the other ones, when they deal with politics, you don't necessarily expect a concrete analysis of the political situation. But those writers were gifted with an insight, and France is, of course, itself a kind of political experiment in which all kinds of things—anti-colonialism, racism, immigration—all come together in a laboratory-like way in which they can be dissected.

So those were the people who we should have mentioned. One of the new themes is virtuality. This is alleged to come from Deleuze. I think it is only later that Deleuze gets to virtuality. What is virtuality? It is possibility, but without the future. It is a possibility that exists in the present. So, if you take Deleuze as a philosopher who is attempting to produce immanence, so that no Freudian unconscious sits below the surface, then you can see how virtuality would play its part in the way in which the present is satu-rated with possibilities. You don't have to say that the virtual is something which hasn't come into being yet. I think that is Deleuze's way of dealing with virtuality. I'm not sure that anybody else follows him in this theme of virtuality, but it certainly reflects the notion of immanence that these people today are after.

A strong politics of the '60s and '70s is still around in France, as you can see with the Invisible Committee. It is a group in the South of France that is supposed to have carried out a few attacks. There was an attack on the railroad system. They have written pamphlets which are somewhat anar-chist. They are very sensible. They go through the situation and tell you: "Life, health, and love are precarious, why should work be an exception?"[1] So let's not work. They have a commune of some kind (see Kristin Ross on the significance of the Paris commune).[2] Anyway, these are no longer Maoist elements—going into the factory and trying to become a worker like the other workers—but they are certainly one outpost in France of a living far-left political impulse. There would also be the story of the far-right impulses, but we don't necessarily need to discuss that today. France had the first far-right, anti-immigration movement in Europe. I won't say it was the first fascist movement, because there are countries where that

1   The Invisible Committee, *The Coming Insurrection* (Los Angeles: Semiotext(e), 2009), 43.

2   See Kristin Ross, *Communal Luxury: The Political Imaginary of the Paris Commune* (London: Verso, 2015).

happened quite early and where fascism still exists, but it was among the first recognizable revivals of a real right-wing party.

Then there is the question of objects. There is a return to object-oriented ontology, a slogan that one of these people made up, I think in America, but which partially comes out of French theory. It was sparked by a young student of Badiou named Quentin Meillassoux, the son of a famous anthropologist. His major book is called *After Finitude*, and it has a two-pronged argument. It has an attack on so-called correlationism. You have a subject-object split. Nothing you can do with that. Spinoza just says that the two are the same. That may help some people. Can one do without the subject and just talk about the object? Can one do without the object and just talk about the subject? Materialism and idealism. What Meillassoux says is that, since Kant, philosophers have been doomed always to go through the correlation of these two things. So they can't talk about the material world and nature without trying to show how consciousness could have a connection to those things. It is hard to see what he proposes instead. I have compared this to a return to pre-Socratic philosophy, in which you talk about things like the mandate of heaven or the way in which the forces of reality move things, but that is, obviously, not a very practical suggestion, although I think it is a way of describing all this object-oriented stuff.

Anyway, Meillassoux proposes that our big problem is correlationism. Others might say that this is the same as the problem of immanence but taken in another direction. How can we talk about them all on the same plane? What can the subject know, and what is out there? How can the gap between these be overcome? How can that be made into an immanence? One of the solutions is the old Lévi-Strauss solution: we are a part of nature, and therefore our minds are a part of nature, so our minds are natural. We don't have to defend the procedures inside of our heads, by which we understand things outside of our heads, because they are all part of one thing. And I suppose that this is the final fallback position if you want to get rid of philosophies of the subject, if you want to break up correlationism. (And, in fact, it is what Hegel calls "speculative thought.")

Anyway, Meillassoux then has a very interesting argument. He says that we know life began—and I'm just going to make it up, because I can't remember—a hundred million years ago. Before that, there was no life. However, we also know some of the things that were around earlier than a hundred million years ago. Many things preexisted human consciousness, and, therefore, if you want to be a correlationist—and you have to, because that is the only thing going on in philosophy, since you necessarily have to give an account of the subject and the object if you want an epistemology—then how can we possibly make statements about things that preexisted the human? So, in a way, his argument—and he says so himself—reproduces one of the classic, crazy religious arguments of the eighteenth century which I mentioned earlier in the semester. Fossils started to be discovered in the eighteenth century, but they conflicted with the exegetically calculated origin of the Earth: the world was created 4,444 years before Christ. But the explanation is very simple. It's like the replicants in *Blade Runner*. We needed a memory, so God deliberately inserted into the world things that looked like they preceded the creation. God built in a perspective of history that otherwise would have been flat. In a sense, Meillassoux is reviving this problem. What is the status of these objects that preexisted human consciousness? How can we claim to understand them when there weren't any people around and there was no human consciousness?

Well, you can think that this is as relevant as you want, but this is the kind of argument that is made in Meillassoux's *After Finitude*. As I say, it has sparked an object-oriented ontology in which you somehow deal with objects without the circuit of correlationism. How is that possible? It takes two forms. One is from Bruno Latour. He comes out of what is called science studies, the new version of the history of science. His most famous book was *The Pasteurization of France*, where he studied Pasteur's revolution and gave a completely new picture of what Pasteur was doing. But then he became a theorist, and he worked out this idea of a democracy between objects and people. If you're looking at the past, if you're looking at events, you cannot privilege human beings. You have to see that there is a symbiosis between technics, objects, and human actors. Those are all on the same level. He calls this a network. Maybe we can get out of the subject-object split that way, Latour says. So he has become the theorist of what is called "actor-network theory," connecting up these movements in time which are a kind of apparatus, including objects and people. And that is, certainly, one of the thematic concerns today, and it seems to some to offer some new kinds of problems to explore.

The other feature of all of this is the media, because the media already is some kind of object. What do we do with it? There the most important figure whom we haven't touched on is Bernard Stiegler, who just died, and who has produced an enormous amount of work sort of under the auspices of Derrida. But he goes back to the sources of Derrida's *Grammatology*, namely André Leroi-Gourhan—the anthropology that is used and in a way criticized in the *Grammatology*—to talk about instruments. He wants to expand Derrida's notion of *écriture*, of writing, to include instruments of writing, which can be thought of as prostheses. I suppose it begins with Heidegger in the sense that Heidegger distinguishes, as I said last time, between objects that are simply there and objects that are there for us, objects ready-to-hand, objects that exist as part of us. These could be prostheses: our books, our writing, our pens, the computer. All those things are *zuhanden*, and in Stiegler they are integrated into a prosthetic process which is an extension of the Derridean notion of the supplement, of difference and of writing. Stiegler went on to perform a kind of culture criticism, in which he proposed a different relationship to technics, as he calls his new, philosophical version of media theory, and it touches on many of the more banal things that we already know about the critique of technology, commodification, and consumerism. But, at any rate, I would say that he has been maybe the loudest voice in contemporary French theory in this area, which tries again to pull various media back into a relationship with the body, and which synthesizes previous theories of the body that come out of Merleau-Ponty with the ontologies that come out of media theory.

There is also the work of Michel Serres, ostensibly about communication theory, but really about everything. He was a polymath. He wrote about all kinds of things. I would have said his major interest was in thermodynamics, but he did write a great deal on culture. His most famous book is called *The Parasite*, which is about noise in communication, where he claims that communication is essentially parasitic. What comes out of his work, a very great influence in France and elsewhere in science studies, is the work of Isabelle Stengers and a Soviet physicist, Ilya Prigogine. Stengers and Prigogine write *Order Out of Chaos*, which was an enormous revelation in France and in the United States as well, in which the whole notion of the thermodynamic is turned around in all kinds of interesting ways. And there have been other French versions of this, such as René Thom's catastrophe theory. A great deal of interest is generated out of this science-inspired work, and it comes into theory in a way that I think it didn't in the '70s and '80s. Obviously there is all the neuro stuff on the brain. Deleuze touches on it a little bit at the very end of his final book,

What Is Philosophy? But other people have done more. Catherine Malabou is one. She wrote a book on Hegel and plasticity.[3] I think that is a terrible word, but she means plastic in the sense of transformations. It is a very interesting part of some current Hegel revivals. She tries to generalize her notion of plasticity to deal with the brain from that perspective. So the philosophy of brain science is also involved in this turn toward science.

I would say the political analyses of the more ontic type—studies of immigration, citizenship, and so on—are reviving the classical themes of political theory in an age when, after American hegemony, it no longer seemed important to raise any of those questions, because the American constitution solves them all. Well, apparently, it didn't, so there is a return, particularly today, of the whole immigration crisis in questions of what citizenship would be. Of all those people, probably Rancière's notion of democracy is the most interesting, but I have mentioned these studies of Balibar.

I haven't mentioned De Certeau, who pioneered some very interesting notions of space. Walking as a trope, for example, is one of his ideas. There is also Paul Virilio, who studied speed, space, and the body, speed as a transformation of these elements of the body. We mentioned very briefly Pierre Bourdieu, his post-Barthesian studies of distinction, the prestige of strata in the work of art, who then went on to do studies of what he called the field of art, in his promotion of sociology as the supreme science. I would say there is almost a tragic view of knowledge here, where all these knowledges produced by the various institutions in Bourdieu are all turned into modes of prestige in a way, and only the sociologist can see through them and judge them.

I have left out the final figure in this. I have considered this person somebody who remains to be invented. On this notion of immanence, what do you do? You say that philosophy is incapable of reaching immanence, and therefore we should somehow get rid of philosophy. All philosophy is, by definition, metaphysical. It has transcendence in it, because otherwise there would be nothing to philosophize about. Therefore, the final position on immanence would be: let's not have philosophy at all. This is, in fact, not an invented position but is the philosophy, if you want to say it that way, of a real human being, who is a philosopher, named François

---

3   Catherine Malabou, *The Future of Hegel: Plasticity, Temporality, and Dialectic*, trans. Lisabeth During (New York: Routledge, 2005).

Laruelle, who calls his work "non-philosophy." And it does indeed consist in examining all these other philosophies and somehow tracking down the transcendence in them. It is a final form of class struggle in philosophy. That is to say, it is the final form of tracking down idealism and getting rid of it. But when you get rid of it, you have gotten rid of philosophy itself.

I think this is a theorization of the whole movement of theory. So he will write books about non-theory. For example, there is a book on non-Marxism.[4] He is a kind of Marxist, but, he says, one must get rid of everything transcendental and philosophical in Marx. One can agree with that. It seems to me, however, that the problem with that approach, with which I have some sympathy, is that all these theorists already had to be doing philosophy for you to have something to undo. That is to say, you require philosophy in order to unphilosophize it. If you just started out, let's say, a peasant who hadn't gone to school, who wouldn't even know who Plato was, and you said, "Look, here's a non-philosopher," that would be a more Rancière-type position, which would hold that you could get everything out of this peasant, just the way Plato in the *Meno* produces all of philosophy out of the head of this little kid. So that would be the starting point, but Laruelle—on whom, by the way, one of our most distinguished graduates, Alex Galloway, has written an interesting book called *Laruelle: Against the Digital*—has to have the previous history of philosophy there to get a non-philosophy out of it somehow. So philosophy, by producing its network of errors and its rich heritage of philosophical mistakes, has provided him with the requisite material to unphilosophize. Anyway, that would be a final position, so he is a good person with whom to stop.

In one of your questions, you asked how to produce new problems. I can't tell you how to do that. Some of these problems interest me more than others. Some of them don't interest me at all. But those are my own limitations. That is precisely the work of a newer theory: to go back and see what the interesting problems are. I would say that you know what they are. People are philosophizing now about ethics, art, the brain. The question is not what is being done, but what should be done, or maybe what is the matter with what is being done. But I think it is not possible for me to lay down a future program of these things. That could be something for some of you, but you would have to know what is going on to go beyond it or

---

4 François Laruelle, *Introduction to Non-Marxism*, trans. Anthony Paul Smith (Minneapolis, MN: University of Minnesota Press, 2014).

to find the new. I think one of the ideas of the postmodern in general—I don't mean to adopt it or push it—is that the whole of modernism was based on the idea of the new. "Make it new" (Pound). Break with the past. Modernism came to an end more or less when people found that they couldn't think of anything new. Then you get postmodernism, which is a practice of the resuscitation of the past, transforming the past, working in the styles of the past, including that of modernism itself. The same would maybe be true of philosophy. But this is all tied to the feeling that your nation-state or your collectivity can imagine a future, and certainly the most successful part of neoliberalism was to have persuaded us that the future is here: We have the market, and we don't need anything else. Maybe that is changing. In the case of France, I have pointed to the kind of thing that the common market meant when France became a member of it—your own national tradition and language is now a part of something larger—and maybe we all have this feeling on the scale of globalization, though we don't yet know what that larger thing is. I would say that the new has to come out of thinking of those newer forms, but since it is something that remains to be thought, I don't think there is anything more to say about it at this stage. Chiasmus: the future of "the problem" is the problem of the future.

April 20, 2021

Index